Becoming Mexipino

LATINIDAD

Transnational Cultures in the United States

This series publishes books that deepen and expand our knowledge and understanding of the various Latina/o populations in the United States in the context of their transnational relationships with cultures of the broader Americas. The focus is on the history and analysis of Latino cultural systems and practices in national and transnational spheres of influence from the nineteenth century to the present. The series is open to scholarship in political science, economics, anthropology, linguistics, history, cinema and television, literary and cultural studies, and popular culture and encourages interdisciplinary approaches, methods, and theories. The series grew out of discussions with faculty at the School of Transborder Studies at Arizona State University, where an interdisciplinary emphasis is being placed on transborder and transnational dynamics.

Marta E. Sánchez, Series Editor, School of Transborder Studies

Rodolfo F. Acuña, *In the Trenches of Academe: The Making of Chicana/o Studies*

Marivel T. Danielson, *Homecoming Queers: Desire and Difference in Chicana Latina Cultural Production*

Rudy P. Guevarra Jr., *Becoming Mexipino: Multiethnic Identities and Communities in San Diego*

Lisa Jarvinen, *The Rise of Spanish-Language Filmmaking: Out from Hollywood's Shadow, 1929–1939*

Regina M. Marchi, *Day of the Dead in the USA: The Migration and Transformation of a Cultural Phenomenon*

Priscilla Peña Ovalle, *Dance and the Hollywood Latina: Race, Sex, and Stardom*

Luis F. B. Plascencia, *Disenchanting Citizenship: Mexican Migrants and the Boundaries of Belonging*

Becoming Mexipino

Multiethnic Identities and
Communities in San Diego

RUDY P. GUEVARRA JR.

RUTGERS UNIVERSITY PRESS
NEW BRUNSWICK, NEW JERSEY, AND LONDON

Library of Congress Cataloging-in-Publication Data

Guevarra, Rudy.

  Becoming Mexipino : multiethnic identities and communities in San Diego /
Rudy P. Guevarra, Jr.
     p. cm. — (Latinidad : transnational cultures in the United States)
   Includes bibliographical references and index.
   ISBN 978–0–8135–5283–5 (hardcover : alk. paper) — ISBN 978–0–8135–5284–2
(pbk. : alk. paper) — ISBN 978–0–8135–5326–9
   1. San Diego (Calif.)—Ethnic relations.   2. Mexican Americans—California—
San Diego—Social conditions.   3. Filipino Americans—California—San Diego—Social
conditions.   4. Community life—California—San Diego .   I. Title.
   F869.S22G78   2012
   305.868′7207307794985—dc23   2011032963

A British Cataloging-in-Publication record for this book is available from the British
Library.

Copyright © 2012 by Rudy P. Guevarra Jr.

All rights reserved

No part of this book may be reproduced or utilized in any form or by any means, electronic
or mechanical, or by any information storage and retrieval system, without written permission from the publisher. Please contact Rutgers University Press, 100 Joyce Kilmer Avenue,
Piscataway, NJ 08854–8099. The only exception to this prohibition is "fair use" as defined by
U.S. copyright law.

Visit our Web site: http://rutgerspress.rutgers.edu

Manufactured in the United States of America

For my parents, Angela and Rudy Guevarra

Contents

Acknowledgments

I can honestly say this project began the day I was born. As a child, I never fully understood what my experience as a Mexipino meant, other than being instilled with a sense of pride for both my cultures. I grew up eating both Mexican and Filipino food and observed the interactions of my relatives at our family dinners and social gatherings, which were always mixed. What did resonate with me, however, were the stories I heard growing up. I remember sitting mesmerized by the family stories I heard at the dinner table whenever my relatives would visit. My grandparents, uncles, aunts, family friends, and parents would reminisce over old family stories that always fascinated me. I had my favorite ones that I would ask them to repeat while my siblings or cousins and I (whoever could stay up that late) listened attentively. Thus began my love affair with our history and the oral tradition of sharing our family narratives. Little did I know that later in life it would be those family stories and the ones I heard from other Mexipinos who told their own histories over the years that inspired me to share these narratives. Collectively, these stories weave together into a narrative that is rich with cultural interactions and identity formations, terms I would later know and be able to articulate as an adult. I honor all my relatives, both Mexican and Filipino, who sacrificed everything to come to the United States. They sought a better life for their families and future generations, and I am the beneficiary. Their stories inspired me and will continue to live on through me. To them I send a loving and heartfelt *muchisimas gracias, agyamanak,* and *maraming salamat po.*

I want to thank my mentors, past and present, who saw something in me and believed in the story I wanted to tell. I have benefited tremendously from their love, guidance, and support over the years. Our time together has been and continues to be a blessing in my life. My mentors include Zaragosa Vargas, Paul Spickard, David Gutiérrez, Catherine Ceniza Choy, Kathy Nakagawa, Carlos Vélez-Ibáñez, Mary Romero, Rick Bonus, Michael J. Gonzalez, and Judy Liu.

I hope to carry your example to my students and be the kind of mentor, teacher, and friend you have all been to me.

A big thank-you to my family, friends, and colleagues who took the time to read my manuscript in parts or in its entirety; thank you all for providing me with the valuable insights and critiques needed to shape it into what it has become. I owe an intellectual debt to all of you. These include my brother Ben Guevarra, Robert Soza, Karen Leong, Django Paris, Marivel Danielson, Jordan Gonzales, Kelly Jackson, Seline Szkupinski-Quiroga, Joanne Rondilla, David Torres-Rouff, Loan Dao, Chris Knaus, Cyndy Snyder, Oscar Fierros, and Tony Zaragoza.

I also want to thank my friends and colleagues who have provided intellectual encouragement throughout my career and supported this project in various ways. These include Tracy Buenavista, Christine Hong, Luis Alvarez, Linda Trinh Võ, Mary Danico, Evelyn Hu-Dehart, Vicki Ruiz, Reg Daniels, George Lipsitz, Raúl Ramos, Yen Le Espiritu, María Raquél Casas, Michelle Tellez, Jason Oliver Chang, Robyn Rodriguez, David Hernández, Victor Hugo Viesca, Melany Delacruz-Viesca, Camilla Fojas, Rafael Zapata, Judy Patacsil, Felix Tuyay and everyone in the Filipino American National Historical Society of San Diego, Lori Pierce, Jonathan Okamura, Dennis Childs, Kip Fulbeck, Jerry Garcia, Gail Perez, Alberto López Pulido, Douglas Daniels, Pablo Landeros, Jeff Moniz, Charlene Tomas, John Rosa, Angelica Yanez, Marc Coronado, Matt Kester, Isaiah Walker, Sharleen Nakamoto Levine, Margaret Hunter, Zeus Leonardo, Diane Fujino, John Park, Ernesto Chavez, Angela Bruening-Miranda, Charlene Martinez Qoalexenze, Natchee Blu Barnd Qoalexenze, Farzana Nayani, Jennifer Noble, Fanshen Cox, Heidi Durrow, Marc Johnston, Laura Kina, Guillermo "Memo" Pastrano, David Montejano, Dean Saranillio, Ingrid Dineen-Wimberly, Lily Welty, George Sánchez, Chrissy Lau, Brianne Davila, Kimberly Hoang, James McKeever, Mike Chavez, Alex Garcia, Lisa Marie Rollins, Fuifuilupe Niumeitolu, Vika Palaito, Kehaulani Vaughn, Jimmy Patino, Victor Gomez, Sarah Griffith, Rani McLean, Natalie Cherot, Zelideth Maria Rivas, Ku'ualoha Ho'omanawanui, Ioane Ho'omanawanui, Sefa Aina, April Henderson, Richard Griswold del Castillo, Rita Sanchez, Denise Segura, Joanie Cordova, Emily Lawson, Rick Baldoz, Murray Lee, Darcy Ritzau, Mérida Rúa, Josef Castañeda-Liles, Alex Fabros Jr., Xuan Santos, Gerardo Aldana, Brandon Yoo, Karen Kuo, Wendy Cheng, Wei Li, Alan Gomez, Mary Margaret Fonow, Paul Espinosa, Marta Sánchez, Lisa Magaña, Edward Escobar, Eileen Diaz McConnell, Maria P. P. Root, Teresa Williams-León, Erika Lee, David Galbiso, Gilbert González, Edward Slack Jr., Adrian Cruz, Mario Garcia, Dawn Mabalon, Helen "HQ" Quan, Mario Montano, Cathy Schlund-Vials, Jose Alamillo, Melinda L. de Jesús, Nancy Magpusao, Anna Gonzalez, Travis Smith, Faye Caronan, JoAnna Poblete, Gina Velasco, Keith Camacho, Wesley Ueunten, Theo Gonzalves, Martin Manalansan, Dylan Rodriguez, Dorothy Fujita-Rony, Emily Ignacio,

Robert Chao Romero, Isabela Quintana, Anthony Ocampo, Ryan Yokota, and John Munro. A special *mahalo nui loa* also goes out to the hui, the Kaluhiokalani family and the Kaerchers.

To my *familia* at Arizona State University and Arizona at large, thank you for providing me with the love, support, and community that have sustained me in so many ways. Our community has been an oasis of hope in an environment that has often been hostile.

I want to thank all the staff at the various archives, historical societies, and libraries who assisted me in my search for documentation about the Mexican, Filipino, and Mexipino experience. Your time and patience in helping me locate every little tidbit of information made this book possible. A gracious thank-you goes to Rachael Ortiz at the Logan Heights Historical Society; Uncle Fred and Auntie Dorothy Cordova at the Filipino American National Historical Society, National Pinoy Archives, in Seattle; Helen Ofield at the Lemon Grove Historical Society; Jeff Crawford and Linda Johnson at the California State Archives; Mary Allely at the National City Public Library; Peter Hanff and Emily Balmages at the Bancroft Library at the University of California, Berkeley; Jeffrey Rankin in Special Collections at the University of California, Los Angeles; Judy Soo Hoo at the Asian American Studies Center and Yolanda Vargas at the Chicano Studies Research Center at UCLA; Chancellor Rodrigo Valdivia and June Daspit at the San Diego Catholic Diocese Archives; James Cartwright at the University of Hawai'i at Mānoa University Archives and Manuscripts; Joan Hori and Dore Minatodani at the University of Hawa'i at Mānoa, HSPA Archives and Hawaiian and Pacific Collection; Lisa Gezelter and Paul Wormser at the National Archives and Records Administration, Laguna Niguel; Rae Shiraki at ILWU Local 142, Hawai'i Archives; Robert Marshall at California State University, Northridge Urban Archives Center; Alexis Moreno at Southern California Library for Social Studies and Research; Bernie Arreguin at the Rose Canyon Historical Society; Andrew Gordon at the San Diego Association of Governments (SANDAG); Jeremy Hollins at the La Jolla Historical Society; Dennis Sharp and Jane Kenealy at the San Diego Historical Society; Marcelo Adano at Museo Histórico Naval de Acapulco; Conrado Palomino at Museo Histórico de Acapulco, Fuerte de San Diego; and to the staff at San Diego State University Special Collections and University Archives, Stanford University Department of Special Collections and University Archives and Hoover Institution Archives, the San Diego County Public Library, Hawai'i State Archives, and the Mandeville Special Collections at the University of California, San Diego. I also want to thank my research assistants over the years who assisted me along the way. Their help has also been vital to this project. These include Mark Leo, Mark Tran, Thomas Rosario, Daniela Schonberger, Rhea Duncan, Lily Robles, Shanna Maschmeier, China Mauricio, Eric Bargemann, Mia Franco, and Shamarah Lang. A special thank-you to Wan Yu for re-creating the population maps on San Diego and to Richard Marciano,

Camille Guérin-Gonzales, Ron Buenaventura, Barbara Tolentino Reyes, and Christian Trajano for your generosity in sharing your research notes and sources with me early on in this project.

I want to thank my editor Leslie Mitchner, the series editors, and the rest of the staff at Rutgers University Press for believing in this project and for taking the time to work closely with me throughout this process. I also want to thank my copy editor Karen Johnson for her patience and painstaking work on the manuscript. You have all made this an enjoyable experience.

The University of California's Chancellor's Postdoctoral Fellowship made funding and support for writing drafts of this manuscript possible. Other funding that helped support this project in its early stages includes the Ford Foundation Dissertation Fellowship; the UC President's Dissertation Fellowship; the Institute for Labor and Employment Dissertation Year Fellowship; the University of California, Santa Barbara, Doctoral Scholars Fellowship; the UC MEXUS Dissertation Research Award; UCSB Center for Chicano Studies Research Grant; the Bancroft Library Study Award; the Organization of American Historians Huggins-Quarles Award; the Pacific Rim Grant; the Western History Association Sara Jackson Award, and the Institute for Humanities Research at Arizona State University.

A special thank-you goes to the families who shared their stories and photographs with me. These include Villarin, Balino Rowan, Balino Fernandez, Guevarra, Martinez, Perrariz Mena, Hollman Garcia, Ayap, Valladolid, Mata, Mariscal, Limjoco, Lleva, Solis, Meneses, Patricio, Duran Gonzales, De Los Santos, Abundis, Lacan, Reyes, Romio, Chavez, Zarate, Arreguin, Rodriguez, Tapia, Gonzalez, Garcia, Lim, Amaguin, Dominguez, Galbiso, Gomez, Lacang, Ramirez, Ochoa-Tafoya, Rivas, Tellechea, Balanag, Ybarra, Zuniga, Monzon, Ortiz, Patacsil, and Johnson. This project would not have been possible without your generosity and time. May this book be a humble gesture to honor all of your contributions. Thank you.

Most of all I want to thank my family. They have watched me toil over this project the last eleven years, yet never stopped encouraging and supporting me in a life that can be isolating at times. The home-cooked meals and good times we shared together enabled me to endure this arduous journey. This includes all my family in San Diego, the Bay Area, Hawai'i, Santa Barbara, Los Angeles, Las Vegas, and D.C. For their unconditional love and support, I am eternally grateful. I hope what I have written will be a small token of my own love and dedication to all of them.

I may have forgotten to mention a few people who were also instrumental to this project. If I have done so, please forgive me. Though this journey has been long, your love and support is appreciated.

Becoming Mexipino

Introduction

MEXICANS, FILIPINOS, AND
THE MEXIPINO EXPERIENCE

On March 15, 2008, Manny Pacquiao and Juan Marquez squared off for the WBC Super Featherweight Championship of the world. The fight was held at the Mandalay Bay Resort and Casino in Las Vegas, Nevada. The fight between Filipino boxer Pacquiao and Mexican boxer Marquez symbolized many things. First, two men—one representing the Philippines and the other Mexico—were competing in a title fight that would garner them and their respective home countries worldwide attention. Their hopes and dreams of economic success were made possible in the United States, where they competed for the title, its cash prize, and bragging rights. Finally, people in the crowd were waving Philippine and Mexico flags, representing the ethnic pride they attached to their respective fighters. Before the fight began, the national anthems of each country were performed. A Filipina represented the Philippines, while a Mexicano performed Mexico's national anthem.

The U.S. national anthem was notable. There to perform it was fourteen-year-old Jasmine Villegas, a multiethnic Filipina-Mexican, or Mexipina. The image of this Mexipina, who sang her country's most revered song, sent a powerful message filled with layers of symbolism. Villegas's mere presence embodied the coming together of two cultures, one Filipino, one Mexican. She signified this union as its product: an American-born, multiethnic Mexipina who embodied this representation of multiplicity in the United States, another reminder echoing President Barack Obama's words about his own multiracial background when he said, "In no other country on earth is my story even possible."[1] Her image indeed tells this story. It is the tale of two communities that participated in this country's economic, social, and cultural development. These communities, one Mexican and the other Filipino, converged, sometimes in competition and in tension but more often in cooperation and coalition to carve a place for themselves and their children. It is a distinct union that has been carried into the twenty-first century. As I watched the event, I knew that this was

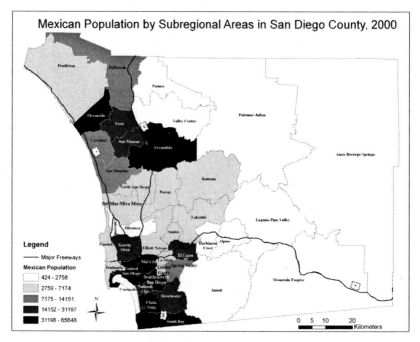

Map 1. *Source*: SANDAG, constructed by the U.S. Census Bureau, 2000 Census Summary File. Map created by Wan Yu, Department of Geography, Arizona State University.

Note: Central San Diego includes Logan Heights (Barrio Logan), Sherman Heights, Golden Hill, downtown San Diego, and Little Italy. The South Bay includes Otay Mesa, Imperial Beach, and San Ysidro. Southeast San Diego includes Paradise Hills, Encanto, Shelltown, and Valencia Park. Mid City includes City Heights, College Area, Kensington, and Talmadge. For complete listing of all neighborhoods in these subregions of San Diego, see *The City of San Diego Neighborhood Maps Index*, http://www.sandiego.gov/neighborhoodmaps/index.shtml (accessed May 7, 2010).

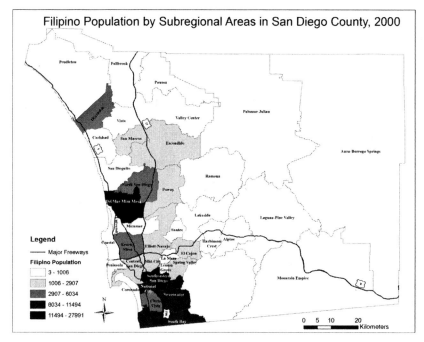

Map 2. *Source*: SANDAG, constructed by the U.S. Census Bureau, 2000 Census
Summary File. Map created by Wan Yu, Department of Geography, Arizona State
University.

more than a boxing match. It was a powerful reminder of just how prevalent Mexipino communities are within the fabric of California, the Southwest borderlands, and U.S. history.

As a scholar who also shares this multiethnic background, I am often challenged by my colleagues and friends concerning my scholarly interest with chronicling the Mexipino experience in San Diego. When engaging in discussions over my research, I am often asked by my fellow historians, So what? Why is this story important? What makes the interethnic relationship between Mexicans and Filipinos so unique and, more so, what is so special about the lives and experiences of Mexipino children? Let me be clear. As someone who is also Mexipino, this is a personal journey to understand my family and the communities we are a part of in San Diego. I am a fourth-generation Mexipino. My father and grandmother also share this multiethnic mix. Growing up in San Diego, I have met a lot of Mexipinos over the years who share similar experiences, growing up in two cultures. Some of them even go back several generations, like my own family. The Mexipinos I have met over the years are also from different generations. It is a distinct experience that is common in the communities where I grew up in San Diego, yet is given little attention by scholars in the fields of ethnic studies, history, and mixed-race studies. Ours is a story that has existed for several hundred years and is a common experience throughout California, Washington, New Mexico, and Mexico, among other geographical sites where Mexican and Filipino communities converge, but no one has fully explored this history. I have thus spent my adolescent and adult years trying to understand what historical and contemporary forces shaped the Mexipino experience in a place like San Diego, California.[2] In doing so, I often ask myself, What makes our collective story possible?

San Diego is home to the nation's second largest Filipino community and continues to be a favorable destination for new Filipino immigrants. According to the 2000 census, San Diego's Filipino community currently numbers 133,112, or 4.5 percent of the total population of the county, making them the largest Asian group in San Diego. Sharing a border with Tijuana, Mexico, San Diego is also home to substantial Mexican and Chicano communities that are continually fed by immigration from its southern neighbor. The Mexican population totals 804,047, or 27.1 percent of the county population, making them both the largest Latino group in San Diego and the county's largest ethnic minority. By 2009, the number of Filipinos grew to 135,272, while those who identified as Mexican increased to 805,326.[3] What is even more intriguing is that with the 2000 census, individuals for the first time could mark more than one racial category. As a result, 15 percent, or 249,000 of those with Asian ancestry, also identified as Latino, while 119,829 of those with Latino ancestry also identified as Asian.[4] Taken together, these numbers are impressive regarding the size of the mixed Asian-Latino population in the United States, which would include Mexipinos in those numbers. This signals larger trends: San Diego and the nation at large are fast becoming a nonwhite majority in the twenty-first century. One can only wonder what the 2010 census will reveal with the mixed-race Asian-Latino population.

Collectively, Filipinos and Mexicans have been central in the economic and social development of San Diego since the early twentieth century. As workers they contributed to the agricultural, fish-canning, service work, and wartime industries that made San Diego an economic juggernaut, especially during the 1930s, World War II, and the postwar years. As home to one of the country's largest naval bases, San Diego also solidified its importance as a major military installation on the West Coast. Despite these facts, San Diego as a region has garnered little historical attention. Indeed, the vast majority of scholarly attention has been given to Los Angeles's ethnic communities and, most notably, its Chicano population. As the gateway to California, San Diego remains in the shadow of its northern neighbor in both social and economic importance. Even more neglected are the histories of its racial and ethnic communities. For example, other than Richard Griswold del Castillo's edited volume, *Chicano San Diego,* and Roberto R. Alvarez Jr.'s *Familia,* there are no other monographs on the Mexican or Chicano experience in San Diego. Similarly, Yen Le Espiritu's *Filipino American Lives* and *Home Bound* are the only full-length studies done on Filipinos in San Diego.[5] Given San Diego's large Mexican and Filipino communities and the interethnic mixing that has and continues to occur, one can only wonder why there is not more scholarship.

More importantly, there is no meaningful analysis exploring the experiences of San Diego's Mexicans and Filipinos in relation *to* each other. Adelaida Castillo-Tsuchida's 1979 MA thesis was the first to briefly touch upon the interactions between Filipinos and Mexicans in San Diego. James Sobredo's 1998 dissertation on Filipino exclusion campaigns also provides a brief comparative analysis of Mexican and Filipino communities.[6] Although limited in its scope, what Sobredo did provide was the implication of where these sorts of interpretive inquiries can take us. Other scholars, such as Paul Spickard, Maria Root, and Karen Isaksen Leonard, have also pointed to the historical interactions between both groups. No other work to date has been done to compare their experiences in a substantive way. It is here that I wish to make these historical interventions and unearth these experiences.

As the field of comparative ethnic studies continues to grow, these sorts of comparisons are vital for understanding communities in rural and urban settings. Studies conducted by Scott Kurashige, Lorrin Thomas, Mark Wild, Karen Isaksen Leonard, Mae M. Ngai, Laura Pulido, Natalia Molina, Paul Spickard, Jonathan Y. Okamura, and Moon-Kie Jung, for example, have led the way in critically examining racial and ethnic groups as both intricate relationships and comparative analysis.[7] This growing body of scholarship is leading the way to interrogate larger questions of what Michael Omi and Howard Winant refer to as "racial formations" and the realities that ethnic and racial groups do not exist in

isolation from each other, but rather in relation *to* each other.[8] This comparative/
relational multiethnic approach, as geographer Laura Pulido notes, "enables us
to see the interaction among various racial/ethnic groups and their influences on
each other."[9] Indeed, it helps us to rethink how we understand race and racial
formations by rearticulating these conversations to include the complexities of
racial hierarchies that go beyond the dichotomy of the black/white binary.[10] My
study contributes to this growing body of work by filling an important scholarly
gap. It expands on these works by exploring how the shared experiences of
Mexicans and Filipinos in San Diego forged a distinct identity over several generations from two ethnicities that share overlapping histories, a similar culture,
and lived experiences. Their relationship, however, was complex, forged through
moments of both cooperation and disagreement, which will be highlighted in
the pages that follow. They also had differential experiences at times, especially
when it came to matters such as citizenship, factors influencing immigration
experiences, and the issue of whiteness that some Mexicans evoked and that
Filipinos could not. Shifting racial positions for both groups, as historian Scott
Kurashige notes in his study on Black Japanese in Los Angeles, "varied over time
and space in conjunction with demographic, economic, and political changes,"
which also affected San Diego in regional, national, and transnational/transpacific
ways.[11] Yet despite these moments of divergence or difference, their relationship
serves as an example for the possibilities of interethnic cooperation and coalition
building. We can learn from their experiences as we continue to live in a country
where different racial and ethnic groups converge in multiple settings.

MULTIPLICITY AND THE MEXIPINO EXPERIENCE

In both historical and contemporary contexts, multiracial/multiethnic settings
ultimately lead to the formation of interethnic and interracial mixing and
mixed-race children through personal relationships, shared experiences, and
overlapping histories. Racial mixing has always been a part of our nation's
history, despite the aggressive attempts of local, state, and federal officials
to prevent these unions (and procreation for that matter) through various miscegenation laws over the past three hundred years. These racist miscegenation
laws were finally declared unconstitutional at the national level with the
Supreme Court case *Loving v. Virginia* in 1967.[12] As a result, interracial mixing
and marriage proliferated, which in turn increased the number of multiracial
children during the baby boom of the 1980s and 1990s.[13] The scholarship that
came out of this time period addressing the multiracial population also increased.
Although much of the early research conducted on interracial coupling
and mixed-race identity were on biracial black/white individuals and families,
research in the field of Asian American and Pacific Islander studies moved
beyond the black/white dichotomy and included the voices of multiracial and
multiethnic Asian Americans and Pacific Islanders. A large portion of these early

studies came out of California and other West Coast states, Hawai'i, and the present-day U.S. Southwest, revealing an experience that was never just black and white, but rather multiethnic, and included Asian, Pacific Islander, Mexican (and other Latinos), and indigenous ancestries. Although some of these stories initially followed a similar nonwhite/white dichotomy, more voices emerged from subsequent studies to include a variety of mixed race/ethnic experiences and interracial/interethnic coupling. The field of Chicana and Chicano studies also had a few early studies addressing the issue of multiethnic and multiracial Mexican, Chicana, and Chicano identity. A small sample of this extensive and growing body of early and contemporary works from both disciplines includes studies by Paul Spickard, Maria P. P. Root, Teresa Williams-León, Velina Hasu Houston, Cynthia Nakashima, Christina Iijima Hall, Rowena Fong, Kip Fulbeck, Stephen Murphy-Shigematsu, George Kitahara Kich, Karen Isaksen Leonard, Gloria Anzaldúa, Kevin R. Johnson, and Martha Menchaca, for example. Collectively, these studies paved the way toward rearticulating and moving beyond the black/white or white/other paradigm of race and mixed-race relations and focusing instead on the understudied histories of mixed-race peoples of Asian, Pacific Islander, and Mexican descent and the rich, complex ways identities are forged and maintained.[14] It is here that my work also makes a theoretical intervention by proposing to include a distinct experience in communities throughout the West Coast and U.S. Southwest, places not included in this body of scholarship. Indeed, I contend that one of the missing stories is the Filipino-Mexican connection and the frequent coupling and multiethnic experience that have existed for centuries yet have never been given full attention in understanding the complexities of race and ethnic relations and multiple identity formations in the growing field of mixed-race studies.

Becoming Mexipino: Multiethnic Identities and Communities in San Diego is a social-historical interpretation of two ethnic groups, one Mexican, the other Filipino, whose paths led them to San Diego, California, from 1903 to 1965. I situate my study between these two historical moments to document the first migration of Filipinos to San Diego in the twentieth century and the impact that the changes in the Immigration Act of 1965 had on both Mexican and Filipino communities. Although African Americans, indigenous peoples, those of Chinese and Japanese ancestry, and whites figure in this story at different historical moments, the major actors in this story are Mexicans and Filipinos and their Mexipino children. This book recounts the story of how predominately Filipino men and Mexican women, key characters in this tale, were part of multiracial communities that lived, worked, worshipped, and socialized together under various contexts with overlapping histories. As Scott Kurashige writes about the black and Japanese American communities of Los Angeles, here I also demonstrate how and why Mexicans and Filipinos "came to occupy overlapping positions within the racial politics and geography" of twentieth-century San Diego and how "race functions in a multiethnic context."[15] Their cultural similarities were initially forged from a shared Spanish colonial past and have resonated through the twentieth century. They formed intimate relationships over several generations and raised multiethnic Mexipino children. As they came of age, generations of Mexipinos forged new identities for themselves that were rich and complex as they navigated through their multiethnic families and communities, creating an experience that continues to be distinct in its own right. Borrowing Kevin Mumford's process of "excavating a genealogy," I uncover the multiple layers of historical narrative that explain how Mexicans and Filipinos came together in the twentieth century and the various "interzones" that facilitate their intricate, interethnic relationships.[16]

The challenging part of telling this story, however, is the dearth of sources available for discussing both Mexican and Filipino communities in San Diego. I painstakingly searched all of the archives available in San Diego and throughout the state of California to find scattered fragments of information about the presence and participation of Mexicans, Filipinos, and Mexipinos in their communities. My search for evidence took me as far north as Seattle, Washington, and south to Acapulco, Mexico. I excavated sources such as newspapers, labor reports, government documents, census reports, city directories, immigration records, baptismal and marriage records, and other primary and secondary sources. Although I tried to weave together their stories as best as I could, there were certain chapters that had fewer sources and less documentation on either group when discussing them collectively. What I had to do is rely on the fragments of information I gathered and use them to the best of my ability, given the lack of sources available. Personal interviews were also vital to this story. The dozens of individual and families I interviewed were helpful in contributing their stories, personal documents, and photographs. These included Filipinos, Mexicans, and Mexipinos spanning several generations. They helped me build a personal archive of sources, enabling me to share their narratives with you. Their collective memories are at the heart of this story, breathing life into the photographs, archival documents, and personal archives I gathered during the course of writing this book.

Before we begin this journey exploring the interactions of Mexicans and Filipinos in twentieth-century San Diego, we need to look back several centuries, to during their first meetings in the era of Spanish exploration and colonialism. This historical episode laid the foundation for their twentieth-century interactions and is important to understand how deep their connections are in the context of this story.

SPANISH COLONIALISM AND THE ORIGINS OF MEXIPINISMO

Cultural similarities are the foundation of the Mexican and Filipino relationship—a relationship that began in the sixteenth century. For more than 250 years, Philippine and Mexican history was intertwined through the Acapulco-Manila Galleon Trade (1565 to 1815), a byproduct of both countries' Spanish colonialism.

This global enterprise under Spain's empire brought about an exchange of luxury goods, agricultural produce, precious metals, and, most of all, people. Filipino and Mexican *indios* and *mestizos* were key actors in the human and cultural exchanges that took place and forged centuries of racial and cultural blending, or *mestizaje* in both Mexico and the Philippines. These relationships extended well beyond what even their Spanish colonizers expected.[17] Indeed, in addition to the agricultural goods exchanged between Mexico and the Philippines, which have greatly impacted both countries, Filipinos and Mexicans cohabited and intermarried for centuries. During the 250 years of the galleon trade, Filipino and Mexican indios and mestizos arrived in each other's countries as slaves, servants, concubines, and soldiers. Given the brutality and forced servitude experienced by the Filipino and Mexican laborers on the galleons across the nine-thousand-mile journey, desertion was inevitable.[18] Upon a galleon's arrival in Manila, its predominately Mexican crew deserted, blending into the local Filipino indio and mixed-race communities. The same phenomenon occurred when galleons reached Acapulco's ports. Thousands of Filipinos jumped ship and also blended into the local Mexican indio and mixed-race populations. This took place for the next 250 years, resulting in Filipinized Mexicans in the Philippines, and Mexicanized Filipinos in Mexico. Although there is a dearth of evidence regarding the Mexican presence in the Philippines during this time, there is a bit more documented evidence of the Filipino presence in Mexico. According to the journalist and author Floro Mercene, for example, mixed Mexican-Filipinos can trace their Filipino ancestry back over fifteen generations. Filipinos and mixed Mexican-Filipinos were also active participants in major events in Mexican history, including independence from Spain and the founding of several Mexican towns.[19]

When Mexicans and Filipinos began intermixing, they found they had a lot in common, such as religion. Under Spanish colonialism, Mexicans and Filipinos were predominately Catholic, which enabled them to participate in religious events and celebrations together, as well as forge stronger bonds through the practice of *compadrazgo,* or godparenthood. This was something that both Mexicans and Filipinos already practiced prior to Spanish Catholicism; it was further reinforced, which strengthened the bonds between them. Spanish colonialism also influenced both groups by giving them a shared language. Other Filipino dialects, such as Tagalog and Chavacano, also have many Spanish words in them.[20] Filipinos and Mexicans also shared various religious and cultural events such as Dia de los Muertos (Day of the Dead) and the coming-of-age ceremonies for young women (the Filipina debut and Mexican *quinceañera*), which are similar in tradition and significance, as well as the spectacle of cock-fighting.[21] These are just some examples of the many cultural exchanges that both groups engaged in, which had a lasting impact on both their countries. These cultural exchanges reinforced the bonds of mestizaje between Mexicans and Filipinos.

Although the galleon trade ended in 1815, these historical ties and cultural bonds laid the foundation for what would be the renewed interethnic relationships and communities in twentieth-century San Diego and other locals throughout California and the Pacific West Coast. Wherever there were Mexicans and Filipinos, cultural interactions were renewed and interethnic relationships and communities were formed. What resulted was a multicultural experience that resonates to present-day Mexican and Filipino cultural expressions. The children from these twentieth-century families and communities are thus part of a long historical, collective memory of Mexipinos who trace their origins to the first interactions that took place during the sixteenth century. It is this cultural, linguistic, and religious foundation that enabled Mexicans and Filipinos in San Diego, for example, to forge multigenerational interethnic families and identities. This foundation however, is just the beginning.

MAPPING THE MEXIPINO EXPERIENCE

Chapter 1 investigates the colonial relationships between Mexico, the Philippines, and the United States. These colonial relationships allowed the United States to draw upon a colonial workforce to help build its western seaboard cities, such as San Diego. Immigration acts that excluded Asians and other European ethnic groups in the late nineteenth and early twentieth centuries worked in conjunction with the unrestricted flow of Mexican and Filipino labor to the United States. Both groups immigrated in mass numbers during the early twentieth century to help build San Diego into a major metropolitan city. For Mexicans this was a transnational experience, while Filipinos engaged in a transpacific migration. The labor of Mexicans and Filipinos fueled the diversified industries of San Diego's agriculture, fish-canning, defense, and service sectors. The U.S. Navy was also a means by which Filipinos came to San Diego, thus serving in the American empire.

Chapter 2 examines how the forces of race and the politics of space shaped the Mexican and Filipino communities of San Diego. Race was the primary factor in the formation of segregated communities, which were a part of larger multiracial spaces where these two groups converged and interacted with African Americans, Asian Americans, and some European ethnics. As whites fled the changing demographics in these aging areas, they used race-restrictive covenants, local and state-sponsored redlining, and even violence and intimidation to confine Mexicans, Filipinos, and other nonwhites to their racially prescribed spaces. Mexicans and Filipinos turned inward for safety, support, and cultural familiarity. These communities were formed primarily in the South Bay, in the Southeast, along the waterfront (e.g., Logan Heights) and in a small section of downtown San Diego.

Chapter 3 explores the social worlds that Mexicans and Filipinos created to cope with the social pressures of racial segregation and discrimination. Within their multiracial communities, Mexicans and Filipinos formed social organizations, such as mutual aid societies and social clubs, as mechanisms of ethnic solidarity and camaraderie. These organizations were also established to fight for the civil rights of those experiencing racial discrimination. These existed both as separate ethnic organizations and as interracial ones that included Mexicans, Filipinos, and Mexipinos. Social clubs, for example, were more prevalent among second- and third-generation teenagers who also created vibrant youth cultures that were distinct in their own right. These youth cultures included fashion, music, and other forms of entertainment, which provided them a nurturing haven from life's drudgeries and a hostile outside world.

Chapter 4 focuses on how labor and racial oppression was critical to the workplace interactions between Mexicans and Filipinos. Since both groups experienced exploitation and racial oppression, they found a common bond on which they developed their own respective labor cultures that varied with the industries in which they labored. They also organized together to fight their oppression by working under coalitions of separate ethnic unions, as well as forming interethnic ones. Work cultures, labor organizing, and the daily interactions that Mexicans and Filipinos experienced in their communities strengthened their interethnic relationships. Labor was thus a vital factor in how Mexican and Filipino communities were established and intimately tied together in San Diego.

Chapter 5 examines the interethnic relationships primarily between Filipino men and Mexican women. Given that both groups shared many cultural, religious, and linguistic similarities and were for the most part immune to the miscegenation laws of the times, they began a network of Filipino-Mexican families that linked together San Diego, the Imperial Valley, and Tijuana, Mexico. These relationships occurred over several generations beginning in the late 1920s. The Mexipino children that came from these unions are the legacy of this multigenerational relationship. Their multicultural upbringing allowed Mexipino children to identify with both aspects of their parents' cultures. Interactions with newly arrived Filipino and Mexican immigrant groups that questioned their cultural authenticity also illustrate how Mexipinos are in tension with their cultures of origin. In response Mexipinos used their multiethnic identity to resist and challenge monoethnic identities. It is this experience, I argue, that demands a reassessment of what it means to be both Mexican *and* Filipino and how group identity and community were, and continue to be, redefined by Mexipinos in the twenty-first century.

The epilogue examines the post-1965 Mexipino experience with their participation in the cultural nationalist movements of the late 1960s and early 1970s in San Diego and, more recently, with transpacific and transnational activism in the Philippines and Mexico. As recent arrivals from the Philippines and Mexico continue to migrate and settle in satellite suburban communities, class tensions also define Filipino-Mexican relations with older, established communities.

The epilogue also looks at the future of Mexican-Filipino relations and how the experiences of Mexipinos help us to understand these relationships through a multiethnic lens.

By telling this story I explore how we can use the shared experiences of Mexicans and Filipinos in San Diego to understand how ethnic communities function in relation to each other in a local context, while tying it to larger multi-ethnic narratives of California, the Southwest borderlands, and U.S. history, which are influenced by transnational and transpacific events. Oftentimes ethnic and racial communities are marginalized and neglected by these very narratives. Their stories have been hidden, even excluded from the dominant narrative of our nation's past, rendering them invisible, or a shadow at best. I attempt to follow in the footsteps of other revisionist historians and ethnic studies scholars who have been able to bring "the margin at the center." Indeed, by probing the historical amnesia that plagues San Diego's past, I can follow historian Richard Griswold del Castillo's attempt to empower Mexicans and Filipinos "with a sense of belonging and of pride in their participation in the rich history of this region."[22] Thus, by examining the intimate, complex relationship between Mexicans and Filipinos in San Diego and exploring how they and their multi-ethnic children carved a place for themselves in the United States, we can begin to appreciate how identities and communities are formed, nurtured, and sustained over generations. Indeed, the multiple generations of Mexipinos are testimony to this unique history of multiethnic communities in the United States. It is a story worth telling.

CHAPTER 1

Immigration to a
Rising Metropolis

When Jesus "Chuey" Garcia came to the United States in 1927 from Guanajuato, Mexico, he ended up working as a cook for twenty-five cents an hour at an El Paso restaurant. From there, he migrated to San Diego, where he worked picking tomatoes and celery for fifteen cents an hour. He also worked various other unskilled jobs, such as digging ditches. He was disillusioned. "Why did I come? My hands looked like the bottom feet of a horse." Ultimately, Jesus Garcia ended up going back to his trade as a cook, and by 1956 he worked his way into owning his own restaurant, Chuey's Cafe. Since its opening at the corner of Main and Crosby Streets (now Cesar Chavez Parkway), Chuey's has been a cultural institution in Barrio Logan, a predominately Chicano community in Southeast San Diego.[1] Jesus Garcia was not alone in his journey to San Diego to toil in the fields and ditches of a growing city that required cheap, manual labor to sustain its economic boom.

Like Jesus, thousands of Mexicans and Filipinos came to San Diego and other areas of California and the Pacific West Coast from the 1900s to the 1930s seeking employment opportunities in the United States. Most Mexicans and Filipinos who arrived were "birds of passage," hoping to make enough money to go back to their homeland, purchase property, and live out their lives among their families and friends.[2] What both groups did not realize, however, was how larger forces of colonialism and global migrations were influencing their lives.

This chapter will explore the colonial relationships and legal immunities that Mexicans and Filipinos utilized to come to the United States during the early twentieth century in order to feed the growing demand for labor that cities like San Diego needed to support their growth. As newcomers to San Diego, they formed both sedentary and fluctuating communities that followed overlapping migratory labor patterns across the Pacific West Coast. The cultural records that emerge from these communities examine how Mexicans and Filipinos began establishing themselves in San Diego.[3] As their numbers increased, by the 1930s there was a cry for their exclusion and, ultimately, expulsion from the United States. Those who survived the repatriation efforts of the Great Depression continued to be the community anchors for subsequent Mexican and Filipino immigrants who settled in San Diego.

MECHANISMS OF MIGRATION

The overlapping migrations of both Mexicans and Filipinos to the United States, and San Diego in particular, are intimately tied to histories of colonialism and immigration policies, which have been both facilitators and responses to globalization. First colonialism and then neocolonialism dictated the relationships between Mexico, the Philippines, and the United States. After the U.S.-Mexican War of 1846–1848, Mexico lost half its territory—now the U.S. Southwest. Since then Mexico and the continental United States have maintained a close network of economic and political ties, which fashioned itself as a colonial relationship. As historian Gilbert González notes, U.S. capitalist interests have dominated economic institutions in Mexico, leaving it dependent on foreign interests. U.S.-built railroads of the nineteenth century (and later, twentieth-century highways), moving in a north-to-south direction, linked both countries.[4] This, along with economic opportunities, facilitated the flow of Mexicans into the United States to meet its labor demands throughout the twentieth century. Its proximity to Mexico would ensure a limitless supply of cheap labor. In the Philippines, however, a more intensive form of colonialism and neocolonialism occurred, which had specific implications for Filipino migrants.

As the United States expanded its empire across the Pacific at the end of the nineteenth century, it illegally seized the Hawaiian Kingdom, and then the Philippine Islands, which had already declared their independence from Spain. The Philippine-American War of 1898 began and continued through the 1910s. The war was just the beginning of an enduring colonial relationship between the United States and the Philippines. As military campaigns came to an end, the U.S. education system was the next step in pacifying Filipinos after their military defeat in the Philippine-American War. Philippine nationalist Renato Constantino called it the "miseducation" of the Filipinos under U.S. colonialism in order to mold them into good colonial subjects.[5] With the Philippines as a colonial possession, there was now a labor pool of inexpensive, brown bodies to travel across the Pacific to the continental United States as colonial subjects. As an economically dependent and U.S. military–inundated country, the Philippines provided both laborers and sailors to travel within the confines of United States and its territories. Given their status as U.S. nationals, Filipinos could move freely in what historian Dorothy Fujita-Rony called the "colonial empire."[6]

In the twentieth century, these neocolonial relationships enabled the United States, and California in particular, to draw upon a cheap labor pool when needed, then to dispose of it when workers were seen as a threat to America's economic, racial, and moral interests. Indeed, as historian Mae Ngai notes, both Mexicans and Filipinos became part of an "imported colonialism" as the result of the United States' geopolitical power, which has influenced global structures of migration. As a transnational (Mexicans) and transpacific (Filipinos) labor force, both groups "challenged cultural and political norms across a broad spectrum, from the properties of interracial sex to nation-bounded definitions of the working class."[7] This colonial relationship defined how the United States saw both Mexican and Filipino workers, who could be counted on during periods of wartime, but ruthlessly betrayed when economic times threatened white wealth.

Immigration policies were used as legal justification to exclude Asians, while bringing in thousands of Mexican and Filipino laborers to work in California's agricultural, fish-canning, and service industries and on the railroads. Although the United States initially relied on Chinese, then Japanese labor, the American Federation of Labor and civic and social organizations soon called for the end of Asian immigration. An anti-Asian movement ensued, which pressured local, state, and national politicians to act. As a result, Asian immigrants became the first targets of racially motivated legal exclusion. First, the Chinese Exclusion Act of 1882, then the Gentlemen's Agreement in 1907–1908, and finally the Immigration Acts of 1917 and 1924 signaled the end of Chinese, Japanese, Indian, and other Asian immigration to in California.[8] The outcome produced a demand for another cheap labor source. Since Mexicans and Filipinos were both exempt from the 1924 Immigration Act, they were the logical groups to replace Asian farm workers. Thus, after 1910 Mexicans were the primary source of labor to meet the expansive growth of California agriculture.[9] As colonial subjects with U.S. national status, Filipinos also had no immigration restrictions. They could travel freely within the territorial jurisdiction of the Untied States. This enabled them to come by the thousands to California.[10] At the same time these events were unfolding, San Diego's city leaders and boosters were moving to secure it as a military city in the West, which enabled federal money to pour in and shape its infrastructure, making it a major metropolitan city. These structures, in turn, needed a workforce to meet the demands for growth and prosperity. Mexicans and Filipinos filled that need.

San Diego: An Emerging Metropolis in the West

San Diego is California's southernmost city, neighboring Tijuana, Mexico. As California's second largest city and the nation's eighth largest, San Diego is home to one of the largest naval stations in the country and has one of the largest economies in the world.[11] The navy continues to be an important part of San Diego's economy as a major metropolitan city. Defense spending, for example, continues to pour into San Diego, contributing more than 11.7 billion dollars a year to fuel its military installations and civilian workforce.[12] As the gateway to

California, San Diego shares a border with Tijuana, Mexico; these two border towns are nestled in one of the world's largest economic zones. San Diego's location thus ensures the continued growth of the Mexican population, now the largest nonwhite ethnic minority in the county. As a naval town and port city, San Diego has also been an area of settlement for Filipinos since the early twentieth century as the United States extended its empire across the Pacific from its western shores. It is currently home to the second largest Filipino population in the country.[13]

San Diego has a rich, complex history, yet little is known about the city or its racial and ethnic communities. When we look at the history of San Diego's economic and social development, for example, we tend to hear the same narrative regarding the role of Alonzo Horton, William Kettner, John D. Spreckels, and other founding fathers of the city, whose visions for San Diego were grand indeed.[14] One cannot ignore how these visionaries sought after vital federal aid for the development of a city that would one day become home to one of the largest military bases in the United States and a center where agriculture, fish canning, ship building, and other wartime industries thrived. Although the nineteenth century saw the foundation being laid for the city, the early twentieth century was a turning point in San Diego's development, as Kettner expanded beyond Horton's and Spreckels's original visions of growth. Kettner secured federal and military spending to develop San Diego into a naval center that became headquarters to the Eleventh Naval District.[15] Construction, agriculture, mining, infrastructure, fish canning, and other industries also thrived during the early to mid twentieth century in San Diego as the population doubled every decade as a result of the navy's increasing labor demands. The favorable climate of San Diego, which was advertised in the 1880s as a cure for many health problems, also contributed to its population growth.[16]

Although we may look to the visionaries and admire the risks they took and fortunes they spent to see their vision become reality, we must not ignore the labor force that actually built the city. Indeed, tens of thousands of workers labored relentlessly, risking their lives in the process of building San Diego and its infrastructure, brick by brick, building by building, and industry by industry. It was the rank-and-file workers who toiled in the rock quarries, brickyards, construction sites, mines, railroads, fish canneries, and agricultural fields so that visionary dreams could become a physical reality. They, I argue, risked just as much and lost their own fortunes along the way, sometimes even their lives. They are the true unsung heroes and heroines in the development of San Diego as a metropolitan city in the West and should be included in the larger narrative of the region's history.

These early industries relied heavily on manual labor, both unskilled and semi-skilled, performed by predominately by nonwhite immigrants. From the early use of Italian, Portuguese, Chinese, and Japanese labor in the late nineteenth to early twentieth centuries, the workforce shifted to become primarily Mexican and Filipino. Although San Diego's economy relied primarily on the navy and defense-related industries during World War II, during its formative years in the early twentieth century, San Diego's economy relied heavily on agriculture and fish canning. As early as the 1920s, agriculture was among the top industries in San Diego, as was the fishing industry, which included several canneries.[17]

California's rapid development during the twentieth century, however, was facilitated by wartime expansion. This was fueled by shipbuilding and aircraft production, especially during World War II. San Diego was no different. Given that San Diego has one of the ten best natural harbors in the world and could hold most of the U.S. Pacific fleet, the navy eyed the city with its prime location and friendly climate. Thus, with the help of men like William Kettner, San Diego established longstanding economic ties to the navy, soon earning the reputation as the "Gibraltar of the Pacific" when it became home to the largest naval station in the country.[18] By the late 1920s and well into the 1930s, San Diego was also gaining a reputation as the "air capital of the West," with Consolidated Aircraft, Solar, and Ryan among the major companies making it their home.[19]

As a result of San Diego's diverse industries, economic and population booms signaled the expansive growth and ensured that San Diego experienced less economic turmoil than other cities, especially during the Great Depression.[20] City boosters and officials, such as Spreckels and, more so, Kettner, were able to continue to gain federal money to create and expand the urban infrastructure of San Diego. This money was also tied to the navy since it was "the primary instrument in the course of urban development."[21] San Diego's industries were so prosperous that between 1939 and 1943 it rose from seventy-ninth in the nation to twenty-eighth as an industrial center. By the 1940s, San Diego became a fast-paced city, leaving behind its image as a "sleepy navy town" or "sleepy border town" and became a "wartime metropolis." San Diego was now an important supplier to the West's regional economy, what Abraham Shragge called a "Federal city."[22]

The need for labor was crucial for San Diego to continue its economic expansion and sustain a growing population from the 1920s to the 1940s. The availability of immigrant labor was necessary to feed this growing metropolis. The United States was in a dilemma, however, since it already excluded Asians and other immigrants from its shores. Without a viable labor force, California, and San Diego in particular, looked south of the border and across the Pacific to meet those labor needs. It was Mexicans and Filipinos who became the major source of labor for San Diego. Their early migrations to San Diego illustrate both the shared and divergent experiences that influenced their move to the region, the early formations of their communities, and how they responded to the xenophobia and nativism that plagued the era of the Great Depression.

MEXICAN IMMIGRATION TO SAN DIEGO

San Diego was once part of Mexico, so there has always been a Mexican community within the city. They lived, worked, and traveled back and forth from
Mexico to visit family and friends, and circular migration was common. Many
of the families that came and settled in the region were part of familial and
extended kinship networks; these networks fostered new arrivals who came to
join relatives and friends in neighborhoods such as National City, Logan
Heights, and Lemon Grove.[23]

Increased immigration of Mexicans to San Diego occurred during the first
two decades of the twentieth century because of two events: the Mexican
Revolution of 1910–1920 and World War I. The Mexican Revolution displaced
and dispersed over a million of its citizens, with the majority of them fleeing to
the United States. The ravages of war resulted in loss of land, poverty, starvation,
and a devastated economic, social, and political structure. Mexican immigrants
sought refuge and economic security in the United States. As political scientist
Wayne Cornelius noted, "For the first (and probably the last) time in American
history, tens of thousands of Mexicans were readily admitted to the United
States ... as economic refugees."[24] Most of these immigrants were ordinary
workers and their families who wanted nothing more than a chance to survive.
Political refugees, merchants, and other intellectuals formed this diaspora of
Mexicans to the United States.[25]

During the Mexican Revolution, tens of thousands of Mexicans made their
way into San Diego, not only from Tijuana/San Ysidro, but also from El Paso
and other ports of entry. For example, longtime Logan Heights resident
Consuelo Zuniga's mother's side of the family migrated to San Diego in 1912 to
escape the political unrest that was going on in Mexico. They first ended up in
Arizona, then made their way to San Diego, where they settled in Logan Heights.
Her father's family migrated from Sonora to Douglas, Arizona. He traveled to
the Imperial Valley, then also made his way to Logan Heights. Both her parents
worked in the canneries. Connie's father eventually started working for Nelson
Construction Company.[26]

The migration of Mexicans during the Mexican Revolution coincided with
the onset of World War I (1914–1918), which created an acute labor shortage due
to the loss of men who went to serve in the military. Rising industries such as
factories, mines, construction, agriculture, fish canning, and transportation
needed a labor supply to sustain the United States' involvement in the war effort.
With the passage of the Immigration Acts of 1917 and 1924, which targeted both
Asian and southern and eastern European immigrants, Mexicans were among
the only immigrants from the Western Hemisphere who were exempt from
these laws, and thus they were able to come in to the United States free of quota
restrictions.[27] From 1918 to 1930, U.S. interests encouraged the influx of Mexican
immigrants to fill labor needs. As one Mexican immigrant stated about the

United States, "The country across the border promises new experience, excitement, adventure."[28] The chance to live free from war, earn a living, and provide their children with school was more than enough to entice many Mexicans to migrate north to the United States. Mexican immigrants found themselves in a position to fill the labor needs of California while sustaining their own economic livelihood. As such, the majority of Mexican immigrants who came to San Diego were laborers.

California was a key state that absorbed a great portion of the Mexican immigrants who came during the early twentieth century. According to Governor C. C. Young's Mexican Fact Finding Committee Report, *Mexicans in California,* the State of California saw an increase of 25,068 Mexican immigrants, or 316.0 percent, between 1900 and 1910, and another 55,077 immigrants from 1910 to 1920, or a 163.5 percent increase. Another 163.5 percent increase from 1920 to 1930 placed the total number of Mexicans in California at around 223,912.[29] Overall, 617,000 Mexican immigrants entered the United States legally, which was approximately one-half of the total legal Mexican population in the country.[30]

Although San Diego did have a much smaller Mexican population than its northern neighbor Los Angeles, its population also doubled every decade from 1900 to 1930, giving it the fifth highest percentage of Mexicans in the state of California.[31] Similarly, when looking at the Heller Committee Report, *How Mexicans Earn and Live,* which was a study based on the Mexican community of Logan Heights during the 1930s, census data was used to show that while Mexicans comprised 1.2 percent of the total population in the United States, they constituted 6.5 percent of the total population in California. San Diego was among the ten counties listed that had the highest percentage of Mexicans within the population. This number, however, can be misleading because the Heller Committee admitted that agricultural workers were not in included in their study due to the migratory nature of this particular group. This would have made the Mexican population much higher than listed in census and state reports, thus demonstrating San Diego's importance as a site of early Mexican community formation.[32]

By 1941, Mexicans comprised approximately 7.6 percent of San Diego's total 11.2 percent minority population. An economic and industrial report on San Diego, however, noted that the proportion of San Diego's Mexican population was small considering that it shared a border with Tijuana, Mexico. State reports have documented that it was because there were not enough industries to keep Mexican workers.[33] Although there may be some truth to these statements, the fact that San Diego has historically been inundated by military personnel and retirees has created what Richard Griswold del Castillo calls "the basis of a conservative, Republican-dominated elite that has sought to develop San Diego as a tourist attraction with minimal attention to the needs of marginalized groups."[34] Indeed, this comment provides valuable insight to the racial mechanics that were working to ensure that the city's nonwhite population always remained minimal, at best. This will be further discussed in the following chapter.

TABLE 1.1

ESTIMATED NUMBER OF FOREIGN-BORN WHITE MEXICANS
IN CALIFORNIA COUNTIES AS OF 1930

County	1910	1920	1930
Los Angeles	11,793	33,644	95,953
Imperial Valley	1,461	6,414	28,157
San Diego	2,224	4,104	7,572

Sources: Will J. French, dir., Mexicans in California: Report of Governor
C. C. Young's Fact-Finding Committee (San Francisco: State of California
Department of Industrial Relations, 1930), 46; and Paul S. Taylor,
"Mexican Labor in the United States," University of California
Publications in Economics 6, no. 1 (1928): 18.

One issue that is not discussed in state and federal reports when looking at
San Diego's population statistics and industries is the fact that San Diego and the
Imperial Valley are historically tied to each other with regards to Mexican migration. This can also be said of Filipino migration, which will be discussed in further detail later in this chapter. If we were to include those numbers from the
Imperial Valley with San Diego's numbers, given the migration of Mexican agricultural workers between the two areas, there would be a tremendous increase
in San Diego's population. Table 1.1 shows population statistics between Los
Angeles, San Diego, and the Imperial Valley.

The reason for including the Imperial Valley is because it was once a part of
San Diego County. It was not until 1907 that the Imperial Valley was made into a
separate county. Both counties have been sites of historical migration, intimately
tied together for both the Mexicans and their Filipino counterparts, who traveled
the same roads together. In these mobile communities, workers circulated
between the two counties as part of the larger migration circuit throughout the
Pacific West Coast. For example, David Galbiso's Filipino-Mexican family, which
included his parents and uncles, owned farmland in Niland, a small farming community located in the Imperial Valley. His uncle Geronimo first migrated to the
United States from Hawai'i, where he worked for the Hawaiian Agriculture
Company in 1924. After his contract was completed in 1926, he left for the continental United States. Geronimo worked in agriculture, traveling back and forth
from Arizona to San Diego, primarily to Spring Valley during the 1940s, where an
established network of Filipino laborers was present. While working in Spring
Valley he was able to earn enough money to go into partnership with his brothers
and purchase farmland in Niland in 1951. It was because of these experiences that
Galbiso called San Diego the focal point for Filipinos who left the Imperial Valley
to settle there. Family and friends who settled in both areas continue to maintain

a network of familial and kinship relations over the years. In fact, every year there is a Niland reunion in San Diego that brings these families together.[35]

Early sociological studies of Mexican immigrants also showed that due to the seasonal nature of agricultural work in the Imperial Valley, ten thousand Mexican laborers out of a population of twenty-one thousand, or nearly one-half, were constantly migrating in and out of the area, making their way into San Diego, among other locations. Similarly, the cities of La Mesa and El Cajon, two other agricultural areas in San Diego County, are situated along the eastern route to the Imperial Valley. Given that they are linked by both Highway 80 and the Southern Pacific Railway, one scholar remarked, "San Diego was an important transit and shipping center for Imperial Valley fruit and truck stops."[36] These routes fed this connection of laborers and agricultural products. This coincided with the labor needs of neighboring San Diego, which also had a fluctuating Mexican population for the same reasons. In December of 1919 the newly built railroad connected San Diego to Imperial Valley to transport railroad, construction, and agricultural workers; it also provided a means to cement the link between both regions.[37] Thus, San Diego's Mexican population was much greater than what is portrayed by Governor Young's report. Including the Imperial Valley to some extent is reasonable, given its close relationship and proximity to San Diego. Although it still had a much smaller Mexican population, San Diego had an impressive increase in its numbers, reflecting the larger trends of population growth. Table 1.2 shows the increase per decade, from 1900 to 1970.

Early U.S. census data is notorious for being inaccurate based on fixed numbers for households interviewed. For one, census information cannot be accurate given the size of most Mexican families, which may not have been fully accounted for; the seasonal nature of agriculture and the mobile communities of workers who followed the crops; the fishing boats that had crews out to sea throughout the year; and the fact that many census takers may have underestimated the Mexican population based on recording only a few households in a given neighborhood. Census takers were known to undercount racial and ethnic populations in low-income communities. Griswold del Castillo also notes, for example, that "the 1930 census also did not count the American-born children of Mexican parents, a group that probably tripled the reported figures."[38] Moreover, the numbers may also be misleading because many Mexicans fluctuated between the San Diego–Tijuana border region, traveling to work or temporarily residing in San Diego. Indeed, Mexicans and Filipinos lived in transient, fluctuating communities. This is especially true for the period up until the 1920s because San Diego and Tijuana had an open border until the formal establishment of the Border Patrol in 1925. Even then, Mexicans continued to cross back and forth to work, shop, or visit family and friends in San Diego.[39] Repatriation drives in the 1930s, as well as Mexicans being lumped together under a white category in the 1940 census, have also made it difficult to estimate the population. As the geographer Phillip Pryde notes, "It is impossible to determine how many

TABLE 1.2

TOTAL MEXICAN POPULATION IN SAN DIEGO, 1900–1970

Year	Total population	Mexican population
1900	17,700	638–893
1910	39,578	1,588–2,224
1920	74,683	3,563–4,104
1930	147, 995	9,266–20,000
1940	203,341	N/A
1950	334,387	15,490
1960	1,033,011	70,000
1970	1,357,387	150,000

Sources: U.S. Census Bureau, *Thirteenth–Twentieth Censuses, 1900–1970* (Washington, DC: U.S. Census Bureau, 1900–1970); and Alberto Camarillo, *Chicanos in a Changing Society: From Mexican Pueblos to American Barrios in Santa Barbara and Southern California, 1848–1930* (Cambridge, MA: Harvard University Press, 1996).

Note: Given the inaccuracy of census reporting on the Mexican community of San Diego due to the migratory nature of a segment of the population, I rely on Albert Camarillo's study, which utilized various variables in calculating the Mexican population of San Diego. See Camarillo, *Chicanos in a Changing Society,* 200–201. Other studies used to help determine population accounts include George B. Mangold, *Community Welfare in San Diego* (San Diego: San Diego County Welfare Commission and City of San Diego, 1929), 20; Lawrence Herzog, *Where North Meets South: Cities, Space, and Politics on the United States–Mexican Border* (Austin: University of Texas Press, 1990), 173; Philip R. Pryde, *San Diego: An Introduction to the Region* (San Diego, CA: Sunbelt Publications, 2004), 75–90; and San Diego Association of Governments (SANDAG), "Mapping the Census: Race and Ethnicity in the San Diego Region," *SANDAG Info 1* (April 2002), www.sandag.org/uploads/publicationid/publicationid_722_1120.pdf (accessed July 18, 2006).

Spanish-speaking residents lived in the country during this time period because such information was not considered important enough to ask about in the census."[40] As Mexicans were making their transnational migration to settle and labor in San Diego, Filipinos were also making their transpacific migration.

FILIPINO IMMIGRATION TO SAN DIEGO

Like Mexican immigrants, the majority of Filipinos who came to the United States during the early twentieth century also initially came as "birds of passage."

With economic conditions in the Philippines in shambles after its war with the United States, there were limited opportunities at home. As colonial subjects looking for a way to survive, thousands of Filipinos were first recruited by Hawai'i's sugar and pineapple plantations. Many moved on to the fish canneries and agricultural fields along the West Coast of the United States in order to come back home with some sort of financial success. They intended to buy land and live out their lives as property owners in the Philippines.

Although the majority of Filipinos left the Philippines for the United States out of necessity and economic survival for the families they left behind, many also came seeking adventure along the way. Ben Villarin, for example, was one of a group of young boxers who came to the United States to train with the famed Filipino fighter Speedy Dado in 1930. Although his career as a boxer never took off, Ben ended up living in Los Angeles, then moving to San Diego and settling in Logan Heights in the 1940s after he met and married his wife, Dorotea. She was a schoolteacher in the Philippines but did some work as an extra in war movies while in Los Angeles. Ben and Dorotea left the Philippines seeking adventure as well as an opportunity to work in the United States. Other occupations facilitated Filipino migration to the United States. According to historian Catherine Ceniza Choy, for example, Filipina nurses migrated to the United States in the early 1900s, an experience shaped by U.S. colonialism in the Philippines.[41]

As with their Mexican counterparts, economic motives, coupled with the thrill of adventure in a new land, were enticing enough to bring them to the United States. As colonial subjects who had the status of U.S. nationals, Filipinos had the freedom to move anywhere within the colonial empire of the United States. Filipinos' status as nationals, however, would come to haunt them later. As quasi-citizens they were neither citizen nor alien, thus they could not own or lease land, nor did they have ample political protection when they faced racial discrimination and violence.[42]

Because Filipinos came across the Pacific, their migration routes differed from those of Mexican immigrants. As early as 1906 Filipinos were sent to Hawai'i to work in the sugar and pineapple plantations. Sugar cane producers would be the main employers of Filipino immigrants to Hawai'i. As early as 1917, U.S. mainland agricultural interests were considering and even advocating for the importation of Filipinos, in addition to Mexicans, as a means to fill the labor shortages, most notably in California, during World War I.[43] Thus, the sugar planters of Hawai'i and the agricultural and fish-cannery employers of California and the Pacific West Coast turned to Filipinos to fill these positions. Filipinos, like Mexicans, were coming in by the thousands between 1920 and 1930 to labor in various industries. Laborers, however, were not the only ones who came from both Hawai'i and the Philippines. A key difference that distinguished the migration of Filipinos from the migration of their Mexican counterparts was that Filipinos came to the United States, and San Diego in particular, by way of the U.S. Navy. Given their colonial relationship with the United States, many

Filipinos also came as government-sponsored students in the early 1900s. A brief look at the diversity of Filipino immigration to San Diego must be examined in order to understand the complex position Filipinos had as colonial subjects and settlers in the United States, as compared to Mexicans, who primarily came as laborers.

The Pensionados Come to San Diego

Prior to their arrival as laborers and sailors to San Diego, Filipinos first came as government-sponsored students. After the Philippine-American War, a colonial government was established, which was ruled by Americans with a secondary level of Filipino administrators as part of the "Filipinization" of the country.[44] Part of this plan was to educate Filipinos in the United States and bring them back to the Philippines, where they would hold government posts. This was the beginning of the Pensionado Program, which lasted from 1903 to 1940. Under this program, five hundred *pensionados,* or "fountain pen boys," as they were also called, came to the United States.[45] The government supported most of the pensionados during the first phase of the program. In later years, two-thirds would be self-supporting students who worked in agriculture, domestic work, and service industries, while a smaller number were given partial support from the government or help from family and friends.[46] Documentation of this first group of pensionados in San Diego was mentioned in various San Diego newspapers in 1903. They noted that "ninety-eight little brown men" were coming to San Diego County.[47] In all, ninety-six students actually arrived in California, landing in San Francisco aboard the steamer *Korea* on November 9, 1903. From there, a group went to Los Angeles by train; nineteen ended up in San Diego three days later. According to newspaper accounts, they were greeted by Mayor Frank P. Frary; W. L. Frevert, president of the San Diego Chamber of Commerce; Hugh J. Baldwin, county superintendent of schools; Frank P. Davidson, city superintendent; Thomas F. Branscome, superintendent in National City; and Miss Myers, principal at Coronado.[48] They spent the day with county superintendent of schools Hugh J. Baldwin at the schools where they were to be placed. From there, they were registered at the Horton House, where they signed in, and then proceeded to dine at the Manhattan in downtown San Diego.[49] They were given a reception at the home of Superintendent Baldwin, where they displayed their "rare musical ability, particularly on the guitar," which showed their hosts that they were "passionately fond of music."[50] While in San Diego the pensionados also amazed local residents, school administrators, and newspapers with their appearance. They were described as "neatly clad young men, well built, though slightly undersized, with well shaped heads."[51] Moreover, the fact that these Filipinos could speak English amazed their American hosts, who were not fully aware of the impact that U.S. colonialism had on the Philippines. Not only did they have some fluency in English, but most of them were also fluent in Spanish and their own local dialect.[52]

School officials also observed the similarity between Filipinos and Mexicans. A report to the Philippine Commission, for example, describes the area of southern California and its heavily Mexican-influenced region and, more notably, mentions that the Filipino pensionados attended the same school with Mexicans. It stated that "the Filipino in many respects is more like the Mexican than he is like any other race I know of."[53] This comment illustrates the shared cultural similarities these outsiders observed and foreshadows how both Filipinos and Mexicans would later be racialized and treated in the United States.

With regards to their other activities and how they fared in school, one newspaper reported that the initial group of Filipino students in San Diego completed their studies with an "honorable dismissal" and departed in June of 1904 back to the Philippines.[54] Though these were not really settled immigrants per se because they returned home, nonetheless, their presence marked the earliest documented arrival of Filipinos in San Diego as the county's first foreign exchange students. Another aspect of this colonial relationship was via the U.S. Navy, which was an avenue for Filipino migration to the continental United States that resonates to this day.

Filipinos in the U.S. Navy

Like many of his countrymen in the Philippines, Ciriaco "Pablo" Poscablo dreamed of coming to America. The navy was one means to achieve this goal. In 1919, he left his hometown of Calasiao, Pangasinan, and traveled to Cavite, where he enlisted in the navy as a musician second-class. His other duties aboard the ship included working as a steward since his responsibilities went far beyond that of a musician in the navy. He was dispatched aboard the USS *Albany* in December of that year. He traveled to San Francisco, where he boarded the USS *Arizona* in 1922. He was discharged in San Pedro, California, in 1923. From there he traveled to San Diego aboard the USS *Melville*. In 1924 he was stationed at the San Diego Naval Training Center, where he received further training. Pablo remained in San Diego for the remainder of his life.[55]

Like Pablo, many Filipinos came to the United States via the navy to "see the world." Although Pablo enlisted as a musician, his duties aboard the ship included working as a steward like most Filipinos who joined the U.S. Navy. As with employment opportunities in the various industries on the West Coast, the navy proved to be another pipeline for Filipino migration to booming naval towns such as San Diego, Los Angeles, San Francisco, and Seattle in the early twentieth century.[56]

The Filipino presence in the navy was also a result of post-1898 U.S. colonialism and militarism in the Philippines. With U.S. control of the Philippines, the military established the practice of recruiting Filipinos since it was more costly to recruit and ship American soldiers from the United States back to the islands. Filipinos entered the U.S. Navy in 1901 as a result of General Order Number 40, which was signed by President William McKinley. This allowed approximately five hundred Filipinos into the navy. As historian Jocelyn Agustin Pacleb noted, "Thus began the Navy tradition of enlisting Filipinos outside of the U.S."[57] By World War I, the navy was the primary means by which Filipinos entered U.S. military service. They were, however, confined to the rank of steward. As stewards, Filipinos were essentially domestic servants for white naval officers. In order for them to obtain U.S. citizenship, they had to serve for at least three years in the military; otherwise, they were ineligible for this benefit.[58]

The recruitment of Filipinos into the U.S. Navy, as Pacleb also noted, "coincided with the migration of Filipina/os to the United States for educational and work opportunities prior to World War II."[59] By the end of World War I, approximately twenty-five thousand Filipinos came to U.S ports where they received their discharges and settled, finding employment in the naval yards as well as in a variety of other occupations.[60] This type of Filipino settlement in the early twentieth century differed from both Mexican immigration in general and the previous migration of pensionados who came in 1903. For one, while the pensionados received their education and went back to the Philippines, many of the early navy Filipinos settled in the United States, being among some of the first Filipino settlers. One of the earliest records of Filipinos landing in San Diego by way of the navy is in 1907, when the USS *Boston* anchored in the city's harbor. By then, only a small group of Filipinos resided in the city. According to Felix Budhi, who came to San Diego in 1908, there were a small number who lived around Market Street. As Budhi observed, "Around Market, Fifteenth, and Sixteenth, a small Filipino community is found . . . [and] a few of the Filipinos owned small restaurants combined with pool and gambling tables. Outside downtown there were only acres and acres of farms."[61]

This was one of the earliest cultural records of Filipino settlement in San Diego. Individuals such as Vicente Elequin and Tony Alcalde were among the small number of Filipinos who also came to San Diego between 1918 and 1919. Alcalde, for example, came to San Diego in 1919. He joined the navy to secure a steady income. As he recalled, the only work available in San Diego at the time was agricultural work or the navy.[62]

After their service in the U.S. Navy, Filipinos also worked in civil service jobs or agriculture.[63] Ricardo Romio, for example, was born in Logan Heights in 1937. His father, who was Filipino, and his mother, who was Mexican, both settled in Logan Heights in the early 1930s. His mother worked at the canneries and his father was in the navy. His father joined the navy in 1918 as a steward. After he got out of the navy, he went to work for civil service in North Island, then at the 32nd Street Naval Base, which bordered National City and Logan Heights. He served in both World Wars.[64] Freddie Ayap's Filipino father was also in the navy. He moved his family to Logan Heights in 1943 during World War II. After his retirement in 1949 he returned to farm work in the community of Encanto before he got a job in civil service as a custodian at North Island.[65]

As a naval center, San Diego has been home to one of the southernmost points of what Dorothy Fujita-Rony called the "colonial empire." Like Seattle, San Diego was a colonial metropolis where Filipinos arrived after traveling across the Pacific to come to the continental United States.[66] Many of them who came did not stay permanently, but left with the ships. Their voyages, however, allowed many Filipinos to set foot in San Diego. Indeed, the navy has been instrumental in the growth of the Filipino community in San Diego. Today, approximately half of the Filipino population in San Diego has some direct or indirect ties to the U.S. Navy.[67]

For many of the Filipino recruits, San Diego would be the first place they visited in the United States. They received training in Point Loma at the San Diego Naval Training Center. As sociologist Yen Le Espiritu notes, "Until 1998, San Diego was the site of the largest U.S. naval base and the Navy's primary West Coast training facility, the Naval Training Center (NTC)." Here, Filipinos came to receive training and spend their liberty on shore. Another study also documented that Filipinos were also employed in the naval yards. Given that they were only employed on a temporary basis, no records are available as to how many were engaged in this type of employment.[68] Although the U.S. Navy provided a means for Filipinos to earn a living and come to the continental United States, the majority of them made their way to labor in California agriculture and travel its migratory circuit.

Migratory Labor in California's Fields

Like Mexicans, the majority of Filipinos who came to the continental United States from 1920 to 1934 were employed in agriculture. Indeed, as much as 59 percent of all Filipino workers were engaged in this industry.[69] Due to the number of Filipinos involved in agricultural work, chapter 4 will examine in detail the conditions in which they labored and their response to grower exploitation. What will be discussed in this chapter is the nature of the migratory labor circuit they worked along the West Coast and how San Diego was a part of this route despite its omission from the historical record.

San Diego was the southernmost tip of the West Coast migratory labor circuit, with a large agricultural industry to feed workers into this system, yet many state and independent studies in the 1930s, such as Bruno Lasker's *Filipino Immigration to the Continental United States and to Hawaii* and Will J. French's special bulletin, *Facts about Filipino Immigration into California*, fail to mention it as a locale for Filipino immigration.[70] San Diego did not register on the map despite the thousands of Filipino (and Mexican) migratory laborers who lived in or passed through San Diego to labor in the county's agricultural fields.

Given the nature of this type of invisible employment, census data is also inconsistent. Regarding actual numbers of Mexicans versus what was included by census takers, the same could be said about Filipinos. Because the majority of Filipinos were laborers in industries such as agriculture in San Diego and nearby

Imperial Valley, their population fluctuated with the seasonal crops, creating a "portable community," a highly mobile population of migratory laborers that came in and out of San Diego. Indeed, as Linda España-Maram noted about these portable communities, "Because most Filipino laborers had to tailor a life in harmony with their migratory work patterns, they created a community that was versatile and, for them, functional. They took their communities with them."[71] Filipinos settled temporarily to harvest San Diego's many crops, only to leave and follow the migratory circuit that took them throughout the state of California, sometimes even as far as Alaska to work in the fish canneries.[72] This is also true for Mexican agricultural workers.

U.S. census data and other reports also do not account for the fluctuating navy population among Filipinos, who oftentimes went out to sea. This affected how communities were formed and, more importantly, how they sustained themselves as workers and sailors fluctuated in and out of San Diego. This created a sort of routine fluctuation of the Filipino community, which expanded when seasonal crops needed to be harvested and when the ships came into town and contracted when the naval vessels and migratory workers left. Table 1.3 provides some indication of San Diego's Filipino population from 1900 to 1970.

Given that state officials and researchers did not bother to include migratory laborers in studies on the Mexican community of San Diego, it is likely that they did not take into account Filipinos who also had similar employment, as well as those who were in the U.S. Navy. Census reports are also misleading given the fact that both Filipinos and Mexicans share many similar Spanish surnames. This could have led census reporters to assume that Filipinos were fewer in number if they were mistaken for Mexican and added to their population statistics.

TABLE 1.3

FILIPINO POPULATION STATISTICS

Year	United States	California	San Diego
1900	–	–	–
1910	2,767	5	–
1920	26,634	2,674	48
1930	108,260	30,470	394
1940	98,535	31,408	799
1950	122,707	40,424	N/A
1960	181,614	67,134	5,123
1970	336,731	135,248	15,069

Source: Yen Le Espiritu, *Home Bound: Filipino American Lives across Culture, Communities, and Countries* (Berkeley: University of California Press, 2003), 101.

Since population counts do not document this, oral testimony is relied upon to give an idea of Filipino and Mexican presence since many of them were often overlooked in the residential areas where they rented homes. That, in addition to the census takers not even bothering to count Filipinos, could have led to a miscount on the actual numbers of them in San Diego.[73]

The memories and photographs of the workers, as well as some newspaper accounts, are among the only cultural records that exist which document how these fluctuating and sedentary communities affected the cultural landscape of San Diego. According to historian Adelaida Castillo-Tsuchida, for example, the earliest documentation of Filipinos who settled permanently in San Diego was in 1908.[74] The presence of these early immigrants would be the cement that held together the subsequent migrations of workers to the city. Porfirio S. Apostol, who arrived in San Diego in 1932 after traveling from Seattle, worked his way down through California. He observed that there were about one hundred Filipinos living in the city.[75] Even by the late 1950s, the Filipino community was considered small by population standards. Filipina resident Nena Amaguin also remarked on the Filipino community's size in San Diego when she settled there in 1958. She remarked that it was "very small. When we came here [there were] only a few Filipinos."[76] Although her statement does suggest that San Diego's Filipino community was small, again it may not take into account the portable communities or those that lived in other areas outside of her own in the downtown sector on J Street, where a small number of Filipino families resided. Filipino and Mexican communities, although small, managed to survive and steadily grow throughout the early twentieth century, being fed and then diminished by the fluctuating mobile communities that came with the crops or navy ships. There were always small, yet stable communities that lived in cities such as San Diego. A more detailed account of these community formations will be discussed in the following chapter.

Gender Imbalance among Early Immigrants

The makeup of the Mexican and Filipino immigrant communities differed in terms of their gender makeup. As previously mentioned, Mexicans who came to the United States during the years 1910 to 1920 to escape the Mexican Revolution were families as well as single men and women. Both men and women came to fill labor shortages during World War I and took advantage of the unrestricted access of immigration laws, resulting in a large, gender-balanced population. Men were not the only ones who came to labor in San Diego and other areas of the United States. Women also came on their own to work and earn a living in *el norte*.[77] Indeed, many Mexican women made the journey up north as widows, single mothers, and individuals. They, along with thousands of others, came to the United States to work and eventually settle in San Diego. Once there, some stayed in Logan Heights or National City, while other families traveled back and

TABLE 1.4

COMPARING THE MEXICAN AND FILIPINO POPULATION
IN THE UNITED STATES, 1925–1929

Group	Single (%)	Married (%)	Widowed (%)	Less than 30 years old (%)
Mexican	55.1	40.6	4.2	71.0
Filipino	77.3	22.5*	0.2	84.3

Source: William J. French, dir., *Facts about Filipino Immigration into California, Special Bulletin No. 3* (San Francisco: California Department of Industrial Relations, 1930), 46.
*Most married Filipinos came without their wives.

forth between communities because of the nature of their work. Irene Rivas, for example, grew up in Logan Heights during the 1920s. Her stepfather used to work for the Santa Fe Railroad and her mother was a housewife. Given the nature of his work on the railroads, her family had to move around a lot, to Campo, National City, and then back to Logan Heights.[78]

Although both Mexicans and Filipinos had a bachelor population in their communities, Filipinos had more of a gender imbalance. According to French's *Facts about Filipino Immigration into California,* the ratio of Filipino males to females was fourteen to one. Other studies rate this even higher, as much as twenty-three to one.[79] The majority of the bachelors who came to the United States were young as well, between the ages of sixteen and thirty. Those men who came to the United States did so without their wives. During the years 1920 to 1929, only 2,079 women came to California, compared to men who numbered 29,013, or 93.3 percent of those Filipinos who came to California. In all, between the years 1920 and 1929, approximately 31,092 Filipinos came to California.[80] A comparison of the Filipino and Mexican immigrant population can be seen in table 1.4.

ROUTES OF MIGRATION

The avenues of migration for both Filipinos and Mexicans to San Diego also tell a story. A sample of Mexican Immigration and Naturalization Records for the years 1935 to 1942, for example, provides an idea as to where they were coming from, their modes of transportation, and where they settled in San Diego. No one Mexican state produced a majority of immigrants coming to the United States; however, the Baja California region did supply a sizable number who settled in San Diego. The vast majority of those sampled came by way of border entries, such as San Ysidro or Calexico. This included walking, using a horse-drawn carriage, or driving an automobile through these border points. Some arrived through El Paso via the electric railway, railroad, and even by ships, which brought Mexican immigrants from Ensenada and other coastal ports along Baja California. The modes of transportation also varied according to the year the individual first came to San Diego, which ranged from the mid-1800s to the 1930s.[81] Although they came by different modes of transportation, those who settled in San Diego went to areas where already established communities were present, such as Logan Heights, National City, Chula Vista, and Lemon Grove.

The majority of Filipinos, however, came to the United States through the ports of Los Angeles and San Francisco. Some also came through the port of Seattle and even came by way of Mexico. Los Angeles and San Francisco had the greatest number of Filipino migrants to enter California. Of the total number of Filipinos in California who entered the state between 1920 and 1929 (31,092), approximately 17,425, or 56 percent, embarked from Honolulu, whereas 10,882, or 35 percent, embarked from the Philippines. The remaining 2,785, or 9 percent, arrived via foreign ports.[82] The reason the majority of those who immigrated embarked from Honolulu, Hawai'i, was the result of labor discontent and expanding opportunities in California and elsewhere along the Pacific West Coast. Many Filipino laborers were also blacklisted and deported to the continental United States. Thousands more left to try their luck with their families and friends who had migrated earlier.[83] In essence, Hawai'i became known as the halfway station between the Philippines and the continental United States, particularly California.[84] Once in San Diego, they had to settle and find a place to call home.

Planting Roots in San Diego

For both Mexican and Filipino immigration to the continental United States, the discourse has been framed in terms of economic opportunity, but the role of family support was just as important, if not more so. Many immigrants came to establish a new home and be the anchor of community building for the subsequent family members and friends who would follow, while others sent money home to support their loved ones. For those family members who followed their loved ones, they began to build an extensive network and community that included family, friends, and extended kin. These relationships were strengthened by their commitment to each other and their cultural values. Anthropologist Roberto Alvarez Jr., who wrote about early Mexican immigration from Baja California to San Diego, observed how the practice of *parentesco,* which included kin ties between blood relations as well as non-kin ties among those who shared history and geographic locations, provided a means by which reciprocity and kinship solidarity were maintained among families and friends. That, along with the practices of *compadrazgo* (godparenthood) relationships, marriage, and, most importantly, *confianza,* or trust, was the basis by which all social relationships, networks, and institutions continued, including both familial and kinship ties among these migrants.[85] As Alvarez pointed out, "Most of the families that arrived were kin to the previous migrants. In a well-practiced pattern, they sought refuge and aid in the homes of close kin. Extended kindred, like home-town networks, continued to provide family bonds and new outlets for the growth of family interrelations . . . Incoming families and friends brought news of loved ones in the south and changes among kin in the homeland."[86]

If it were not for the role of already established families and kin that had set the foundation for others to join them, the experience would have been more difficult in an already alienating environment. This was also true for Filipinos, who relied on connecting with the few families that were present once they arrived in San Diego. Family and kinship ties were central for the survival of both Mexican and Filipino communities. Though the disbursement of families and friends occurred throughout San Diego County as they moved out of the original areas of settlement, they nonetheless continued to stay connected. They got together during religious, familial, and other social events such as weddings, baptisms, anniversary parties, family get-togethers, and funerals. These gather-ings, though at times less frequent than in the past, illustrate how these ties have remained despite the geographical mobility and settlement of families.

Though some of these early communities have changed dramatically, such as Lemon Grove, Logan Heights, National City, and Chula Vista, some of these families or their descendents still remain, maintaining roots to the homes they once knew. Industries have changed, such as the closing of the local fish canner-ies in Logan Heights and surrounding areas, as well as the end of agriculture, specifically lemon orchards in Lemon Grove. These have given way to other wartime industries during the postwar era as well as technological industries. What has risen are the service-related industries that employ thousands of Mexicans and Filipinos. Yet for Filipinos, a mainstay in their own communities has been the navy, as more naval families arrived in San Diego, increasing existing communities or establishing new ones outside of the South Bay and Southeast sections of San Diego. But as more Mexicans and Filipinos continued to pour into the United States, local, state, and national officials began calling for their exclusion and, ultimately, their removal.

EXCLUSION AND REPATRIATION

Although Mexican immigration during the 1900s and 1910s was virtually ignored by immigration officers due to the labor needs of railroads, mining, and agricul-ture during World War I, by 1919 Mexicans were required to apply for admission when they entered a U.S. port of entry.[87] By the end of the 1920s and well into the dawn of 1930, the U.S. attitude toward its Mexican and Filipino populations went from one of necessity due to the labor shortages of World War I to one of disdain. Nativists and white labor accused both groups of taking away their jobs. Despite the need for both Mexican and Filipino labor, by the late 1920s both groups were the targets of xenophobic whites who saw their numbers increasing too rapidly. Because the numbers of both Mexicans and Filipinos were rising prior to the years leading up to the Great Depression, politicians, conservative labor unions, and white labor saw them as a threat.[88] Of the estimated 45,208 Filipinos in the continental United States, approximately 30,470 came to California, which fueled the cry for their exclusion.[89]

Economic competition was the supposed reason behind the call for exclusion since Filipinos were allegedly displacing whites in various occupations, such as hotel, restaurant, and agricultural work.[90] This was absurd given the fact that service work and agricultural jobs were already racialized as "Filipino work" or "Mexican work." Nonetheless, white laborers still made these ridiculous claims even as they sought to avoid these jobs.[91] Mae Ngai notes that as the United States was shifting its relationship with the Philippines from a colonial to neocolonial model, the move to end Filipino immigration and exclude them from U.S. shores was a calculated "movement for decolonization and exclusion."[92] This was in response to the hysteria that was being drummed up by politicians and labor groups that saw the continuous flow of brown bodies from the Pacific and south of the border as a threat to the racial, moral, and economic livelihood of the country. Indeed, the unwarranted alarmist attitude was the cause for many editorials, commentaries, and even state reports on the "Filipino and Mexican problem." Such problems were the topic of many nativist groups, such as the Commonwealth Club, American Legion, Veterans of Foreign Wars, America for Americans Club, California Joint Immigration Committee, State Grange, Native Sons of the Golden West, the California State Federation of Labor, and the American Federation of Labor, many of which held conventions and passed resolutions calling for the exclusion of both Mexicans and Filipinos. Judge George J. Steiger of San Francisco, for example, also questioned their ability to assimilate, stating, "We all must agree that the Filipinos do not and cannot assimilate with our people."[93] By racially constructing Filipinos and Mexicans as outsiders and thus unable to assimilate with whites, momentum was gained in the public sphere for their exclusion and removal.

From the individual to the institutional level, workers, politicians, and organizations called for an end to both Mexican and Filipino immigration to the United States. What distinguished these groups from each other was the series of legislative measures targeting Filipinos specifically. The cause for alarm was made notably by individuals such as Congressman Richard Welch of California, who introduced a bill (H.R. 13900) on May 19, 1928, to the House of Representatives calling for the exclusion of Filipinos and classifying them as "aliens" in order to solve the so called "Philippine Problem." He, among others, helped fuel the flames for anti-Filipino sentiment by calling Filipino immigration "the third Asiatic invasion of the Pacific Coast."[94] He advocated for closing the doors on immigration, stating, "Filipinos are not our own people," despite the fact that they were still U.S. nationals. Congressman Charles Colden also proposed bill H.R. 9281 in 1934, which would have restricted both Mexicans and Filipinos by placing quotas on "immigration from the Republic of Mexico and the Philippine Islands."[95]

Senator Samuel Shortridge proposed an amendment to the Harris immigration bill (S.51), stating that he was a "friend of the Philippine people and would give them independence at this very hour if I had the power." This statement showed that he was in favor of Philippine independence, not because he was a friend of Filipinos, but because he wanted to prohibit their entry into the United States. By granting Philippine independence, Filipinos would immediately have their status changed from national to immigrant, which in turn would allow for their exclusion.[96] This assumption can be gathered through a previous statement he made regarding his view of Chinese exclusion, where he stated, "We stopped the Chinese from coming to our shores not because we hated them, but because we loved our own."[97]

This statement is problematic for two reasons. First, exclusion of the Chinese and the subsequent targeting of Filipinos for exclusion were based on race, which was imbedded in the language of the exclusion and repatriation acts. Whites saw Filipinos as a threat, and they were not discreet in their motives. Second, the fact that racial violence toward Filipinos was so intense demonstrates the racial climate in which they were living. It was an intensity that surpassed even the animosity toward Mexicans during this time. If Shortridge was so concerned about "our people," he would have suggested that the United States did not need Filipino labor so long as there were Mexicans. In other words, he noted, "We do not have to look 6,000 miles across the Pacific to get this seasonal labor. It is overabundant in Mexico."[98] This shows that issues were far more complex than labor when dealing with Filipinos. Shortridge was successful in crafting his language to show an air of genuine concern, all the while distracting the public from his real intentions, which were anti-Filipino.

Eventually, the bills were defeated. Yet it did not stop its proponents, chiefly U.S. labor unions and politicians, from virtually ending both Filipino and Mexican immigration to the United States. As one individual noted in his address to the Commonwealth Club of California during a meeting on the issue of Filipino immigration, "If the presence of particular races is detrimental to our interests, that fact would seem ethically to justify action to control the evil."[99] Mexicans were also targeted, whether foreign or U.S. born. As one Americanization teacher noted, "He [the Mexican American] is really not part of the real America. Because of language and color he is foreign even to the so called 'hyphenated' American citizen; he may always be."[100] Filipinos and Mexicans were both demonized and dehumanized. Their presence was framed as an invasion that had to be curtailed. Thus the social, economic, moral, and health problems that they supposedly contributed to U.S. society needed to be dealt with by excluding them from the United States as well as calling for their repatriation or, rather, deportation.[101]

In response, both the Mexican and Filipino communities wrote their own editorials and commentaries attesting to their law-abiding ways, contributions to the city and state economy, and their desire to be a part of the United States.[102] Yet their presence came at a time when economic insecurity was at its height, with the collapse of the stock market in 1929 and the resultant Great Depression that lasted throughout the 1930s, leaving the United States in economic turmoil. It was during the 1930s that the treatment of both Mexicans and Filipinos was at its worst. For Filipinos, however, they faced greater violence than their Mexican counterparts. Filipinos were the victims of violent race riots, such as those that occurred in Exeter, Watsonville, and the Imperial Valley, among other areas of California and the West.[103] Because of the perceived economic and social competition that they had with white men over white women and "white jobs," Filipinos were beaten, stabbed, robbed, chased out of numerous towns, and even killed by bombings and shootings at the hands of white men in various cities throughout California. Mexicans were also viciously attacked. The Ku Klux Klan, for example, had an active chapter in San Diego and was responsible for many acts of violence against Mexican migrant workers. According to the civil rights and labor activist Robert Galvan, these violent acts of terror included migrant workers being hanged from trees in rural areas, buried alive, and lit on fire "to see them dance." The racism and terrorism against Filipinos was so intense that writer Carlos Bulosan noted, "I came to know afterward that in many ways it was a crime to be a Filipino in California."[104]

Despite the fact that numerically Filipinos were never a real threat to white labor, they were still the targets for exclusion, as was the case for both the Chinese and Japanese before them.[105] San Diego Assembly District candidate George B. Bowers, for example, argued that immigration from Japan, Mexico, and the Philippines was "not a problem of the future; it is a problem of today."[106] Ironically, this fear created an unholy alliance between those Filipinos pushing for independence and nativists who wanted to rid themselves of their "Filipino problem." Continued pressure by groups such as the American Federation of Labor, the Sons and Daughters of the Golden West, and the Commonwealth Club and efforts by Philippine officials resulted in the adoption and passing of the Tydings-McDuffie Act of 1934, which recognized Philippine independence but required it to be under U.S. rule until 1946.[107]

The passing of the Tydings-McDuffie Act was supposed to answer the problem of Philippine independence. This act did not solve the "Philippine problem." The act did not provide for either economic or national security of the Philippines, which still had complex economic and strategic interest for the United States.[108] With the stroke of a pen, Filipinos no longer possessed national status but were instead reclassified as immigrants. This virtually ended Filipino immigration to the United States from the thousands in previous years to a mere fifty Filipino immigrants per year after 1934. This was in essence an exclusion act.[109] This move proved to be devastating to the Filipino population, which immediately ceased to grow as it once had. The move to exclude Mexicans, however, failed.

Nativists such as Congressman Welch and Senator Hiram Johnson, among others, orchestrated the immediate repatriation of Filipinos, who were now seen as "indigents" leeching off welfare rolls, despite the fact that these claims were unsubstantiated. As nationals, Filipinos were ineligible for public relief despite paying taxes.[110] This fact was buried under the inflammatory rhetoric by public officials and conservative labor leaders, which further exacerbated public fear. A year later, the Filipino Repatriation Act passed, which was, in essence, a one-way ticket to the Philippines with the legal means to keep Filipinos from reentering the United States, despite the lofty excuse that it was for the benefit of Filipinos who wanted to go home. It was, in fact, as contemporary Filipino writer Manuel Buaken noted, a deportation and exclusion act.[111] The Immigration and Naturalization Service (INS) scheduled "deportation parties" to round up Filipinos across the United States. Many Filipinos carefully read the stipulations of the act, which stated, "No Filipino who received the benefit of this Act shall be entitled to return to the continental United States except as a quota immigrant under the provision of [the Tydings-McDuffie Act]."[112] They were well informed of the issue and thus were resistant to the hollow provisions of the Repatriation Act.

Despite the excuses that white politicians and city officials made that Filipinos were a burden on relief rolls, in fact, as a community, Filipinos pooled their resources together, rather than depending on welfare, for fear of being shamed and losing face.[113] Indeed, as Linda España-Maram notes regarding the Filipino community of Los Angeles, through the practice of *utang na loob* (mutual support) and other forms of mutual aid, Filipinos sustained each other through "a sense of responsibility for one another's welfare," which enabled them to avoid depending upon U.S. institutions for assistance. It was a sense of pride in not having to rely on outside support, but rather on each other.[114] This would be the same reason why they did not take advantage of the "voluntary" efforts for them to be repatriated at the onset of the Filipino Repatriation Act of 1935. In fact, only 2,190 took advantage of this act. Some left voluntarily due to their disillusionment because of their treatment in the United States. Of that number, 95 percent were men.[115]

In San Diego and the Imperial Valley, repatriation was also underway as newspapers advertised for the free transportation back to the Philippines.[116] Yet, by and large, the majority of Filipinos did not take advantage of this act because they did not want to go home as failures. To go back to the Philippines at the government's expense was shameful for many Filipinos. It was an admission of defeat for these young men, so, rather than be disgraced, they endured their treatment in the United States. As historian Adelaide Castillo-Tsuchida remarked, "To the average Filipino, it would have meant 'losing face' and suffering humiliation, or *mapapahiya,* to return home as a repatriate."[117] Rather, they stuck it out and used various survival mechanisms such as family, extended family, and community support to stay and endure the harsh years of the Great Depression. In the end, Filipino repatriation was a failure.

Their Mexican counterparts, on the other hand, fared a lot worse in terms of repatriation efforts. Mexicans, like the Filipinos, were blamed for the Great Depression, yet even more so because of their larger population in the United States. Immigration was virtually uninterrupted for two decades prior to the Great Depression, which enabled Mexican communities to grow at an escalating rate. Their substantially larger numbers made them a target for more forceful action. This included congressional legislation that was introduced in 1929 making unlawful entry into the United States a felony, along with a series of federal deportation campaigns also known as "repatriation."[118] As the historian Zaragosa Vargas notes, President Herbert Hoover mobilized public opinion against the Mexican population and "made Mexicans the prime targets for government persecution, regardless of whether or not they were citizens of the United States."[119] Mexicans were accused of burdening local economies through public relief and the taking of "American" jobs when they should be saved for white Americans.

In response to this allegation, Griswold del Castillo provides an important insight. As he notes, unlike what the popular imaginary constructed, which was that Mexicans were taking jobs and burdening welfare rolls, "Mexican nationals nationwide were among the least likely to rely on county welfare or charitable services, and the vast majority of them were already unemployed."[120] The majority of Mexicans did not want to go on relief rolls because it was an insult to be supported by the government. They would rather work several jobs or have multiple incomes from everyone in their family working rather than go on relief. This was true for Connie Zuniga's father during the Great Depression. He said he could never bring himself to collect welfare because it was a thing of pride. Instead, Connie's father worked numerous odd jobs in addition to his work in construction. Similar to the Zunigas, other Mexican families in San Diego also opted to work rather than go on relief during the Depression. Joe Lerma and his siblings, for example, helped contribute to the family income by working after school at the fish canneries or selling tacos and tamales.[121] Jesus Ochoa, who was the eldest of five children, helped his mother, who was the sole provider as a widow, by selling newspapers after school. His mother worked at Van Camp fish cannery. In 1940, he worked at the Civilian Conservation Corps camp in California, which was established by President Franklin Roosevelt during the Depression to provide work for unemployed men.[122]

Despite these facts, in Southern California as early as 1931, efforts were already being made to deport Mexicans. Memos were being circulated between the Los Angeles Chamber of Commerce and city officials, which stated: "By all means the Government should proceed to deport all undesirable aliens at this time, particularly those who are a burden to the community and if it can be speeded up I see no reason why it should not be done. . . . The main thing however, is to keep from upsetting the whole Mexican population by wholesale raids and other methods which are misunderstood by the Mexican and set that Mexican afloat."[123] Despite their concerns over disrupting the Mexican population with wholesale raids, that is exactly what occurred. Studies on Mexican repatriation provide ample evidence of deportation raids as the immigration and police officers rounded up Mexicans, both citizens and noncitizens, and sent them across the border. These agents of the state did not bother to distinguish the difference. Their racial uniform as "Mexican" was enough to subject them to deportation.[124]

Indeed, being Mexican became the physical marker that singled them out for racial profiling and, ultimately, deportation. As a result, entire families and large sectors of Mexican communities were deported through a concerted effort from national, state, local, and charitable agencies. As the mechanisms of repatriation, or deportation, targeted Mexican immigrants, U.S. citizens of Mexican descent were also affected. The deportation of U.S. citizens clearly violated their civil rights.[125]

Fear also facilitated their departure. As the historian George Sánchez notes regarding Los Angeles's Mexican community during the repatriation drives, fear resulted "in encouraging Mexicans of varying legal status—including American-born citizens of Mexican descent—to contemplate leaving." The involuntary roundups and coercion to leave was stressful. Many fled for fear of deportation.[126] Estimates vary, but contemporary studies suggest that up to one million persons of Mexican descent were repatriated back to Mexico during the years 1930 to 1935 in an effort to stabilize the country's economic woes by ridding itself of its "Mexican problem." Of this number, an estimated 60 percent were U.S. citizens by birth, a majority spoke English, and many had lived in the United States all their lives. This accounted for 20 percent of the Mexican population in the United States, a staggering number that fell victim to this forced removal.[127]

Although the size and growth of San Diego's Mexican communities were also affected, not all of San Diego's Mexican community was deported. Jose "Joe" Galvan, for example, worked the celery fields of the South Bay and did pick-and-shovel work on Works Progress Administration (WPA) projects during the Great Depression.[128] John Rubalcava's family was also one of the fortunate ones who had job security and was among those that were not deported. Most of John's family was either working or in school, which enabled them to be spared the humiliation and devastation of being repatriated. As John recalled, "I saw the ship down on Broadway, when we were sending them back, because I had some friends, and they were waving at me." He was around seven or eight at the time as he watched the ships depart from the marina on Broadway in San Diego.[129] Herb Ibarra also recalled the scene that took place during the repatriations in San Diego: "My mother knew that a relative of ours was on one of the boats, so she took me with her to San Diego Harbor. I won't ever forget the boats, the humanity packed onto the decks under armed guard. We saw our relative on the boat and we waved, but the guards wouldn't let us talk; wouldn't let anybody off the boat. I saw all of this, looking between the legs of adults."[130]

In San Diego County, the number of Mexicans and Mexican Americans who were formally repatriated was 1,913. According to historian Camille Guérin-Gonzales, this was twice the number of people who were on relief.[131] The number of Mexican families on relief in San Diego was relatively small, yet they were pressured by relief agencies to return to Mexico. Arthur Louch, who was head of the County Welfare Department, stated that between 400 and 500 Mexican families were on public assistance in San Diego. Although Louch also noted that 375 other alien nationalities were on public assistance, only Mexican families were targeted as being a burden on San Diego's economy. This does not even take into account U.S. citizens who were also on relief, which no doubt far surpassed any other group. Louch's goal was to deport Mexicans in San Diego before they became "spoiled by inactivity and public aid." Yet those who wanted to work and could find jobs in public works projects were thrown out for preference to U.S. citizens.[132]

Those who were persuaded to leave San Diego contacted Mexican consul Enrique Ferreira for financial assistance. They were transported by boat and railroad. Over half of San Diego's *repatriados* settled across the border in Baja California, such as Colonia Libertad in Tijuana. Overall, 70 percent settled along the Mexican border states of Baja California, Sonora, Sinaloa, Chihuahua, and Coahuila. Given the close proximity of these areas, it is highly likely that once they were able to, these same Mexican and Mexican American families returned to San Diego and other U.S. border cities because that is where they considered their home to be, especially for the majority of repatriates who were U.S. citizens.[133]

As a result of these mass deportation drives, whole communities were disrupted. Families and friends were torn apart and uprooted from their homes. Housing, businesses, and communities were lost, leaving behind the hopes, dreams, memories, and the lives that they once knew.[134] The economic insecurity of the U.S. public, as well as their fear, nativism, and lack of compassion toward Mexicans and Filipinos, put those Mexicans and Filipinos in a humiliating and unjust situation. With nearly 20 percent of the Mexican population and 7 percent of the Filipino population in the United States repatriated during the Great Depression, it was as Ngai noted, "a racial expulsion program."[135] These efforts, though a failure in many respects for both communities, show how, despite the move to exclude and remove both groups, they, in fact, continued to grow throughout the twentieth century. The demand for labor, especially during World War II, would be the catalyst for a renewed growth of both communities.

———

As Mexicans and Filipinos continued to immigrate to San Diego, they were coming into a city that had already decided where they could live. Although both groups came to live in areas where there were preexisting Mexican and Filipino populations in San Diego, they soon found out why. The politics and social implications of race had a strong hold over the city's nonwhite communities. The city was growing overall as more whites and nonwhites came into San Diego, which doubled the population every decade. What brought Mexicans and Filipinos to San Diego was primarily the need to fill the labor demands that the city required to continue its exponentially rapid growth. Yet as they came to labor for San Diego's economic development, they would not share in the freedom to live where they wanted or be able to move up the socioeconomic ladder. Their citizenship did not matter either. They were confined to barrios or "ghettos" in larger multiracial communities. As we will see in the following chapter, Mexicans and Filipinos were up against an unseen, albeit powerful force in their pursuit for economic, political, and social equality.

CHAPTER 2

The Devil Comes to San Diego

RACE AND SPATIAL POLITICS

In 1928, Filipino writer (and later World War II veteran) Manuel Buaken came to the United States to seek an education and make a place for himself in his newly adopted country. Upon his arrival, he obtained a job working at a Los Angeles restaurant. However, when he sought housing, he faced a humiliating experience. When inquiring about renting a place to live, an older woman rudely turned him away by replying, "Only whites in this neighborhood." He tried six other places, only to be turned away from all of them. Manuel described his experience: "I spent the entire day going from door to door, trying to rent a place to live but without success. At the end of them I was tired physically, and weary mentally; my personal pride was entirely subdued; I was wounded deeply in heart and in soul! For on that day I had tasted more pangs of life's bitterness than all the sordidness of this world I have ever known before, and learned what calamity and what tragic consequences race prejudice can inflict on a man's life!"[1]

Buaken was not alone in his humiliation and disillusionment based on the treatment he received because he was Filipino. Racial discrimination was a major factor that kept Mexicans, Filipinos, and other nonwhites confined in racially segregated areas in San Diego. From racial zones after World War I to race restrictive covenants through the 1960s, racial segregation affected racial and ethnic communities for generations in San Diego.[2] These structures and institutions of racism were most notable where Mexicans, Filipinos, and other nonwhites lived. They were all the targets of racial covenants.[3] Race restrictions did not go unnoticed by early civil rights and race relations organizations. They sought to shed light on the injustices that nonwhites experienced as a result of racial discrimination in housing. In cities all over the United States racial segregation became a major issue. San Diego was no different. As the

American Council of Race Relations documented in its 1946 study of San Diego's racial problems, "Racial segregation and discriminatory practices are the principle means by which the majority carries out its beliefs. These apply universally to Negroes, but also to Mexicans, Chinese, Filipinos, Japanese, and East Indians, wherever these groups appear in sufficient numbers to arouse color consciousness."[4]

Mexicans and Filipinos built a world of their own within the confines of these segregated, isolated, multiracial communities. They constructed a safe haven where they could be themselves and find, if only for a brief moment, an escape from the social pressures and daily frustration associated with racism and discrimination. Although there were multiple factors that created the social space for Mexicans and Filipinos, I argue that race and its intersections with class were at the forefront. Racial segregation was so profound that the remnants of this hideous past can still be seen in these same communities, which remain predominately nonwhite. The racial segregation that occurred in San Diego is best exemplified by Stephen Pitti's metaphor of the "devil" for white racial ideology, which was the mechanism used to oppress Mexicans in San Jose, California.

In San Diego race and its intersection with class were also crucial in how its white population found ways to construct a racial divide for its nonwhite residents and maintain what historian George Sánchez calls "zones of whiteness."[5] Invoking the "devil" of white racial ideology thus ensured that Mexicans, Filipinos, African Americans, Asian Americans, and indigenous peoples were for the most part separated and confined to living in separate multiracial communities or reservations (for indigenous peoples) since the mid-nineteenth century. Despite the fact that there were prominent Asian Americans and African Americans in San Diego, they were still segregated well into the twentieth century.

For Filipinos and Mexicans, their place in the racial hierarchy of exclusion is interesting to note. For one, although Filipinos held the status of U.S. nationals and owed "permanent allegiance to the United States," they experienced a quasi-citizenship status that did not provide them with any civil rights protection. As such, they were racially segregated and treated like any other nonwhite group.[6] For U.S.-born Mexicans, their case was unique. Although they were considered "white" by law, they did not experience any difference in treatment save for the few who phenotypically looked white and asserted their whiteness for social mobility. As historian Paul Spickard notes about the majority of Mexicans, "In their social relationships they were manifestly treated as Brown, not White."[7] Their whiteness and even citizenship were ambiguous at best since their social realities and racialization as "Mexican" included them in the company of those excluded, along with Filipinos and other nonwhites.[8] Thus, when newly arrived Mexicans and Filipinos came to San Diego, they entered a city that had already established itself since the late nineteenth and early twentieth century as an Anglo town.

Indeed, San Diego's white population conjured its own "devil" to both exploit its Mexican and Filipino workers and confine them to certain sectors of the city and county in order to maintain San Diego's zones of whiteness.[9] The politics of space were intertwined with what Michael Omi and Howard Winant call "racial formations," which, when imposed on housing, for example, bring about "a process of historically situated projects, in which human bodies and social structures are represented and organized."[10] This was how San Diego was able to create and maintain racialized spaces, which inevitably led to a collective identity of struggle and resistance among its nonwhite communities. This segregation was done through de jure and de facto means. Not only did the "devil" sustain white identity and communities in San Diego, it also forged multiracial communities and identities. Mexican and Filipino communities, then, were a part of this collective identity as nonwhite, oppressed people who forged a bond with African Americans, Asian Americans, and others in these larger multiracial spaces. Thus, their collective identity and the activities they engaged in enabled them to survive the devil's chokehold on San Diego's multiracial enclaves.

From the onset, whites did not want to live by or mix with racial and ethnic minorities in San Diego. In order to separate themselves, they utilized federal housing policies, real estate agents, and practices such as racially restrictive covenants to create what George Sánchez refers to as "geographies of difference," which were "rooted in inequalities based on social class and an inclusive sense of 'ethnic otherness.'"[11] Mexicans and Filipinos in San Diego did not have the political influence to expand their residential space or move outside the confines of their multiracial communities and barrios. Since white residents were the majority, they utilized their political and racial solidarity to control the city and who could live where. This gave them the freedom to move out of the "old" part of San Diego and build new residential suburban areas that were free from nonwhite residents.[12]

San Diego had such a bad reputation for its race relations that, according to labor historian Jim Miller, "in 1965 the Fair Employment Practices Commission called San Diego one of the most segregated areas in the country and linked that segregation to employment discrimination."[13] Since San Diego wanted to create an image conducive for tourism, it had to separate itself along racial, ethnic, and class lines. As Miller notes concerning San Diego's development, "The city of San Diego was not built on Anglo-Saxonism alone. . . . From the beginning, San Diego's elite knew that if they were to build a garden city free of not just the ethnic conflicts but also the class strife that plagued other cities, they would have to devise a growth plan that avoided the importation of an unruly working class."[14]

For San Diego's nonwhite communities, race and class would be determining factors in their segregation, and at times when class was not the issue, race would always be invoked. Several factors influenced racially segregated housing patterns of Mexicans, Filipinos, and other nonwhites. These included

voluntary segregation, white flight, restrictive covenants, availability of housing
and discriminatory practices at the hands of real estate agents, as well as local,
state, and government institutions.[15] These mechanisms confining San Diego's
Mexican and Filipino communities will be discussed throughout this chapter.
First, let us examine the early formations of these communities.

THE BARRIOIZATION OF SAN DIEGO

The move to segregate Mexicans, Filipinos, and other nonwhites in urban areas
such as San Diego followed the process that historian Albert Camarillo called
"barrioization." For Mexicans, this process occurred after the Americanization
of Southern California in the late nineteenth century. According to Camarillo,
because of their political powerlessness and economic disadvantage, "Mexicans
everywhere struggled to maintain their communities. . . . [T]hose communities
that persisted did so only after their Mexican citizens adapted themselves to
their new existence in a residentially segregated, poverty-stricken barrio."[16] This
process occurred as San Diego continued to grow and become more urbanized,
forcing its Mexican and other nonwhite populations close to industrial areas
where housing was older and rundown.

Although scholars such as Camarillo and others describe the barrio as a
Mexican space, many of these barrios were a part of larger, multiracial spaces.
As Sánchez notes on the multiracial makeup that defined the Boyle Heights
community of Los Angeles, for example, there is an assumption that the multiracial communities of the present testify to how the legal and political struggles
of previous generations enabled geographic mobility of nonwhites to newer
suburban communities. What is forgotten, however, is the racial segregation
that actually created early multiracial communities to begin with and how these
communities interacted with each other on intimate levels that often times went
beyond racial or ethnic lines among those that were confined to these spaces.
This was one of the arenas were Mexicans and Filipinos interacted. Thus, racial
diversity in segregated communities is nothing new and actually stems from the
earliest practices of racial segregation. Sánchez writes, "We have collectively
forgotten the history of racial interaction in the past, and the particular way in
which the legacies of racial conflict in Los Angeles are erased from the urban
landscape."[17] This was no different in San Diego's barrios, such as Logan Heights
(also known as Barrio Logan) and National City. Although they may be predominately Chicano and Latino today, prior to the late 1960s they were multiracial communities including Filipinos, African Americans, Asian Americans,
Chamorros, and other nonwhites. This is what defined the multiracial communities and barrios of the early twentieth century. Political powerlessness and
economic displacement forced these multiracial communities to remain within
the confines established by white political, geographic, and economic control.
Indeed, as geographer Wendy Cheng observes about the intersection of race and

property, "homeownership is a central element of the perpetuation of racial inequality vis-à-vis literal property."[18]

By the early twentieth century, Mexicans and Filipinos considered these communities and barrios their homes as they struggled to make ends meet.[19] Logan Heights was the second and newer pocket of Mexican population in San Diego (the first one being Old Town), yet it was more important in the barrioization process because it was an urban area located close to the waterfront—an industrial/residential zone where many also worked. Over 25 percent of the city's Mexican population lived in this area. The small population of Filipinos who lived in the same areas also endured the same racial discrimination. This process was how the politics of race and space defined the barrios and multiracial enclaves of San Diego.[20]

The fact that San Diego did not have a large Mexican or Filipino population at the time did not mean it was not an important destination for newcomers. Mexicans, Filipinos, and other nonwhites were left with areas along the industrial waterfront to the south of downtown and the corridor area running through downtown San Diego; other communities were located in the adjacent southeastern section and the South Bay region of San Diego, which extended all the way down to San Ysidro. These areas were all located below the I-8 Freeway, which was south of the Mission Valley area. The I-8 Freeway historically served as the racial dividing line between the old and new areas of San Diego, which were developed and maintained. As Lawrence Herzog observed on transboundary urban space in San Diego, "nearly 70 percent of the entire Spanish-surname population of San Diego resided within the city of San Diego in Barrio Logan and San Ysidro."[21] Longtime residents such as Connie Zuniga noted the longstanding presence of Mexicans in these areas: "There was a lot of Mexicans in the area [Logan] and I think a lot of people just gravitated to that area. . . . [F]or some reason everybody knows about Logan and you end up in Logan; all the Mexicans did. . . . [Y]ou look at the history of Mexicans in San Diego; they all started out in Logan Heights."[22]

San Diego's Mexican and Filipino residents lived in the downtown and waterfront areas of Logan Heights as early as the 1900s.[23] Mexican and Filipino communities were also established in National City, Chula Vista, Imperial Beach, San Ysidro, and a small section of downtown San Diego prior to 1910. In National City, for example, there was a small Mexican community present during the early 1900s, which went as far back as Logan Heights.[24] Joe Montijo, a longtime Mexican resident of National City, recalled that his family settled in National City in 1849. Similarly, National City elementary school photographs dating to 1906 show a large number of Mexican children. Other National City residents, such as John P. Mendez's family, settled in the area as early as 1912.[25] According to historian Adelaida Castillo-Tsuchida, Filipinos were also living in the downtown section of San Diego as early as 1908. In Chula Vista, Filipinos were also present as early as the 1910s because of their presence in the citrus industry. One former resident of Chula Vista said: "I remember the Chinese first when I came, just scattered around in Chula Vista. Very quick after the Chinese were here the Filipinos started coming in. There got to be quite a few of them working in the fruit, some of them in the packinghouses, some picking lemons."[26]

San Ysidro, because of its proximity as a border town to neighboring Tijuana, also evolved into an ethnic enclave. As a port of entry, it was also important for the Mexican migrants who crossed over into San Diego.[27] Yet Logan Heights was the historical nucleus of Mexican settlement in San Diego during the twentieth century and continues to be one of the oldest remaining Mexican and Chicano barrios in San Diego. Photographic evidence also points to Logan Heights as an early area of settlement for Filipinos since the late 1920s.[28] Several state and federal reports designate Logan Heights as having the largest concentration of Mexicans in the city of San Diego. National City and Logan Heights remained the primary areas of settlement in San Diego through the 1960s.[29]

Sampling a portion of housing tract census forms from 1930 for the area of downtown San Diego and the Logan Heights area also confirms the fact that the majority of Mexican and Filipino residents did indeed live in and around these areas. Mexicans were also found within the vicinity of what is now called Little Italy due to its proximity to the fish canneries and Logan Heights. This was as far as Mexicans and Filipinos were able to go within the downtown and surrounding sections. Point Loma to the north was the dividing line where whites, well-to-do Portuguese, and other European ethnics resided. Small pockets of Mexican and Filipino populations could also be found in Spring Valley, Lemon Grove, Encanto, La Mesa, and El Cajon in the eastern part of the county, as well as Oceanside and Escondido in the northern part of the county, working in agriculture and construction. Lemon Grove, for example, had a sizeable Mexican community in the 1930s. As populations in these areas continued to grow after 1950, they also became newer areas of multiracial settlement.[30]

During the years 1910 to 1926, both Mexican and Filipino migration into San Diego increased, yet most migrants still resided within these already established communities. Census information is also verified by a 1937 Federal Writers' Project report, which listed San Diego's Mexican community as being located between Sixteenth and Twenty-Fifth Streets, along Logan and National Avenues.[31] Due to the onset of the Great Depression and the repatriations, which occurred because of the country's economic crisis and decreased immigration from Mexico and the Philippines, housing patterns for Mexicans and Filipinos did not change much. It would not be until World War II and well into the 1950s that both groups would shift and begin moving further into the southeastern sections of San Diego. The Mexican community of Logan Heights, however, remained the second largest in California from the 1940s to the 1950s.[32]

Mexicans and Filipinos began to move toward the northeastern sections of San Diego in the 1960s, which distributed their numbers into other parts of the city. The majority of Mexicans and Filipinos, however, still resided in the Southeastern and South Bay regions of San Diego.[33] During the post-1960s both Mexicans and Filipinos were able to move out of Logan Heights and National City, locating further into Chula Vista, Imperial Beach, San Ysidro, Paradise Hills, and Encanto. As one observer noted in San Ysidro, "We've gotten an influx of African Americans, Pacific Islanders, especially Filipinos."[34] Smaller pockets of these communities continued to live in Spring Valley, Lemon Grove, La Mesa, and El Cajon but were often separated from white suburban areas. These areas became open for settlement as they became old and whites moved to newer suburbs.

Although a few Mexicans and Filipinos were documented as living beyond the racial confines of the South Bay and Southeast, they were still segregated. These particular families or individuals constituted an exception, where they did not pose a threat to the surrounding white community. These included Filipinos who labored as houseboys or chauffeurs to prominent white families and oftentimes lived in the employer's house or close by. Mexicans who chose to identify as white and claimed a "Spanish" identity or lived as domestic workers or groundskeepers for prominent whites also lived in these areas. One such neighborhood where there were several Filipino, Mexican, and African American families was located on Cuvier and Draper Streets in La Jolla, which was an older, rundown section. This section in La Jolla was known as the "servants' quarters." These families labored in the nearby small-scale agricultural fields of La Jolla or as service workers and janitors or in small restaurants that catered to an overwhelmingly rich, white community.[35]

The quality of housing was another issue that Mexicans and Filipinos had little control over. Given that the waterfront areas of Southeast and South Bay San Diego were comprised of older, rundown neighborhoods, these areas also provided low-cost rental housing. This made it affordable for semi-skilled and unskilled workers to support a family, or multiple families, who resided in the dwellings that were available to them. Indeed, the lower cost of housing for both rentals and purchase in these older neighborhoods where whites had vacated was desirable for these families, who could afford to live there, as opposed to other sections of the city.[36] These houses were old and dilapidated, but it was their only option. An early social survey completed in 1914 on San Diego's housing situation in the area showed the following: "There are distinct slum conditions in San Diego in shacks along the waterfront and among the Mexicans, Negroes and Whites, in the tenement houses and cottages of the district south of 'F' Street, and west of 16th Street to the waterfront."[37]

This was the barrioization of San Diego's multiracial communities. The 1930 Heller Committee Report on the Logan Heights community of San Diego described the housing conditions for the Mexican families in greater detail. The report noted that overcrowding was common and 80 percent of the families in the study lived below normal living standards with unsatisfactory sanitary conditions, despite the fact Mexican Americans had higher incomes than other nonwhite groups. Mexican Americans could afford to live outside of Logan Heights and other older areas, yet they did not. This was also the case for Filipinos, who remained for the most part in these neighborhoods. This is one indicator that both groups were refused housing or intimidated from moving into other communities where whites resided. The level of segregation in San Diego was higher than all other California cities, suggesting a lack of opportunities and overt discrimination.[38] According to a 1946 Intergroup Relations in San Diego report, "On the whole, the Mexican-American group in Southern California is the most isolated group in this area."[39] As many of these studies point out, racial discrimination was the single most driving factor in segregating San Diego's communities.[40] It weighed more than the cost of housing or socioeconomic forces. Let us now examine the mechanisms of discrimination that were the primary social forces at work.

MECHANISMS OF DISCRIMINATION

Racial discrimination took on various forms, which, taken together, confined Mexicans and Filipinos in prescribed areas. Whites demonstrated an unwillingness to live with racial and ethnic minorities by moving out to newer suburban neighborhoods, a discriminatory process called "white flight." As nonwhites continued to move into the older, deteriorating homes in San Diego's southeastern communities, white residents sold their homes and moved to newer suburbs further north and east. As a result, areas like Logan Heights became known as "the residential section of the Negroes, Mexicans, and Orientals."[41] This was further validated by one San Diego resident who recalled how the racial makeup of the southeastern section of San Diego began to change during the 1920s and 1930s when whites moved out as African Americans and Mexican Americans moved in.[42] According to LeRoy Harris's study of African American and Mexican communities in San Diego, white flight was "the withdrawal from, or refusal to enter neighborhoods where large numbers of Negroes are moving or already residing. . . . [O]nce this happens, the remaining whites seek to leave, and this seems to confirm the existing belief among whites that complete transformation of a neighborhood is inevitable once Negroes begin to enter."[43]

Additionally, as an American Council on Race Relations report noted, as racially restricted enclaves like Logan Heights were beginning to be known as Jim Crow areas, whites continued to move out or refused to live there. This continued the cycle of maintaining segregated communities. As long as whites did not want to live with nonwhites, the attitudes and practices only reinforced this sort of housing inequity.[44]

Another issue that will be debated is voluntary segregation. Scholars point out that racial and ethnic minorities separate themselves from larger society because they chose to live in areas where they felt more comfortable, in spaces where there is common culture, language, and interest. In time, these groups would eventually be absorbed and assimilated into the larger society, becoming, in essence, white.[45] Although this sounds ideal for the immigrant experience in the United States, these authors do not take into account that this only applied to European ethnics. For African Americans, Mexicans, Chinese, Japanese, Filipinos, and other nonwhites in San Diego, this was not their reality. They could not easily assimilate, no matter how hard they tried. They wore what historian Ronald Takaki called a "racial uniform," which did not allow them to assimilate and become part of mainstream society.[46] In fact, their racial uniform only added to their foreignness or otherness, which in turn kept them isolated in their multiracial communities. Edwin B. Tilton, assistant superintendent of schools in San Diego, shared his disdain regarding Mexican schoolchildren, illustrating their otherness: "The Mexicans at Sherman School have bad social habits and are not clean. American parents don't want their lily white daughters rubbing shoulders with the Mexicans with their filthy habits."[47] Similarly, Frank Penuelas recalled how his teacher made him stand in front of the room and called him a "dirty Mexican who had no respect" because he took off his wet shoes before entering the classroom when it was raining.[48] Both remarks typified white stereotypes regarding Mexicans: that they were unclean, inferior, and unfit to interact with mainstream society. When Mexicans, Filipinos, and other nonwhites ventured out to public places and sites for recreational activities, they were discriminated against and made to feel uncomfortable by whites. One San Diego reporter noted, "They [nonwhites] couldn't sit on the ground floor of most theatres. Many didn't know they could vote."[49] This only further contributed to their staying within the confines of their own communities. The Intergroup Relations in San Diego report noted, "Outside of this district [Logan Heights] minority groups were made to feel out of place and uncomfortable in the recreational program of other areas." San Diego resident Paul De La Cruz also remarked that one of the biggest problems Filipinos faced was discrimination.[50] Armando Rodriguez, who grew up in San Diego, recalled, "The only reason I got to know places outside the barrio was because my mother cleaned houses in Golden Hill and North Park."[51] These examples thus show that it was not a matter of voluntary segregation but rather self-preservation to remain within their communities. Every time they ventured out they faced the inevitable hostile remark or refusal of service. It was what kept Filipinos and Mexicans from feeling like they belonged to mainstream society. For Mexicans and Filipinos, it was easier to remain in their racially segregated neighborhoods where the insults and hostile environments were not present. In these racialized spaces they were surrounded by their own cultures, languages, and interests. It was all they had. As a result, they constructed their own world apart from mainstream society and turned inward to support each other.

SAFE HAVEN FOR THE WEARY

In 1989, the Filipino Men's Forum met to identify and honor some of the remaining Filipino old-timers who were still alive at the time in San Diego. They were among the first Filipinos who came to San Diego during the early twentieth century. One of those who were to be honored was Bonifacio Dacumos. As A. B. Santos recalled, "When I was desperate for help and had no money to pay rent, he took me in, fed me and he even taught me how to iron my clothes. There were times then that I only ate once a day and when he learned this, he took care of me." Santos went on to become one of the most successful Filipino realtors in San Diego. Despite his success, he never forgot the kindness this *mangong* (older brother) extended when he was first getting settled and trying to survive in San Diego.[52]

This story illustrates an important point. Given that Filipinos and Mexicans were not made to feel welcome in areas outside of their communities, they often had to turn inward for compassion and support from each other. It was how they survived as a people, especially during tumultuous times like the Great Depression and the wartime years. Their shared experiences of racial discrimination and marginalization, coupled with a familiar culture, provided them with the safety and familiarity that justified their choice to live in these multiracial communities. It enabled them to endure.[53] As Governor C. C. Young's Fact Finding Committee report, *Mexicans in California*, suggests:

> The tendency of the Mexican to live in a racial group is strengthened by several conditions. On arrival he seldom speaks English and consequently is dependent upon the Spanish-speaking group for adjustment to his new environment. The Mexican commonly performs unskilled and consequently low paid work, so that his choice as to quarters is restricted. In Mexico the laboring classes have been used to very simple living with only the most primitive sanitation, and owners are naturally reluctant to rent their buildings to Mexican tenants if others can be found. In addition, there exists a prejudice against the Mexican which manifests itself in the common classification of the Mexican as "not white."[54]

As this observation clearly notes, the experiences of Mexicans and Filipinos arose out of a set of circumstances that revolved around racial discrimination and isolation. As the passage suggests, owners of rental properties sought other tenants before choosing the rent to Mexicans. Moreover, being classified as "not white" also contributed to their social isolation as mainstream society exhibited its prejudice against them. Thus, it was not merely their choice to self-segregate. Rather, the spaces that already had existing Mexicans, Filipinos, and other nonwhites were borne out of segregation, which allowed new residents to enter a safe, familiar, and economically viable environment. For Mexicans, circumstances such as a familiar culture and language made it easier for them stay in certain neighborhoods or barrios. Richard Griswold del Castillo noted about the Mexican barrio: "The barrio gave a geographical identity, a feeling of being at home, to the dispossessed and poor. It was a place, a traditional place that offered some security from the city's social and economic turmoil."[55]

Since the vast majority of Mexicans and the entire Filipino population of San Diego could not assimilate because of their race and skin color, they turned to their culture and cultural institutions to maintain their identity and dignity apart from the outside world. Many Mexicans also planned on returning to Mexico after working in the United States, so they decided to stay in a familiar cultural environment rather than venture out beyond these spatial boundaries that did not welcome them. As temporary residents, they did not see a need to assimilate into a culture that they did not intend on being a part of.[56]

Indeed, for many Mexican immigrants, their racialization and the treatment that accompanied it were also a factor in why they stayed in their own spaces. During the early twentieth century sociologist and contemporary observer Emory S. Bogardus also described the problems Mexican immigrants faced from whites with regards to housing. Numerous instances were cited where Mexicans were denied housing in certain neighborhoods at the protest of (white) neighbors who opposed them moving in. Others who were able to move in, such as a prominent Mexican businessman, where threatened. Even if Mexican immigrants became citizens, it was pointless because of the racial discrimination and segregation they faced. In the Imperial Valley, Elmer Heald, district attorney, went on record, saying, "I think it would be better if we picked up a whole lot of Mexicans and sent them back to Mexico. They are very undesirable. They don't assimilate into Anglo-Saxon citizens."[57] They had no protection because even laws were used against them. The value of citizenship was worthless because of the perpetual foreignness and social ostracism that Mexicans faced. Filipinos also observed the limits that their quasi-citizenship provided. As Filipino resident Tony Alcade recalled, they too encountered problems obtaining housing because homeowners refused to rent to them. The racism they endured with regards to miscegenation, for example, only reinforced that citizenship in all its forms did not necessarily mean equality.[58]

Mexicans and Filipinos found that living in a familiar space was all they had because they were not welcomed elsewhere. Even if one could afford to live outside of the older barrios, it did not mean white residents were waiting to welcome either group with open arms into their communities. Intimidation and violence was also inflicted on nonwhites who tried to move into white neighborhoods, so there was no reason why they would subject themselves or their loved ones to this treatment. Mexicans and Filipinos, because of their racialized bodies, were seen as undesirable and unfit to live in white neighborhoods. For those that tried, they were met with resistance by their white neighbors.[59] Lillian Lim grew up in Berkeley, California. As a child she distinctly remembers being in the car and watching her parents as they dealt with discrimination.

She recalled, "I remember going to places and then being turned away at the door. Just because it was the wrong neighborhood, the wrong neighborhood for anyone of color." Although her family now resides in San Diego, those painful memories remain.[60] Given this sort of treatment, voluntary segregation does not account for their longstanding communities. A more accurate statement would be that they were denied any form of voluntary option. They simply had no choice but to remain in their multiracial communities. Race restrictive covenants and violence ensured this would be enforced.

RACIAL COVENANTS AS WHITE SUPREMACY

Whites in San Diego did not want to live side by side with Mexicans, Filipinos, or any other nonwhite groups. In order to prohibit the movement of Mexicans and Filipinos into their communities they invoked the "devil's" spirit in the form of racial segregation. Indeed, racial segregation was the greatest factor impacting urban space.[61] As Kevin Mumford argues, the "interzones" of race and boundaries in urban cities were produced and reproduced to facilitate "the intricate, intimate encounters between people designated as different." This was achieved through social structures, institutions, and geographical space. Mumford writes, "Social racism, at least in part, is responsible for the production of geographies and institutions, and cultures."[62] Race restrictive covenants were the best weapon segregationists utilized to keep their communities white. Race restrictive covenants served as the vanguard for white flight and reinforced geographic boundaries in San Diego. Whites not only had the economic means to move out of older neighborhoods, but did so in order to avoid race mixing with nonwhites. They wanted to maintain the desirability of their communities by moving to newer suburban developments that were free from racial and ethnic populations. By engaging in these practices, whites were, as historian Mary Ting Yi Lui writes, "transforming these urban neighborhoods comprising of ethnically diverse populations into both cultural and special constructs that reinforced and reproduced Euro-American notions of racial and cultural superiority."[63] As a result, the southeastern section of San Diego, for example, consisted predominately of multiracial neighborhoods well into the 1940s.[64] In order to keep nonwhites confined in these sections, surrounding white neighborhoods discriminated against them and barred them from moving into their areas throughout the 1930s and 1940s. These practices ensured that areas such as Logan Heights would remain "prototypical low-income, inner city ghetto[s]," by 1950. Racial segregation was so profound in these areas that it affected all aspects of their social environment. Communities like Logan Heights were described as follows: "The substandard conditions of the San Diego Mexican community, as reflected by their occupational status, living environment, and health problems, were magnified by their segregation. Separate schools, churches, and businesses existed for the Mexican community."[65]

Through racially restrictive covenants, whites were able to successfully keep Mexicans, Filipinos, and other nonwhites from moving into their neighborhoods. This was one of the many social and institutional means that whites used to separate themselves. That, coupled with limited economic and social mobility, hindered the choices Mexicans and Filipinos had in terms of housing. One Mexican American recalled: "This residential location process was hardly accidental, of course. Limited occupational mobility and lower per capita income restricted the housing choices of Mexican American families. San Diego social space is marked by considerable segregation of Hispanics and Anglos. Equally, Mexican Americans have been unable to maintain political control over the built environment, even in the city's most Hispanic territories."[66]

For those who did own housing in areas such as Logan Heights, they could not gain enough from the sale of their homes to move out. Through economic racism, Mexicans and Filipinos, among others, were confined to their neighborhoods. This preserved the pattern for spatial segregation as Mexicans "remained both economically and spatially excluded from better occupational and housing opportunities."[67] It became so normalized that, as one San Diego resident recalled, "segregation was a fact of life."[68] In 1946, the American Council on Race Relations in San Diego also noted a similar pattern of racial segregation and housing within Logan Heights. They addressed the issue of how white residents in other areas were resistant to the movement of African Americans (among other nonwhites) into their communities, thus keeping their neighborhoods from becoming like Logan Heights, which the report cited as an interracial community. Residents in these white communities also addressed their fear that property values would be lowered. The report observed: "Through community inertia, increased dilapidation, deterioration, plus the enforcement of racial restrictions in other areas, Logan Heights is rapidly becoming a segregated neighborhood. White families, aware of the social stigma attached to living in a Jim Crow district, endeavor to move out, and since they are acceptable elsewhere, only the racial minorities who cannot leave will eventually remain. This trend is not to the advantage of San Diego."[69]

An examination of federal, state, and independent reports and oral histories demonstrated that multiracial communities like Logan Heights continued to be segregated through white resistance. Race mixing was the overriding factor in their resistance. This had an impact on nonwhite communities for generations. Mexican residents who grew up in San Diego recall how racial segregation was prevalent in their lives. One Mexican couple remembered, "This city was segregated. If you were Mexican and brown, you lived in Logan Heights or National City or Shell Town. You were not allowed to buy in certain areas or rent. Upper class Mexicans lived wherever they wanted."[70] This statement is telling given the de facto "nonwhite" status and treatment the vast majority of Mexicans experienced with regards to fair housing. I contend that upper-class Mexicans who had the freedom to move out were light-skinned, economically well off, and claimed to be Spanish rather than Mexican—a move to whiteness that enabled them to live outside these racially prescribed spaces.

For the vast majority of Mexicans, segregation defined their lives. Lauro Vega, who grew up in 1929 in National City, recalled, "In the barrios, at that time we didn't think anything about it, but it was segregated. If there were whites in the neighborhood, they had to go to another school a mile down."[71] Similarly, Filipino residents in San Diego noticed the confinement of their communities, which also limited their choices of where to live. Charito Balanag, a resident of San Diego, noted that Mexicans and Filipinos were "pushed together. There was discrimination."[72] The fact that Filipino residents such as Balanag could see how both groups were confined together acknowledges their shared experiences with racial discrimination. These testimonies thus illustrate some of the similar tactics used to keep them separated from whites. Young's report also points out how restrictive clauses prohibited Mexicans, among other nonwhites, from living in white areas. The report indicated: "In addition, other boards cited clauses inserted in deeds and sales contracts calculated to confine Orientals, Mexicans and Negroes to certain districts. Although most of these clauses seek to restrict the occupants of these premises to 'persons of Caucasian race,' in some instances the Mexican was definitely specified as prohibited from occupancy."[73]

Overcrowded housing in these communities was also a product of racism. Houses were rundown, had poor sanitary conditions, and were neglected by their absentee landlords. This also led to health problems in these communities. Indeed, as George Lipsitz wrote, "Housing affects health conditions, with environmental and health hazards disproportionately located in minority communities."[74] Logan Heights, for example, was rezoned from a residential to industrial area in the 1950s, which allowed white-owned junkyards to inundate the community. These junkyards were located beside schoolyards and homes, among other areas.[75]

What made racial segregation in housing more tragic was the fact that state institutions were also involved in upholding and perpetuating them. During the 1920s, the National Association of Real Estate Boards (NAREB) implemented a strict code of ethics that prohibited their members from selling homes to nonwhites, thus promoting racial segregation. Sociologist Jesus Hernandez wrote, regarding the activities of NAREB, "The use of race as an important intervening variable in determining property value directed a nationwide network of realtors, community builders, mortgage lenders, and appraisers to be race-minded in land development, property exchanges, valuation, and in determining access to housing credit. Consequently, race became an important organizing factor for the real estate industry, its affiliates, and its clients."[76] The policies of NAREB changed little in the subsequent decades, denying generations of Mexicans, Filipinos, and other nonwhites fair housing. In fact, NAERB was known as a "segregated trade association that advocated discriminatory practices and effectively barred nonwhites from access to its multiple-listing services."

Their code of ethics in the 1940s maintained racial restrictions by instructing that a realtor "should never be instrumental in introducing into a neighborhood a character of property or occupancy, members of any race or nationality, or any individuals whose presence will clearly be detrimental to property values in that neighborhood."[77]

In 1946 the American Council on Race Relations, whose headquarters was in Chicago, responded to racial segregation by recommended that new housing patterns be "developed on a completely interracial basis. . . . San Diego does not have to create a segregated neighborhood. It can provide an example of interracial living which would be an inspiration to other cities."[78] Despite efforts by the American Council on Race Relations to advocate for more multiracial communities, its words were not heeded. The problem of segregated housing continued well into the 1960s in San Diego as well as all across the United States. That the majority of Mexicans and Filipinos continued to live in the same communities provided visible evidence that they were not experiencing the social mobility they hoped for.[79]

Housing deeds were one of the major documents that included race restrictions. A sample of declarations of restriction in housing deeds in San Diego, for example, showed that out of twenty-nine deeds, twenty contained such racial restrictions. Although these clauses varied, they all usually mentioned that housing "would not be sold, leased, rented, or occupied by any person other than one of the Caucasian race."[80] Others were more specific, detailing exactly which racial or ethnic groups were to be excluded. Racial restrictive covenants throughout different San Diego neighborhoods show that these restrictions stretch as far back as 1888 and as recently as 1957.[81]

Housing development pamphlets for neighborhoods like Loma Portal (situated in Point Loma) and other areas of San Diego north of downtown indicated similar clauses, dating back as far as 1906. These various housing developments had specific restrictions that stated, for example, "Property in Loma Portal, shall never be sold to any except members of the Caucasian race." Similarly, other racially restrictive clauses in San Diego neighborhoods such as City Heights and Valencia Park also stated:

> No lots sold to any but the Caucasian race.
> We are enforcing building restrictions and white race occupancy with all lots sold.
> No lot shall even be lived upon or used or occupied by any person with blood that is not entirely of the Caucasian race[82]

These various racially restrictive clauses in house deeds and housing pamphlets where given to real estate agents to be enforced. In other neighborhoods, like Talmadge and Kensington, the reasons for restriction included the following: "The district at the present time is all white with the exception of three or four families, and we want to keep it from becoming the same as Logan and

Imperial which were white districts a few years ago with good property values, now they are mixed districts with rents and property values reduced 50%. . . . [T]hese restrictions make it known that it is a permanent white district and prevent it being offered for sale to people not of the Caucasian Race."[83] As these examples illustrate, Mexicans, Filipinos, African Americans, and other nonwhites were barred from moving into newer, suburban neighborhoods throughout San Diego. These practices thus continued to demarcate the color line in housing.[84]

In addition to the racially restrictive clauses in deeds, real estate agents, apartment and house managers, builders and developers, mortgage bankers, and other institutions promoted the racial exclusion of Mexicans and Filipinos, among other "non-Caucasians," in San Diego.[85] Real estate agents played a key role in residential segregation. Stuart Palmer observed that real estate agents served as the informal gatekeepers of their nonwhite communities: "The real estate agency and its associated financial institutions, at a somewhat higher level of control, exert an influence which is equally powerful as that of the neighborhood association. . . . [T]he practices of real estate firms in regard to selling and renting housing to racial minorities, together with the policies which these practices either implement or aid in formulating, provide a direct and often final determination of the accessibility of the existing housing supply."[86]

This description demonstrates how real estate agents defined where minorities were able to live, geographically separate from white communities.[87] As new subdivisions were built, real estate agents continued to enforce similar racial restrictions prohibiting "undesirable elements," which usually meant "Negroes, Mexican Americans, and Orientals." An exception to this was A. B. Santos, a Filipino who obtained his real estate license and in 1952 became the first agent to sell a home to a Mexican American family in Valencia Park. This caused an uproar among members of the real estate board, who, as Santos recalled, "told me to my face I was a disgrace to the business." Although Santos was among the handful of nonwhite agents who tried to resist racial restrictions in housing against nonwhites, for the most part real estate agents contributed to the continued segregation of Mexicans and Filipinos in San Diego and remained the supporters of the racial dividing line.[88]

The federal government was also a conspirator to these discriminatory practices. The Federal Housing Administration (FHA), for example, was guilty of insisting that racially restrictive covenants be implemented in order for residential projects to receive FHA-insured financing. In fact, the FHA even drafted a model covenant to be used in housing sales it financed. This move prevented declining property values as a result of having mixed neighborhoods; thus nonwhites remained in old, dilapidated housing.[89] In its *Underwriting Manual* in 1938, the FHA stated, "If a neighborhood is to retain stability it is necessary that properties shall continue to be occupied by the same social and racial classes."[90] Up until the 1950s FHA policies stated that realtors could lose their license if they sold to a Mexican or other nonwhite family. Even during the Kennedy administration, the FHA refused to comply with his orders for fair housing loans for minorities under Executive Order 11063. Lipsitz noted, "White resistance to Kennedy's executive order reflected and exacerbated popular support among whites for racial discrimination."[91] Lipsitz's statement demonstrates that the federal agencies sanctioned racial segregation with housing, even to the point of refusing a presidential executive order. Despite these concerted efforts in support of racial segregation and restrictive covenants, whites still had the audacity to assert that Mexicans, on the whole, were "socially irresponsible people who prefer to remain in conditions of poverty."[92]

Another government agency involved in upholding racial segregation was the Home Owners' Loan Corporation (HOLC). A predecessor to the FHA, HOLC was established under Franklin Delano Roosevelt's New Deal programs and legislation in 1933. HOLC was created to protect homeowners from foreclosures during the Great Depression. HOLC both systematized appraisal methods and initiated the practice of redlining, a practice of discrimination based on geographic location. As part of their City Survey Program they mapped residents by race and ethnicity.[93] These Residential Security Maps were used by HOLC agents as redlining maps with areas marked by different colors indicating the level of desirability of the neighborhoods. This was one way HOLC agents could maintain white neighborhoods in any particular section of the city. HOLC created Residential Security Maps for cities that had a population of forty thousand or higher.

In 1936, San Diego was one of the cities mapped; this mapping included the San Diego proper area, Paradise Hills, Encanto, Coronado, and La Jolla. Agents noted areas where large concentrations of nonwhites resided. The language used to describe these neighborhoods was telling. In the HOLC area descriptions, each section of the city was designated with a combination of a letter (A–D) and color code (green, blue, yellow, and red). These combinations went by desirability or, more properly, security threat to whiteness. For example, A/Green areas were considered the best, were homogeneous, and were in-demand "hot spots" for white residents. Some of these descriptions would also note if the residents in these communities were "100% or all white" and had "no infiltration of any inharmonious influences." These included neighborhoods like Normal Heights, Point Loma, and most of La Jolla and Coronado. B/Blue areas were still desirable and consisted mostly of white residents. C/Yellow areas were the buffer areas around the red sections, indicating that they were "rapidly declining, leaning towards red areas," and lacking homogeneity. D/Red areas, which were considered the worst, were located in Logan Heights and other parts of Southeast San Diego, East San Diego (City Heights), Encanto, a small segment of downtown San Diego, and Paradise Hills. An older section of La Jolla known as the "servants' quarters," was also included; it was "populated with the serving class of whites, negroes and Mexicans." These areas were characterized by hazardous,

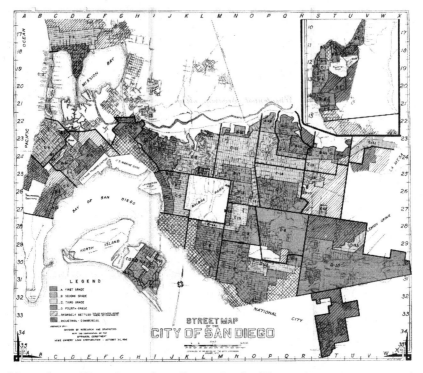

Map 3. *Source*: Home Owners Loan Corporation San Diego region map, 1936.
Courtesy of Richard Marciano, Sustainable Archives and Leveraging Technologies
(SALT), Testbed for the Redlining Archives of California's Exclusionary Spaces
(T-Races), http://salt.unc.edu/T-RACES/ (accessed May 1, 2010).

"detrimental influences . . . undesirable population or infiltration of it" or the
"predominance of subversive racial elements."[94]

What is interesting to note about these descriptions is that they always mention the class of people in the neighborhoods, whether or not there is an "immediate threat of foreign infiltration," and, specifically, if there are Mexicans in the
neighborhood. By designating foreignness, Mexican, Negro, or other "subversive elements," HOLC residential maps were utilized to maintain the color line
and, ultimately, white communities. By informing white residents of potential
undesirable elements in their neighborhoods (e.g., nonwhites), redlining maps
were used by HOLC to institutionalize racial discrimination by making it applicable beyond an individual basis. Thus, HOLC was responsible for bringing the
notion of "neighborhood" into the public discourse as a unit of discrimination,
and this discrimination was enforced through federal policy in localized situations in San Diego.[95]

In addition to real estate agents and other state agencies, a concerted effort of
residents in white neighborhoods ensured these covenants were enforced
through "Neighborhood Improvement Associations" and private action.[96]

It came to the point that even Mexican residents were pressured not to sell to other nonwhites such as African Americans. Connie Zuniga shared an incident regarding her father's decision to sell his home in Logan Heights. She recalled: "There was a lot of ritzy people that lived in Golden Hill . . . [and] there was subtle discrimination. I remember when I was in the fifth grade my father needed some money, so he decided to sell the house that we had bought right next to us, and he sold it to a black man. Well we had a conversation with people coming down from Golden Hill, little old white ladies knocked on our door and let my father know that he would have to take the property back because it was a covenant that you could not sell to black people."[97]

As Zuniga's statement implies, race had a major impact on where they could and could not live; it also influenced what they could do with their property, even if they owned it. It shows the extent to which whites went to impede the movement of nonwhites into white neighborhoods, especially in the newer housing developments.[98] Many individuals who were victims of racially restrictive covenants wrote the governor of California, criticizing the fact that these covenants were "undemocratic and [were] a creation of race-conscious among the caucasians [*sic*]. . . . Racial intolerance is produced by man-made legislation; and racial tolerance can be produced by man-made legislation."[99] Despite these letters, and the 1948 Supreme Court decision ruling against restrictive covenants, de facto exclusions kept occurring. Rather, these clauses were informally maintained throughout the 1950s and well into the 1960s by both real estate agents and homeowners. A sample of housing deeds in San Diego was documented by LeRoy Harris: the latest date for the racial restrictive clause was during 1957.[100]

These practices, however, did not go unchallenged. In 1945 Filipinos, with help from the San Diego Race Relations Society, an early civil rights group that advocated social justice for the city's nonwhite communities, challenged racial segregation and won.[101] This was not the only case to be challenged. Between 1963 and 1966, San Diego also had a total of twenty-seven cases filed with the State of California Fair Employment Practices Commission regarding racial discrimination in housing. Most people, though, either did not file a complaint or did so only when they could no longer accept the humiliation of constantly being refused housing based on their race or ethnicity.[102]

There were also allies in the fight for social justice and fair housing. William Byron Rumford, for example, was the first African American to serve in California's state legislature. Rumford and his allies in the civil rights struggle pushed for and were successful in getting the Rumford Fair Housing Act passed into law in 1963. As a result, housing discrimination based on race was outlawed as public policy. The following year the San Diego Fair Employment Practices Commission filed the first suit against a property owner and manager in National City. The claim was on behalf of an African American woman who was denied housing; she won. The apartment owner was thus ordered to rent the apartment to her.[103] This was a victory for nonwhite groups seeking equal access to housing. Despite these victories, white resistance to forced rental or sale of individual property continued. Agents of discrimination also gathered to combat the civil rights legislation.

Real estate groups in San Diego took on the battle in favor of racial segregation throughout the state of California. They fought to have the Rumford Fair Housing Act repealed with Proposition 14 because it "violated the basic right of a property owner to sell his property to anyone of his choice." Proposition 14 was placed before California voters and passed by a two-to-one margin both statewide and in San Diego. This attested to the fact that white residents in both California and San Diego in particular did not want to be told what they could do with their property, which also meant they wanted the freedom to engage in racial discrimination. White homeowners in San Diego used this argument to keep their neighborhoods "respectable." Then the California Supreme Court declared Proposition 14 unconstitutional and reinstated the Rumford Fair Housing Act.[104]

This was a blow to those in favor of racial segregation. Since many realtors in San Diego were now considered racist because they supported Proposition 14, the San Diego Realty Board in 1964 made it necessary for their members to adhere a new Code of Practices that bound them to "offer equal service to all clients without regard to race, color, religion, or national origin in the sale, purchase, exchange, rental, or lease of real property."[105] This was a defeat for real estate agents who engaged in racial discrimination, yet segregation continued in San Diego and throughout the United States for the next twenty years. Lipsitz noted, "White resistance manifested as refusal to abide by fair-housing laws [that] continued to guide federal policy in the 1970s and 1980s."[106]

Mexicans and Filipinos faced yet another obstacle when venturing outside their communities—violence. This was another informal means to socially control the movement of nonwhites out of their communities, whether it was to look for housing outside of their neighborhoods or just to visit public spaces. As one magazine observed: "The ultimate stage of the sickness known as prejudice is violence. It may take the form of hoodlumism, vigilante action or terror. Recent incidents directed at Negroes, Jews, Japanese, Mexicans and Filipinos have a clear relationship with the Nazi philosophy of hate; the difference is only in degree."[107]

Individuals as well as the state, such as police officers, participated in acts of intimidation and violence, thereby maintaining public segregation. Filipino author Carlos Bulosan wrote about several incidents in San Diego where white men attacked him when he ventured outside the Filipino and Mexican districts in San Diego. He recalled: "I was still unaware of the vast social implications of the discrimination against Filipinos, and my ignorance had innocently brought me to the attention of white Americans. In San Diego, where I tried to get a job, I was beaten upon several occasions by restaurant and hotel proprietors."[108]

Longtime Logan Heights resident Ricardo Romio also recalled his experiences with racial discrimination as a teenager. When Ricardo and his friends wanted to venture outside their Logan Heights neighborhood and into other areas of the city, they were stopped by police officers. Romio noted that it was the police who enforced the color line, which separated areas like Logan Heights from other parts of San Diego: "One time I went out of town, I went up to North Park to the skating ring and a cop got us over there and took us to the back alley and knocked us around and told us get out of there and go back to your own part of town. . . . [T]hey don't want our kind up there."[109] As both Bulosan's and Romio's experiences suggest, violence was used to police the color line in San Diego, serving as a stark reminder as to where nonwhites did or did not belong. The fact that law enforcement also engaged in these acts of violence only illustrates the extent to which racial discrimination and segregation was prevalent in San Diego.

THE DEVIL INFILTRATES THE CATHOLIC CHURCH

Racial discrimination did not just occur in housing. In fact, the racial segregation of space went beyond housing to included churches, employment opportunities, and public spaces. Institutions such as San Diego's Catholic Churches were no stranger to the devil's influence as the color line was also drawn in places of worship. Even in terms of where to pray, there was the subtle impact of discrimination on Mexicans and Filipinos. According to one Logan Heights resident, "all the Mexicans went to Our Lady of Guadalupe." There was a church in adjacent Golden Hill, Our Lady of Angels, but they were made to feel unwelcome there. Thus, the Mexican community found a place to worship at Our Lady of Guadalupe Church, which was completed in 1922. A larger church and rectory were built up the street and dedicated in 1931. This was done to accommodate Mexican parishioners, who comprised 63 percent of the church's congregants.[110]

Since they lived in the same multiracial communities and were predominately Catholic, Filipinos went to the same churches as Mexicans. Longtime Logan Heights resident Lanny Villarin recalled that mostly Mexicans and Filipinos went to Our Lady of Guadalupe, Saint Jude, and Saint Anne's Catholic Churches. Filipinos also attended Christ the King Church, in Southeast San Diego.[111] In looking at the ethnic and racial makeup of various parishes throughout the San Diego Catholic Diocese, those churches with the most Mexican and Filipino parishioners were located within or in very close proximity to communities that were predominately Mexican and Filipino. This suggests the covert practice of racial discrimination and segregation also applied to where one worshipped, even though the majority of Mexicans, Filipinos, and a substantial number of whites in the area were all Catholics.[112] The churches that had substantial Mexican and/or Filipino membership are listed in table 2.1.

As the table suggests, even in the place where one would hope to find compassion and equality—the Catholic Church—the devil's ugly head reared itself to perpetuate racial discrimination. Mexicans and Filipinos, both immigrant

TABLE 2.1

CHURCHES WITH LARGE NUMBERS OF MEXICAN, FILIPINO,
AND OTHER NONWHITE PARISHIONERS

Church	Racial/Ethnic Makeup	Community
Our Lady of Angels	Mexican	San Diego
Saint Anthony of Padua	Mexican, Filipino, Guamanian	National City
Saint Rose of Lima	Mexican	Chula Vista
Saint Anne	Mexican	San Diego
Saint Mary	Filipino, Mexican, Guamanian	National City
Our Lady of Mount Carmel	Mexican, Filipino	San Ysidro
Our Lady of Guadalupe	Mexican, Filipino	San Diego (LH)
Saint John of the Cross	Mexican	Lemon Grove
Saint Rita	Mexican, Filipino, African American	San Diego
Our Lady of Guadalupe	Mexican	Chula Vista
Saint Charles	Filipino, Mexican	San Diego (IB)
Saint Jude Shrine of the West	Mexican, Filipino, African American	San Diego
Christ the King	Filipino	San Diego
Most Precious Blood	Filipino, Mexican	Chula Vista
Saint Michael	Filipino, Mexican	San Diego (PH)

Sources: "Parishes in Chronological Order of Establishment," San Diego Catholic Diocese Parishes Directory, 61. Information on ethnic and racial makeup of parishioners was provided by Chancellor Rodrigo Valdivia, San Diego Catholic Diocese. During my initial visit to the San Diego Catholic Diocese on June 24, 2004, Valdivia provided information regarding racial and ethnic makeup for various churches in San Diego. Information regarding Mexican and Filipino parishioners was also gathered by finding out which parishes offered a Spanish and/or Tagalog mass. Valdivia also provided this information. Additional information regarding the date of dedication of Our Lady of Guadalupe Church was obtained from Albert López Pulido, "Nuestra Señora de Guadalupe: The Mexican Catholic Experience in San Diego," Journal of San Diego History 37, no. 4 (Fall 1991): 237.

Note: (LH) represents Logan Heights, (IB) represents Imperial Beach, and (PH) represents Paradise Hills.

and U.S.-born, were subject to the racial hostility of white society and its institutions. These practices continued to segregate them. This limited both Mexicans and Filipinos to living, working, attending school and church, socializing, and seeking recreational activities within their isolated multiracial spaces. Thus, as both groups lived confined, segregated lives, they began to construct their own social world that took care of their own needs.[113]

CREATING MULTIRACIAL SPACES

In his book *Interzones*, Kevin Mumford examines the relationship between blacks, whites, and Filipinos in the racially blurred "interzones" of vice districts in Chicago and New York, where these various groups interact on both a social and intimate level. Although these interzones have a negative reputation attached to them because of their multiracial character, as Mumford notes, these "interracial relations on the margins remain central to understanding the character of modern American culture."[114] Indeed, given that the color line during the twentieth century confined Mexicans and Filipinos to living in a collection of multiracial interzones in San Diego, they utilized these spaces for multiple functions in response to the social pressures of racial segregation. These spaces helped them to cope with their conditions by allowing them to feel a sense of safety and security from the outside world that was often unwelcoming to both Mexicans and Filipinos. In many ways these multiracial enclaves, or barrios, were a cultural oasis that defied the trope of the devil by providing a space for families to reside, an ethnic labor market, and an atmosphere where one could find refuge and healing from an often hostile environment. It was the community ethos within this space that created social stability and shaped a collective identity among its residents. Because of their shared identity and community space, these areas had significant meaning to the Mexicans and Filipinos who lived in these multiracial communities.[115] They were not the geographical territories outsiders characterized as "enshrouded in darkness, disease, and criminality," but rather a safe haven for its residents.[116] As one Filipina recalled, the Filipino district that she lived in, which was called "skid row," was "not a scary place because it was home to her." She would be sent with her siblings to go shopping, oftentimes walking at sundown, yet always felt safe. Rather than seeing the Filipino bachelors who frequented the area as dangerous, sex-crazed men, she experienced them as friendly individuals who always treated the children with kindness, sometimes buying them candy.[117]

Families welcomed newcomers and provided community for those who had none. They were responsible for the cultural retention and survival of their communities, creating this safe haven for new and old residents alike. Indeed, cultural retention and a shared experience with racial segregation functioned as mechanisms for survival within both Mexican and Filipino communities. Lazaro Lupian's family, for example, settled in San Diego during the early 1920s.

Lazaro's father worked many jobs to support his family. He worked as a ditch digger and bartender. He was able to land a job at the U. S. Grant Hotel, where he worked first as a dishwasher and then later as maitre d.' Lazaro's mother, Manuela, was one of the first to open a Mexican restaurant in their barrio in San Diego. "Mi Casita" was very popular. Lupian recalled, "She was a good cook and her food was well known." She was also known for her generosity and kind heart. During the turbulent times of the Great Depression she often fed the field workers. As Lazaro noted, "If they had money they paid for lunch. If they didn't, the workers still ate lunch."[118] Similarly, a young Filipina by the name of Angel recalled her father frequently bringing home one or two other Filipinos. "He felt sorry for them—they had not eaten in days . . . in later years these men would reappear at their door and repay the family for their generosity."[119] It was that sense of community that enabled Mexicans and Filipinos to endure the social and economic pressures they faced. Their generosity for each other was the cultural glue that cemented their relationships, which in turn defied the devil and its hideous grasp on the racial politics of the city.

The areas also provided a sense of home away from home, where familiar sights, sounds, and smells could be found. As Rick Bonus notes in *Locating Filipino Americans*, these spaces included Filipino- and Mexican-owned or managed barbershops, restaurants, pool halls, and other establishments that catered to their communities by "demarcating a space of one's own within a larger unfamiliar world . . . a piece of home from the past."[120] These establishments also provided a sense of familiarity and comfort to those who were alienated from mainstream society by reinforcing their identities as Filipinos and Mexicans. Here, Filipinos and Mexicans could do their shopping, eating, and also meet up with friends and family to talk and share the latest news. Goods and services provided by Filipino- or Mexican-owned businesses reminded their ethnic patrons of the *sari-sari* (convenience) stores or *puestos* of their homeland, conjuring up a sense of nostalgia, where the sights, sounds, and smells provided comfort and fellowship.[121]

Finally, these spaces provided a sense of normalcy and permanency in an environment where Filipino and Mexican men (with or without families) were always on the move. Their transient, migratory life always kept their sense of home as mobile. Having a physical location where both Mexicans and Filipinos could hang out and find a sense of home, safety, and normalcy provided them with a reason to endure the senseless acts of discrimination and racism they felt on a daily basis. Many of these aging manongs had no family, so other Filipinos provided a sense of family for them.[122] They picked them up and took them to their homes to celebrate holidays and special events. These families were also the only ones who were available to identify the bodies of those who died alone. Nena Amaguin recalled her role among the old manongs whom she visited and brought home. She stated: "I used to pick them up (from downtown). . . . [T]here are Filipinos who have been old and living in a small shack there . . . there were five or six of them in a dinky house . . . then some of the older people died and they don't have nobody, nobody even buried them. . . . [T]here's so many of them that don't even know their family. Some are farmers, some from Stockton and then they live here in San Diego because of the weather."[123]

Nena also helped sailors who were on liberty in San Diego. Her family was among those who invited them over for social functions and dinners. She noted, "You know, the sailors before, they have no place to come. You know, the Filipino sailors, they have to hang there, eat there [downtown]. There's no place . . . [and] that's why we always had so many."[124] Another Filipino recalled, "Some sailors even had 'Kababayans' [friends] that would pick them up at the barracks and spend the weekends with them having picnics."[125] Indeed, many Filipino families provided a home for sailors who were far from their loved ones. Lanny Villarin's family also hosted groups of Filipino sailors who were visiting San Diego. Many of their family photos show the presence of visiting sailors. He recalled fond memories of him and his siblings entertaining them while his father cooked *lechon* (roasted pig) in their backyard in Logan Heights.[126]

SOCIAL LIFE IN SEGREGATED SPACES

In *Becoming Mexican American,* George Sánchez describes how ethnicity was forged through a shared experience of living in the United States. It was a collective identity that was reinforced through the process of creating a stable environment where families and communities could survive and thrive. He writes, "Through the daily struggle to survive in an oftentimes hostile environment, these newcomers constructed a world for themselves, shaped by both their memories of their past lives and by the realities of their present situation."[127]

Indeed, as nonwhite working-class groups, both Mexicans and Filipinos created a social world within their multiracial neighborhoods that went beyond just single ethnic identities. Rather, their socioeconomic situation and similar experiences with racism not only helped strengthen their ethnicity, but also enabled them to share in common struggles of racial and social oppression. This was evident, for example, in one particular area where predominately Filipinos and other nonwhite groups congregated in a section of downtown San Diego known as the tenderloin area, or "skid row." Although much has already been written on Filipino districts and their primary establishments of interracial social contact, such as taxi dance halls, a short description of San Diego's tenderloin district is necessary to put into context how the interzones of their social life and intimate interracial interactions occurred in this particular space.[128] In this segregated space, predominately Filipino bachelors, a handful of mixed Filipino families, Mexicans, Asian Americans, and African Americans lived and/or spent their leisure time, escaping the social pressures of the outside world. Residents in this area were workers who had steady employment in the service industries, seasonal agricultural workers, and some navy families. Some Filipinos lived and worked in a number of the downtown hotels and restaurants.[129] This area encompassed the blocks of Fourth through Sixth Avenues and Island, Market, and J Streets and was also home to many other Asian-owned businesses and tenants such as Chinese and Japanese. Some Filipinos also rented out space and operated their own businesses.

Filipinos and Mexicans were residents of skid row as early as the 1920s. Trapped in downtown and with limited means, Filipino men used available rental space efficiently. Migratory field hands who lived off seasonal income especially had to be cost conscious, and sometimes as many as ten or twelve Filipino men shared a single hotel room or small apartment. In 1932, for example, Porfirio S. Apostol and twelve other Filipinos rented a room at the Earl Hotel for eight dollars a month. Those with more steady employment in service-related work in the downtown district were able to have a bit more stability in regards to their living situation. Others, like Ciriaco "Pablo" Poscablo, lived in the area with their Mexican wives and Mexipino children.[130]

Although visiting Filipino sailors could join local families for picnics and other recreational activities, the Filipino district with its nightlife was one of the only places they could go in order to enjoy their weekends on shore. Filipinos could not hold dances in other area hotels, such as the U. S. Grant, Coronado, or El Cortez ballrooms, despite the fact that many Filipinos worked in these hotels. In order to keep from being humiliated and angered, and to avoid racial confrontation and discrimination, Filipinos tended to steer clear of these spaces. Instead they enjoyed themselves close to home.[131] Within the district the popular spots were the taxi dance halls, which provided Filipinos an opportunity to dance with and date white, African American, Mexican, and other Latina women. As one Filipino migrant noted about the city's Filipino district, "Oh, you should have seen Market Street then. It was like the Las Vegas strip with all those bright lights and dancing girls."[132] Although the majority of those who frequented the taxi dance halls were Filipino, single Mexican men also went to these establishments. Virgil Garcia recalls going down to the Filipino district, which was located in Chinatown. He also remembered it as "skid row." He recalled: "There was a Filipino pool hall there . . . [and] we used to go eat; they [Sun Café] had real cheap, fifty cents per lunch. . . . I knew that area pretty good. Of course, they had their own Fandango nightclub too! Me and my buddies would go down there and have a few [beers]."[133]

One of the most popular dance halls in San Diego was the Rizal Dance Hall, located on Market Street. As the center of recreational life it was the rendezvous point where, Linda España-Maram noted, "Filipinos could cement and rejuvenate personal bonds, share food, swap stories, and surely gossip about the *kababayan* [countrymen] among the migration circuit."[134] As outsiders, Filipinos, Mexicans, and other marginalized groups in San Diego formed this tenderloin subculture, which allowed them to be themselves and find recreation and some sort of normalcy from their everyday working lives.

The taxi dance halls were not the only establishments where Filipinos and Mexicans could find entertainment and intermix with each other in social and intimate contexts. Filipinos and Mexicans used these forums to form interethnic relationships that contributed to the growth of their communities. These dance halls were part of a larger, vibrant nightlife that included restaurants, barbershops, gambling dens, pool halls, and other small businesses that catered to their clientele. This was the social arena where Filipinos, Mexicans, and others sought out recreation, camaraderie, and a good time. Consuelo Zuniga recalled: "There used to be a Filipino district in downtown. They had bars down there . . . down on Fifth Street. . . . [I]t was like little nightclubs. It was mainly populated by Filipino people. You know, we had the Filipino Hall on Market Street. . . . [W]e used to go dancing there; they'd have a wedding there."[135]

Pablo and his wife, Felipa, welcomed Filipino sailors who visited the area. In their apartment on Market Street, right above the Sun Café, they entertained their guests.[136] Afterward Pablo joined the other Filipino sailors downtown to hang out in the district and play pool. His grandson Rudy remembered watching him play pool with the other manongs, dressed in their khakis and flannel shirts; the pool hall was filled with smoke and the sound of their Ilocano dialect and pool balls cracking all around him.[137]

San Diego City Directories for the years 1920 to 1965 provide a glimpse into the tenderloin's businesses, which were owned by Filipinos and Mexicans. A sample of these establishments indicates that as the communities grew within the confines of their geographic spaces, so did their businesses. This may be a result of the continued confinement of businesses in certain areas, which only had so many spaces available. Numerous Filipino- and Mexican-owned businesses were concentrated in these same areas. With regards to Filipino businesses, there was the Luzon Café, which was located on Market Street between Third and Fourth Avenues. Owned by Marcelo and Trinidad Marzo, the Luzon Café was a popular place where the old manongs gathered to eat and hang out with each other when they frequented the district. The café was also a place where many Filipino stewards on liberty went to eat inexpensive food and meet their friends and women.[138] Right next to the restaurant was the Luzon Pool Hall. Another Filipino restaurant was the Manila Café on Market Street. There was a barbershop owned by Marciano Padua, which was located on Third Avenue and Island Street.[139] A man named Hermipaco, or "Paco," owned another barbershop that was popular among the Filipinos in the 1930s. It was located on Fifth and Market Street. As Pedro Lacqui, a Filipino migrant who lived in San Diego during the 1930s, remembered, many happy times were spent at the barbershop. There, the old manongs came to gossip and listen to the local *rondalla* groups that came to play for them.[140]

Other eateries included the Bataan Café, located on Fourth and Island Avenue during the 1940s, which was owned by the Custado family. Hugo Marzo and Julio Advincula owned the P. I. Café on Fourth Avenue. There was also the

Mabuhay Café on Island Street. It was a restaurant that also served as a bar and dance spot. Rolando Mata recalled that at the Mabuhay, you could order beer and eat *tapa* (dried meat) and request short orders like *pancit*. There was also music that played from the jukebox. He recalled, "It's dark; lights are dim. Music most of the time they play, you know, dancing music: Latin, jazz, and some bouncy music." It was in the Mabuhay where he met Mary, a "mestiza" (Mexipina) who often frequented the place with her Mexican girlfriends.[141] It was in establishments such as these where mixing occurred between Filipinos and Mexicans. Mata's observation also illustrates taxi dance halls were not the only rendezvous points for Filipinos and Mexicans.

Mexican businesses in skid row were also numerous. One of the earliest was the Cooperativa Mexicana, Incorporated, located on 530 Market Street.[142] City directories also show a number of Mexican-owned businesses from 1920 to 1965. There were several barbershops, including Los Tres Mosqueteros on Fifth Avenue. There were also other Mexican barbershops (listed by owners' surnames) on Fifth Avenue and Market Street. Other Mexican-owned businesses included Tito's Barbershop on Fifth Avenue, Fiesta Café on Market Street, Chico's Restaurant on Fifth Avenue, and the Acapulco Café, among others. In nearby Logan Heights, they also had their own bars and restaurants, such as Chuey's Café on Main Street and El Carrito Café on Logan Avenue.[143] Other businesses, such as bars, catered to the fish cannery workers. Consuelo Zuniga recalled: "There was a place . . . old Chuey's . . . that was the hang out for the cannery people. They would go there after work and have a beer and a social life and that was quite a hang out. And there was another bar in Logan; it was called Porky's. That was where the fishers, the fishermen hung out; not so much the cannery people but the fishermen."[144]

Outside of downtown San Diego, Filipino and Mexican businesses also thrived. In National City, for example, there was Toledo's Produce on Palm Avenue, which was owned and operated by a Filipino-Mexican couple. James Toledo ran the family farm, an eight-acre plot of land on what are now Plaza Boulevard and Palm Avenue. There he and his wife sold their produce, as well as Filipino and Mexican food, through their *sari-sari* store, the first in San Diego.[145]

For Filipinos and Mexicans who lived in San Diego, these ethnic-owned businesses and segregated communities and churches were the hub for the cultural interactions and information exchanges that were, in essence, the foundation of these communities. Given the nature of their geographically mobile communities, migrant workers and sailors, for example, could find each other through advertisements and word of mouth in these permanent spaces. This was a way for mobile communities to create a "home" wherever they went, complementing permanent communities during the 1920s through the 1960s. Because seasonal workers could "tailor a life in harmony with their migratory work patterns, they created a community that was versatile, and for them, functional. They took their communities with them."[146] These intertwined communities and places of business thus developed as a necessary survival mechanism, tying together sedentary and permanent communities in San Diego. Although home and community did not necessarily translate to permanency, the roots of dozens of established families tied everyone together in an intricate web of familial, kinship, and friendship networks. What cemented their relationships was the fact that many Filipinos and Mexicans were homesick and they shared a collective experience of racial discrimination, marginalization, and violence.[147]

These spaces, although confined and limited, did enable both Filipinos and Mexicans to establish small businesses that catered to their communities, and at the same time provided a space where they intermixed with each other. It was within these racially segregated spaces that Filipinos and Mexicans·began forming interethnic relationships, facilitated by the dance halls, restaurants, and other community institutions such as Catholic Churches. This was one way in which the Mexipino population began to grow and flourish within multiracial communities.

As these communities began to expand throughout the early twentieth century, residents remained involved in their own ethnic organizations and social functions. Historically, they had no choice. When either group tried to be a part of mainstream society they were shunned and, at times, met with hostile words and acts of violence to make sure they "knew their place." Whites ensured that Filipinos and Mexicans would be denied access to both public and private functions and social gatherings at public places such as theaters, restaurants, and nightclubs where whites would be present.

In response to racial discrimination, they turned inward, sought refuge, and thrived within their own communities. Their communities were self-sustaining for the residents, providing everything they needed.[148] These communities were the hubs that newly arrived immigrants were drawn to because of their established presence and the availability of goods and services that catered to their needs. As one Logan Heights resident noted, their barrio was known as "the womb" because everything you needed was in the community.[149] Older residents, because it was ingrained in them to do so, continued to live in or visit their neighborhoods; this is a stark reminder of how racism serves to confine and keep groups historically separated and contemporarily seeking the same sort of comfort and familiarity.[150]

Another mechanism for survival was through social organizations, which were just as vital for these communities as small businesses. Occupying the same social space, they complemented each other to provide camaraderie and community for all who participated. As residents created this social world to bring themselves comfort and a sense of belonging, they also used it as a means to foster the growth of ethnic social organizations and to meet the various sociopolitical needs of their communities.

CHAPTER 3

Survival and Belonging

CIVIL RIGHTS, SOCIAL ORGANIZATIONS, AND YOUTH CULTURES

In San Diego during the twentieth century, racial segregation and the specter of discrimination facilitated the need for Mexicans and Filipinos to turn inward and build their own social worlds within larger multiracial spaces. Within these spaces Mexicans and Filipinos organized themselves into ethnic-based social organizations. These organizations were vital for the survival of both Mexican and Filipino communities in San Diego. They had numerous functions. First, they provided an avenue for residents to come together and participate in social functions and events and be recognized for their achievements, whereas in mainstream society they were often marginalized. It was because of this alienation that both Mexicans and Filipinos gathered to celebrate their own cultural, historical, religious, and social events. These organizations also took on several forms. These included umbrella associations, smaller regional associations, and labor unions. These groups also sought to create a space for themselves and worked collectively to build community centers.[1] As sociologist Jon Cruz has noted about the formation of the Filipino community in Washington, the same could be said about San Diego's Filipino and Mexican communities in that community building was "far more than simply a means for people to socialize." Their organizations and goals in community building were used to establish networks based on identity and shared experiences, promote their needs, mobilize resources, organize social and cultural activities, and protect their communities both socially and politically. This was all done in an effort to strengthen their emotional bonds to each other.[2]

Mexican and Filipino immigrants oftentimes based their organizations and clubs along ethnic lines, with a regional or homeland association. Given that they were both often excluded from mainstream clubs and organizations (both social and labor ones), they depended on their own ethnic group to foster a sense of family within and between their respective communities. This is not to say that they did not work together to form interethnic solidarity. In fact, as the next chapter will show, Filipino and Mexican social organizations were one of the catalysts for interethnic unionism between both groups. Rather, they formed separate ethnic organizations to address the particular needs of their communities while sustaining their specific identity, culture, history, and dignity as human beings. These groups were formed as a means not only for mutual fellowship and camaraderie, but also for protection from the outside world. Many of these social organizations and clubs were fraternal in nature. Mutual aid societies and fraternal organizations were often transplanted from their home countries in Mexico and the Philippines with chapters in the United States.[3] Social clubs and organizations also functioned within the confines of their communities, often holding meetings and social events at members' houses, local church recreation halls, and other establishments that did not deny them the use of their facilities. Often, such establishments were themselves owned or operated by racial and ethnic minorities.

Social organizations were a means to foster extended family and kinship ties, reinforcing the bonds they already had as members in the same community. Given that Mexicans and Filipinos were heavily invested in family and extended kin, these organizations served to broaden the ties between those they included in their fold and protect and defend members in the midst of alienation, marginalization, and even violence. These organizations, and the communities they represented, resisted and reacted on many levels to such treatment, using "reactive and defensive, proactive and offensive cultural strategies."[4] These included organizing, letter writing, lobbying public officials, and staging demonstrations. Throughout the twentieth century Mexicans and Filipinos fought for their civil rights pertaining to education, social equality, and political representation. These activities maintained their dignity as both groups faced mounting pressure from intimidation, violence, and even deportation by local and state officials, most notably during the Great Depression and throughout the postwar years. Both Mexicans and Filipinos fought on behalf of their communities and often in coalition with each other. This was especially true concerning union organizing. Many of these same ethnic social organizations had members who were also involved in union organizing. Indeed, as historian Zaragosa Vargas notes in *Labor Rights Are Civil Rights*, "The labor struggles of Mexicans were inseparable from the issue of civil rights. . . . [J]ust as racial discrimination led Mexicans to pursue the righteous path to unionism, it pushed them into the struggle for social justice."[5] The same could be said for Filipino social organizations and for labor activists such as Pablo Manlapit and Philip Vera Cruz, for example, who saw the two issues as being intimately connected.

Social organizations were also emotionally supportive for those who felt the pains of prejudice and discrimination. Within their organizations, Filipinos and Mexicans could assume roles of responsibility and shine through their hard work, as opposed to their virtual invisibility as civilians and laborers in a white world. They were treated with respect by their fellow members and given a space to feel important.[6] For Filipinos and Mexicans, social organizations and clubs were essential for surviving, especially for newly arrived immigrants. These groups provided a means of "socialization for new arrivals and a comforting retreat from cultural shock."[7]

Although both groups formed social organizations along ethnic lines, their common fight against racial oppression oftentimes facilitated interethnic coalitions. These interethnic coalitions also united them with other racial groups under the banner of civil rights, which will be discussed later in this chapter. For the second and third generations, their organizations and clubs facilitated intermixing between U.S.-born Mexicans, Filipinos, Mexipinos, and African Americans. It was these cultural sites where interethnic relationships thrived. Let us now turn to these organizations that formed in response to racial oppression and marginalization as well as those that sustained both ethnic and interethnic collective identities.

EARLY SOCIAL ORGANIZATIONS

By the early twentieth century, Mexicans and Filipinos were establishing their lives in San Diego, forming communities, and laboring in the city's various industries that fueled its economic development. Despite their contributions, they continued to remain in socially segregated, multiracial communities and were prohibited from using various public institutions and services. The Mexican communities of San Diego, like those in other areas in the United States, responded by developing their own institutions to take care of their members since there was no one else to turn to. Mutual aid societies, or *mutualistas,* as community institutions, for example, were central for Mexican immigrants and Mexican Americans. Mutual aid societies provided benefits and services for their members and families in working-class/working-poor communities. This mutual assistance included insurance, funeral expenses, disability, and other forms of support. They also addressed social injustice in the public sphere, such as racial discrimination and prejudice. Historian David Gutiérrez writes, regarding Mexican mutualistas: "Their use marked the birth of an oppositional strategy that acknowledged the common oppression Mexican Americans suffered in American society while offering an alternative, positive label that countered the stigmatized status many Americans sought to impose on Mexicans."[8]

Mutual aid societies also participated in and promoted the celebration of Mexican cultural holidays and events, such as Independence Day, or Fiestas Patrias (September 16), Dia de la Revoluccíon (November 20), and Cinco de Mayo (May 5).[9] Some of these organizations also celebrated both Mexican and U.S. holidays to show their patriotism to both countries. Within the Mexican community in San Diego, there were several active organizations. Among the earliest ones documented in San Diego was the Mexicans of San Pasqual, in 1900.

It was a fraternal society headed by John Novorra, who was said to be one of the most influential Mexicans in San Diego. The society was for mutual protection and support of the Mexican communities. As with other mutual aid and benevolent societies, it paid for the funeral expenses of deceased members, as well as providing a monthly allowance from the association if the member was married.[10] Another early Mexican organization was La Sociedad Beneficia Mexicana "Benito Juarez" Sociedad de National City. Established during the early 1900s, this fraternal organization also provided funeral expenses for its members and mutual support and even sent the bodies of deceased members back to Mexico.[11] Other mutualistas in San Diego, or with ties to the neighboring Tijuana region, included the Unión Patriótica Benéficia Mexicana Independiente and La Junta Patriotica Mexicana.[12] These early organizations were essential to the everyday survival of their members, who were coming to San Diego to fill the labor demands of the city.

Mexican Independence Day/Fiestas Patrias (September 16) was the most important Mexican holiday and was celebrated in San Diego and in Tijuana. *El Hispano Americano,* a Tijuana newspaper, described the celebration in 1934, when la Sociedad Caballeros de la Gran Tenochtitlán sponsored the event with the cooperation of the Mexican consul of San Diego, Enrique Ferreira, who also spoke there. In addition to Mexican Independence Day, the organization was also responsible for celebrations honoring Cinco de Mayo in San Diego; one such celebration was held in Germania Hall in 1934.[13] In 1935, several San Diego Mexican social organizations also participated. Newspaper accounts of these events provide some indication as to the existence of additional social organizations in San Diego. These included the Unión Mexicana de Obreros y Campesinos, las Logias Minerva y Balboa de la Alianza Hispano-Americana, and las Comisiones Honorificas Mexicanas del Condado. Not much else is mentioned about them in San Diego newspapers.[14] Other Mexican Independence Day events were sponsored and hosted by the Mexican Consulate in San Diego as well as event committees such as the Mexican Patriotic Committee in the 1930s. Other smaller celebrations were held in various parts of San Diego, including Logan Heights.[15]

One specific and well-known place that hosted many of these celebrations among the large Mexican community of Logan Heights was the Neighborhood House, which was located on 1809 National Avenue. Established as a settlement house by white social reformers and liberals in the 1920s, the Neighborhood House was meant to foster cultural understanding with the immigrant populations in Logan Heights while engaging in Americanization efforts in the community through cultural, educational, and social activities. It also set up a health clinic.[16] Dinners were held there to commemorate Mexican celebrations; included were councilmen and former mayors of San Diego as well as community members and organizations such as the Service Clubs Presidents' Council.[17] Other groups active in the Mexican communities of San Diego varied according to community. Some were active as extensions of Catholic or other Christian churches while others were strictly for social purposes.

Another of the major Mexican organizations in San Diego was the Alianza Hispano-Americana. Established in 1894 in Tucson, Arizona, the Alianza Hispano-Americana was a fraternal society that also provided mutual aid for its members, including insurance policies for funeral expenses, social activities, and other services. More importantly, they provided support, which was "similar to that given by families and traditional communities." This was provided in the form of social and entertainment activities, support in time of need, and other activities for the members and their families.[18] It was a national fraternal society with lodges located throughout the United States and Mexico. Many social organizations, such as the Alianza, were oftentimes the prelude to social movements and worked with labor unions, getting involved in strikes, such as the Imperial Valley strike in 1928. The Alianza, for example, provided its members with organizational skills and instilled in them a consciousness to address oppression and exploitation, which also appealed to labor union members.[19]

In San Diego and the Imperial Valley, the Alianza had several lodges. In the 1913 list of lodges, San Diego had one. Another lodge was active in San Ysidro in 1933. By 1942, that number had grown to nine in San Diego County, three in the city of San Diego and one each in Otay, National City, El Cajon, Lemon Grove, Vista, and Escondido. In the Imperial Valley there were four lodges, one each in El Centro and Calexico and two in Brawley.[20] Although not much is mentioned regarding the activities of the Alianza Hispano-Americana in San Diego, there are references to members participating in Mexican Independence Day celebrations during the early 1930s.[21] What the Alianza was known for, however, was its involvement in civil rights issues for the Mexican communities in the United States. By 1955, the Alianza had a Civil Rights Department established as part of the organization.[22] Other groups that came out of the postwar period included the Mexican American Movement, which was formed in 1945 to promote higher educational achievements, which, it contended, would be "a means of overcoming the problems of prejudice, segregation, discrimination, social inequality and inferiority complex."[23]

In the 1950s, there was the Hermandad Mexicana Nacional (Mexican National Brotherhood), which was an organization of Mexican workers who were predominately Spanish-speaking immigrants. Led by San Diego union leaders Phil and Albert Usquiano, the Hermandad Mexicana Nacional established chapters throughout the county, including the San Diego, National City, Oceanside, and Escondido. Most of the members were also affiliated with unions, such as the Carpenters Union and Laborers Union. The Hermandad Mexicana Nacional was formed after World War II in response to the activities of the Immigration and Naturalization Service to cancel work visas of Mexican workers who held jobs in San Diego but resided in Tijuana. These workers had the right to live as permanent residents of the United States but were forced to live with their families across the border due to housing shortages caused by the economic and population boom of World War II. In 1951, the Hermandad Mexicana Nacional fought to protect the rights of these workers and won many cases involving their employment and residency. These chapters in San Diego eventually became part of the Mexican American Political Association (MAPA) in the 1960s.[24]

MAPA was formed in Fresno in April of 1960. A nonpartisan group, MAPA's purpose was to be "an effective instrument for the Mexican-American community to use in its effort to place capable and talented Mexican-Americans in elective and appointed offices." On December 28, 1964, they held a conference with California governor Edmund Brown. The conference also included other prominent members of California's Mexican American community. In fact, three members were from San Diego, Charles Samarron, Larry Montoya, and Armando Rodriquez.[25]

The Filipino community also had extensive social clubs and organizations that included both immigrant and U.S.-born members. However, there is a dearth of scholarly information on Filipino social organizations. Most information regarding the existence of Filipino social organizations and clubs was found in San Diego city directories. Other information was gathered from the private collections of members who were involved in these organizations and clubs. They provide great detail as to the activities these organizations were involved in. One of the most popular holidays among the Filipino community in San Diego was the annual celebration of Rizal Day on December 30. This brought out the "entire Filipino colony of San Diego," as noted by the *San Diego Union*.[26] Rizal Day was to commemorate the life and death of Dr. Jose Rizal, a Philippine hero and martyr whose execution ignited the Philippine revolution against Spain in 1896. Rizal Day was *the* holiday for Filipinos during the 1930s, which also coincided with the rise of Filipino organizations. Articles in the *San Diego Union* throughout the 1930s highlighted the events. At these functions, the Filipino community was able to enjoy national and culturally specific festivities, which included feasting and dancing, while maintaining their patriotic ties and loyalty to the Philippines.[27]

There were a wide variety of Filipino social organizations, including church related, fraternal, mutual aid, social, regional, and labor related. Filipino social organizations were documented in San Diego prior to the 1920s. One of the earliest records obtained was an event sponsored by the Philippine Organization of San Diego (or the Filipino Organization), a commemorative celebration for Rizal Day in 1919.[28] Members held their event at Liberty Hall, which was located on Ninth and G Streets. Members included Felix Budhi, who first came to San Diego in 1908 by way of the U.S. Navy. There were also listed another thirty-one members in this organization, at least eight with navy ties. This event illustrated there was, indeed, a small Filipino community in San Diego prior to the 1920s, and it had organized.[29]

Organizations such as the Filipino Club of San Diego were active in the early 1920s. Although it was listed as a social club, one Filipino noted, "It was really organized for gambling purposes."[30] Other social clubs included the Rizal Day Club, the Filipino Sporting Club of Coronado, Improvement Association, and the Filipino Athletic Club, which was headed by Vincente Elequin. According to Elequin, who was a well-known leader in the Filipino community and headed several organizations in San Diego, the Filipino Athletic Club had over one hundred members by 1928; they were involved in organizing picnics and basketball games. They also co-sponsored Rizal Day celebrations with the Rizal Day Club. These organizations provided a space for the Filipino community to celebrate its cultural events.[31] On December 30, 1935, for example, several clubs got together to celebrate Rizal Day at the San Diego Hotel, including the Filipino Community Rizal Day Organization, the Caballeros De Dimas Alang, Jaena Lodge No. 11, General Lucban Lodge No. 23, Filipino Community Association of San Diego, Filipino Athletic Club, Unity Club, Filipino La Jolla Club, and the Sporting Club of Coronado.[32]

There were other notable events celebrated in San Diego. In 1935, for example, over two hundred people came under the auspices of the local Filipino Community Commonwealth Association to celebrate the commonwealth status of the Philippines. The Filipino community celebrated the anniversary of this event one year later, with events being held by both the Filipino Community Association of San Diego and the Filipino Sporting Club of Coronado. By 1965, the celebration of Philippine independence grew to nearly forty-five hundred people in attendance and included a dance sponsored by the Cavite Association of San Diego at the El Cortez Hotel.[33]

One of the oldest fraternal societies that had an active chapter in San Diego was the Caballeros de Dimas-Alang. Established on January 20, 1921, in San Francisco, California, it was a transplanted fraternal society from the Philippines.[34] Its purpose and objective was for "social intercourse, mental improvement, mutual aid, benefit, and protection." It provided economic aid to members when one of them was ill or suffered misfortune. It also helped obtain employment and encouraged business when its funding allowed it. Members established branches throughout California, including San Diego. The Jaena Lodge No. 11 was located at Market Street.[35] For many Filipinos, the organization was a means to escape the "American hosts who only tolerated [them] for [their] cheap labor" and to go where they could "stand proud and tall alongside persons who suffered the same fate."[36] Organizations thus nurtured a collective identity of struggle and survival for Filipinos who were far away from their homeland. They also provided a space where members could express their frustrations and find strategic ways to resist the social pressures they faced on a daily basis.

Another social organization was the Filipino Federation of America, Incorporated. Headed by Hilario Moncado, the organization had many objectives, some of which included religious ties: "promoting friendly relations between Filipinos and Americans, develop true Christian fellowship, the education advancement of each member, and advance the moral and social conduct of each member."[37] They had branches throughout the Pacific West Coast and Hawai'i. San Diego was among the California cities with a local branch (Branch No. 9), which was established July 16, 1928, at 325 Speckles Theatre Building at the corner of Second and Broadway.[38]

Social organizations and clubs gathered their communities to celebrate not only holidays, but also special occasions such as birthdays, baptisms, and weddings. Since space to hold these functions was limited outside of the communities, oftentimes members pooled their resources together and built the space themselves. Filipinos wanted to establish a permanent site that they could feel connected to, which, in turn, would let San Diego know that they were a part of the city's social composition. They also wanted to feel a sense of belonging to their new home, which led to community institution building. As early as 1931, San Diego's Filipino community met to discuss plans to build a community center. Seeking the aid of those sympathetic to their cause, and wanting to be a part of the larger society of San Diego, the community association stated: "The object of the association is to organize a recognized body to represent its race in the Interracial and international council of San Diego; to take active part in both social and civic bodies of the city; to create good spirit and unity among Filipinos; to take pride in our own race and demand just and equal treatment everywhere and oppose all discrimination on account of color; to promote better friendship and more sympathetic relations between Filipinos and other races; to promote better representation of our race in the community in which we live and to give possible assistance to any Filipino who deserves it."[39]

Years later, the community center became the Filipino American Veterans Hall (FAVA), located on Market Street. Established in the late 1940s, FAVA Hall served as the community's main event center where various Filipino organizations and clubs held their dances, pageants, and other social, religious, and cultural celebrations.[40] According to Delfin "Del" Labao, a longtime resident of San Diego, "From 1950 to 1962, FAVA was the center of activity for the Filipino Community of San Diego."[41] FAVA Hall still stands as the Filipino community's oldest recreation center. Prior to that, many events in the 1930s were held at the Philippine Hall on 631 Sixth Avenue as well as other venues such as Germania Hall and the Elk Club.[42]

In addition to having localized social organizations or branches, Filipinos in San Diego were also part of a larger entity that united Filipino community organizations across the nation. The Filipino Inter-Community Organization of the Western States had three separate organizations as members: the Philippine Council of San Diego, located on Market Street, and two general member branches in the Imperial Valley region. On August 28, 1946, San Diego's branch hosted several hundred delegates for the eighth annual convention at the chamber of commerce and a welcome dance at the U.S. Grant Hotel, where many Filipinos were employed. This particular event was a rare occasion in terms of its location, given that Filipinos were oftentimes not allowed to hold social events in downtown hotels prior to the 1960s.[43]

For both Filipinos and Mexicans, most of the early social organizations were comprised of men. Women had auxiliary branches of these organizations, but none of their own. These social organizations, for the most part, were male dominated. It would not remain this way. One of the most notable and prominent social organizations in the Filipino community is the Filipino American Women's Club (FAWC). Formed on January 13, 1949, FAWC (previously known as the Filipino Women's Club) is San Diego's oldest and longest-running Filipino American social club still in existence. FAWC was responsible for being the "first to present and promote Philippine culture" to mainstream society. Its original members included Ruth H. Abad, Alice L. Hawkins, Teodora R. Miraflor, Helen E. Padua, Dionisia Padua, Julia Elegado, Mary Manzano, Anita Pastor, Mary Somera, Concordia Hill, Alejandra Abrenilla, Isidra Fernandez, and Maxima Aspiras.[44] FAWC was instrumental in many social and cultural functions that brought attention to the Filipino American community. Since the majority of the women were married to Filipinos in the navy who were members of the Filipino American Veterans' Association (FAVA) Hall, they had a space to hold their functions. In addition to being married to navy men, some of these Filipinas were also married to farm workers and service workers in the urban sector of downtown San Diego. The goals of the organization were to "defend the rights and demand justice for Filipinos; promote the welfare of Filipinos."[45] FAWC also fostered cultural awareness by providing a positive image of the Filipino American community by teaching other ethnic groups about the history, language, food, and music of the Philippines. As Charito Balanag, a former president of FAWC, recalled about the origins of their organization, "You know people got together, but there was no formal society. So Ruth [Abad] said let's form an organization." Abad also wanted to do this because, as Balanag recalled, "there was no organization for the women."[46]

At first the men made fun of Ruth Abad and the other women; they said, as Balanag recalled, "she is over fifty years old . . . the concept of the men were different because a woman's place were at the home and not to go out to the world to be educated." They also didn't think the women would get along.[47] The men's reaction could be attributed to the fact that they were threatened by their wives' assertiveness and willingness to play active, public roles in the community. Despite their initial skepticism, the women of FAWC proved them wrong. FAWC grew both in membership and importance for the Filipino community of San Diego. Indeed, FAWC not only promoted their culture and celebrated events but also provided familial support and consolation to each other in order to maintain those bonds of family and community. This was another way they provided a safe haven for each other. Virginia Gomez, also former president of FAWC, recalled, "If someone is in need of a service, we go and help them. You know we wanted to help one another, and each other."[48]

As membership grew in FAWC, they soon extended its activities to include a Thanksgiving dinner for Filipino recruits at the Naval Training Center and sponsored the Sampaguita Ball (named after the Philippine national flower). FAWC also focused on "the welfare of disadvantaged women and children," working closely with several charities at home in the United States as well as in the Philippines. FAWC also held many "Nepa Salo-Salos," or Filipino get-togethers, to provide a social and recreational outlet for members, their families, and visiting Filipinos. As preservers of Philippine culture, language, and history, members of FAWC engaged in teaching children Filipino dress, dance, and songs.[49] Many of these functions took place at the Filipino American Veterans' Association (FAVA) Hall on Market Street. The reason they held their events there was because other venues, such as the U. S. Grant, Coronado, or El Cortez Hotels, oftentimes did not allow them to hold their dances there. This discrimination was evident despite the fact that these same Filipinos worked in these hotels and restaurants.[50] Balanag recalled, "What I gathered from the old-timers here was that Filipinos . . . could not have dances in the big hotels. That was a no-no."[51]

Another interesting thing to note about FAWC was its membership practices. When the issue of including Mexican and white wives of Filipino men came up, the majority of them voted to keep membership for only Filipinas. Of those who were in the minority who voted to include them was Ruth Abad, who was, in fact, racially mixed (Filipino-white). This incident, as sociologist Yen Espiritu notes, reminds us that "the 'Filipino' community was never all Filipino."[52] It also suggests Filipinos and Mexicans did not always work together, but rather had their own separate agendas, which were based along ethnic lines. By the time members like Virginia Gomez were active, FAWC did have members who were mestizas, including Filipino-Mexican, Filipino-Panamanian, and Filipino-white mixes.[53] These experiences would foreshadow the interethnic makeup that defined subsequent generation social clubs and organizations.

Cultural awareness and civic engagement were not the only things that immigrant and U.S.-born Mexicans and Filipinos advocated for. Indeed, for the generations that struggled to make a difference in their communities during the early twentieth century, one of the major issues that they grappled with was civil rights. In San Diego the struggle for civil rights created moments of spontaneous organizing to address a particular incident of racial discrimination among the Mexican community of Lemon Grove as well as a multiracial alliance of early activists who fought for social justice and equality for all oppressed peoples—a struggle that they engaged in collectively through the San Diego Race Relations Society.

THE LEMON GROVE INCIDENT

In addition to living in racially segregated neighborhoods, Mexicans in San Diego County were also pressured to attend segregated schools. During the 1930s in the rural community of Lemon Grove, for example, school officials singled out the children of Mexican immigrants to attend a separate school from white children. The Mexican students were predominately U.S. citizens by birth, whose families migrated from Baja California to work primarily in the area's lemon orchards (among other industries).[54] Known as the "Lemon Grove Incident,"[55] the case of *Roberto Alvarez v. The Board of Trustees of the Lemon Grove School District* would be the first successful court challenge against school segregation in U.S. history, predating both landmark Supreme Court cases *Mendez v. Westminster* in 1947 and *Brown v. Board of Education* in 1954.[56]

On July 23, 1930, the local Parent-Teacher Association (PTA), with the endorsement of the local chamber of commerce, requested from the Lemon Grove School Board the separation of white and Mexican children at Lemon Grove Grammar School.[57] On August 13, a special meeting was called by the Lemon Grove School Board, which voted to send Mexican children in the area to their own special school because of supposed issues surrounding overcrowding, sanitary conditions, and deteriorating morals.[58] These racially segregated schools, much like ones established in other parts of California and Texas, were labeled "Americanization schools" to justify the segregation of Mexican school-children.[59] On December 16, 1930, the school board voted to go ahead with its plans, yet parents were not notified that their children were to be sent to a segregated school until after the Christmas vacation.[60]

When Roberto Alvarez and his classmates went to school on the morning of January 5, 1931, they were stopped by Lemon Grove Grammar School principal Jerome T. Green. He was only admitting white students into the school and directing the Mexican children to a two-room building on Olive Street, which was later called the Caballeriza (the barn) by the Mexican community. Roberto and all the other Mexican schoolchildren (except three) ran straight home. When the children informed their parents of what occurred, they were outraged. The parents knew this was racial discrimination. In response, they refused to send their children to the segregated, makeshift school. A total of seventy-five of the students remained at home, which the local press reported as "the Mexican student strike."[61]

The parents immediately formed the Comite de Vecinos de Lemon Grove (the Lemon Grove Neighbors Committee). They appealed to the Mexican community, the press, and the Mexican consul. Mexican consul Enrique Ferreira aided them in hiring a lawyer and filed a class-action lawsuit against the school district.[62] *La Opinion*, the largest Spanish-language newspaper in California, wrote editorials in support of the Mexican schoolchildren. Roberto Alvarez was the lead plaintiff in a lawsuit by the Mexican community of Lemon Grove against the school district.[63]

The school board denied it was segregating the Mexican children during the trial. Board members informed the court that they build the separate school so that "backward and deficient children could be given better instruction than they could be given in a larger school."[64] The plaintiff (Alvarez) and ten additional witnesses demonstrated that they were actually segregated based on inaccurate generalizations regarding the intelligence of Mexican students and the assumption that they did not speak English despite the fact that most were American citizens and English was their primary language. Alvarez was chosen as the lead plaintiff because he had an excellent academic record in the Lemon Grove School District, disproving the argument that Mexican American students needed to be separated from the white children because they did not speak English well and were remedial.[65]

In March 1931, the court ruled in favor of the Mexican parents and against the Lemon Grove School District. San Diego Superior Court judge Claude Chambers ordered the reinstatement of Mexican American school children, stating that "the equal but separate segregation statements violated the Constitution."[66] Having lost the court decision, the school board decided that "only a spirit of good will prevailed and it was decided that everything was to continue exactly as it did prior to January 5th."[67]

Although this was a major victory for Lemon Grove's Mexican community, it did not end school segregation for all nonwhite groups. According to historian Richard Griswold del Castillo, "their segregation violated a state law that allowed for the segregation of African American and Indian children. Thus the verdict did not challenge racial segregation per se, and it would remain for later court cases to outlaw that injustice for all students of color."[68] The Alvarez case also did not set a precedent to desegregate others schools outside of Lemon Grove after 1931. The case remained a local incident.[69] The issue of school segregation and unequal educational opportunities would remain a problem, resurfacing again in San Diego County with *Carlin v. San Diego Board of Education* in 1967.[70] Despite the Lemon Grove incident's not reaching national attention, what it did demonstrate was that the Mexican community would fight for its civil rights and challenge efforts by segregationists to deprive its children of an equal education.

While the Mexican community of Lemon Grove organized itself to combat racial discrimination and segregation, other alliances across racial and ethnic lines also surfaced in the early 1920s, some preceding the Lemon Grove incident, and continued to fight for the civil rights of all nonwhite groups in San Diego County well into the 1940s. The San Diego Race Relations Society would be among the first interracial organizations that advocated for both Mexicans and Filipinos in the region.

EARLY MULTIRACIAL COALITIONS FOR CIVIL RIGHTS

The San Diego Race Relations Society was founded in the early 1920s. Led by Dennis V. Allen, its membership included African Americans, Mexicans, Chinese, Italians, and other ethnic whites.[71] As a multiracial group fighting on behalf of racial equality and good relations, it spearheaded many activities

regarding race relations in San Diego, most notably to combat racial discrimination in the public sphere. It also was involved in programming and events that
brought together various racial and ethnic groups to celebrate the diversity of
San Diego and build community together.[72] Given the work that the San Diego
Race Relations Committee was doing, it led the way for a larger, independent
commission known as the California Race Relations Commission, which was
established and appointed by then governor Frank Merriam in 1937. The
California Race Relations Commission had three members from the San Diego
Race Relations Society, Dennis V. Allen, Cuahtemoc A. Hernandez, and Rev.
Kei T. Wong.[73] A meeting was held in San Diego, at the San Diego Hotel, where
Allen was appointed commission chairman. Members met at other occasions in
other California cities, such as Los Angeles and Santa Barbara. Yet, despite their
work in race relations, the current governor at the time, Culbert L. Olson, did not
fund their commission, which was already being funded by the members themselves. In order to help with the financial situation of the commission, Allen wrote
the governor in 1946, appealing for financial support of this noteworthy and
much needed commission that dealt with racial problems throughout the state
and was being neglected by the governor at the time. The lack of support by the
state was forcing the commission to end its operations—a clear indication that
civil rights were not on the agenda of the state. Allen wrote in his letter: "Because
of the lack of funds and official recognition, I feel that you should know that the
Commissioners appointed long since discontinued operation with efforts to keep
the Commission alive. . . . [T]he Commissioners felt a public slight on the State's
failure to somehow assist us in meeting operation expenses."[74]

Allen went on to discuss the activities of the San Diego Race Relations Society
in public programming and its campaign to ensure that the Fair Employment
Practices Act was being upheld by the state. Yet, despite the fact Allen alleged
that "many public officials are members of the San Diego Race Relations
Society," the lack of racial equality in San Diego at the time only reinforced what
was going on in the larger arena of race issues in California.[75] Despite the lack of
support, the San Diego Race Relations Society continued its efforts at fighting
for civil rights.

In August of 1944, the San Diego Race Relations Society got involved in a
racial discrimination case in Escondido. In a letter to Mayor Edgar E. Clover of
Escondido, on August 30, 1944, Dennis Allen testified that four Mexican nationals were denied service at the Rendezvous Cocktail Lounge. When asked why
service was denied to these individuals, the employee replied that the owner had
instructed him to do so. They were denied service despite the fact that the men
were neatly dressed and had not been drinking. The men were obviously humiliated by this act of racial discrimination, so much that the Mexican Consulate
of San Diego intervened, sending a formal complaint to the San Diego Race
Relations Society. A letter was also sent to Governor Earl Warren describing the
situation. The San Diego Race Relations Society called for an investigation on

this matter as well as an end to such discrimination.[76] This illustrates how the multiracial coalition of civil rights activists continued its efforts at community building by advocating for the rights of those who were the victims of racial discrimination.

In 1945, the San Diego Race Relations Society was also called in to aid two Filipinos who were refused housing in the Golden Hills area of San Diego (Twenty-Fifth and Broadway). According to local Filipino resident Delfin Labao, in response to this act of discrimination, the San Diego Race Relations Society staged a demonstration protesting the actions of the white homeowners who refused to sell the homes to these Filipinos. The homeowners eventually relented, thus giving the San Diego Race Relations Society its first major victory against housing discrimination in San Diego.[77] The San Diego Race Relations Society illustrates how a coalition of African Americans, Mexicans, and other groups formed a multiracial organization to fight for a common cause that affected them all: racial discrimination. Within this particular setting, they also empowered themselves, challenging racism and bringing attention to the racial climate that existed in San Diego. They worked together to push their agenda for civil rights.

Although the children of these civil rights activists would also participate in similar struggles, taking on the helm of righteous resistance from their parents, they also were involved in creating a youth culture that defined their generation. These second- and third-generation urban youth formed social clubs that both involved community and were socially engaging through music and dance. The youth culture they developed enabled them to find their own voice in the public arena as they created a sound and image all their own.

SOCIAL CLUBS AND YOUTH CULTURE

The groups formed by subsequent generations of U.S.-born Mexican and Filipino youth from the 1940s to the 1960s had a more social-community orientation to them, which facilitated intermixing between them all. They formed social clubs and were a part of youth cultures that took on a different dynamic than those organizations of their parents (both immigrant and U.S.-born). Their social clubs provided not only a means for having fun and socializing, but also a chance to make a difference in their communities, like their parents had done. During the 1940s, the Lucky 13 was one such group. Formed by thirteen teenage Mexican American girls in the community of Logan Heights, the Lucky 13 was primarily a social club and held meetings at the Neighborhood House. They were all the children of fish cannery workers. One day they decided to form a club but had to find a name that suited them. Lucky 13 member Dora Hollman Garcia recalled, "We were all thinking of a name for us . . . Las Amigas, and then she [Mrs. McClure] says, you know there's thirteen of you, how about the Lucky 13? So, we voted on it at the next meeting." Dora also goes on to mention that more girls joined the Lucky 13, including a few Filipinas who lived in the neighborhood, which was a testament to their camaraderie.[78]

The Lucky 13 used to have sewing groups and members played the piano at the Neighborhood House. More often, they planned teenage dances. They held dances and other events as a means to provide some form of entertainment for their peers. Delia Chavez recalled how a group of them who were in their early teens took sewing and cooking classes at the Neighborhood House. The Lucky 13 performed community service. They gathered to bake and to sing Christmas carols for residents at local retirement centers.[79] Given that most of the events occurred at the Neighborhood House, the girls from the Lucky 13 got to interact with the boys from the neighborhood. In fact, as Delia Chavez recalled, "The majority of the girls married boys from the neighborhood. I didn't, but a lot of them did."[80] As they got older, they became part of the Senior's Club, which held USO dances for the servicemen in the back of the Neighborhood House. Another group that facilitated the social interaction between Mexican, Filipino, and Mexipino youth in Logan Heights was Our Lady of Guadalupe's Catholic Youth Organization (CYO). In addition to having sports teams, the CYO also held chaperoned dances for the neighborhood youth. Logan Heights resident Armando Rodriquez noted, "The CYO dances were a highlight of my youth well into my twenties."[81]

Filipino Americans who came of age during the 1940s and 1950s also formed social clubs as a means to organize themselves and negotiate their identities as both Filipino and American. These included interethnic clubs, which were formed by both Filipinas and their mixed-race peers. The first was the Filipino Genies, or "FG's." A rival club, the Mestiza Debs, was composed of all mixed-race Filipinas. Although both groups were service clubs, they centered a lot of their activities around social activities such as dances. As Anne Santos Slangle recalled, "Parties were a big thing."[82] Most of these girls were children of Filipino families who were present in San Diego since the 1920s, if not earlier. Family names included Santos, Esquerra, Magagy, Kistner, Tamayo, Isturis, and Custado, among others.[83] The Esquerra family, for example, owned a Filipino restaurant on Market Street, which was the site for many of FG's meetings. Unlike Filipina clubs, there is no documentation available regarding Filipino boys' social clubs. Rita Kistner recalled, "There were very few Filipino boys in school with them."[84] This may be due to the fact that most of the Filipinos who were their peers were involved in mixed-race social clubs with Mexicans and African Americans, rather than being a part of ethnic-based social clubs.

Sports teams were also vibrant during the late 1940s and early 1950s. Many were formed under the direction of coach and athletic director Augie Escamilla from the San Diego Boys' Club. The club catered to the Mexican, Filipino, and African American youth in Southeast San Diego. Basketball, baseball, boxing, and other recreational sports were important to the youth who attended the club. Not all of the sports teams, however, were part of the Boys' Club. Basketball teams like the Toltec Club were also popular, which, according to Freddie Ayap, included a mix of Mexicans, Filipinos, and mixed-race Filipinos.[85]

In addition to sports teams, Mexican, Filipino, and African American youth in San Diego were also a part of a thriving zoot-suit culture, which was popular during the 1940s. These coming-of-age youth were donning the drape-shaped zoot suits and dancing to the tunes of Duke Ellington and Lalo Guererro, among others. Their bebop and jitterbug dances were part of their zoot culture.[86] Dances were held in the Neighborhood House in Logan Heights. Many of these zoot-suiters also went to the Filipino district, where they continued to frequent the nightclubs and social hot spots that welcomed them.

Clad in their zoot suits and shoes, they were making a statement, which, as one former Pachuco (zoot-suiter) recalled, "contributed to a dress code, a dress code that stated: We're not from Mexico, we're American."[87] But their zoot suits were more than a statement of Americanism. These young, urban, working-class Mexicans, Filipinos, and others who were marginalized by race, class, and age were also resisting their treatment by mainstream society. For those who embraced the zoot culture, Linda España-Maram writes that it was a "subcultural gesture that refused to concede to the manners of subservience." Indeed, for both Mexicans and Filipinos who wore the zoot suit, it enabled them to shed their work uniforms, which symbolized servitude; and thus they "challenged stereotypes of being submissive, unassertive, and always eager to please." As España-Maram further suggests, "The drape shape represented an open challenge to the dominate society's perception of poverty-ridden 'dirty' Mexicans and Filipinos."[88] It was a way for both brown and black youth to engage in an urban culture that flew into the face of white America by creating "fresh meanings of gender, race, and nation as they lived in wartime America."[89] The attire, music, and swagger that these brown and black youth participated in created a shared experience of community building that resisted the social pressures of white America. Their fashion and culture of resistance, however, was met with violence. These young brown and black youth became the targets of the war at home, which white sailors, police officers, and civilians waged during World War II in Los Angeles and San Diego. San Diego resident Edward Galván recalled: "Back then the cops were mostly white and they sure used to hassle the hood. Two of these cops were from the old Prohibition days. They used to take scissors and horse pliers and cut the shamps—duck tails—off the Pachucos' clothes or take the soles off their shoes."[90]

Indeed, the intimidation and violence directed at young Mexican, Filipino, and African American youth who donned these outfits have been well documented, especially in areas like Los Angeles, where the Zoot Suit Riots were the most violent.[91] San Diego did not escape the fear or violence that spread throughout Los Angeles and beyond. In fact, many sailors who participated in the Los Angeles Zoot Suit Riots of 1943 were stationed in San Diego. Newspaper accounts on June 10, 1943, for example, reported that groups numbering up to several hundred servicemen swarmed through downtown San Diego and neighboring communities like Logan Heights and National City, searching for zoot-suiters who supposedly infiltrated the city. Although there were minor incidents and some of the zoot-suit-clad youth were pursued, most who were targeted were able to escape the worst of the mob violence. The *Los Angeles Examiner* also reported that "a mob of more than 100 sailors and marines stormed down a main street after several youths wearing the outlandish garb, but the zoot suiters made a getaway before fists began to swing."[92]

Other national newspapers reported that clashes occurred involving thousands of civilians and servicemen. Hundreds of Mexicans, Filipinos, and African Americans were injured and arrested; oftentimes this included both zoot-suiters and civilians who fit the racial profile. As the *Chicago Defender* reported, "The trouble spread from the downtown section of the residential sections of both Negroes and Mexicans which border together from Logan Avenue to Imperial Avenue in the Logan Heights district . . . [and] it developed into the worst racial outbreaks in the entire history of this city."[93] Tensions increased over the next two days to the point that military patrols and police were called in to subdue the conflict between servicemen and zoot-suiters. On June 12, 1942, military police picked up servicemen who were apprehended by local police for being a part of the roaming patrols out looking to beat up zoot-suiters. They were jailed along with twelve Mexican youth, whom the police reported were part of a National City gang.[94]

Civil rights activists such as Luisa Moreno, who was also a labor organizer, condemned the violent acts of racism that young zoot-suiters experienced at the hands of hundreds of white servicemen, civilians, and even the police, who were supposed to protect them yet turned the other way or even arrested the victims as instigators of the riots. The police were even involved in the beating of zoot-suit-clad youth in San Diego. Frank Penuelas recalled, "There were a lot of beatings by the police at the time. . . . [T]hey'd take the kids down to Benson's lumberyard and make them take off their clothes and beat them." The navy even went so far as to cover up these disturbances by military personnel against zoot-suiters and civilians.[95] Civil rights groups such as the Citizens Committee Against Discrimination also condemned the violence that occurred without provocation, blaming the news for stirring up hysteria in San Diego as it did in Los Angeles, which they labeled "a campaign of race incitement."[96]

What is important to remember about these incidents is that during World War II, both Mexican Americans and Filipinos (U.S.-born and immigrant) volunteered by the thousands to show their loyalty to their country. Ironically, they flocked to serve in the U.S. armed forces to preserve and protect democracy abroad despite not experiencing it at home. It is estimated that over eighty thousand Filipinos in Hawai'i and the continental United States rushed to their local recruiting centers to enlist. Although Filipino immigrants were at first refused the opportunity to fight in the U.S. armed forces, President

Franklin D. Roosevelt signed into law a revision of the Selective Service Act. This allowed the formation of the First and Second Filipino Infantry Regiments, U.S. Army (numbering over seven thousand), which participated in the liberation of the Philippines from Japanese occupation, among other campaigns. Mexican Americans also served valiantly in both the Pacific and European war fronts with over five hundred thousand enlisting in the U.S. armed forces and earning more medals of honor than any other ethnic group.[97]

Ironically, despite fighting under the U.S. flag overseas, Mexican and Filipino communities did not experience the freedom that democracy evoked at home. Rather, the violence only illustrated, as George Sanchez notes, "the Anglo American cultural intolerance of racial and cultural differences, and the special difficulties of a generation of youth suspended between two cultures." Yet it was this culture of difference that enabled young Mexicans and Filipinos to find their voice and participate in their own urban youth subculture. It allowed them to find a sense of belonging in a marginalized existence. Indeed, as historian Luis Alvarez also points out, "Zoot-suiters deserve the recognition for creating an awareness and a record that there was racial and ethnic difference, even at a time when cultural differences were being stifled."[98]

Despite the wartime sacrifices of both Mexicans and Filipinos, they still faced racial discrimination in housing, education, and employment and in the public sphere, as documented in *Look* magazine, which reported, "Filipinos and Mexicans on the West Coast are barred from 'white' restaurants, segregated in theatres."[99] Their struggle would continue well into the 1950s and 1960s as returning veterans from World War II used their wartime experiences to empower themselves in fighting for democracy at home. It was also during the postwar years that the next generation of Mexican and Filipino social clubs took on a different form.

POSTWAR SOCIAL CLUBS AND YOUTH CULTURE

During the post–World War II years, Mexicans and Filipinos continued to participate in the youth culture that was developing both a style and musical sensibility. The 1950s and 1960s had their share of social clubs. Many of them were multiracial in membership. One of the first and most influential clubs was Los Gallos (the Roosters); members included Salvador "Queso" Torres, Ricardo Romio, Roberto Martinez, and Haracio and Hiram Piña, among others. Torres recalled, "We started that club [with forty-two members] to show people who we were—not in a violent way, but in a proud way . . . and from being part of it, we developed a social consciousness. And we had good times."[100] Los Gallos even sponsored younger clubs, like Los Chicanos and Los Lobos. These clubs organized benefit dances as well as holiday parties for children in their community. As a founding member of Los Chicanos, Henry "Leaky" Diaz noted, "We rented loudspeakers and invited people to bring their kids to the old

Coronet theatre.... [T]he theatre showed cartoons and we gave the kids gifts."[101] Other groups included the Yellow Jackets and El Nido Teenage Club. According to Freddie Ayap, there was also the 38 Club, which was located on Thirty-eighth and National Avenue. Most of the social clubs held dances for their peers and sponsored picnics and other social activities. Connie Zuniga said, "During the fifties . . . there were a lot of Mexican clubs. There used to be dances every single week."[102]

There were also teenage clubs for girls, like the Cheetahs, the Blue Notes, and the Drifters. Los Gallos used to have joint meetings with them all the time and have dances together. Ricardo Romio also reported that some of these groups were multiracial like Los Gallos. They had members who were Mexican, Filipino, mestizo (Mexipino), Chinese, Japanese, and African American. They were all mixed.[103] When asked what the social clubs were like in Logan Heights, Romio stated: "We started Los Gallos. It was a social club, and all the other clubs around were getting bad reputations, always in the papers for rat packs, they called them, doing all kinds of bad stuff. And we just did the opposite. We gave a Father's Day dinner; we helped people; we did things to help people in the community. And one time we got invited to see the governor and we went to Sacramento."[104]

Given the previous racial violence that plagued the wartime years, especially for young brown and black youth who were stereotyped as gang members, teenage clubs of the 1950s and 1960s wanted to shape a particular image of themselves. As Los Gallos member Romio recalled, their club wanted a clean image, so in their neighborhood they were involved in a lot of activities, such as community service. He recalled: "We would go out of our way to do things in the community and let them know who we were and what we were doing, and why we were doing it. Like, we had that show at the corner theater for kids on Christmas. We passed out candy and stuff like that. We had Santa Claus come down there for them to see Santa, just things like that. And then the Father's Day dinner, we went up to Sacramento . . . all the things that we could think of that would help people out in the neighborhood. Anytime, somebody was in trouble or needed help for something, we helped them out and we gave them a little card, a Los Gallos card." According to Romio, their social club was one of the few that did this in the neighborhood. He commented, "The Yellow Jackets used to laugh at us. They used to make fun of us all the time."[105]

That did not stop them from being involved in their community. Los Gallos also used to have its meetings and dances at the Neighborhood House. When members wanted bigger venues they started looking for halls such as Code Six, which was located on B Street up by Golden Hills.[106] This was how subsequent generations of U.S.-born Mexicans, Filipinos, and Mexipinos utilized their social clubs as they came of age between the 1950s and 1960s. They wanted a sense of belonging as they grappled with balancing their ethnic Mexican, Filipino, and American cultures. The social clubs were the places where they continued to intermix and blend their cultures, nurturing another generation of Mexipinos who were a part of these groups. Another way youth were able to continue their intermixing of people and culture quite successfully was through music.

FORGING A MULTIRACIAL POPULAR CULTURE

In his study on popular culture, George Lipsitz contends that music was a mechanism of defense by which African Americans responded to racism, exploitation, and oppression. Other groups that shared in this oppression found a means by which they too could artistically express these experiences. Lipsitz writes, "Black culture contains the most sophisticated strategies of signification and the richest grammars of opposition available to aggrieved populations."[107] One of these musical genres was rock and roll. Originating in working-class black and white communities, this musical style resonated with San Diego's Mexican, Filipino, Mexipino, and African American youth. They began forming bands and playing gigs at various local spots in their communities. Music and dancing provided an escape from the harsh realities of racism. As historian Douglas Daniels noted, it was the entertainment, music, dancing, and socializing that "made racism seem less important."[108] People from different racial and class backgrounds mixed together without the constraints of outside norms. The combination of social organizations, clubs, and music enabled them to create their own social world and escape the confines and social pressures related to their racially segregated condition. Within their multiracial spaces, they mixed together, creating and participating in the popular culture of their generation.[109]

During the 1950s and 1960s, Mexicans, Filipinos, Mexipinos, African Americans, and some whites, among others, comprised many of the multiracial bands in the neighborhoods, contributing to the youth culture, which was rock and roll in Southern California. San Diego was no exception. In fact, there was a vibrant musical culture that developed with many local bands. One such band was the Kingsmen. According to Lanny Villarin, there were two Filipinos in that group. Villarin observed that the intermixing and cultural blending of these bands always included Filipinos. He noted, "We had a lot of Filipinos in those different bands. . . . I don't really remember an all-Mexican band. They always had some Filipinos stuck in there."[110] He also mentioned other groups that were in the music scene in San Diego included Joe Houston, the Bostics, and Benny and the Velvetones.[111] Rachael and the Chorals released a record in 1957 with the Velvetones. The lead singer, Rachael Ortiz, was from Barrio Logan. There were also Johnny Otis and Big Jay McNeeley.[112] As a spectator and participant in the dance and music scene of his generation, Villarin recalled a lot about the bands that played in his neighborhood. One of his favorite memories concerned local music legend Big Jay McNeeley: "We used to have dances down at the Neighborhood House, and we had a really good time. . . . [W]e used to go to dances downtown at the Palladium. We used to have battle of the bands. I remember after a dance he [Big Jay McNeeley] ended up at a party in Logan Heights and he came out of the house playing the sax and walking down the street playing the sax. That was one of his trades. There was stuff like that all the time."[113]

One of the most famous Mexican American singers to come out of San Diego's multiracial rock-and-roll scene was Rosie Hamlin, of Rosie and the Originals. Hamlin (birth name Mendez) lived in National City yet also spent time with relatives in Logan Heights, including her aunt Rachael Ortiz (of Rachael and the Chorals).[114] Through her uncle's girlfriend she met musicians David Ponci, Noah Tafolla, Tony Gomez, and Carl Von Goodat, all of whom later became the Originals. At the age of fourteen, Hamlin penned a poem called "Angel Baby." Rosie and the Originals decided to record the song. According to Hamlin, it was recorded on a two-track in an airplane hanger in San Marcos, California. She recalled, "You couldn't even find a recording studio in San Diego then."[115]

After they pressed a copy of their record, Rosie and the Originals took it to Kresge's Department Store in San Diego to see if they could play it in the listening booths. The song made such a commotion among the youth that a distributor for Highland Records asked them to bring their master to a meeting. Three weeks later, their song was on K-Day Radio with Alan Freed. In his introduction to the song, he said, "This is by a fifteen-year-old girl from National City, California, named Rosie."[116]

"Angel Baby" released in late 1960, peaking on the Billboard charts at number five in 1961 when Hamlin was just fifteen years old.[117] Recorded for Highland Records, it was their biggest hit to date, selling millions of records. Despite the fame that the record created for Rosie and the Originals, like most artists of that time, they were cheated out of their royalties. She even had to prove that she wrote "Angel Baby."[118] When "Angel Baby" took off on the music charts, Hamlin had to leave Sweetwater High School in National City during her first year in order to hit the touring circuit and promote her record. Rosie and the Originals went on to tour with Alan Freed's rock-and-roll tour, which included the likes of Jackie Wilson, Carla Thomas, Ben E. King, Bobby Rydell, Chubby Checker, Bobby Darin, the Shirelles, Little Anthony and the Imperials, the Marcells, the Isley Brothers, Dell Shanon, Johnny Otis, Big Joe Turner, Big Momma Thornton, Fats Domino, Chuck Berry, and Little Richard. She also got to work with Freddie Fender as well as numerous East Los Angeles groups such as Malo, Tierra, and El Chicano. Hamlin also got to open for the Rolling Stones when they played in San Diego. Even John Lennon recorded a rendition of "Angel Baby." He commented, "Little Rosie was one of my favorite American artists."[119]

When Hamlin first started to gain recognition for "Angel Baby," Villarin remembered that she asked him to sing during his club meetings at Saint Jude's Catholic Church. As he recalled, "Her song, 'Angel Baby,'" was "the biggest hit of anybody in San Diego. We had a lot of hits, but 'Angel Baby' was the biggest hit in the whole area."[120] Rosie Hamlin's success was nurtured in the multiracial communities of National City and Logan Heights. In these spaces of intermixing and cultural blending, her and other multiracial bands in San Diego set out to define their generation through music. Despite the contributions of Rosie and the Originals and other groups to come out of San Diego's rock-and-roll scene, not much is mentioned about the area's artists. Rather, Southern California's Mexican American rock-and-roll scene tends to focus more on Los Angeles. This topic of research begs for further inquiry.[121] Nonetheless, "Angel Baby" remains one of the most popular oldies that still blares from lowriders and the homes of America's Chicano youth, who relate to the music from that generation.

The youth culture of the 1950s and 1960s ushered in another means by which Mexicans and Filipinos interacted with each other, reinforcing the bonds between both groups in their communities. Indeed, a love for music and the opportunity for young Filipino American men to dance and find companionship with Mexican American women in these settings provided another reason for them to forge more intimate ties, which often led to dating and marriage.[122]

—————

Despite the fact that whites racially segregated Mexicans and Filipinos, restricting them to certain sections of San Diego, and at times using intimidation and violence to keep them confined in their multiracial spaces, both groups flourished. Within their communities, social organizations and clubs thrived. They addressed the needs of their communities and formed networks that fostered a sense of solidarity through emotional and cultural bonds. They created ethnic-based as well as larger multiracial organizations to fight for their civil rights and resist their treatment as second-class citizens. Their children helped develop and sustain thriving youth cultures that were very American in their multiracial sound and sensibilities. Their shared experiences with social ostracism, racism, and, at times, violence kept them emotionally connected to each other as they continued to live, work, socialize, and worship in their multiracial communities. It is within these communities, as bell hooks noted in *Killing Rage,* that the space for people to heal and find normalcy in their lives was provided.[123] Mexicans and Filipinos found time to be with family and friends and heal through recreational activities, music, and prayer. In doing so they were involved in the cultural retention and survival of their communities, creating a "home away from home" atmosphere, which was a safe haven for residents, and especially for new immigrants. On a larger scale, they created a cultural awareness of their communities, most notably from the 1940s through the 1960s, as they sought acceptance in broader society. This enabled them to overcome some of the racial barriers they faced in San Diego. Their participation in the music scene, for example, clearly illustrates that they were becoming part of America's popular culture by contributing national hits—all from the confines of their segregated communities. But those who labored in San Diego's various industries endured continued racial discrimination and low wages. Mexicans and Filipinos, however, did not stand by idly. Rather, they organized and resisted in the workplace.

CHAPTER 4

Race and Labor Activism in San Diego

In 1936, Mexican and Filipino celery workers in Chula Vista, the southern area of San Diego County, struck against the Chula Vista Vegetable Exchange. Although functioning as separate ethnic unions, the Mexican Union of Laborers, the Filipino Labor Union, and the Field Workers of San Diego County united against the celery growers to demand a wage increase to thirty cents an hour and the guarantee of a four-hour shift minimum if employers requested them to work for the day. Representing the Filipino and Mexican labor unions were Chris Mensalvas and Joe Espinosa.[1] City newspapers reported that alien Mexicans who were striking were threatened with deportation. Police were present to patrol the picket lines; however, there were no reported incidents of violence.[2] This was not an isolated strike. During the 1920s and well into the 1930s, a series of strikes, both nonviolent and violent, occurred between Mexican, Filipino, and other ethnic farm workers against the various fruit and vegetable growers that were operating across California. San Diego's Mexican and Filipino farm workers were part of a larger movement of agricultural laborers during the early half of the twentieth century that struck throughout the state of California as they fought to secure a living wage and better living and working conditions. San Diego's farm workers were not alone but rather one strand in an intricate web of labor organizing and strife that was occurring across the state. They, along with fish cannery workers, faced many hardships as they sought to organize, sometimes as separate ethnic unions but more often as part of larger interracial coalitions in a hostile environment that did not welcome any form of labor resistance. San Diego's political climate, with its pro-business and anti-union reputation, is well documented. Local political and business interests were not afraid to use violence against any form of social and economic justice movement that originated among racial and ethnic minorities. San Diego sought to remain, as David Reid noted, "a kind of Anglo crusader kingdom."[3] Thus, growers, operatives, vigilantes, local authorities, and even the state attempted to crush local movements among Mexican and Filipino laborers.

As a colonized workforce, San Diego Mexican and Filipino laborers were relegated to the most menial positions.[4] In agriculture, for example, both Mexicans and Filipinos were usually field hands. They earned substandard wages while working in extreme heat from sunup to sundown, whereas whites were either foremen or worked in the packing sheds, which usually had union representation as skilled labor. This was also true for most other industries with a racialized wage system. In the fish canneries of San Diego wage disparities were further complicated by both race and gender. Despite union representation, women typically earned less than men and worked in gender-specific jobs. By and large, however, the majority of positions that Mexicans and Filipinos occupied were at the rank-and-file level and strictly on the bottom rungs of the labor market. This was also true for service-oriented positions. In these various occupations workers faced discrimination, isolation, and substandard wages. Mexicans and Filipinos sought to alleviate their conditions by organizing, both separately and in alliance, to combat unfair labor treatment. Indeed, Mexicans and Filipinos in San Diego organized with thousands of others across the state to gain higher wages, union recognition, and better living and working conditions. These unions were an extension of their communities. In Logan Heights, for example, cannery workers held mixed events such as formal and informal meetings at each other's homes, union-sponsored picnics, and other community events. The social activities and union meetings strengthened their relationships as workers and community members. These ties, which often included familial and extended kinship relations, bound them together.

In this chapter I examine the role of the workplace and how mutual participation in various industries affected both Mexican and Filipino communities in San Diego during the early half of the twentieth century. I contend that the intersections of race, class, and gender with labor were crucial factors in the daily interactions between Mexicans and Filipinos. They were the key elements in defining both communities in how they were formed and sustained by the industries they were involved in, especially as they related to agriculture and fish canning. Undoubtedly, the social relationships they forged stemmed from their shared experiences on the job and social status in a racist environment. Mexicans and Filipinos, however, experienced what Laura Pulido calls "differential racialization." Pulido writes, "Different groups are racialized in distinct kinds of ways. What this means is that a particular set of racial meanings are attached to different racial/ethnic groups that not only affect their class position and racial standing, but are also a function of it."[5] This differential racialization did impact how Mexicans and Filipinos organized independently of one another at first, and at times tension did exist between them; but in many instances they labored together, sharing common working-class experiences, which were influenced by their shared racial oppression. This was most evident in the agricultural fields where predominately Filipinos and Mexicans organized together.

Some scholars have pointed to the ways in which Filipino and Mexican interethnic labor organizing during the 1930s was unsuccessful due to differential racialization, which affected how their coalitions persisted, and the role white supremacy played in preventing them from occurring, oftentimes through the use of violence. What I will show is in this chapter, however, is how Filipinos and Mexicans, despite their differential racialization, were able to build solid coalitions with each other, and other racial/ethnic groups to a lesser extent, in order to mobilize and work on basic bread-and-butter issues, such as higher wages. The numerous examples in this chapter will demonstrate that the interethnic relationships between Filipinos and Mexicans did not just produce risky coalitions but rather facilitated a legacy of meaningful labor organizing that enabled both groups to find common ground together under a larger multiracial class consciousness and build upon their other overlapping histories of colonialism, migration, racialization, and civil rights struggles.[6]

Although Mexican women were also present in the fields and packing sheds of San Diego and were involved in labor activism, the agricultural field was a male-dominated industry because of its migratory nature and grower preference for "gang labor."[7] Race and its intersection with gender were most evident in the fish canneries, which employed a substantial number of women. In fact, the majority of workers in San Diego's fish canneries were ethnic Mexican women. Their sheer number and participation allowed Mexican women to exert power and influence within their unions. Mexicans and Filipinos were also overrepresented in certain industries along ethnic lines, a result of their differential racialization. Independent from their Filipino counterparts, Mexicans in San Diego, for example, dominated the railroad and construction industry in the early 1910s and 1920s, where they worked as manual laborers. These industries served as gateway employment for their entrance into other occupations such as agriculture and fish cannery work. Mexicans and Filipinos also worked together in the service sector, but they never organized into unions during the early twentieth century. It was Filipinos who tended to dominate this particular occupation because of their previous colonial status as naval stewards.

With the development of San Diego's various industries during the 1910s through the 1940s, immigrants filled the void of unskilled and semi-skilled labor. These individuals worked in the city's growing agricultural, fish-canning, and service-related industries. As San Diego became known as a "city in motion," a workforce was needed to keep it moving. Yet from the annals of labor history, these ethnic and racial workers, especially in San Diego, were left on the margins or, at best, relegated to a footnote in historical studies that focused on labor movements principally concerned with skilled, white labor. These sources excluded defining categories of analysis, such as race, ethnicity, and gender. This is evident in the *San Diego Labor Leader*, for example, an AFL paper that focused predominately on skilled, white labor. When examining this newspaper, what is most interesting is what is *not* mentioned, which normally included the presence and labor struggles of ethnic workers in San Diego.[8] Such neglect suggests that San Diego's workforce was predominately made up of white males. This, of course, is absurd. Interviews previously completed with Mexicans and Filipinos attest to their presence. The fact that these workers were not mentioned has been detrimental to the historical knowledge of their existence in San Diego. To historians and contemporary writers of the time, they were not important enough to mention, which is why oral histories have been vital in illustrating the presence of these workers in various establishments. Oral histories and photographs were thus the primary source of information I relied on to document the lives of both Filipino and Mexican workers in San Diego.

Ignoring the Mexican and Filipino presence has had a twofold effect, the first being that San Diego has developed a racially exclusive historical narrative and consciousness, the second being that San Diego's prominence can be largely attributed to the unacknowledged work of Mexican and Filipino workers. Examining the social and cultural commonalities that these two communities had with one another, it is obvious that the workplace had a huge impact on their interactions. What historical records do show is that Mexicans and Filipinos were oftentimes present together in various San Diego industries. We will now turn our attention to the industries that employed Mexicans and Filipinos.

Serving Empire: From Stewards to Service Workers

A. B. Santos, a longtime Filipino resident of San Diego, worked at the Hotel Del Coronado in the 1920s. He also lived in a dormitory, working as a helper in the executive dining room. He was paid twenty dollars a month plus housing. As he recalled, there were a number of Filipinos who worked at the hotel, including six in housekeeping, eight to twelve busboys, two dining room helpers, and the head of the dormitory. Santos was the only Filipino (or Asian, for that matter) to graduate from Coronado High School, and he later worked as an insurance agent. Indeed, he was an exception, yet Santos could sell insurance only to Filipinos and other Asian Americans. He was prohibited from selling insurance policies to whites. He recalled that most Filipinos he knew had limited opportunities because "Americans believed that Filipinos and other Orientals were just dishwashers and cooks because these were the only jobs of Filipinos in the navy and these were the only ones they knew."[9]

As Santos's statement implies, Filipinos were forced into racialized occupations that were service- or domestic-oriented despite their educational background. The lack of opportunities to move into other occupations because of racial discrimination was something both Filipinos and their Mexican counterparts shared. Racism also played a role in what they were paid. If Filipinos and Mexicans worked alongside whites in restaurant work, for example, they were paid less. Manuel Buaken shared this frustrating experience: "What made the work hardest was that I knew Americans working on all-around kitchen jobs, on relief routines such as I was handing, were paid wages of from $35 to $45 a week at a time, and there I was getting $18."[10] The lower wages Filipinos and Mexicans received, compared to white workers, demonstrated the way racism affected them economically. Filipinos and Mexicans felt the sting of this injustice, yet they were not organized, so they could not collectively respond to their wage disparities.

Although Filipinos and Mexicans were a part of the service sector, working in restaurants, hotels, and resorts, it was the former who filled the majority of these positions. As an extension of their previous work as stewards in the U.S. Navy, Filipinos were seen as an ideal domestic and service workforce. This transition from stewards to service workers only reinforced the racial and colonial relationship Filipinos had with white America. A California state report on Filipinos noted, for example, how they were fast becoming the preferred labor force in domestic and service related work: "Filipinos are taking the places of white workers in many of the occupations in which they find employment upon arrival into California. This is especially true in hotel, restaurant, and domestic occupations. Many such jobs as bell boys, bus boys, elevator boys, house boys, waiters, dishwashers, janitors, porters, gardeners, cooks, kitchen helpers, pot washers, house workers [sic], and other hotel, restaurant, and domestic occupations . . . , which were formerly held by white men and women, are now held by Filipinos."[11]

In San Diego, some of these establishments included Mercy Hospital, El Cortez Hotel, Hotel Del Coronado, the Golden Lion Tavern, and the Casa de Mañana in La Jolla. From 1935 to 1938, Paul De la Cruz worked as a busboy at the Golden Lion Tavern, earning ten dollars a week. Pablo Poscablo worked as a kitchen helper at Mercy Hospital from 1955 to 1960. Juanita Santos, because of her degree in pharmacy from the Philippines, was able to secure a position in the pharmacy at Mercy Hospital, a position that was very rare for any Filipino (or Filipina) at the time. Typically, most Filipinos were relegated to working in the kitchen. The year was 1959.[12] Filipinos even served as houseboys and chauffeurs for rich white families in San Diego. Such was the case of Pedro Lacqui, who worked as a chauffer for Edward Chrysler (of Chrysler autos) and his family in La Jolla.[13]

In addition to the pay, the attitudes Filipinos and Mexicans had to endure from their employers and customers added to their frustration. Buaken observed at his job as an apartment janitor, "I had to crawl on my knees to please them [tenants]. I had to be submissive and servile and eternally patient; had to be known for my wholehearted willingness to serve others—or else!"[14] Although most Filipinos and Mexicans had to endure this inhumane treatment because of their racialized work, a handful were able to move up the ranks in their places of employment in San Diego. Carlos Cruz, for example, was a former navy steward who arrived in San Diego from Guam in 1929 and got a job working at El Cortez Hotel. He was able to work up to executive chef at the hotel by 1945, which was a rare promotion for Filipinos at this time. Max Meza, who came from Guadalajara, Mexico, in 1953, worked his way from dishwasher to busboy, then to waiter in the main dining room at El Cortez.[15]

Filipinos and Mexicans also worked at local high schools doing similar types of service-related work. This included positions as kitchen help or grounds keepers in wealthier areas such as La Jolla. High school annuals in La Jolla provided some insight into the occupations filled primarily by Filipinos and Mexicans. This was the case for both Pablo Poscablo and Amando Amansec, who were part of a Filipino kitchen crew at Bishop High School in La Jolla in the mid 1960s. By the late 1960s, the kitchen staff also included Mexican workers, such as Consuelo Fernandez, who immigrated to San Diego from Michoacán, Mexico, by way of Tijuana.[16] These workers lived in an older, rundown section of La Jolla that was known as the "servants' quarters," which provided workers close proximity to their places of employment. This neighborhood included Cuvier and Draper Streets, where Poscablo and Fernandez lived alongside other Filipino, Mexican, and African American families.[17]

In addition to their presence in La Jolla, Filipinos and Mexicans were also employed at the Hotel Del Coronado, which was situated in another wealthy part of San Diego on Coronado Island.[18] In the areas surrounding the Hotel Del Coronado and other establishments, single Filipinos were provided housing in dormitories by their employers; some shared their limited space with other ethnic groups such as Mexicans, Chinese, and Japanese. As one Filipino resident recalled, they all lived at the "foot of Orange towards North Island, East Avenue, and down by the base side." They also intermingled with the nearby African American population. This area of Coronado also had a "servants' quarters" that was in close proximity to the hotel and other places of employment. They labored as cooks, waiters, busboys, bellhops, bartenders, and janitors at the Hotel Del Coronado.[19]

Although previous reports noted that Filipinos were employed in domestic and service jobs once held by white men and women, Filipino writer and contemporary observer Manuel Buaken, who lived and worked in California during the 1930s, noted that whites, even if given the chance to do service work and other similar jobs, refused to do them because it was beneath them. Buaken said, "None of these people who were desperate for work would accept a dishwasher, busy boy, or porter job at those wages."[20] Service jobs and other unskilled labor had been racialized as "Mexican" or "Filipino" work. For Filipinos and Mexicans, employment opportunities were limited. They took what they could get as a matter of survival. It was one of the factors that stifled any labor organizing in the service sector at the time. Two other types of employment, however, helped facilitate the interactions between Mexicans and Filipinos through labor organizing. These were agriculture and fish canning. As "interzones" of labor, these two industries, and the labor organizing that occurred, initiated the interactions and long-term relationships between both groups.

AGRICULTURE AND LABOR ORGANIZING

Today, agriculture is a billion-dollar industry in San Diego. It ranks fourth among industries for the city's income.[21] Avocados rank as the city's key "signature crop," with eggs, tomatoes, and strawberries as other major crops. Historically, agriculture has been a major industry in San Diego since the late nineteenth century. Citrus crops, primarily lemons and oranges, were planted commercially in San Diego in 1869 and soon created an economic boom lasting until 1939. By the end of World War II and well into the postwar period, however, the agricultural industry declined as urbanization and population growth slowly ate away the citrus fields.[22] Along with the military and fish canning, agriculture was one of the city's major industries. The introduction of various fruits and vegetables to California's agribusiness by the Chinese, Japanese, and Koreans created an economic boom for the industry.[23] Of all the industries present in San Diego, agriculture, in particular, was dependent upon cheap labor. As California's agricultural industry experienced massive growth and productivity during the early twentieth century, growers relied more and more on a labor pool that could be exploited in order to maximize profits so that agriculture could continue to gain power as a major industry in the state. The work pool was comprised of racial and ethnic minorities who were predominately immigrants.

By the early twentieth century, agriculture was recognizably the state's largest industry. As noted by a former director of the Los Angeles County Farm Bureau, George P. Clements, "Agriculture is the foundation upon which all other industry is built. . . . Agriculture represents 60% of all commerce, 68% of all national commerce, and creates 50% of all new national wealth."[24] It was so lucrative that during the Great Depression of the 1930s, when other industries were struggling, agriculture remained profitable.[25]

By the late 1920s and well into the 1930s, the agricultural industry was fueled by local Mexican and Filipino labor. They usually had established small communities in these towns, while others were part of the migratory labor force that was passing through.[26] In Lemon Grove, for example, a substantial number of Mexican families working in the lemon orchards settled in the area from the Baja California region.[27] Workers also came from nearby communities. Logan Heights was one urban area that also had local residents working in agriculture. Longtime Logan Heights resident Bertha Ramirez remembers her mother working in Spring Valley picking vegetables such as green beans and tomatoes during the layoff period at the canneries. Freddie Ayap's father also worked in the tomato fields of Encanto when he retired from the navy.[28]

The need for workers for these labor-intensive crops helped facilitate the growth of local communities, especially where labor was needed year round. Chula Vista's and Lemon Grove's citrus industries employed multi-generations of Mexican and Filipino fruit pickers through the entire cultivation and harvest cycle. Joe Montijo, who grew up in National City during the early

1900s, remembered large numbers of Mexicans working in the lemon orchards in Chula Vista. He recalled, "In Chula Vista, at that time, lemons were plentiful. Chula Vista, at that time, had the biggest packing companies of the world. That was before Riverside ever started on their lemons." Longtime Chula Vista resident Robert Holmes also noted that Filipinos were in the area working as lemon pickers and in the packing sheds around 1912.[29] Given its importance in citrus and vegetable production, San Diego has long been an area that contributed to the economic growth of the state of California, yet San Diego is rarely mentioned for its economic contributions.

San Diego has also been overlooked as a site along the West Coast's migratory labor route for Filipino farmworkers. Early reports such as the state of California's *Facts about Filipino Immigration into California* and Bruno Lasker's *Filipino Immigration to the Continental United States and to Hawaii,* for example, omit San Diego County among its agricultural locales where Filipinos migrated to find work. Recent studies also overlook San Diego's role in the migratory labor circuit despite the fact that early observers of Filipino migrant labor in the 1930s suggested otherwise. Other than Paul Taylor's early observations in the 1930s and Richard Griswold del Castillo's recent *Chicano San Diego,* there is also a dearth of information regarding San Diego as a site for Mexican workers in the same migratory circuit.[30]

San Diego has long been a part of the corridor of labor migration on the West Coast that occurred between California and the fish canneries of Alaska. Filipino fish cannery workers, or Alaskeros, worked alongside other Asians, American Indians, and Mexicans in the seasonal work of fish canning.[31] As they made their way down through the Pacific Coast to the state of California, both Filipinos and Mexicans followed the seasonal crops as well. The circuit took them through Northern California, the San Joaquin Valley, Los Angeles, and finally to San Diego and the Imperial Valley. At the southern end of the state they labored in citrus groves and the lettuce, celery, melon, pea, and tomato fields. The fact that these migratory laborers followed the crops down to San Diego and brought in fluctuating, mobile communities of both Mexicans and Filipinos demonstrates that San Diego was linked to the migration circuit. Filipino writer and contemporary observer Carlos Bulosan mentioned San Diego on several occasions in his autobiography, *America Is in the Heart.* His written memoirs reveal his travels up and down the Pacific Coast with other Filipinos in search of labor in the fields and canneries.[32] Similarly, economist Paul S. Taylor noted that agricultural laborers in California undertook an extensive migratory labor circuit. It expanded from the Imperial Valley all the way to the Sacramento Valley and all the fields in between.[33] As California's agricultural industry experienced tremendous growth throughout the early twentieth century, its demand for cheap labor to sustain and fuel its expansion was insatiable. The combination of a large labor pool of workers and continued federal investment in aqueducts and other infrastructure helped Californian agriculture become the single largest industry in the state. Mexican and Filipino farmworkers came to fill this void from the mobile communities traveling the migratory circuits and the local communities, and some Filipinos came across the Pacific Ocean from Hawai'i.

Mexican and Filipino migrants gravitated toward California because of employment opportunities that were left open after Asian immigration was put to a virtual halt.[34] They would fill this void yet do so in competition with each other. As Mae Ngai writes, "If Filipinos competed with other ethnic groups for farm work, it was not with whites, but Mexicans, and to a lesser extent, with Japanese, South Asians, and Koreans."[35] This enabled the state's agricultural interests to utilize a large labor force, which they soon became dependent upon. Noting the economic importance of Mexican labor George P. Clements stated, "We cannot get along without the Mexican laborer."[36] Agriculture was the largest sector for employment for both Mexicans and Filipinos by 1930. An estimated 33 percent of all Mexicans and 59 percent of all Filipinos were engaged in agricultural work.[37] On the continental United States, Filipinos and Mexicans were relegated to "stoop labor" positions in agriculture, which were racialized as "Mexican jobs" or "Filipino jobs." White laborers refused these positions because they thought they were beneath them. One agricultural economist noted, "Some jobs are for Anglos, others are for Mexicans. . . . It is stoop labor, and we have never been able to get our domestic workers to stay with it."[38] Mexicans and Filipinos performed most agricultural jobs, and California growers exploited these farmworkers, pitting them against each other to drive wages down for all ethnicities, which led to interethnic tensions between both groups. Indeed, it was Filipinos and Mexicans who bore the brunt of this labor exploitation through their differential racialization. Writer, lawyer, and contemporary observer Carey McWilliams noted, "With the exception of the Mexican, the Filipino has been the most viciously exploited of any of the various races recruited by the California agriculturalists to make their vast army of cheap labor."[39] It was their shared oppression and the observations they made in unison that facilitated the bonds between both communities, thus enabling Mexicans and Filipinos to organize together.

Although Mexicans and Filipinos were needed to build up California's economy, both groups were the targets of nativists and American labor. Samuel Gompers, head of the American Federation of Labor (AFL), for example, was known to be both anti-Asian and anti-Mexican. Gompers adopted what one historian called "both an anti-immigration stand and a racist argument" to justify the AFL's resolutions at national conventions to demand an end to both Asian and Mexican immigration to the United States.[40] Others remarked, "With the Mexican comes a social problem. . . . It is a serious one. It comes into our schools, it comes into our cities, and it comes into our whole civilization in California. . . . We take him because there is nothing else available."[41] Similarly, Filipinos were also seen in an unfavorable light. According to Clements, the Filipino was "the most worthless, unscrupulous, shiftless, diseased, semi-barbarian that has ever come to our shores."[42] As disposable workers, they were only wanted for their labor and then were to be discarded when their work was completed. As one individual noted, "We will let him in so we can use him and when he can serve us no longer we will ship him back."[43] Filipinos were also seen by growers as a commodity; growers characterized them as less than human: "It must be realized that the Filipino is just the same as the manure that we put on the land—just the same."[44]

Initially, growers who hired either Mexican or Filipino workers, depending on the employer's preference, did so with the assumption that they were hiring cheap labor that was, first, unintelligent and only good for hard labor and, second, passive, powerless, and easily exploited. Growers thought that they could exploit their nonwhite labor force indefinitely, without any repercussion. One grower remarked, "Mexican labor is satisfactory when placed in occupations fitted for. They apparently fit well on jobs not requiring any great degree of mentality, and they do not object to the dirt."[45] The inhumane treatment Mexicans and Filipinos experienced by growers was mounting, which led to their discontent in the fields.

Militancy arose as a response to grower exploitation and racial oppression. Labor militancy caught growers off guard because of their initial views that Mexicans and Filipinos would not organize. Growers felt both groups were content to labor in backbreaking work for pitiful wages. Moreover, the leadership potential and ability of Mexicans to organize was doubted. In 1929, writer Helen Walker wrote, "It is very much easier for him to follow, to obey, to imitate, than it is for him to lead, to command, or to originate. His Latin temperament alone explains this."[46] In 1930, Republican governor C. C. Young also shared his racialized view of Mexicans by stating, "He does tasks that white workers will or cannot do. He works under ... conditions that are often too trying for white workers. He will work in gangs. He will work under direction, taking orders and suggestions."[47]

These statements completely ignore the fact that Mexicans were excluded from leading or commanding others in the workplace unless it was within their own ethnic organizations and unions. For the most part, Mexicans and Filipinos were relegated to taking orders and were prevented from moving up in their respective occupations due to racial discrimination. Others also viewed Mexicans as incapable of organizing into unions: "He is easily satisfied; he does not organize troublesome labor unions. He is cheap labor."[48] According to sociologist and contemporary observer Emory S. Bogardus, "Like other unskilled workers, the unskilled Mexican does not form labor unions. He is not educated to the level of unionization. Union men say that the Mexicans won't organize, and that he works so cheap that no white laborer can compete with him."[49] This statement neglects the fact that Mexicans were organizing with the Japanese as early as 1903 in Oxnard, California. In a show of working-class solidarity, Mexican members refused to be chartered by the AFL because the AFL did not want to include the Japanese in its ranks.[50] These early twentieth-century sociologists also ignored the fact that Mexicans had already been organizing during the 1920s in the Imperial Valley under the Confederación de Uniones Obreras Mexicanas (CUOM).[51]

Throughout the early twentieth century, the AFL continued to bar Mexicans and Filipinos from their union ranks. One scholar noted, "The period between 1900 and 1936 was the apex of craft unionism, which all too often excluded Mexican skilled as well as unskilled workers."[52] Despite being excluded, Mexicans and Filipinos organized themselves along ethnic lines at first, seeking recognition of their unions. Unfortunately, they were forced to accept charter status by the AFL, rather than direct affiliation, which was intended to segregate them both racially and nationally from white "American" workers.[53]

The AFL has a long history of being both anti-Filipino and anti-Mexican when it comes to immigration issues and organizing workers. The AFL, which was comprised primarily of trade and craft unions, has been characterized as a major group that had racist policies toward nonwhites in the United States.[54] Mexican labor was seen in a favorable light prior to 1924, when Gompers's and the AFL's focus was on excluding Asians from labor unions and immigration to the United States. Between 1924 and 1930, however, with increased Mexican immigration and competition between Mexican and "American" (white) laborers, there emerged more anti-Mexican sentiment.[55] Given that the AFL was predominately concerned with skilled white labor, it did not bother to organize and grant membership to semi-skilled and unskilled nonwhite workers. These conditions were worse in San Diego, where the AFL only granted Mexican workers permits but did not allow them membership in its union. The absence of union memberships jeopardized their job security, seniority rights, and the right to collectively bargain with employers.[56] The AFL had a reactionary policy of discriminating against Filipino, Mexican, African American, and other nonwhite workers. When the AFL did organize white workers in agriculture, they usually did so with "casual white labor."[57]

Although the AFL in San Diego tried to organize agricultural workers between 1919 and 1936, as historian Nancy Miller noted, "they were short-lived and had limited success due to the weaknesses and the racism that permeated the [San Diego] Labor Council, but the interest revealed by these actions distinguished the local council's position from that of the national AFL which in effect did nothing."[58] The few Mexicans who did have permits with the AFL in San Diego were now being excluded for taking jobs away from white workers. In response, Mexican workers formed their own union called the Mexican Laborers Local 349.[59] Mexican workers who had a loose affiliation with the AFL were also afraid that the AFL would not protect them since many workers were being deported or threatened for organizing in San Diego and nearby Imperial Valley fields.[60] The labor militancy and organizational skills of the Filipino farm workers also caught the attention of the AFL, yet instead of taking them into their fold, AFL leadership labeled them as the "Filipino labor menace." The AFL accused them of being unfair competition to white labor and denied them union membership. Thus, Filipinos also turned to organizing themselves in their own ethnic unions.[61] These incidents demonstrate why Mexicans and Filipinos formed ethnic unions. Since they were both refused membership in the AFL and attacked for their militancy in response to being exploited, they had no choice. Mexicans and Filipinos had to rely on themselves to protect their interests, so they formed their own ethnic unions, which gave them an organizing mechanism to combat grower exploitation.

Mexican and Filipino militancy erupted throughout the agricultural fields of California. Growers, however, tried to undermine the efforts of Mexican and Filipino ethnic unions. As Mexican militancy in the fields increased, for example, growers sought to crush their efforts by hiring Filipinos as scabs to replace them. As with Mexicans, growers initially considered Filipinos as highly desirable laborers and ideal workers. Growers believed that Filipinos were "more docile, low paid, and hard working, unlike the Americanized Mexicans." One grower remarked, "The Filipinos are considered very desirable workers because they are willing to work under all sorts of weather conditions, even when it is raining and the fields are all wet."[62] Similar to Mexican workers, Filipinos proved the growers wrong when they organized themselves to combat grower exploitation. This practice was an extension of their social organizations and mutual aid societies that addressed the labor rights of workers.[63] The fact that labor disputes were erupting throughout the state indicates the nature of the exploitative environment in which Filipinos and Mexicans worked.[64] In response, Filipinos and Mexicans struck under separate ethnic unions. These included, for example, the Filipino Labor Union (FLU), the Filipino Labor Association, the Filipino Labor Supply Association, the Mexican Labor Union or Confederación de Uniones Obreras Mexicanas (CUOM), the Confederación de Campesinos y Obreros Mexicanos (CUCOM), the Mexican Agricultural Workers Union, and the American Mexican Union.[65]

Independent labor organizations stemmed from the growers attempts to divide and control the labor resources and wages by keeping their workers practically isolated from each other. If they could keep the ethnic groups separated, growers believed that they could (1) have an excess of labor readily available, (2) have the groups compete over wages, thus driving down the price of labor for their own profit, and (3) prevent them from organizing into larger unions. The growers' tactics were initially successful in the Imperial Valley. Mexicans and Filipinos organized separately and, at times, were in conflict with each other, as witnessed by one farm worker who noted that they did not get along with each other.[66]

The divisive tactics in California reflected those used by the sugar planters in Hawai'i between Filipinos and the Japanese.[67] By having two competing ethnic groups, California growers assumed that they would not communicate with each other because of language differences. One labor report on Filipinos in

California observed: "At times growers prefer to have the contractor employ a mixture of laborers of various races, speaking diverse languages and not accustomed to mingling with each other. This practice is intended to avoid labor troubles, which might result from having a homogenous group of laborers of the same race or nationality. Laborers speaking different languages and accustomed to diverse standards of living and habits are not as likely to arrive at a mutual understanding which would lead to strikes or other labor troubles during harvesting seasons, when work interruptions would result in serious financial losses to the growers."[68]

In the same manner that Filipinos tried to join forces with Japanese laborers against sugar planters in Hawai'i, Filipinos also saw the similar plight they faced with their Mexican counterparts in California; thus they used their experience in Hawai'i and sought to organize across ethnic lines to combat their exploitation. The growers never anticipated that cultural and language similarities that existed because of Spanish colonialism would inadvertently facilitate labor organizing between Filipino and Mexican workers. Many Filipinos, for example, spoke Spanish. Filipinos were also fast becoming the vanguard of labor activism in California. They were key to labor organizing and oftentimes were recognized as being more militant than their Mexican counterparts, which can be attributed to their previous experiences in Hawai'i.[69] Filipinos militancy, however, made them more of a threat to growers. In a report entitled *Labor Unionism in American Agriculture,* Stuart Jamieson of the U.S. Department of Labor documents the activities of Filipino militants in the agricultural fields of California. According to Jamieson, their exploitation as well as their commitment to economic justice fueled Filipino militancy, which resulted in the formation of agricultural labor unions and strikes. McWilliams also noted, "The Filipino, militantly race conscious, began to protest against his exploitation in California at an early date, and has grown increasingly rebellious."[70] In addition, other scholars have also highlighted the role of Filipino farmworkers who built a "reputation for militancy and radicalism" in California: "Although never plentiful in number, Filipino farmworkers had a profound impact on labor relations in California farms. Their militancy and organizing expertise provided inspiration and leadership for farm-worker unionizing efforts in California throughout the 1920s and early 1930s."[71]

Filipinos fought against the low wages they earned doing stoop labor. Their dissatisfaction with their wage rates is best illustrated by their militant wildcat strikes that caused much disruption in the fields. These strikes did not always achieve union recognition, but they did provide them with higher wages. Their militancy proved that they were not to be underestimated. Filipinos, like their Mexican counterparts, were definitely not docile. In fact, they were fast becoming a threat to grower control over the workers. As historian Howard DeWitt remarked, "this is an early indication that Filipino unionization was a serious part of California agriculture."[72]

This collective consciousness and solidarity helped them overcome prejudices that might have divided them.[73] Growers and shippers tried to use their own propaganda to minimize interethnic unionization of Filipino and Mexican laborers, stating: "Mexicans and Filipinos will never for any length of time stay organized in a closely knit union, as practically all the field labor is itinerant and moving from one location to another in the state. They lose contact to a large extent with their organizations and leaders and thus lose interest in the movement."[74] Their predictions were far from accurate. Filipino and Mexican workers and labor organizers continued to organize across the state, hence the continuous labor strife in California's agricultural fields. The growers' strategy eventually failed as Filipinos and Mexicans continued to disrupt the growers' plans. This culminated with the organization of interethnic unions, often initiated by Filipinos and with leadership provided by both groups.

As previously mentioned, Filipinos were more aggressive in labor organizing because of previous experiences in Hawai'i. In his book *Reworking Race: The Making of Hawaii's Interracial Labor Movement*, Moon-Kie Jung examines how Filipino, Japanese, and other racial groups in Hawai'i that were involved in the International Longshoremen's and Warehousemen's Union (ILWU) were able to draw upon a working-class interracialism to transform their racial and class interests and re-imagine a new interracial political community as it pertained to their labor struggles on the islands. He notes, "Interracialism should be conceptualized as an affirmative transformation of race that, discursively and practically, deals with and rearticulates extant racial divisions."[75] This theoretical concept can be applied to how Filipinos and Mexicans aligned themselves to combat worker exploitation in the agricultural fields of California. Although their early efforts at organizing as a coalition of ethnic unions were "risky coalitions" at first, they were necessary, as was the fragile coalition of Japanese and Filipinos in Hawai'i, to gain some sort of economic justice.[76] Yet in the context of California, whose enormous agricultural industry was exploiting and oppressing its workforce on much grander scales, Filipinos utilized their experiences in Hawai'i and applied them with their Mexican counterparts, thus rearticulating their own racial and class divisions and uniting under a banner of interracialism for the good of all workers. It was a strategy, I contend, that Filipinos and Mexicans utilized to forge their interethnic alliances in San Diego and the Imperial Valley. Indeed, the link between Hawai'i and California with regards to labor activism has been long overlooked in previous studies documenting early organizing between Filipinos and Mexicans and begs for further research and scholarly inquiry.[77]

Given that Filipinos were able to bring this lesson with them to California, they saw opportunities with Mexican workers and strategically started transforming their own labor movements utilizing this concept of interracialism in the 1930s. It was Filipinos, I argue, who initiated these interethnic coalitions with Mexicans and other groups by moving beyond what David Gutiérrez calls "ethnonational and class solidarity" among Mexican workers. Thus began a legacy of interracialism in labor organizing that predated the iconic merging of Filipino and Mexican farmworkers under the United Farm Workers Movement, which catapulted Cesar Chavez to worldwide notoriety.[78]

During the 1930s, Filipino labor organizers appealed to their fellow rank-and-file workers to join with Mexicans and other groups under the communist-influenced Cannery and Agricultural Workers Industrial Union (CAWIU) and have a "perfect militant struggle for living wages, against discrimination of races, [and] for unemployed relief." Interethnic organizing was a response to growers who tried to pit Filipino workers against Mexican workers under the pretense of patriotism. Growers claimed that it was the Filipinos' patriotic duty to drive the Mexicans out before the Mexicans drove them out. Growers told them that the "Mexicans were no good" and, because the United States was not their country, Filipinos should drive them out. In response the Filipino workers shouted down the growers' intentions. Their actions reflected unity with their Mexican counterparts, which showed that Filipinos were implementing interracialism in California.[79] The Filipino community press also advocated for an interethnic organizing effort between all workers. As one Filipino newspaper reported: "It follows that those who have no power can not have justice; and in order to have an equal justice, one must have equal power. On the same principle, the Filipino workers as well as the other workers must understand that the justice of their cause lies in UNITED EFFORT, equally powerful as their highly organized enemies, who, from time immortal, denied them of their daily bread."[80]

Up until that time, most labor organizing occurred under separate ethnically based unions.[81] The CAWIU, however, was effective in utilizing Filipino know-how with interethnic organizing and bringing all workers under a collective banner that advocated "the Communists' antiracist, egalitarian idealism."[82] Consequently, the CAWIU had a large number of Mexican and Filipino workers as active elements who even provided some of the leadership in the union. Active membership in the CAWIU was decisive for Filipinos. The union was also one of the few voices that came to their defense during the anti-Filipino riots that occurred in Watsonville and other areas of California.[83]

As mentioned in chapter 3, *mutualistas* (mutual aid societies) and other social organizations provided Mexicans and Filipinos with the foundation to organize their workers. As Camille Guérin-Gonzales notes, mutualistas initially "provided a forum for workers' complaints against employers and often negotiated conflicts between workers and employers." It is no surprise that labor unions and strike leaders emerged from mutualistas. Indeed, David Gutiérrez writes, "Many of the earliest strikes were coordinated by local mutualistas."[84] This provided workers with self-protection and the camaraderie required to collectively fight for improved working conditions for all farmworkers.[85] Filipino farmworkers were also known for their militancy and radicalism in the fields, which appealed to the CAWIU when it organized farmworkers in the 1930s. With the

CAWIU behind them, Filipinos used their experiences to organize with Mexicans, perpetuating the interethnic unionism that they learned in Hawai'i. Together, Filipinos and Mexicans were a force to contend with in the fields.[86]

Interethnic unions spread like wildfire throughout the state during the 1930s. Approximately 140 strikes involving over 127,000 workers occurred in California alone during this time.[87] These events were the result of individual ethnic unions, interethnic union alliances, and multiethnic unions. In the San Diego–Imperial County district, Mexican laborers filed numerous complaints through the State Labor Commission during 1926. Over 378 cases claimed that the growers refused to pay the workers their wages, which totaled $16,444.97. Of the final amount, $8,198.35 in wages were still pending. Since San Diego also handled cases filed in the Imperial Valley, both counties were intricately tied to the labor strife.[88] In 1933 the *Statistical Summary of Agricultural Strikes in California* also documented that the majority of strikes occurred due to workers wanting wage increases, with union recognition coming second. The majority of these strikes (24) were led by the CAWIU; 21 strikes alone involved 32,800 workers. The 4 strikes that involved a total of 4,750 workers were defeated. San Diego, however, was home to one of the successful strikes. The wages of 400 tomato workers were raised. The Imperial Valley had 3 strikes involving 3,700 workers, 2 of the strikes saw gains, 1 was defeated.[89]

Stuart Jamieson's labor report provides an interesting account of Filipino and Mexican interethnic unionism in California. Interethnic strikes under the leadership of the experienced Filipinos were successful in California during the 1930s. San Diego and nearby Imperial County had more than their fair share of labor disputes. These strikes involved Mexican, Filipino, and, on some occasions, other workers who struck with their own ethnic unions and in cooperation with one another. For example, in 1930, 8,000 Mexican, Filipino, and Chinese workers in the Imperial Valley struck for higher wages and improved working conditions under the Trade Union Unity League (TUUL), which was also affiliated with the Communist Party.[90]

Mexicans and Filipinos in San Diego continued to organize and strike throughout the 1930s. In 1932, for example, Mexican and Filipino strawberry workers organized together with the help of Communists in San Diego.[91] In January of 1933, Chula Vista celery workers in San Diego County requested a wage increase and union recognition. They were labeled as "agitators" and demonized for their organizing activities.[92] In the Imperial Valley, over 1,000 pea pickers struck in November of 1933. A representative of the Regional Labor Board was sent to settle the strike. Mexican and Filipino workers in the northern region of San Diego County also filed a complaint against the Japanese Tomato Growers with the National Labor Relations Board. The workers demanded a raise from fifteen cents an hour to twenty-five cents. Over 125 workers were involved. The case was settled in December of 1933. In June 1934, a series of strikes and some rioting took place in San Diego County. The labor dispute

pitted Mexican and Filipino workers against Japanese and Anglo vegetable growers. The National Labor Relations Board also intervened in the mediations.[93]

Mexican celery workers also struck in Chula Vista. They demanded a wage
increase to thirty cents an hour from the Celery Growers' Association. Although
reports about ranchers brandishing loaded shotguns and workers fleeing were
reported, growers eventually conceded to the workers' demands.[94] Another case
was filed against the Japanese Celery and Vegetable Growers in June of 1934. The
incident involved 1,500 Mexican and Filipino workers in San Diego County. The
case was settled when growers agreed to pay twenty-five cents per hour in July of
1934. In San Ysidro, Pedro Lozano, president of the local branch of the Mexican
Labor Union, led Mexican workers in a strike against Japanese growers. The
union demanded an increase in wages from ten to twenty-five cents an hour to
thirty to thirty-five cents an hour.[95] Similarly, 4,000 pea pickers went out on
strike against pea growers in the Imperial Valley. In June of 1934, Mexican orange
pickers in Lemon Grove struck against the Lemon Grove Fruit Growers'
Association, demanding a raise from four cents a box to six and a half cents.
Alarmed, the growers called in the sheriff for help. In the end, an agreed wage
scale of twenty-five cents per hour was reached between the workers and growers. In Mission Valley, Mexican celery workers walked out of the fields, striking
against the San Diego County Celery Growers' Association. These other strikes
occurred almost simultaneously with the one in Lemon Grove.[96]

The following month, another strike occurred in Chula Vista. The Japanese
melon growers immediately settled the labor dispute. The settlement secured
two dollars per day and a minimum three-week employment or twenty-five
cents per hour wage for indefinite periods of work for the Mexican workers.
The Regional Labor Board in San Diego and the Chula Vista Chamber of
Commerce handled the case. The strike's success can be credited to the successful efforts of the workers to keep scabs (otherwise known as strike breakers)
from entering the fields while melon crops began to rot.[97] In August of 1934, over
2,500 workers were involved in labor disputes against several growers in the
San Diego region. Several months later the Mexican Agricultural Union led a
strike of over 2,000 workers against the Sundry Vegetable Growers in San Diego
County. E. H. Fitzgerald, labor commissioner, was called in to settle the dispute
so that crops would not be lost.[98]

Given the rising militancy of Filipinos and Mexicans in the 1930s, growers,
with the help of vigilantes and the police, waged their own campaign of violence
and terror against the strikers. During a labor dispute in December 1930, for
example, police arrested strikers, while a group of five white men were responsible for the bombing of a Filipino labor camp. The assault on the camp claimed
the life of Aristo Lampky, a twenty-one-year-old Filipino, and injured several
others.[99] These acts of terrorism only strengthened the resolve of the strikers,
who continued to resist together. This led to more violence, especially in the
Imperial Valley. According to one state report, Imperial County has long been

the center of large and violent strikes in California.[100] Between 1933 and 1934, an estimated 8,000 to 10,000 Mexicans and 5,000 Filipinos were in the valley, available for hire as stoop labor. Growers and labor contractors exploited workers, who labored for twenty-five to thirty cents an hour in 130 degree heat. Thousands of Mexicans and Filipinos, as well as a small number of East Indians, African Americans, Japanese, and whites, joined in the strikes under the CAWIU in the lettuce, cantaloupe, and pea fields. This was known as the "Great Imperial Valley Strike." Growers, with the help of the police, private armies, vigilante mobs, and the persuasion of the press, committed horrible acts of violence and intimidation against the agricultural workers and their allies, including labor organizers, American Civil Liberties Union lawyers, journalists, and the International Labor Defense.[101] The situation was one of "near crisis" and almost reached uncontrollable dimensions. Chester Williams of the American Civil Liberties Union compared the situation in the Imperial Valley to war, making an analogy to how the growers and their allies reacted to worker discontent and organization.[102] Indeed, deputized vigilantes, who, as one scholar noted, "were drawn from the American Legion, the Ku Klux Klan, and the Silver Shirts, committed some of these horrible acts."[103]

According to one report, unlawful raids and arrests were made; workers were terrorized with fire, bombings, and violence. Property was also destroyed. Many of the strikers were kidnapped or chased out of town under threat of violence or deportation. Others were killed, and a number suffered injuries for having demanded an increase in wages to thirty-five cents an hour. Carlos Bulosan recalled the violence that occurred, stating, "In the Imperial Valley, news came that a Filipino labor organizer had been found dead in a ditch."[104] Prisoners were also locked in stockades and put in chain gangs, and blockades were established to keep food and moral aid away from these individuals. Guns were also used against unarmed strikers and citizens.

Incidents of violence were duly reported. For example, in Brawley, Niland, and El Centro (all in the Imperial Valley), during January of 1934, the police, deputies, American Legionnaires, and vigilantes raided worker meetings at Aztec Hall. They threw tear gas into the hall and proceeded to club the workers as they came out. Despite the workers' resistance, they were eventually dispersed and arrested. Azteca Hall was destroyed when the Fire Department flooded the building; 350 people were injured and 150 of the victims were arrested. Other workers were beaten unconscious, while an ACLU lawyer was kidnapped, beaten, and robbed. There were also other countless beatings by the police and vigilantes. Growers even hired gunmen as strikebreakers, who were deputized by the sheriff. These included 700 men who were "taking the law into their own hands." In the aftermath of the violence, an infant died from complications due to the tear gas that the police discharged into a crowd of women and children.[105]

To alleviate the violence, the federal government sent federal conciliator General Pelham D. Glassford to the Imperial Valley to hear the testimony of both parties and to report back to the appropriate officials. From the start, it was obvious that Glassford's agenda was to disrupt communism in the Imperial Valley and put an end to the "red" organizing. He stated, "My investigation has shown that this union [CAWIU] is indisputably, though indirectly, connected with a wide-spread Communist program." Glassford's attempt to establish that the workers had communist ties and his criticism of the strikers' tactics to boy-cott the harvest and threaten the growers' profits were reasons to build a case to curtail workers' constitutional rights.[106]

Glassford's openly pro-grower stance was not without criticism. As vigilante violence and intimidation continued against the workers and ACLU representa-tives, the Open Forum stated, "General Glassford is nowhere to be found. . . . [H]e has completely capitulated to the growers."[107] To make matters worse, local newspapers labeled the workers as "reds" and "communists" to minimize their struggle for union recognition and higher wages. These labels were used by growers, vigilante mobs, and the state apparatus to justify the use of violence against the workers.[108]

The growers also had another ally. Mexican consul Joaquin Terrazas worked directly with growers to break the strike and create division among the workers. At the request of federal mediator Campbell MacCulloch, Terrazas was respon-sible for organizing Mexican workers under a separate ethnic union, the Asociación Mexicana del Valle Imperial (Mexican Association of the Imperial Valley) to negotiate their own demands. The growers supported Terrazas in what was essentially a company union.[109] Terrazas was also reported to have threatened workers with more arrests and deportation. His alliance with the growers was obvious.[110]

Terrazas sought to create tensions and divide workers by stating, "Filipinos, Americans, and Negroes will probably not listen to anything I have to say."[111] His impartial attitude toward other workers only fueled tensions between them. Similarly, MacCullouch also tried to embellish reports to the National Labor Relations Board about Filipino and Mexican tension, claiming that the constant clashes between Mexicans and Filipinos were because they "cordially hate each other." This statement was meant to instigate tensions between Mexicans and Filipinos. The allegation was obviously false since both groups were at the helm of union organizing. Indeed, as the Open Forum noted, "The Filipino group is actively organizing. The leaders assured us that this time effort will be made to join with all other groups of workers, regardless of color or race."[112]

It was clear that the multiethnic union of workers, who were predominately Mexican and Filipino, desired to be organized under the CAWIU and refused to be a part of Terrazas's company union. It was under the CAWIU that Mexican and Filipino workers experienced true democratic unionism and a sense of belonging that they could never find in a company union.[113] Workers in the Imperial Valley and organized labor in San Diego requested that the U.S. Department of Labor and the National Labor Relations Board step in to allow them to choose their own union since they were being pressured to join the company one. As the *San Diego Labor Leader* reported, this was questionable since the National Industrial Recovery Act outlawed company unions.[114]

Knowing full well that the CAWIU would win a union election, Imperial Valley growers and shippers as well as federal, state, and local authorities worked to prevent it. Even the bias of National Labor Relations Board representatives MacCullouch and Glassford were, as Gilbert González noted, "so blatant that they behaved like paid agents of the growers and shippers."[115] As a result, agribusiness and its affiliates moved decisively to recognize the Asociación Mexicana as the official union. Many Mexican workers joined the Asociación Mexicana as a result of fear, intimidation, and threats of being blacklisted for refusing to comply with the growers and Terrazas's wishes.[116] Terrazas was thus successful in coercing Mexican workers to join his union at the cost of their alliance with Filipinos and other workers for economic justice. In the end, Terrazas's betrayal of the workers, in addition to the growers meeting "the militancy with unbound terrorism," led to the ultimate defeat of the CAWIU in the Imperial Valley.[117] Although not much is documented regarding the relationship between Filipinos and Mexicans after this ordeal, one could speculate there was a sense of betrayal felt by Filipinos. This may have caused some tension between the two groups; however, interethnic organizing between Filipinos and Mexicans persisted. Their continued alliance in the fields demonstrates the type of interracialism that Moon-Kie Jung describes, though it sometimes did fail. Yet the minor examples provided illustrate why they saw a need to organize together; this need enabled them to press forward and mobilize despite some minor setbacks orchestrated by growers and the state.

In addition to Terrazas's betrayal of the strikers, the San Diego Chamber of Commerce also sanctioned the terrorism inflicted on Mexican and Filipino workers and their leaders because they were considered communists. The San Diego Labor Council, however, supported the strikers in the Imperial Valley and denounced the San Diego Chamber of Commerce's decision because the strikers were not "'reds' or Communists but 'poor Mexican laborers.'"[118] It was the workers' right to organize under the National Recovery Act. The San Diego Labor Council even passed a resolution in support of the strikers, yet, despite its support for the workers and cries of foul play against the growers and their allies, the council did little to organize agricultural workers under the AFL. Instead, the CAWIU was actively organizing workers who appealed to them because the communists promoted "anti-racist, egalitarian idealism."[119]

The violence occurring in the Imperial Valley spread to neighboring San Diego between the months of May and July of 1934. Following his speech at the Hammer Club, Chester Williams, executive head of the International Labor Defense, was warned to leave town. Other individuals involved in the labor organizing efforts were shot at and beaten by both vigilantes and the police. On the lawn of the East San Diego Library, for example, two organizers from the International Students'

League were arrested and clubbed in a raid by police at their meeting.[120] The right to organize for economic justice and free speech was not tolerated by Imperial Valley and San Diego growers. The San Diego Chamber of Commerce cooperated with the growers to fight the "rising menace" and the reluctant San Diego Labor Council remained unmoved by the horrific scene.[121]

Despite these acts of intimidation and violence, Filipinos and Mexicans continued to organize in San Diego during 1935 and 1936, illustrating their resolve even under these intense pressures. Rather, the violence and oppression they experienced collectively only strengthened their bonds in labor unionism. Dozens of other strikes occurred in San Diego during 1935.[122] In January of 1935, Mexican workers in the Chula Vista lettuce fields struck against the growers, claiming they had violated an earlier agreement. This strike lasted until July of 1935 and was resolved through arbitration. In May of 1935, a small strike of 85 orange pickers occurred in San Diego County. It was a joint effort by CUCOM and the Vegetable and Citrus Federal Labor Union (AFL) over wages.[123] In the same month, 250 members of the Mexican Union of Agricultural Workers went on strike against the El Cajon Citrus Growers Association over hours and wages. In January of 1936, independent Filipino, Mexican, and Japanese unions in southern California organized together as the Agricultural Workers Unions of America with key leadership coming from CUCOM, the Mexican union.[124]

Filipino and Mexican agricultural workers struck again in February of 1936 against the H. P. Garin Company in San Diego, demanding union recognition, thirty cents per hour in wages, and 60 percent union preference.[125] Growing strikes in California during 1936 reflected what one labor report noted as "a renewed militancy and strength among farm-labor unions organized both by the A.F. of L. and by unaffiliated Mexicans and Filipinos."[126] Although the CIO had turned their attention away from agricultural to cannery and packing shed workers, in San Diego over five hundred members of the San Diego County Mexican Agricultural Workers Union voted to have CIO affiliation. This demonstrated that the CIO still had some influence in the agricultural fields, especially in San Diego.[127]

All of these examples demonstrate an important point. Given that Mexicans and Filipinos shared an experience of racial oppression and poor treatment by their employers, this facilitated their interethnic organizing, oftentimes instigated by Filipinos. Together they faced mounting pressures and violence from growers and their allies, including vigilantes and the state. The meetings they attended, the organizing they participated in, and the terrorism they endured together cemented an alliance that spilled over into their everyday lives and included building relationships and a shared community that traveled the same migratory routes; this alliance grew within the rural communities in which they lived. These experiences continued to shape their relationships as they found common ground laboring and organizing together in San Diego and the Imperial Valley's agricultural fields.

Filipinos and Mexicans continued to organize together well into the late 1930s and early 1940s. In 1938, for example, various Filipino labor organizations across the West Coast voted to form the Filipino Agricultural Laborers Association (FALA). Yet, knowing the value of interracialism with their Mexican counterparts, the Filipino membership decided to change its name to the Federated Agricultural Laborers Association, which invited Mexicans and other ethnic groups into its fold. FALA then struck against the asparagus industry in 1939, winning a significant victory. By 1940, FALA had a membership that exceeded thirty thousand.[128]

Filipinos and Mexicans proved that they were a powerful force to reckon with in California's agricultural fields. As a result of their coalitions and interracialism, Filipinos and Mexicans won some of their greatest gains, higher wages, better working conditions, and union recognition.[129] Within this context, both groups created a workers' culture forged from labor activism. Indeed, when it came to basic bread-and-butter issues for workers against exploitive growers, as Jamieson's labor report noted, "militant unionism seemed to be the only effective means by which labor could win economic gains."[130] In the fish canneries of San Diego, labor organizing also occurred on a massive scale, but with a different gender dynamic and outcome.

Fish Canneries: Race, Gender, and Labor Cultures

Along with agriculture, San Diego's fish canneries were also a rising industry during the early twentieth century. Falling behind the U.S. Navy, the tuna fishing industry ranked second in San Diego's major industries.[131] From 1932 to 1950, San Diego led the nation in tuna canning. During the years 1945 to 1950, San Diego canneries were so productive that the city was known as the "tuna canning capital of the world."[132] Canneries such as Sun Harbor, for example, produced record numbers of canned tuna in 1947. Sun Harbor reported in its newsletter, the *Sun Harbor Catch and Can News*, that it was "packing more cases of tuna than it has in its entire history." Sun Harbor cannery contributed to San Diego's fish-canning industry by producing a record-breaking five million cases of tuna in 1947. By August of 1948, they were quoted as being "the most productive tuna packer in the world and one of the leading sardine canners."[133]

The organizing of San Diego's canning industry began in the early 1900s. In 1909, Alex J. Steele and Edward Hume opened San Diego's first cannery, the Neptune Seafood Company. The major product canned was sardines. World War I dictated that Neptune and other canneries in California focus on the production of sardines for the military.[134] Yet the unstable supply of sardines eventually vanished from California waters. It wasn't until 1911 that another cannery, the Pacific Tuna Canning Company, operated at the foot of F Street in San Diego. San Diego Packing Company was also another early cannery. It was located in the backyard of the Azevedo family in Point Loma. San Diego's early fishermen crews consisted of Chinese, Japanese, Slavic, Portuguese, Italian, and Mexican men and women. It was the Japanese, however, who revolutionized the tuna industry with the introduction of pole-fishing techniques. By 1919, San Diego's Japanese fishermen dominated the waters, catching 85 percent of the tuna in California.[135] Borrowing the successful methods of Japanese fishermen, Italians were able to harvest fish at greater rates, thus adding to the success of the tuna-fishing industry in San Diego.[136] The demand for tuna after World War I increased the profits of both fishermen and canneries alike. As a result, by 1925, San Diego had eight canneries, including Neptune, Pacific Tuna Canning Company, Van Camp, and Westgate, which employed around twelve thousand people. Other canneries followed, such as Cohn Hopkins and Sun Harbor.[137] Tuna fishing was a major industry in San Diego, and the local communities provided much of the labor. In addition to the fish canneries, there was also the Old Mission Packing Company, which canned pimentos, chili peppers, tomatoes, and olives.

San Diego's canneries were a major employer of local residents, especially Mexican American and immigrant women. In fact, these ethnic women comprised the majority of the cannery workforce. A report by the Heller Committee indicated that the majority of the employed Mexican women they interviewed in Logan Heights were cannery workers.[138] Filipinas living in these communities were also employed in the canneries. A longtime San Diego Filipina resident, Charito Balanag, noted, "The canneries were the only jobs that were open to us."[139] Similarly, Elvira Esparza said that the cannery workforce was comprised of Mexican women, Filipinas, and some Anglos.[140] Although the presence of Filipinos in the canneries was documented in the oral histories I conducted among Filipino and Mexipino residents in these communities, as well as other testimonies, not much exists to detail the extent of their participation. However, Filipinos lived in the same communities. Oral interviews and other written evidence corroborates their presence in the canneries, so I rely on these sparse records to show they were a part of the cannery culture and labor activism that existed. In order to integrate their lives into the larger picture of cannery work and the worker culture that developed, I have had to rely primarily on the experiences of Mexican women to tell the story of cannery workers in San Diego.

A sample of San Diego County Naturalization Records, for example, reveals that from 1935 to 1942 the majority of Mexican applicants employed by the fish canneries lived in Logan Heights, National City, and the downtown area around Little Italy. The canneries also sustained Point Loma to the north, where the majority of Portuguese fishermen resided. Similarly, a 1939 Works Progress Administration (WPA) report on San Diego also noted that cannery workers were among the largest number of workers in the community of Logan Heights.[141] Cannery work was one of the many waterfront industries that employed local residents and had a lasting economic impact on their communities. Fish canneries provided year-round employment and part-time work during the seasonal lows.[142] The industry also provided other jobs related to the canneries. Logan Heights resident Salvador Torres noted about the canneries, "It was one of Logan's main job industries. . . . [T]hey provided jobs to cannery workers, fishermen, ship builders and longshoremen." Although residents noted that "*everyone* in Logan worked for the canneries," it was predominately Mexican women who were employed as cannery workers.[143]

Indeed, the experiences of Mexican women and the connections among work, gender, and culture, as well as the networks that were established by women, facilitated their unionization during the 1930s and 1940s. These rank-and-file workers and the "cannery culture" they created in the workplace provide a clear understanding of how work influenced the daily lives of the workers. Historian Vicki Ruiz wrote, "This was an intermingling of gender roles and assembly line conditions, family and peer socialization, and at times collective resistance and change."[144] Work in the canneries helped women assert primary leadership roles and organize other women in the United Cannery, Agricultural, Packing, and Allied Workers of America (UCAPAWA), which in essence made it a women's union.[145] Photographs included in *Sun Harbor Catch and Can News*, *Van Camp News*, and *Tuna Topics*, for example, illustrate that women were a major part of the cannery workforce.[146]

Indeed, one can get an insight into the gendered experience that developed in the fish-canning industry. Unlike the agricultural fields, where Mexican and Filipino men were primarily employed, fish canneries provided unprecedented opportunities for women, especially Mexicans, to labor and contribute to the family income. Being that men's wages were oftentimes not enough to sustain large families, women and teenage children contributed to the family income.[147] Many of the local cannery workers began working in their early teens. During the 1940s and 1950s, many teenagers preferred to work in the canneries and other waterfront industries over pursuing an education because of the money it provided to help support their families.[148] As Emma Lopez recalled: "The big thing was, you really didn't need a college education. You didn't need a high school diploma, so why are you wasting time when you go to the cannery and make the big bucks. So a lot of them quit school to got to the cannery and work, so that's what a lot of them did."[149] These opportunities were available in the nearby canneries where friends and family members were part of an extensive network of long-established cannery workers. Given that Mexicans and Filipinos also worked together in the canneries, this also contributed to their mixing, thus sustaining their interethnic relationships.

The gender difference in the canneries was also evident in the type of labor that men and women performed as well as the wages they were paid. In the canneries women exclusively cleaned and packed the fish into cans. Bertha Ramirez remembers her mother working at Sun Harbor and Westgate canneries as a fish cleaner.[150] Some women, like Sue Talamantez, a Logan Heights resident, worked in the fish canneries for over forty-eight years. Talamantez packed and cleaned fish and progressively worked her way up to the quality-control unit. Mexican and Filipino men were primarily fish butchers as well as crewmen on the docks that unloaded the fish to the canneries. They also worked as can washers, in labeling, and in the warehouses, stacking cases of canned tuna and loading them up for distribution.[151] Virgil Garcia observed that the canneries provided the majority of jobs for both women and the men. He recalled the men's jobs: "They sliced the fishes on down and take the guts out and there was a variety—some of them were in the cooking room and they had all these fish in big racks and they'd take the racks and push them into the big ovens." Similarly, Connie Zuniga's father, Ralph, worked at Van Camp cannery for nine years as a fish cutter and in the boiler room.[152]

Jobs in the canneries were based not only on gender but also according to race. Logan Heights resident Elvira Esparza described the cannery floor as follows: "If any Anglo women working, they were the packers, the Mexicana was the cleaner, got the dirty job, it was always like that. There was a lot of discrimination."[153] Mexican women were thus relegated primarily to working the low-end jobs in the canneries and, overall, women were paid less than men on an hourly basis. For example, in 1939 women earned fifty-five cents an hour while men earned sixty cents. This could be attributed to the fact that Mexican women's jobs in the canneries were part of a gendered and racial hierarchy in the workforce.[154] Their wages were expected to be supplementary to men's and not the sole income, except for some cases where women were single parents. Even if, in reality, the female Mexicans' wages were the main source of income, they were still considered secondary workers and had an obligation to take care of their family first. As anthropologist Patricia Zavella noted, "they believed that work was an extension of family responsibilities."[155]

The cannery culture that developed among San Diego's Mexican and Filipino women was a product of a collective identity that women and men created primarily through family and peer socialization, gender roles, and their collective resistance against their employers. This culture was fostered through what was known as the "piece rate" system. Women were paid based on their production levels as opposed to men who worked hourly wages.[156] Although men were paid better hourly wages, women could earn more than men if they were fast workers. Logan Heights resident Hortencia Carrazco recalled, "The men were paid by the hour, the women were making more because it was piece work at the time."[157] As a result, women in the canneries had a stronger sense of a collective identity because they worked closely together and shared in their gendered wage experience. Kinship and familial networks among Mexican women were also important to maintain the cannery culture because they depended on each other as they worked side by side in the harsh conditions of the canneries. It is also in this context that Mexicans and Filipinos formed intimate relationships as they participated in this cannery culture together. The cannery workers developed and fostered a sense of "big family," which tied their communities together in various levels, not just within the workplace. These ties were so strong that, as one observer noted, "the hard work forged a bond among workers that was strong enough to withstand economic downturns, cannery closings, and the aches and pains of a lifetime of manual labor."[158] Indeed, entire communities in San Diego were often employed in the canneries. Jenny Dominguez, whose family lived in Logan Heights, remembered: "Everyone I knew was employed by the canneries. My mother, aunts, sisters, friends, everyone. If you wanted a job, you just went to a family member who worked at the cannery and asked. Usually they could get you hired. It seemed like the whole community worked at Van Camps."[159] Similarly, Connie Zuniga noted that the canneries employed everyone in Logan Heights. As she recalled, "Everybody worked down at the canneries. . . . [T]hey were dressed in white with little caps and they smelled. You could smell the fish, I mean oh my gosh! They would come home and scrub their hands with lemon to get rid of the smell. . . . But in those days you worked piece rate . . . [and] these were known as the cannery queens. . . . [I]t was something that the women could do because there was not a lot of jobs for women."[160]

When asked how the canneries affected the community, Ricardo Romio, a longtime resident of Logan Heights, replied, "It made them closer because everybody lived in the same place. Everybody knew each other. There was a closeness with the people, not like now."[161] Working with community members inevitably developed a sense of closeness. The canneries also provided many workers with their social life since they worked extensive hours outside of their shared communities. The canneries themselves even put on dances at their union halls and provided the space for outside activities. The *Sun Harbor Catch and Can News, Tuna Topic,* and *Van Camp News* not only reported on each company's success, but also provided workers with personal news regarding their fellow workers, such as weddings, baptisms, births, promotions, and even deaths. These notices were oftentimes written in English and Spanish. This cannery culture perpetuated a sense of big family, where members took care of each other in time of need. Jose Ramirez, for example, a cannery packer at Sun Harbor, thanked his fellow workers in the company's newsletter for the money donated for his child's funeral services and the willingness of the workers to donate blood to his sick wife. This close-knit cannery culture illustrates how close workers were and how strong feelings of family and community were reinforced through these networks within the workplace.[162]

Work at the canneries changed depending on the unpredictability of the day's catch. Usually the work was in the morning, but sometimes workers would be called in the middle of the night to process the fish. John Cota recalled: "It didn't matter when the boat came in. It could be nine in the morning or at midnight, when the fish came in we had to start working and we didn't stop until we were finished. It was a different life but that's the way it was."[163] On occasion, only specific segments of the workforce were called. Canneries had very loud whistles to call the workers to the canneries. These could be heard all through

Logan Heights. The whistles alerted workers of the different work shifts and, inadvertently, served as a clock for the community. Virgil Garcia remembers his mother worked at Van Camp cannery as a fish cleaner: "The cannery used to blow a whistle; you could hear it all over the community. Beep for one table; beep, beep for two tables; beep, beep, beep for three tables. That's how it worked. And a lot of people didn't have phones or no communication. That's how they knew there was work for them."[164] Bertha Ramirez recalls that when she was a child her mother used to work the night shift, then come home early in the morning: "I remember she'd come home; I was six years old at the time and she always smelt of mackerel; that's what they used to clean. . . . She'd come home in the wee hours of the morning, seven, eight o'clock in the morning." Similarly, Hortencia Carrazco noted, "When the mackerel would come in the people would run in to work. Sometimes there were big loads, tons and tons of fish. It had to go out before it spoiled. I was too young then, but my brothers used to go and work."[165]

Since San Diego was a major fish cannery city, employment was year-round. Although employment in the canneries was principally for the adults, teenagers also worked there. Delia Chavez remembers that teenagers only worked at the canneries during the summertime: "If you'd hear the whistle blowing sometimes in the middle of the night and they wanted workers, the guys would get up and they'd go to work. I mean anything they could get because . . . there wasn't much money around . . . [and] they needed to earn money."[166] Carrazco recalled: "When I started working I was about fourteen or fifteen years. I started working at Van Camp in 1943. I went to work to help the family. I had no choice, I had to help my mother, my parents, the younger kids. My mother had a lot of children. There were ten of us. I'd go back to school and the next summer I'd go back to work."[167]

Mexipino Ricardo Romio and his friends also used to go down to the docks and find work on the fishing boats that delivered their cargo to the canneries. As the boats came in, they would holler to the fishermen, "Hey, need some help?" Romio went on to state: "You would jump on the boat, and that was hard work. We had to get down in the hole, and the fish were packed in ice. You had to break them loose, and they lowered a bucket and you fill the bucket and they take the bucket out, and they bring it back and load it again, until you got the whole thing unloaded. . . . [Y]ou'd be down there for quite a while . . . and you'd come out there smelling."[168]

These examples demonstrate that in San Diego cannery work sustained generations of families by providing them with employment.[169] Detailed descriptions of the workers going and coming from work are given by their children as "a mass of white uniforms walking to work everyday, only to return home tired and smelling of fish."[170] Romio also remembers the cannery workers being predominately women. He observed: "They always come walking down our street, the ladies from the canneries, and I would see them all wearing white."[171]

Those who lived in the community were employed year-round, according to Virgil Garcia, whose family also worked in the canneries.[172]

Life in the canneries was not without difficulties. Many former cannery workers recalled the long hours of standing on their feet, oftentimes as long as ten hours per day. Cleaning also took its toll on the women. Many of them suffered from arthritis caused by the repetitive motions of cleaning the fish.[173] Former cannery worker Delia Chavez recalled, "I remember one lady, . . . she said, 'Aye los manos' [Oh, my hands]. They were really arthritic and they were still working, taking aspirin to keep working, to keep going, you know."[174] When work was plentiful, hours were extremely long. Carrazco pointed out: "It was rough in those days but I was making good money. In those days $100 a week was a lot of money. I worked over time. We used to work late, I remember when we had a big order from the Navy or the Army, I was like fifteen years old. We would work until 9:00 or 10:00 o'clock at night. Sometimes we were working Saturdays and Sundays. A couple times we worked the whole month without a day off."[175]

Similarly, Elvira Esparza recalled how she earned 33 cents an hour. In such an unpredictable industry, a workday could last up to twelve hours. She stated, "One day we worked from seven in the morning to seven at night, y todo mojado, uno llega [and we were all wet], standing in the water, but I kept with it 'cause I knew I had to work."[176] Although working conditions and long hours took their toll on their bodies, Bea Avina noted the good pay she received, "The conditions weren't exactly great, but nobody seemed to mind because the pay was so good. . . . In fact, there wasn't any job that we could get that even came close to the pay at the canneries."[177] The ability to make their own money—and good money at that—empowered women in these cannery communities as consumers and, as we shall see later in this chapter, union organizers.

Despite the pay, cannery work had its drawbacks. One of the main complaints of fish cannery work was the smell. Salvador Torres described the areas around the canneries as "the smelliest part of all of San Diego."[178] The smell also permeated into the workers themselves. Cannery workers had the smell of fish stuck in their hands and hair. Some women even had to cut their hair short to help get rid of the smell.[179] Virgil Garcia, whose mother worked at the cannery, recalled, "One day my mom was washing her uniform. 'Ma,' I said, 'My God, la pesca apesta fuerte [the fish smells real strong].' And she turned around and jumped on me. She said, 'Si, pero el dinero no apesta, que no?! [Yes, but the money doesn't stink, right?!]' So she put me in my place. . . . Yeah, it was stinky."[180] The smell was also embarrassing for those who had to ride the bus back home. Rude bus passengers exacerbated the workers' embarrassment when they held their noses and pointed at the tuna drippings on their uniforms.[181]

For some, the smell and taste became overbearing. Ricardo Romio's mother worked at Van Camps cannery since he was a young boy. Ricardo described her experiences as follows: "I remember all the cannery women coming from work and smelling like fish. She worked really hard to support us . . . because my dad was always gone. . . . [A]fter my dad got out of the service, I started staying with him and working at the cannery myself. I used to go down there and unload the fishing boats, so everyday I would bring home these big fish, tunas. My dad . . . he was eating fish everyday and he was really enjoying it. But after a while, man, everything started tasting like fish. I fry an egg; it taste like fish. So I quit bringing them home. I started selling them on the way home."[182]

Eventually, the drudgeries of the job facilitated workers to demand higher pay. Wages were substandard at the fish canneries until workers began to organize and demand higher wages and improved working conditions in the 1930s. One of the first unions to organize cannery workers in San Diego was the Fishermen's and Cannery Workers' Industrial Union, which was affiliated with the Trade Union Unity League (TUUL) in April of 1934. They set out to organize cannery workers in Van Camp Seafood Company for higher wages and union recognition. The owners refused to recognize the union and instead tried to form a company union and intimidate workers into joining it. In order to force workers into signing up for the company union, management informed them that they would not receive their paychecks. Cannery owners used intimidation to discourage the workers who were being organized by the TUUL (an affiliate of the Communist Party). A letter written by O. C. Heitman, from the National Recovery Administration (NRA), informed the executive secretary of the Los Angeles Regional Labor Board, Campbell MacCulloch, that there were approximately one thousand individuals congregated outside of Van Camp demanding their own union instead of a company union. His concern was that bringing in the AFL would cause more trouble since "the Red Ranks are increasing and membership has almost doubled." This was in direct contrast to a letter written by A. K. Johnson, manager of Van Camp Sea Food Company in San Diego, who tried to minimize the organizing efforts that took place in the cannery while pointing out the communist affiliation of union organizers. Peter J. Taylor, secretary of the Fishermen's and Cannery Workers' Industrial Union in San Diego, contacted Charles H. Cunningham, state enforcement officer for the NRA, to come in and settle the dispute.[183]

In May of 1934, Van Camp locked out the strikers and used the police to suppress the strike. According to Taylor, several arrests were made, including one Elena Navarette for a trumped-up assault charge against a police officer. Furthermore, Taylor noted in his letter to the Los Angeles Regional Labor Board: "On the present basis, of police terrorization and the lockout, it is apparently a crime for workers to organize and strike for higher wages and better conditions, even when they are striking for enforcement of the minimum wage law. It is plain to the workers when the cannery employers violate the law, nothing is done. When the workers act in their own interest, the law intervenes with force and violence; or sets up red-tape procedures which defeats action on behalf of the workers."[184]

Taylor's criticism was valid based on the way law enforcement was used to suppress the strikers. He also questioned the impartiality of the Labor Board in helping the strikers. Taylor believed this to be a result of red-baiting, which was aimed at their organizing efforts.[185] Although not much else is mentioned regarding this strike, by 1937 another union came in to organize the workers at Van Camp and the other fish canneries in San Diego. It is within this context that the United Cannery, Agricultural, Packing, and Allied Workers of America (UCAPAWA), under the auspices of the Congress of Industrial Organizations (CIO), began organizing cannery workers.

UCAPAWA was formed on July 9, 1937, in Denver, Colorado, when delegates from eighty-two locals representing Mexican, Filipino, Japanese, African American, and other underrepresented groups came together to form a new union. This new union was formed under the CIO in response to the need to organize unskilled workers from all racial and ethnic backgrounds, both men and women, who were often marginalized from the labor movement and excluded from unions such as the AFL. As David Gutiérrez notes regarding Mexican labor, for example, "UCAPAWA also established important precedents in its efforts to recruit and organize Mexican American men and women workers into the ranks of an American labor organization."[186]

For marginalized racial and ethnic groups, the ability to be a part of and participate in an American labor organization was empowering. The decision by the CIO to include all workers regardless of race, ethnicity, and gender demonstrates its approach to a true democratic movement with regards to labor. It was within UCAPAWA that women began to participate in larger numbers as union workers and assume leadership roles. This empowered them not only on the job but also in their communities, where they had an equal voice to their male counterparts. As historian Vicki Ruiz notes, "The CIO was at that time a maverick arm of the AFL. The CIO recruited unskilled workers along industrial lines in contrast to the standard craft union approach."[187] Because the AFL focused primarily on skilled white labor, many racial and ethnic groups, in addition to women, were excluded from its ranks. In fact, in San Diego the AFL on several occasions excluded Mexicans from membership in its unions.[188] Thus, the success of UCAPAWA was in its ability to recruit workers across racial, ethnic, and gender lines, especially those from unskilled and semi-skilled segments of the workforce who, like agricultural workers, were usually ignored by AFL trade craft unions and their affiliates that were not interested in organizing nonwhites and women into their unions.[189] The union's real success, however, rested in local leadership because it believed in developing a true democratic trade union from the "bottom up." As a result, many cannery locals, where Mexican women comprised the majority of the workforce, provided their own leadership.[190]

This was certainly the case in San Diego. Since women made up over 75 percent of the workforce in San Diego's fish canneries, they dominated the union. As Salvador Torres recalled, when men tried to bring up their issues at union meetings, "the women would tell them men to 'shut up' and they would discuss issues in the fish room and packing room. They would actually say, 'shut up.'"[191] This statement illustrates an important point. Given the participation and dedication that Mexican women had in the canneries and the effectiveness of their organizing among each other, they were able to exert their power and influence over the men. Thus, the gender balance of power seemed to be in the hands of women at the local level. It is within this context that Luisa Moreno stands out as one of the most recognized labor organizers in San Diego.

In 1937, Luisa Moreno, a labor organizer who was in charge of organizing UCAPAWA in Southern California, moved to San Diego. With the assistance of Robert Galvan she began to organize thousands of fish cannery workers in San Diego under UCAPAWA Local 64.[192] The first cannery organized under Local 64 was Van Camp Seafood Company, the largest cannery in San Diego. In March of 1939, UCAPAWA Local 64 signed an agreement with Van Camp. The company recognized the union and granted a preferential shop and seniority rights, an eight-hour day, higher wages and overtime pay, all of which affected the seven hundred employees of the new union, 75 percent of which were women. As labor historian Zaragosa Vargas noted, this major victory for Local 64 made it "one of California's leading UCAPAWA locals."[193] This victory could be attributed to the strength and effectiveness of the female leadership and the multiracial rank-and-file membership. Moreno then set her eyes on the other canneries, organizing workers from the California Packing Corporation, the Marine Products Company, the Old Mission Packing Corporation, and Westgate Sea Products. According to UCAPAWA News, Local 64 was successful in organizing workers at Old Mission Packing Company, with almost half of its workforce signing up with UCAPAWA.[194] That was no easy task since San Diego was known to be an antilabor town that resisted labor organizing with violence.[195] San Diego was also a stronghold of the AFL.

Scholars such as Carlos Larralde and Richard Griswold del Castillo, who have written on Luisa Moreno, provide much about what we know in regards to her labor organizing activities in San Diego's fish canneries.[196] They demonstrate not only the intense resistance mounted against Moreno in San Diego while organizing cannery workers, but also the gains that were made under the leadership of Local 64. In 1940, for example, Van Camp signed a major agreement with Local 64 that included a definite union shop, a guaranteed eight-hour workday, overtime provisions, seniority rights, and improved working conditions—all of which, combined, were a first for the industry, according to UCAPAWA News.[197] In addition to the gains that Local 64 made at Van Camp, scholars have suggested that Local 64 was also successful in organizing the other canneries. This was also highlighted by UCAPAWA News, which claimed, "Fish Cannery Local 64 in San Diego is rapidly becoming the largest and most active union in town."[198]

Despite the ambitions of Local 64 in San Diego, it was only successful in securing a closed shop in the Van Camp cannery.[199] According to various articles in the *San Diego Labor Leader*, the AFL already controlled the majority of the fish canneries of San Diego. By the 1940s, the AFL had secured contracts for all of the canneries except Van Camp, which was under UCAPAWA.[200] As a resident of San Diego, Luisa Moreno was in charge of organizing the city's canneries in 1940; however, given that the AFL already controlled all of the canneries except Van Camp, it is likely that Moreno had limitations in securing UCAPAWA as the bargaining agent for all cannery workers in San Diego. Given the early political ties that labor had in organizing the agricultural fields, such as the CAWIU and the Communist Party during the 1930s, most notably in the Imperial Valley, there was more resistance to Moreno and UCAPAWA when she came to San Diego. When examining the overall picture of labor-organizing efforts and unions, the CIO and its union affiliates like UCAPAWA were definitely more radical in their approach to organizing workers across racial, ethnic, and gender lines, U.S.-born and immigrant alike. Their stance as being radical was tied to their membership base, which was predominately racial and ethnic minorities. There also seems to have been more leadership roles given to racial and ethnic minorities and women in UCAPAWA both at the local and national level. As Ruiz notes, women were even more radical than the men in their organizing efforts, with some gaining prominent positions in the union, such as Moreno, who was the international vice president of UCAPAWA.[201]

It is highly likely that given Moreno's status as a resident alien (who had already petitioned for citizenship), as were Robert Galvan and other rank-and-file members, the CIO was equated with "foreignness." This was in contrast to the AFL, which was promoted as an "American" union with a predominately white membership and leadership at the national level. Thus, cannery operatives in San Diego tolerated the AFL as a bargaining unit. Given its already conservative nature, San Diego was more likely to accept working with the AFL, as well as exercise some control by working with it, as opposed to negotiating with individuals like Moreno and Galvan, who were labeled as communists and had this cloud of suspicion hanging over them and their union for their radical approach to union organizing. I contend that, given the political climate of the time, being more radical meant being less American when dealing with nonwhite workers in San Diego's fish canneries, despite the fact that Moreno had already stated that "UCAPAWA was a *left* union, not a Communist union."[202] Nevertheless, the fear of communism and UCAPAWA's reputation as being a Communist Party–affiliated union as early as 1938, and the radical approach to organizing San Diego's fish cannery workers over bread-and-butter issues, put the AFL and cannery operatives on the offensive to ensure that Local 64 did not extend its membership beyond Van Camp cannery.[203]

Moreno's and Galvan's alleged affiliation to the Communist Party added to their notorious reputation among cannery operatives and local AFL leadership, who conspired against both Moreno and Galvan, imposing parameters over their organizing efforts in San Diego.[204] Indeed, when competing with the communist-affiliated or left-leaning unions in the canneries, the AFL had to be more open in organizing Mexican and other nonwhite workers. Although this was true regarding local AFL policies as they pertained to agriculture, this seems more applicable to the fish-canning industry. It was in the canneries that the local leadership of the AFL did "show at least some recognition of the need to break out of its narrow craft and racist isolation if it were to maintain its position in the labor movement."[205] It was this offensive strategy that Moreno had to deal with.

In addition, Moreno and Galvan also had to contend with the Ku Klux Klan, the Silver Shirts, and other white supremacist groups that were vehemently anti-Mexican and were used by canneries such as Van Camp, California Packing Corporation, and Marine Products Company to violently break up union organizing by Moreno and her allies. Galvan, for example, was almost killed by the Ku Klux Klan in San Diego. As labor activist and peer Bert Corona recalled, "The Klan spotted Galvan and almost hanged him. Exhausted, he ran into an army patrol that saved him." Galvan ended up breaking his leg in the escape. Moreno's experiences also convinced her that "tuna executives and the growers had employees that were members of the Klan." Yet despite any fear she had privately, in the public sphere she battled them in order to unionize workers in canneries like Van Camp.[206] Moreno would not give in to the intimidation and violence. She depended on the solidarity of the workers and her allies to empower them through these difficult times.

Although Moreno was making headway with the Van Camp cannery, UCAPAWA did not have the money necessary to compete with the AFL in San Diego. Thus, the jurisdictional disputes and union competition that occurred in the city's fish canneries indicated that the AFL was not going to give up its large portion of the twelve thousand fish cannery workers. For example, when elections were held at the various fish canneries in San Diego, such as West Gate and Sun Harbor, from 1940 to 1942, UCAPAWA Local 64 suffered defeat at the hands of AFL Fish Cannery Workers' Local 21251.[207] At Sun Harbor cannery, the AFL defeated UCAPAWA during the National Labor Relations Board (NLRB) election by a vote of three to one; thus it remaining AFL-controlled.[208] The AFL tried to move in on Van Camp, but Local 64 was able to successfully stay under UCAPAWA and the CIO. The AFL, however, was able to take control over Old Mission Packing Company from Moreno's earlier efforts of organizing them by October of 1940. Old Mission was now under the fold of the AFL, which also controlled Westgate Sea Products Company, California Packing Corporation, Sun Harbor Packing Corporation, and the Tuna Fishermen's Packing Corporation.[209] Among the gains the AFL noted were a five cents an hour wage increase for men and women, which, according to piece rate work for women, gave them an hourly wage as high as sixty-five cents an hour. By 1941, the AFL was notifying CIO workers at Van Camp that their wages were "far below the industry-wide AFL scale."[210] Despite these claims, union members at Van Camp remained loyal to Local 64.

Despite the national views of the AFL, which were conservative and racially exclusive, sources indicate that local leadership in the AFL was taking a different route in organizing the fish canneries in order to combat UCAPAWA Local 64. Local AFL unions had to be more accommodating to win over the cannery workforce that was predominately nonwhite.[211] Given that the majority of the fish cannery workers were Mexican, it was them, along with their Filipino and other coworkers, who participated in local leadership positions and organized other rank-and-file members. AFL members like Sue Talamantez, for example, remained part of the union for over forty years.[212] Cannery sources also point to key organizers for AFL Fish Cannery Workers' Local 21251 such as Fred Martinez, Marina Gomez, Jennie Juaregui, and Guadalupe Arredondo, who were elected officers during the 1940s. Given their Spanish surnames, they were most likely of Mexican descent. This particular aspect of labor organizing within local AFL unions begs for more research.[213]

Despite the tension and competition that was going on with the AFL and UCAPAWA, the fact remains that it was the cannery workers themselves who were responsible for the gains they received through their unions. Regardless of whether the labor organizers were communist-affiliated, politically to the left, or part of the AFL, they only played supportive roles. David Gutiérrez writes, "It was the workers themselves who supplied the drive and commitment to pursue their goals in an extremely hostile and at times violent atmosphere." Since a cannery culture existed in the fish canneries, it was easier for Mexican women and their male coworkers to organize among themselves to obtain higher wages and better working conditions.[214] It was the cannery culture that empowered workers to endure the hardships of union organizing and cannery operative resistance and violence. Although local policies were more favorable to Mexican and other nonwhite workers, national leadership and higher positions in the AFL still continued to be held by whites, indicating a different policy on the national level.

The AFL continued to control all of the fish canneries except Van Camp well into 1941. By 1942 and with the United States' entrance into World War II, both the AFL and CIO agreed to a "no strike" pledge during the war as requested by President Franklin D. Roosevelt. Any labor disputes during this time would be handled through the War Labor Board. During the "no strike" pledge, wages continued to increase for cannery workers both in Van Camp and the other AFL controlled canneries, which at this time totaled six.[215] By 1943, the AFL became home to a joint union of cannery workers and fishermen, which united to become the Cannery Workers and Fishermen's Union in San Diego. This alliance was used to mount increasing pressure against UCAPAWA. Indeed, the postwar years continued to see competition between the AFL and UCAPAWA over San Diego's cannery workers.[216]

By early 1950, UCAPAWA, now known as the Food, Tobacco, Agricultural, and Allied Workers of America (FTA), continued to struggle in organizing other cannery workers outside Van Camp cannery.[217] They waged unsuccessful attempts at Westgate–Sun Harbor and San Diego Packing Company while trying to fight off the AFL-Teamster coalition in a larger union drive across California. The Teamsters used many tactics to swell their union ranks, including intimidation, political maneuvering, cheating during election process, violence, coercion, and, more effectively, red-baiting. These tactics began to crack the foundation of FTA's union membership as red-baiting alienated key labor organizers and their allies in an era where patriotism was demanded of citizens, even oppressed workers seeking true democratic unionism. Although FTA workers resisted the Teamsters, the FTA diminished rather quickly with a "takeover" of FTA affiliates in Los Angeles and San Diego. By 1950 only Local 64 remained.[218] The rise of McCarthyism and the "Great Fear" of communism and unions having to abide by the Taft-Hartley Act hindered what little gains were won by organized labor with the Wagner Act in 1935. This, as Ruiz noted, "spelled the end of democratic organization." According to the San Diego Labor Leader, the FTA was finally expelled by the CIO for having "Communist tendencies and undemocratic practices." By December of 1950, UCAPAWA/FTA was finished.[219] Moreover, according to local newspaper reports, the Immigration and Naturalization Service (INS) deported key figures such as Luisa Moreno, Robert Galvan, and five Filipino labor leaders, claiming that they were "dangerous aliens" for allegedly being affiliated with the Communist Party.[220] Not much else is known about Local 64's organizing activities since then.[221] The AFL now controlled the fish canneries, but even it could not stop foreign competition, environmental laws, and outsourcing, which eventually marked the end of the fish canneries in San Diego.

———

The experiences of agricultural and fish cannery workers in San Diego between the 1920s and 1940s were complex and wrought with instances of what Moon-Kie Jung called interracialism. In the agricultural fields Mexicans and Filipinos created coalitions from separate ethnic unions or established larger interracial ones to fight grower exploitation and racial oppression. Despite experiencing differential racialization and dealing with moments of tension and divergence, they mobilized together, recognizing the advantages of uniting to have their common demands met. They were not alone as they joined thousands of Filipinos, Mexicans, and other racial/ethnic groups throughout the state of California in a series of strikes, most notably during the 1930s. Given the seasonal and migratory nature of agricultural work, however, most mainstream unions, UCAPAWA included, decided to abandon the organization of farm workers and instead focus their attention on packing shed and cannery workers.[222] Under communist-influenced unions such as the CAWIU, they were able to utilize Filipino interethnic organizing skills and recruit across ethnic lines. What usually spelled the end to such organizing efforts was the violence and red-baiting that occurred. As a result, most labor organizing continued under a coalition of ethnic or newly formed interethnic unions such as the Federated Agricultural Laborers Association (FALA).

As the United States entered World War II, many Mexican and Filipino farm workers joined the armed forces to fight abroad. Others went into the cities to take advantage of the opportunities that opened up in the defense industries, which had previously excluded racial and ethnic minorities. This allowed them to obtain better-paying jobs. This included Mexican, Filipina, and African American women. According to Griswold del Castillo, hundreds of thousands of Mexican American women were employed in defense industries. For those working in the aircraft industry, they had to endure racial discrimination and sexism. Their story, as Griswold del Castillo suggests, needs further inquiry.[223] Taking the place of Mexican and Filipino farmworkers, who were now fighting overseas or working in defense industries, were thousands of Mexican *braceros* who, through the Bracero Program (1942–1964), came to labor in the fields as part of the war effort.[224]

With regards to the fish canneries during World War II, both the AFL and CIO unquestionably supported the war effort by agreeing to a "no strike" pledge.[225] This kept workers from striking whenever they had grievances. In a sense the "no strike" pledge hindered union growth in order to support the war effort. Despite the pledge, there were still labor shortages due to the men who went off to war. Women came in to replace the men in defense industries. These new opportunities in defense-related work competed with fish canneries. Unlike the agricultural industry, where braceros came in to fill the labor shortage in the fields, fish canneries still had a large female labor force; yet World War II brought unforeseeable changes to San Diego. At one end, the government purchased large quantities of canned tuna for the military, keeping the industry alive; however, the government was also responsible for closing several of the canneries when the Japanese Americans, who owned the fishing boats, were removed to internment camps and the majority of the tuna fleet was overhauled as patrol boats for the war effort.[226]

Individuals like Moreno and Galvan, who were involved with UCAPAWA, became the target of the House Un-American Activities Committee (HUAC) as a result of McCarthyism and the anticommunist hysteria that was prevalent during the postwar period. Moreno and Galvan were among a number of "dangerous aliens" deported from San Diego because of their civil rights and labor activities.[227] The CIO was not immune to the anticommunist hysteria. Mounting pressure to conform forced the CIO to expel UCAPAWA.[228] As for the fish canneries, they were facing multiple difficulties. Although the canneries sustained San Diego's economy after World War II, the tuna industry's decline was "sharp and permanent."[229]

Foreign competition with the Japanese in the 1950s proved too much for local San Diego fishermen. They could not compete with the Japanese and their lower prices, which the canneries preferred. Although the availability of fish to be canned benefited the cannery workers who still had jobs, as opposed to the fishermen, it spelled the beginning of the end. Stricter government regulations, as well as cheap foreign labor, influenced the canneries to go abroad. In July of 1984, Van Camp moved its operations out of San Diego to Puerto Rico. Bumble Bee (which purchased Westgate cannery) followed suit, moving its operations to America Samoa that same year.[230] With the canneries gone, San Diego's local communities found themselves without employment in an industry that had sustained them for generations. The impact on gender roles was also significant. The closing of the canneries in San Diego, for example, was the end of an era. Men were forced to pursue employment in the shipbuilding and aircraft indus-tries, while many women went back to being housewives or sought employment in other fields.[231]

Filipinos and Mexicans in San Diego were part of a larger movement of laborers throughout the state of California and in various industries who struck for a living wage and union recognition as well as better living and working conditions. Moreover, they organized to find dignity in the work that they did, which was often the most arduous and least appreciated labor because it was racialized as soon as they filled those positions. For agricultural and fish-canning work in particular, both groups organized together in the quest to work across ethnic lines and find strength in numbers. Because Mexicans and Filipinos shared similar experiences with discrimination, violence, and intimidation at the hands of their employers and white workers, they found a common bond as they organized within a rearticulated racial and working-class consciousness, or interracialism.

Unionism was not without its problems. At times there were tensions between the two groups, especially when growers pitted them against each other, and fractures did occur, such as what happened in the Imperial Valley in 1934. By and large, however, as they organized together and found more victories in coali-tion with each other, Mexicans and Filipinos continued to cooperate. Moreover, the use of violence and intimidation by growers, fish cannery operatives, vigi-lante groups, and even the state, especially concerning agricultural workers, only served to keep the two communities united in an effort to secure their demands, even if it meant injury and possibly death. Steadfast in their convictions, Mexicans and Filipinos saw their struggle as not just for labor rights, but for civil rights as well. As historian Zaragoza Vargas noted, the link between labor and civil rights is undeniable.[232] Because labor was racialized and their civil rights were also being violated on account of their race, Mexicans and Filipinos fought these issues on both fronts.

Labor unions, which were forged from the worker cultures that developed in San Diego's agricultural fields and fish canneries, enabled generations of Mexicans and Filipinos to interact with each other. As these stories suggest, their shared experience of combating their oppressive employers, the sense of family and community, and the labor cultures that were forged were key factors in the

FIG. 1 Ciriaco "Pablo" Poscablo came to San Diego via the U.S. Navy in 1924. He met his wife, Felipa Castro, in the early 1930s. Her family had migrated from Baja California to what is now the Otay Mesa area of South Bay San Diego. Their marriage in 1938 would be the beginning of four generations of multiethnic Mexipinos. COURTESY OF THE GUEVARRA FAMILY.

FIG. 2 Mexican social and fraternal organizations were established in San Diego as early as the 1900s. Pictured is La Sociedad Beneficia Mexicana "Benito Juarez" de National City, circa 1900s. DE MARA COLLECTION. COURTESY OF THE NATIONAL CITY PUBLIC LIBRARY.

FIG. 3 Second- and third-generation Mexicans and Filipinos also formed their own social organizations and clubs from the 1940s to the 1960s. Pictured is the first meeting of the "Lucky 13" social club at the Neighborhood House, Logan Heights, circa 1944. According to member Dora Hollman Garcia *(back row, third from left)*, their social club had both Mexican and Filipina members COURTESY OF DORA HOLLMAN GARCIA.

FIG. 5 Socorro Ortiz of Logan Heights and Frank Mendoza of National City at 1239 McKinley Avenue, National City, circa 1945. They married in 1948 and settled at 3760 Logan Avenue, where they raised her four younger sisters, Josie, Lydia, Trinidad, and Rachael. COURTESY OF RACHAEL ORTIZ.

FIG. 4 [OPPOSITE] The Filipino Club of La Jolla was one of the earliest Filipino social organizations in San Diego. Most of the women pictured in this 1934 Mayflower Dance are Mexican and Filipina. COURTESY OF THE FILIPINO AMERICAN NATIONAL HISTORICAL SOCIETY, SEATTLE, WASHINGTON.

FIG. 6 Given the shortage of Filipinas in San Diego, Filipino men oftentimes married Mexicans and other Latinas who shared a similar culture, religion, and language (to some extent). Pictured are Restituto and Ignacia Perrariz and their children, circa early 1930s. COURTESY OF IRENE PERRARIZ MENA.

FIG. 7 Mary Poscablo, a second-generation Mexipina, is pictured here with her uncle Amando Amansec, circa late 1940s. Amando came to San Diego via the U.S. Navy, where he, along with most Filipinos of that time, was confined to the rank of steward. After his military service he worked as a cook and in other service-related jobs with Mary's father, Pablo. COURTESY OF THE GUEVARRA FAMILY.

FIG. 8 Mexicans who settled in the town of Lemon Grove in San Diego County worked in the lemon orchards and packing houses. Pictured are Candelaria Beltran Royce *(fourth on right)*, her aunt Francisca Beltran Alvarez *(first on right)*, and her stepmother, Micaela Beltran *(last on right)*, at the Lemon Grove Fruit Growers Association Packing House, circa late 1920s. COURTESY OF LAURETTA ROYCE JOHNSON.

FIG. 9 Nick Balino met his wife, Rose Audrey Ramirez, when he was working a soup line. He initially came to the United States in the early 1920s to go to school but eventually ended up working as a cook at the Twins Inns Restaurant in Carlsbad. Their family includes four generations of Mexipinos that extend throughout San Diego County. Photo circa 1934. COURTESY OF KATHERINE JEAN BALINO ROWAN AND SUZANNA BALINO FERNANDEZ.

FIG. 10 Simplicio Galbiso *(far left)* is pictured with other Filipino and Mexican farmworkers, circa 1950s. Filipinos and Mexicans were the dominant workforce in California agriculture, including San Diego and Imperial Counties. COURTESY OF DAVID GALBISO.

In the photograph, the banner reads:

1st Communion Class
Our Lady of Guadalupe
Church
San Diego, Calif May 4, 1941

FIG. 11 Since most Mexicans and Filipinos were Catholic, they oftentimes attended the same Catholic churches in their communities. Pictured here is a first communion at Our Lady of Guadalupe Catholic Church in Logan Heights (Barrio Logan), circa 1941.

COURTESY OF RACHAEL ORTIZ, LOGAN HEIGHTS HISTORICAL SOCIETY.

FIG. 12 Filipinos and Mexicans who worked alongside each other oftentimes also spent their leisure time together, forming stronger bonds of community. Pictured is the Villarin family with friends in La Jolla, circa late 1940s. COURTESY OF LANNY AND TED VILLARIN.

FIG. 13 Josefa and Simplicio Galbiso (*couple holding hands*) are pictured with family and friends in the early 1940s. They eventually settled in the farming town of Niland, in the Imperial Valley, which was linked to San Diego's migrant communities. COURTESY OF DAVID GALBISO.

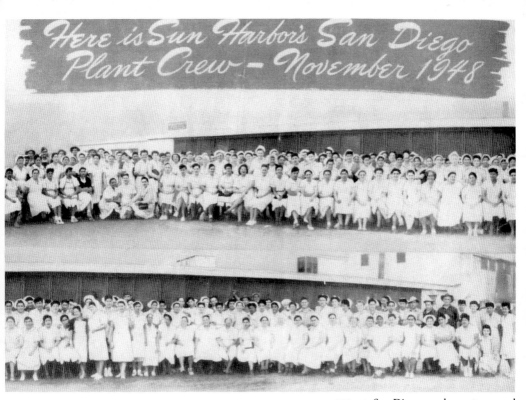

Here is Sun Harbor's San Diego Plant Crew – November 1948

FIG. 14 San Diego was home to several canneries, which employed entire communities along the waterfront. During the 1950s, San Diego was known as the "tuna canning capital of the world." Although the majority of these workers were immigrant and U.S.-born Mexicans, Filipinas and other ethnic groups also worked in the canneries. This photograph was taken at the Sun Harbor cannery in 1948. COURTESY OF RACHAEL ORTIZ, LOGAN HEIGHTS HISTORICAL SOCIETY.

FIG. 15 Filipino families oftentimes took in visiting sailors on liberty in San Diego. They hosted and invited them to community events. Pictured are the Villarin family, which includes Dorotea (mother) and her children, Florence, Bernie, and Lanny, and two unidentified sailors, circa 1950s. COURTESY OF LANNY AND TED VILLARIN.

FIG. 16 The Patacsil (Filipino) and Diego (Filipino-Mexican) families celebrating Christmas together, circa 1950s. As *compadres* and *comadres,* their friendships were deepened by their relations as godparents, fostered through baptisms and other Catholic ceremonies. COURTESY OF JUDY PATACSIL AND LILY VILLARIN BAQUIAL, FANHS SAN DIEGO CHAPTER ARCHIVES.

FIG. 17 Irene Perrariz Mena, a Mexipina, was actively involved in the Chicano movement during the 1970s. She is known as the honorary grandmother of the Brown Berets of Aztlán in San Diego, where she and her family are still involved. COURTESY OF IRENE PERRARIZ MENA.

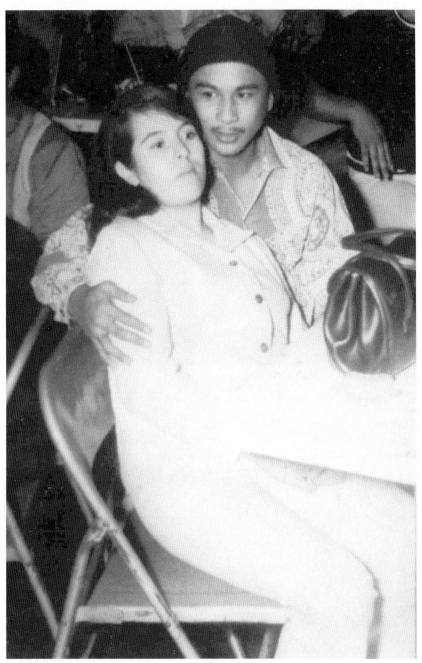

FIG. 18 Rudy Guevarra, a third-generation Mexipino, and his fiancé, Angela Fernandez, in Tijuana, Mexico, circa 1970. Given that Tijuana shared a border with San Diego, many Filipinos also frequented the area and formed communities there that were linked with neighboring San Diego to the north and the Imperial Valley to the east. COURTESY OF THE GUEVARRA FAMILY.

FIG. 19 Bertha and Salvador Lleva and their children, Leticia, Gina, and Karina, circa 1982. They would go on to have another daughter, Marlene (not pictured). Bertha met Salvador in Tijuana in 1971. They moved to San Diego in 1980, settling in the community of Logan Heights. The Llevas eventually moved to Encanto in the early 1990s. COURTESY OF THE LLEVA FAMILY.

FIG. 20 Mexipinos were involved in the immigration rights marches in San Diego during 2006. Pictured are Marlene and Gina Lleva with author Rudy Guevarra Jr. PHOTO COURTESY OF AUTHOR.

personal relationships that developed between Filipinos and Mexicans. As members of multiracial communities forged from racial oppression, Mexicans and Filipinos settled, worked, worshipped, socialized, and married each other, forming interethnic, multicultural families that produced several generations of multiethnic Mexican-Filipinos, or Mexipinos. The families that came out of these experiences, and how their multiethnic children were shaped by living in San Diego, is the subject of the next chapter.

CHAPTER 5

Filipino-Mexican Couples and the Forging of a Mexipino Identity

When Felipa Castro met Ciriaco "Pablo" Poscablo in San Diego, little did she know the impact their marriage would have on their family for generations to come. Born and raised in Baja California, Mexico, Felipa migrated with her family to Tijuana, then made her way north to the Otay Mesa area in the South Bay region of San Diego County during the early 1930s. Her future husband, Ciriaco, arrived in San Diego in 1924 from his hometown of Calasiao, in the province of Pangasinan, Philippines, via the U.S. Navy. Their courtship was brief, and they filed for a marriage license in 1938. What is interesting to note about their marriage is that on their license she indicated she was a "Mexican Indian," despite the fact she was light enough to be considered white. Felipa, however, made sure she was not perceived as white. Rather, Felipa consciously chose to indicate on their marriage license that she was Mexican Indian in order to marry her Filipino husband. In doing so, she resisted the racial restrictions of the time that prohibited miscegenation between whites and nonwhites.[1] She had to assert her Mexican Indian identity in order for the marriage to be recognized by the state. Her choice to identify as "Mexican Indian" reveals an ironic twist of following the legal codes that opposed miscegenation between Filipinos and whites; this also affected light-skinned Mexican women after 1933.[2]

As the historian Peggy Pascoe notes in her book *What Comes Naturally,* in an effort to uphold racial segregation, miscegenation laws were implemented and enforced to prohibit the mixing of whites with nonwhites. Some of the earliest miscegenation laws in the United States—a consequence of white enslavement of Africans—were passed in Maryland and Virginia in the 1660s, prohibiting interracial marriage and cohabitation between blacks and whites. Other states followed suit with their own versions of the miscegenation law, which were maintained up until the Civil War. During the post–Civil War period, fear of miscegenation led to another onslaught of legal barriers and social pressures, which spread to the Western states and other territories in the Southwest.[3]

In these geographic regions, racial formations and the banning of inter-racial intimacies went beyond the black-white binary of miscegenation laws. California, and the U.S. Southwest, for that matter, had a complex multiracial makeup that also included indigenous peoples, Mexicans, Filipinos, Asians, and Pacific Islanders. These large multiracial populations challenged the foundations of these legal barriers, which were already inconsistent at best. Miscegenation laws, however, were adapted to prevent all nonwhites from marrying whites, "despite wide difference in their individual racial formations and specific structures of oppression." By 1933 Filipinos were also included into the fold of "the unmixables."[4]

From the 1860s to the 1960s, the American legal system maintained that interracial marriage was "unnatural," so prohibiting these unions through miscegenation laws became paramount to legally maintaining white supremacy. Yet as Pascoe notes, the "unnatural" argument was more about the interlocking notions regarding the social conceptions of race, maintaining white supremacy and its political implications for the country, which was absorbing large popula-tions of nonwhites as the United States extended its empire continentally and transnationally.

Marriage became "the foundation for the larger racial project of white supremacy and purity."[5] It was a social institution that had many implications as it pertained to property rights, citizenship, and the choice of whom to love. Issuing a marriage license also meant producing racial definitions, which were to be upheld by county licensing clerks. Pascoe notes that their job at racial "guess-work" and their power to grant or deny marriage licenses based on someone's race made them the gatekeepers of white supremacy and purity.[6] In order to cir-cumvent this sort of racial profiling and the uncertainties of miscegenation laws regarding Mexicans (since some had skin complexions that were less threatening to whites), Felipa chose to assert her nonwhite ancestry as a Mexican Indian, jettisoning her ability to be mistaken as white. She thus manipulated the absurdity of miscegenation laws to marry Pablo, since legally California did not prohibit the marriages of Filipino men to Mexican women.[7] Although Felipa and Pablo's marriage was not meant as a political statement, it had political ramifications by resisting the miscegenation laws of their time as part of what Maria Root calls the "quiet revolution fueled by love."[8] Their action, along with that of other couples who defied these legal barriers and took their cases to court, finally succeeded with *Perez v. Sharp* (1948) in California and nationally with *Loving v. Virginia* (1967). Both the California and U.S. Supreme Court declared miscegenation laws unconstitutional because they "violated the Fourteenth Amendment's guarantee of equal protection of the laws."[9]

Felipa and Pablo would go on to have five children who would be first-generation Mexipinos. Their children, grandchildren, great-grandchildren, and great-great grandchildren would also be born Mexipinos, carrying on a legacy of the interethnic mixing and intimacies that were prevalent in San Diego between

Filipino men and Mexican women. As previously mentioned, the gender imbalance of Filipino males to females encouraged them to marry outside their ethnic group. Although Filipinos married white women prior to miscegenation laws denying them that right, they also married American Indians, African Americans, Japanese, Chinese, and, more frequently, Mexicans and other Latinas.[10] The choice of brides usually depended on where Filipinos resided or frequented. It makes sense, then, that intermarriages between Filipinos and Mexican women were prevalent in locales such as San Diego and other areas of California where both communities have historically converged.[11]

In order to understand the frequency of Filipino-Mexican intermarriages over several generations in San Diego and how they formed their multiethnic families within the setting of their respective communities, I interviewed dozens of individuals, including Filipino-Mexican couples and their multiethnic Mexipino children.[12] Their stories are at the heart of this chapter, capturing the rich political and cultural complexity of Filipino-Mexican couples and the distinct Mexipino experience that was forged from these families and communities in San Diego. In framing these experiences, I explore how the children defined themselves over several generations within the context of their families and communities and their process of nurturing and sustaining those identities.

In order to highlight this distinct experience, I compare them with Filipino-white couples and their children. I do this to illustrate how, in many instances, Filipino-white relationships were more politically and culturally complicated, wrought with different kinds of cultural and racial tensions, as opposed to Filipino-Mexican couples, who did not face the same sort of problems or social pressures. Rather, their overlapping histories provided rich, complex layers of shared experiences that began with Spanish colonialism. The stories that follow will demonstrate how this is a distinct experience.

Indeed, having a shared Spanish colonial past, Filipino men found many things in common with their Mexican (as well as other Latina) partners, including Catholicism, Spanish language, and other familial, kinship, and cultural ties.[13] Sociologists in the 1930s, such as Bruno Lasker, noted the shared similarities between Mexicans and Filipinos. Recognizing their common experiences through Spanish colonialism, he stated: "Mexicans in the West have more rapidly come to a friendly understanding with the Filipinos than Protestant groups. The Mexicans, moreover, sharing with the newcomers a history of Spanish domination and likewise being partly of Spanish blood, more frequently fraternize with them, even though there are differences in their dialects and though they are often in direct competition, both social and economic."[14]

A Filipino resident of San Diego provided similar observations when he stated, "We share more similarities with Mexican-Americans than with Asians. . . . We have that combined Spanish and American influence that has blended with our own traditional heritage."[15] Rolando Mata, a Filipino sailor who lived in San Diego, also remarked, "Mexicans and Filipinos almost have the same culture. Like in our culture we were ruled by the Spanish . . . [and] our culture is identical in many ways. Even our food . . . the way we treat our elders, very polite you know."[16] Outsiders have often mistaken Filipinos as Mexican due to their skin color and the fact that a number of them speak Spanish.[17] Regidor Patricio's experiences demonstrate this ethnic perplexity. When Regidor was in Tijuana he was mistaken as a Mexican. He recalled, "Yeah, they didn't know I was Filipino." When he shared his ethnic heritage with them they were surprised.[18] Such testimonies suggest that these physical similarities made social relations easier between the two groups, which led to many relationships between Filipino men and Mexican women. Beginning in the 1930s and continuing throughout the rest of the twentieth century, their children became a distinct byproduct of these unions. When asked why there were a lot of these Filipino-Mexican children, Connie Zuniga, a longtime Mexican resident of Logan Heights, replied: "During the war [World War II] a lot of Filipinos who got out [of] the Philippines by being stewards and they ended up becoming citizens and I think they gravitated to Mexican women because they were Catholics, family oriented. . . . [F]ood is a big factor, like in the Philippines—food, *la comida*—the traditions."[19]

Shared cultural similarities were an important aspect to their relationships. In addition, Spanish colonialism and the cultural mixing that existed since the late sixteenth century left other colonial footprints, namely, their phenotypical resemblances and shared Spanish surnames. Filipinos were even considered a "Spanish-speaking group" by early sociologists such as John Burma because of their similarities with Mexicans.[20]

By marrying Mexican women, Filipinos also avoided the romantic hardships that came with interracial relationships with white women. Filipino-Mexican couples also did not face the social ostracism that Filipino-white couples faced by white society. Sociologist Paul G. Cressey observed this in his 1932 study on taxi dance halls. He wrote, "A few intimate friends may make an exception and admit them [Filipino-white] to their society, but the community as a whole will not. Thus arises the pathetic isolation of the interracial couple." Filipino sociologists, such as Benicio T. Catapusan, recognized the racial intolerance against white women who married Filipinos. They were considered social outcasts within the racial hierarchy of whiteness.[21]

Although many studies about Filipinos in the United States focus on men and their bachelor societies, I contend that their communities were more complex than that. Filipino communities were more than bachelor societies. In San Diego, oral testimonies I conducted and photographic evidence I collected reveal that a handful of Filipino families were present who coexisted with an even larger group comprised of Filipino men with predominately Mexican and other Latina wives.[22] Josephine Armijo, a Mexican who married Simplicio Galbiso, described her community in Niland, California: "Many were bachelors. The rest were married with families. . . . [W]e had a sisterhood with our Filipino men.

The community spirit was great. There were regular gatherings for baptismals, birthdays, the occasional funerals, weddings, end of harvest parties, and many other special occasions. This was a village with an extensive network."[23] Indeed, multiethnic families formed the backbone of Filipino communities that existed both in rural areas and within larger urban neighborhoods, sharing racially segregated, confined spaces with Mexicans, African Americans, Asians, and other nonwhite groups. Ricardo Romio, for example, remembers the community of Logan Heights being very diverse: "The crowd I hung out with, we were all really mixed. There was no separation."[24] Filipino bachelors were connected to these larger multiethnic families and communities and were not separate entities who remained on the fringes.

San Diego's geographical location as a border town with neighboring Tijuana contributed to its ethnic and racial complexity as Mexican immigrants arrived in many of the county's communities. Similarly, the Imperial Valley to the east was also connected as the laborers and their families frequented San Diego. These three locations were intimately connected in this experience as Mexican-Filipino families formed an extensive network between all three locales.[25] San Diego thus became the site where substantial numbers of Mexicans and Filipinos came together over several generations beginning in the late 1920s and early 1930s.

Although Los Angeles has been studied as a site for interracial marriage by early sociologists such as Catapusan, San Diego has also been a locale where generations of Filipino-Mexican marriages took place, both in the county and in neighboring Tijuana and the Imperial Valley. In either case, given their shared social and cultural characteristics, Filipino-Mexican couples comprised the largest numbers of mixed-race unions in these regions. Even contemporary scholars have noted that Filipino-Mexican marriages were numerous.[26] Their multiethnic children have thus been part of a distinct experience that is acknowledged but rarely examined. As Mexipina Gina Lleva noted, regarding the knowledge of San Diego's Mexipino experience, "People in L.A. that I'll meet, they'll be like, oh yeah, she's Mexi-Filipino; there's a lot of those in San Diego. They'll say that. I'm like, really? Is there a support group?"[27]

It has been difficult to fully document all the Mexipinos who live in San Diego. Although some may have similar mixed features that are familiar to other Mexipinos, many are oftentimes mistaken as just Mexican, Filipino, or other ethnicities such as Pacific Islander, Middle Eastern, and American Indian.[28] Given their ethnic ambiguity, Spanish surnames, and the fact that prior to the 2000 census an individual could not mark more than one racial or ethnic category, census reports are also misleading for Mexipinos.

In interviews with Mexipinos in San Diego, they recalled socializing with others like themselves. As these Mexipinos continued to recollect their childhood memories they realized that there were a substantial number of them in their neighborhoods. As Mexicans and Filipinos continue to interact, new generations are being born into a distinct multicultural experience that has shaped generations before them. This large but little-documented group continues to amaze scholars and even fellow Mexipinos who discover that they have met yet another Mexipino as they continue their journey of self-discovery in San Diego. Yet before we can examine their experiences, let us explore the events that set the tone for what became a multigenerational phenomenon.

Prohibiting Love and Intimacy

The story I shared in the beginning of this chapter regarding Felipa Castro and her Filipino husband, Pablo Poscablo, was referenced to raise an important issue. Filipino-Mexican couples in San Diego were able to marry and start their families virtually free from the racial and social pressures of white America; this was not the case for Filipino-white couples. They faced marginalization, violence, and legal measures to prohibit their love and right to marry after 1933. The bond of intimacy that was prevalent between Filipino-Mexican couples enabled them to extend their networks of interethnic couples within the larger Filipino and Mexican communities, giving rise to the Mexipino population, which will be discussed in further detail later in this chapter. The following section will describe how, unlike Filipino-Mexican couples, Filipino-white ones were burdened with ostracism, racial tensions, and dismay over their mixed-race children.

Early Filipino writers of the 1940s, such as Carlos Bulosan and Manuel Buaken, described the experiences they and their countrymen faced in the United States. This was most apparent when it came to whom they could and could not date and marry, especially as it pertained to white women.[29] This was based upon white male sexual insecurity about Filipino sexuality. Basing their sexual fear on racial stereotypes, white men described Filipinos in much the same way as they did African American males. Depicted as oversexualized predators, Filipino men were targets because a large number of them sought the companionship of white women. Given the racial climate, the situation became more problematic because a lot of white women were also attracted to Filipinos, which infuriated white men. Testifying before the House Committee on Immigration and Naturalization in 1930, one white man said, "The Filipinos are . . . a social menace as they will not leave our white girls alone and frequently intermarry."[30] Some references to Filipinos by white men include the following:

"The love-making of the Filipino is primitive, even heathenish . . . more elaborate."

"The Filipinos are hot little rabbits, and many of these white women like them for this reason."

"Filipino boys, with perfect candor, have told me bluntly and boastfully that they practice the art of love with more perfection that white boys, and occasionally one of the [white] girls has supplied me with information to the same effect."[31]

Organizations such as the Native Sons of the Golden West and the Commonwealth Club were up in arms over Filipinos dating and marrying white women. Former superintendent of the Philippine education system and president of the University of California Dr. David P. Barrows simplified the Filipino and his social problems as being "almost entirely based upon sexual passion."[32]

The underlying motive behind this racist thinking was that the relationship between Filipino men and white women threatened white purity. The idea of having mixed-race Filipino-white children was also unacceptable for many white men. Judge D. W. Rohrback, for example, who was known to dislike Filipinos, described them as "little brown men about ten years removed from a bolo and breechcloth."[33] In a statement regarding miscegenation between Filipinos and white women, Rohrback stated, "At the present state of affairs there would be 40,000 half-breeds in California within ten years."[34] Vaughan MacCaughey, editor of the *Sierra Educational News,* also warned that this race mixing would create "a new type of mulatto, a new type of breed, an American mestizo."[35] Similarly, C. M. Goethe's article, "Filipino Immigration Viewed as a Peril," shared the same stance regarding the children of Filipino-white couples: "The Filipino tends to interbreed with near-moron white girls. The resulting hybrid is almost invariably undesirable. The ever increasing brood of children of Filipino coolie fathers and low-grade white mothers may in time constitute a serious social burden . . . [and] immediate exclusion is tragically necessary to protect our American seed stock."[36]

Filipinos' relationships with white women were met with extreme animosity. The violence Filipinos faced at the hands of white men is well documented. These included anti-Filipino race riots in Yakima, Washington, and all throughout California between 1928 and 1930. These were orchestrated by inflammatory remarks by white officials like Judge Rohrback and carried out by white mobs.[37] The fear of creating a hybrid, mongrelized race was part of the sensationalized rhetoric that portrayed Filipinos as a sexual menace and fueled violence. These sentiments not only were about white women, but also were true for light-skinned Mexican taxi dancers who were considered white.[38] For the majority of Mexican women, who were usually nonwhite in appearance and already resembled this hybridization or *mestizaje* (racial and cultural mixing), they could avoid the social pressures white women faced and marry Filipino husbands. For white men, it didn't matter if Filipinos married Mexican women just as long as they did not cross the color line. Sociologist Nellie Foster wrote, "There has been no restriction as to the issuing of licenses to Filipinos and non-whites."[39]

Many of the relationships that occurred were fostered in social spaces like taxi dance halls. They were the primary settings where Filipinos found recreation and love outside of their labor camps and other urban areas where they were employed. In addition to taxi dance halls, there were restaurants, pool halls, and gambling joints where Filipinos could congregate and meet single women.

In the taxi dance halls, the well-dressed Filipino men, wearing McIntosh suits, mingled with white, Mexican, and African American women.[40]

Filipinos who tried to marry white women also faced legal obstacles in the form of miscegenation laws. As Peggy Pascoe notes, by denying their marriages, the state engaged in the legal reproduction of race and racism. Beginning in the late 1920s and throughout the 1930s, Filipinos faced an uphill battle through the courts as they argued for the right to marry their predominately white and, to some extent, light-skinned Mexican wives. Up until 1930, it was up to the licensing clerks to decide if they wanted to issue marriage licenses to Filipinos.[41] San Diego County made it clear that it would not issue marriage licenses to Filipino-white couples. This gained the attention of the Spanish-language media in neighboring Tijuana, where some couples fled to be married.[42]

Filipinos, however, did not stand by idly to this injustice. Rather, they took legal action to demand the right to marry their white wives. Although they saw some minor victories in the early 1930s, two bills were introduced by U.S. Senator Herbert C. Jones to include Filipinos in existing miscegenation laws. Senate Bills numbered 175 and 176 were amended to include Malay into the existing laws that prohibited nonwhites from marrying whites. The legal code stated, "*All marriages* of white persons with negroes, Mongolians, *members of the Malay race,* or mulattoes are illegal and void." Both bills passed unanimously in the Senate and were signed into law on April 20, 1933.[43] Describing the dire situation that Filipino men were put in, sociologist Yen Le Espiritu writes: "When Filipino men refused to be just working bodies and instead flaunted their sexual bodies, they were racialized as sexually threatening. This perceived threat then provided 'justification' for anti-Filipino forces to brutalize their bodies, to enact laws to prevent Filipino-white marriages, and to exclude them from immigrating to the United States. By restricting the migration of Filipinas and by enacting anti-miscegenation laws that prevented Filipino-white marriages, anti-Filipino forces, in effect, outlawed home life for most heterosexual Filipino immigrants. In other words, Filipino migrants . . . were denied a family life."[44]

Filipina scholars Linda España-Maram and Rhacel Salazar Parreñas have also noted the racial dimensions of the law regarding Filipinos in sexual relationships as they pertained to white women in the context of the taxi dance halls. This practice of denying Filipinos a family life was done through the process of controlling and preventing their social reproduction. A combination of the limited number of Filipinas, miscegenation laws, and violence perpetrated by white men ensured that "Filipinos would be unable to produce second-generation Americans."[45]

Although this was true with respect to their involvement with white women, this was not the case with Mexican and other nonwhite women. In fact, many mixed Filipino families thrived within larger multiracial spaces in cities like San Diego, where they married Mexican women. It is this distinct experience of Filipino-Mexican couples, I argue, that helps us to reexamine and rearticulate the families and communities that not only grew but thrived, since they were able to reproduce multiple generations of U.S.-born Mexipinos. Filipinos thus were able to have the family life they desired with their Mexican wives and Mexipino children. Some of these couples were present in San Diego as far back as the early 1920s. Felix Budhi, for example, met and married a Mexican woman by the name of Irma in Ensenada, Mexico. They lived in a section of downtown San Diego where a few other Filipino and Mexican families resided. Others, like Len Monzon, who was in the navy, married Barbara Quines, a U.S.-born Mexipina, in San Diego during the late 1940s. They raised eight children together. Photographic evidence gathered in San Diego up to the postwar years also illustrates the frequency of Filipino-Mexican families, which outnumbered all others, including Filipino-Filipina families.[46]

A Filipino-Panamanian, for example, noted that "many of the wives of Filipino Navy men were Spanish, from Panama, Colombia, and Mexico. A lot of us were half. So, we were the majority."[47] In San Diego during the 1930s when Filipino organizations celebrated Rizal Day, many Filipino men brought Mexican, Panamanian, and other Latina partners to these functions. There, as one newspaper reported, they enjoyed the festivities "while escorting pretty señoritas." There was no mention of Filipinos bringing white women, which is telling of the infrequency of these couples in San Diego at the time. Photographic evidence of social functions also suggests this. Some white women were seen at various Filipino functions in San Diego; however, there were visibly more Mexicans and other Latinas present.[48] Filipino men found that they had a lot more in common with their Mexican wives, could relate better on a cultural level, and were accepted into the Mexican families and community with virtually no hostility. This is not to suggest, however, that the relationship was perfect. Some scholars, such as anthropologist Edwin Almirol, interviewed Filipinos who discussed the undesirability of Mexican wives and focused solely on their differences.[49] However, as most observations noted, such as Bruno Lasker's study in 1931, Mexican women were oftentimes considered the "most suitable spouses" because of their shared similarities with Filipinos. Lasker also stated: "Some of the most successful Filipino marriages are those where the wives are Mexican. Partly because of a similarity of cultural background and of language, often also of common membership in the Catholic Church, Filipinos of a desirable type are accepted into the best Mexican families, and there is no tradition of social superiority on either side."[50]

Veteran Filipino scholars Fred and Dorothy Cordova have also noted that, given the shortage of Filipinas, the Filipino community always consisted of multiethnic or multiracial couples and, because of the cultural similarities of Mexican and Filipinos, these couples seemed to be the most successful of them all.[51] Josefa Armijo Galbiso, for example, recalled the similarities with her Filipino husband, Simplicio: "Because of the Spanish influence in both of our cultures, Simplicio and I found so much in common and joy in our lives.

We found it in our Catholic faith, child rearing practices, and life's goals for our-selves and our children."[52] Moreover, a sample of San Diego County naturaliza-tion records for the years 1935 to 1942 also indicated that a number of Mexican women who filed for their citizenship were married to Filipinos at the time. Most of them were from the Logan Heights area.[53] Longtime resident Lanny Villarin remembers growing up in Logan Heights and seeing Filipino-Mexican couples. He said, "Back in those days they [Filipinos] had to marry somebody, and a lot of them [the women] were Mexicans, a lot of them were South Americans, just as long as they weren't white."[54] Other Filipinas also observed that there were a number of Filipino-Mexican couples. As Charito Balanag recalled, "there was quite a few [Filipinos] that married Mexican women."[55]

Since Mexican women and Filipino men were phenotypically similar and shared Spanish surnames, the licensing clerk usually did not care whether the wife was Mexican. As previously mentioned, although Mexicans were consid-ered legally "white" by law, they were not treated as such. In fact, both the de jure and de facto treatments of Mexicans in terms of racial discrimination and exclu-sion were very similar to the Filipino experience. The exception to the rule was a Mexican who was phenotypically white and mistaken as a white person. Only then were there any questions as to whether or not a Filipino could marry a Mexican woman. On the other hand, there was no opposition to darker-skinned Mexican women marrying Filipinos.

Adding to the complex social networks in a transnational context, Filipino men also went across the border to Tijuana, where they married Mexican women and established communities. Gina Lleva, for example, said that her mother, Bertha, was part of a small community of Mexican women living in Tijuana who dated Filipinos or had Filipino husbands. She stated, "Well, my mother tells me that she met him [her father] through another friend who was also dating a Filipino man. . . . [I]t was like a circuit, a community . . . a circle of women who had been dating Filipino men."[56] Similarly, Rafael Patricio recalled how his parents met. His father, Regidor, was in the U.S. Navy. He used to go with his friends on liberty to Tijuana, where he met his wife, Maximiana, who worked at a local restaurant. Patricio noted, "My dad and his buddies used to eat there and that's how the romance started." This was during the 1950s. They, too, were part of the Filipino-Mexican communities in San Diego and neighboring Tijuana.[57]

FILIPINO-MEXICAN FAMILIES AND COMMUNITIES

Karen Leonard's study of the interethnic relationships between Punjabi men and their Mexican and Mexican American wives in the Imperial Valley, California, provides a useful framework to examine how ethnic identity is invented and reinvented as a coping mechanism to address isolation within one's own com-munity.[58] Although Filipino-Mexican families did not face the same sort of isolation within their larger communities, much can be gained from Leonard's insights into the complexities of interethnic relationships and familial networks. Mexican and Mexican American women, for example, created an extensive female network that not only enabled them to support each other, but also provided the means to introduce others from their ethnic group to Filipino men. In doing so, these women asserted their agency by actively pursuing relationships that proved successful, with love and respect as key components to a successful marriage. Leonard made similar observations, how love and respect played a key role in those marriages that succeeded, despite the high divorce rates of Punjabi-Mexican couples. In contrast, Filipino-Mexican couples had few divorces.[59] Inevitably, the network these women created contributed to more Filipino-Mexican marriages in San Diego, Tijuana, and the Imperial Valley.[60] Indeed, familial and kinship ties were key to how the Filipino and Mexican communities evolved.

The welcoming atmosphere of Mexican families and their communities provided Filipinos with a greater sense of home as they established roots with their Mexican wives who shared similar experiences of isolation, cultural values, and community. These were the first multiethnic families that existed alongside the few Filipino families in San Diego. It was the sizable multiethnic families, however, which demonstrated that intermarriage was so extensive among Filipinos. As Susan Koshy notes, "by 1946, more than half of the immigrants' children were biracial."[61] Consequently, the families also provided a new and different definition of family and home for both Filipinos and Mexicans—a new sense of home beyond the "traditional" family. Indeed, as sociologist Yen Le Espiritu observed in her study on Filipinos in San Diego, "the Filipino community was never all Filipino."[62] Although Filipino men may have been sexual competition for Mexicans, and several fights did occur between them over women, they were minor incidents resulting from jealousy. As one Filipino migrant observed, the jealousy was over the fact that Filipinos "got most of the girls."[63] Gina Lleva also recalled, "You'd have the Mexican men who lived in Tijuana or like even my mom's brothers who, you know, were not very happy with that." However, she continued, "As they met my father they liked the way he was with my mother . . . [and] he was accepted more."[64] Part of the fact was her mother's family did not know what a Filipino was, but upon meeting her father and seeing the way he treated her mother, they were accepting. Gina noted that Filipino men treated Mexican women differently than Mexican men did, which was the reason why there was a community of Mexican women dating and marrying Filipinos. As she recalled her mother's experience, Gina pointed out, "All the women that she met, they would always tell her like, 'Oh, you know the Filipino men, they're good men.'"[65] This statement demonstrates that Mexican women chose to marry Filipino men and spoke well about them to their families and friends because Filipino men did not follow strict patriarchal family structures like some Mexican men did. Filipino men, for example, helped in the kitchen by cooking (a trait many learned as stewards in the U.S. Navy), which was appealing to

Mexican women. Maite Valladolid also shared why she thought her Mexican grandmother married her Filipino grandfather: "I don't know, but I just know that . . . this is my opinion. A lot of Mexicanos are very machistas [men who exhibit hypermasculinity], and I think when you have very strong women who, you know, who on their own came out to the United States and willing to make a better life for themselves and just not for their husbands. . . . I think they look for a strong independent man but who's not willing to be a machista . . . but I don't know. I've never asked. All I know is he [grandfather] did everything for her [grandmother]."[66]

Both Gina's and Maite's statements demonstrate the intimate power Mexican women exerted by choosing *whom* to marry, which in those cases were Filipino men. By recommending Filipino men to their relatives and friends, they continued this process of having control over how they would be treated in their marriages. Witnessing how Filipino husbands treated their wives and noting the cultural similarities between both groups, Mexican families became more accepting and welcomed them into their communities.[67]

Some Mexican families did not initially welcome the Filipino boyfriends and husbands. Tony and Lily Siquiz's story illustrates this initial apprehension. They began their courtship in 1939. When Tony asked for her father's permission to marry her, he refused him because he was Filipino. They ended up eloping to New Mexico and marrying in 1940. Given that her father's approval was important to them both, they decided to tell him the news. Lily shared that tense moment: "When we got back the first thing we did was go see my father and he was OK with it." Tony added, "He became a good friend." They went on to have eight children and celebrated fifty-five years of marriage in 1995.[68] Maximiana Patricio also recalled how her family initially treated her Filipino husband, "Decian mucho. Especialmente los hermanos de mi mama [They criticized me a lot. Especially my mom's brothers]." This was their initial reaction to Maximiana's dating a Filipino but their concern soon changed. Her son Rafael explained: "My observations after all these years, they're very happy with them. They are very accepting; they understand that there's a very big cultural difference, but still a lot of similarities. They love to come to the house and my dad cooks for them. . . . [S]o yeah, they're very happy of their relationship . . . [and] because of the similarities it was easy to accept [them]."[69]

The acceptance of the Mexican families and community in Tijuana was why some Filipinos chose to live there with their Mexican wives and children. Regidor Patricio recalled that many of his friends were also married to Mexican women. As he noted, "We all lived in Tijuana because we all married Mexicans."[70] This was something Rolando Mata also observed about the relationships between Filipino men and Mexican women. Although he and his navy friends dated and married Mexican and Mexipino women, he recalled the couples who lived across the border: "As a matter of fact a lot of Filipinos got married to Mexicans because Tijuana was close."[71]

Filipino-Mexican networks were widespread even within families. When asked about how his mother's family felt about her marrying a Filipino, Ricardo Romio replied, "They never said anything about that because my aunt, her sister, married a Filipino."[72] The Mexican men were oftentimes *compadres* with their Filipino friends. Inadvertently, these friendships reinforced compadrazgo, the familial and kinship bonds that friendship entailed. Mexicans and Filipinos both shared similar family values that were practiced through what were called "familial-social affairs" such as birthdays, baptisms, marriages, and funerals. These strengthened kinship and extended kin ties as family networks grew.[73]

FAMILIAL BONDS: COMPADRAZGO, CATHOLICISM, AND LANGUAGE

Compadrazgo, or "godparenthood," strengthened ties between family, extended family, and family friends as they baptized each other's children and formed stronger ties between each other. As anthropologist Robert Alvarez Jr. noted, this practice illustrated the confianza, or "trust," that was the basis of compadrazgo. Such social relations are exceptionally important especially because they entail a high sense of responsibility, respect, and intimate familial relations.[74] Compadrazgo existed in both cultures. The only difference was grammatical. For instance, Filipinos referred to compadrazgo as *compadrinazgo*. *Kumpari* and *kumari* are the Tagalog variants for Mexican compadre and comadre. Both functioned much the same way with regards to ritual kinship ties and religion.[75]

Catholicism also played a role in fostering their relationships. Filipinos and Mexicans for the most part were Catholic. This provided an opportunity for them to participate in their children's religious upbringing, which, along with the compadrazgo system, strengthened ties between both communities. Most of the Mexipinos I interviewed were also baptized and, in most cases, raised Catholic. Alan Duran Gonzalez's family, for example, attended Our Lady of the Sacred Heart Church in East San Diego. He currently attends Our Lady of Mount Carmel in San Ysidro, where he resides. Gina Lleva was also raised Catholic. Although both of her parents were Catholic, she stated, "My father pretty much left it up to my mother to instill the Catholic religion in us."[76]

Churches such as Our Lady of Guadalupe in Barrio Logan (Logan Heights), Saint Mary's and Saint Anthony's in National City, Saint Jude's in Shelltown, Saint Michael's in Paradise Hills, Saint Charles's in Imperial Beach, and Saint Rita's and Christ the King Church in San Diego are parishes where several generations of Filipino and Mexican communities converge.[77] A sample of baptismal records for Saint Anthony's Catholic Church in National City showed that during the years 1956 to 1965 approximately 7.8 percent of the baptisms recorded were from interethnic couples. Of those seventy-eight interethnic couples that baptized their children at Saint Anthony's, seventy-four were Filipino-Mexican couples. The godparents (sponsors) were mixed, including other Filipino-Mexican, Mexican, Filipino, Filipino-white, and Mexican-Japanese couples.[78] These godparents were a reflection of the way in which Mexicans and Filipinos interacted within their multiethnic community, which played itself out in religious rites, child rearing, and support networks. These included baptisms, confirmations, and marriages. Beyond religious rituals, the shared Catholic culture fostered a sense of extended family. In the event of the parents' deaths, the godparents often took responsibility of the godchild. They understood the social, economic, and religious responsibilities and whole-heartedly participated in them.

Language was another factor that enabled Filipinos and Mexicans to find some common ground. Tagalog, for example, includes thousands of Spanish words in its vocabulary. Chavacano, another dialect, has even more Spanish words. Although many words are spelled differently, they sound very similar and mean the same thing. Moreover, many Filipinos in San Diego during the early twentieth century already spoke or learned Spanish in order to communicate with the Mexican communities around them. When Rafael Patricio's parents met, for example, his father spoke Spanish with his mother. Although his Spanish was not fluent, he was able to communicate because she taught him fluency. He had also learned some of the language prior to meeting her from another Mexican woman he had previously dated. Maite Valladolid's grand-parents also communicated in Spanish. She shared the following story:

> She [grandmother] would tell stories. . . . [S]he kept letters that when he would go off to Fresno or go off to the *campos* and travel to work during the seasons, he would always send her letters. And you could tell when he would write them, and you could also tell when someone who spoke Spanish helped him, 'cause he had very broken Spanish, and the following letter you read it was beautiful Spanish; she was like, "He didn't write that." He tried, he learned Spanish for her, and in their home they only spoke Spanish. And they were learning English so the kids would learn English, and he actually didn't teach my mom or any of my aunts or uncles Ilocano. My aunt would tell me stories; she was like, "Please, please teach me Ilocano," but he goes, "No, no *mija*. You know Spanish and you're learning English; it's going to be too hard." He just didn't want to teach them. From what I hear he adapted a lot to the Mexican culture. And my grandparents, they just spoke Spanish in the home, a little bit of English but mainly Spanish, and they always had their white rice [laughing].[79]

Their story illustrates an important point. Given that Filipinos were living among and dating primarily Mexican women, they took it upon themselves to learn Spanish if they did not know it. Filipinos were able to adapt easily because of their shared colonial past, which resonated with the familiar cultural environ-ment of San Diego's Mexican communities. Gina Lleva's father did not speak much Spanish but eventually learned from her mother. They have since used

Spanish as the way to communicate with each other, rather than English.[80] Others, like Ricardo Romio's father, spoke Spanish, and it was the primary language in his home. It was also how Irene Mena's father and mother communicated. As she recalled, like her father, "the old-time Filipinos spoke Spanish."[81]

The relationship between Filipinos and Mexicans was indeed an amicable one. Their interethnic relationships extended beyond the couple to include family, extended family, fictive kin, and their larger communities. It forged a mutual respect between both Mexicans and Filipinos. As one Filipino said, regarding his Mexican friends, "Our traditions are like one. I feel warmth when it comes to Mexicans. We inherited similar cultural things, the Mexicans and Filipinos."[82] The friendly and harmonious relationships with Mexicans were very different than those of Filipino-white couples. Unlike Filipino-Mexican couples, Filipino-white couples had many cultural obstacles to overcome. These cultural differences constantly led to one partner feeling alienated from his or her spouse's circle of friends and family. As one Filipino recalled, "When among my wife's American friends I cannot make myself feel a part of the groups . . . [and] at times I feel reluctant to talk because of my peculiar accent." Similarly, a white wife of a Filipino stated: "When my husband's friends speak in their dialect, I listen to them with eagerness, trying to grasp the nature of their conversation. When the group laughs, I also 'giggle' with them just to make them feel that I am really a '*makabayan*' [a member of the group]."[83]

These experiences were unlike what Bruce Rowan experienced. As a white man married into a Filipino-Mexican family, he observed the interactions of his wife, Katherine Balino, with her relatives (she was Mexipina). He noted that their relationships were more intimate than those he knew of from other interracial families. Her family and friends got along so well, and he thought this was how all Filipino-Mexican families and communities were.[84] As an outsider to this experience, Bruce found it normal to see Filipinos and Mexicans together. This relationship worked because both groups shared similar traditions centered on family, both immediate and extended. Rachael Ochoa-Tafoya, for example, also saw the importance of family: "I guess the traditions are very close; the backgrounds are very close. . . . I guess I see a closeness in regards to the traditions and family being, it should be, number one in our life always. That's what we were taught growing up, and then religion being important. I guess that's it, being a tighter family unit."[85] Similarly, Rafael Patricio noted how their commonalities made for an ethnic combination that worked. As Patricio explained: "I think because we were both minorities and trying to make it through this society, we had that in common. So, it's easy to do things together. I think that's the big part right there. . . . I think just because of the skin color, the hair, the customs, everything made it so easy. It's like the perfect fit."[86]

Rashaan Meneses also recalled the comforting atmosphere where Mexicans and Filipinos blended together at family functions, sharing in each other's company, food, and music. As Meneses pointed out, "Mexicans and Filipinos are

very much alike. Religiously they are. Culturally they are very, very family oriented. They both have a shared history . . . [and] they've gone through the same
struggles with civil rights and everything. I think in our family they just naturally
gelled. I mean, we're very proud. I mean, when we see our aunts and uncles we
make jokes about being both and how we like to switch between the two. They're
just very symbolic."[87]

The importance of family was definitely a major factor in why Filipino-
Mexican relationships were so successful. Both shared a tradition of having parents, cousins, and other relatives live with the immediate family. They did not see
the immediate family as separate, but rather part of a larger extended one that
oftentimes lived together or in close proximity to one another. Let us now focus on
the children of these families who grew up forging distinct multiethnic and multiracial identities and how they navigated through their respective communities.

American Mestizos and Mexipinos

Another issue that defined Mexipino children as distinct from mixed-race
Filipino-white children was their racial comfort and the level of acceptance by
their respective communities. One of the many issues Filipino-white couples
faced was the prospect of having children. Sociologists in the 1930s considered
these Filipino-white children, or "American mestizos" as they were called, "the
beginning of a new racial group."[88] Although the children were both Filipino and
white, the fact that they were multiracial became a racial dilemma for whites.
Indeed, white women may have fallen in love with their Filipino husbands and
as a couple may have endured isolation from white society, but white women
"do not feel that their conscience permits their bringing into the world children
with such an anomalous racial heritage and with so uncertain a future in our
racially hostile society."[89] A former taxi dancer shared her views on marriage and
children: "I didn't really think of marrying a Filipino until I met Mariano. . . .
[F]or a time I let myself think seriously of marrying him, but down deep I knew
I could never marry a Filipino. One thing I could never get straightened out was
the question of the children. What would they be? They'd be neither Filipinos
nor Americans."[90]

Although race was a cause for concern, generations of American mestizos
were born and raised within the Filipino community. Some were also living in
marginalized spaces within larger cities.[91] Many of their experiences have
become exoticized stories mainly due to their partial white ancestry. They were
also not completely accepted by either the white or the Filipino community.
Phenotype has unquestionably influenced their coming of age as multiracial
Filipinos within interracial families.[92] These experiences suggest that their
identities were fraught with difficulties. For Mexipino children, however, race
did not become such a burden. Their acceptance into the Mexican and Filipino
communities was more widespread since they grew up in nonwhite households

where both parents were usually multiethnic and working class. These multiethnic children did not have to face such staunch racial dynamics, ostracism, and isolation. They were part of larger multiracial communities where Filipinos and Mexicans were mixing for generations.

From Mestizo to Mexipino: Forging New Identities

Mary Poscablo grew up in San Diego's Filipino district where she and her sisters were exposed to the experiences of the early manongs and visiting sailors who frequented the area. In addition to English, Mary also spoke fluent Spanish because of her Mexican mother. Mary identified as a Filipina, however, because she felt a deep connection to her father and his friends, who were constantly present in her life.[93] Other Filipinos who recognized her multiethnic heritage also called her a mestiza. Rolando Mata, who dated her for some time, recalled that because she was mestiza, her beauty and popularity in the Filipino district made her "the toast of the town." Mary often frequented the Filipino district with her Mexican friends who also dated Filipinos. She eventually married a Filipino sailor by the name of Ben and started her own family. In addition to her friends, Mary's two sisters also married Filipinos who were in the navy, and one happened to be Rolando's best friend.[94] What this story suggests is that prior to a Mexipino identity, early multiethnic Mexican-Filipinos were labeled and/or identified as mestizo. As generations of mestizos were born in San Diego throughout the twentieth century, they began to shape a language and experience that suited their multiplicity. I will explore ways in which a Mexipino identity was forged from the term *mestizo* and redefined to represent multiple generations who shared this multiethnic experience.

Location was key to this distinct experience. A substantial number of the Mexipinos I interviewed in San Diego were from the Southeast, the South Bay, and along the waterfront, such as Logan Heights and National City. In these communities, Mexicans, Filipinos, and Mexipinos grew up together in larger multiracial spaces that were predominately Mexican. Given the large Mexican population in these communities and their continued blending with Filipinos, the children of these Filipino-Mexican couples oftentimes looked more physically Mexican. This enabled them to be more readily accepted into the Mexican community. In fact, many of my interviewees recalled that their friends did not even know that some of them were Mexipino. They had the same last name and looked similar to their other Mexican friends. Sometimes their friends assumed that they were just Mexican or Filipino until these Mexipinos told them about their multiethnic background. There was never a moment when they felt rejected. Rather, they were accepted by their peers and participated in both largely Mexican or mixed Mexican and Filipino communities. Virgil Garcia recalled Mexipinos who lived in Logan Heights; "I had good friends that lived three houses down from us that were Filipino-Mexicans."[95] When asked if she remembered if there were any Mexipinos in Logan Heights, Connie Zuniga replied, "Sure, a lot of Mexican-Filipinos. My best friend, Robert, was . . . but mostly those that I knew were culturally Mexican. . . . The mother was Mexican and they were very Mexican culturally, the music, food, they hung out with Mexicans . . . [and] they grew up with the guys."[96] She continued: "If you look at the yearbooks, like at Memorial, you see a lot of Filipino kids or mestizos, you know, Mexican-Filipinos. . . . [T]here was Filipinos in Ocean View, a lot of Filipinos in the area. I just never thought about it because they hung out with the Mexicans, so you didn't think of them as Filipinos. You thought of them, you know, as one of the guys . . . [and] you didn't think about it. . . . [T]hey went to the same parties . . . [and] they went to the same Mexican dances . . . [and] they dated Mexican girls."[97] Irene Mena also noted that "there [were] a lot of Mexican-Filipinos in Logan." She recalled there being at least ten Filipino-Mexican families between Logan Heights and the downtown area of Park Boulevard.[98] When asked if he realized how many Mexipinos lived in Logan, Ricardo Romio replied, "I just never really thought about it. . . . [C]ome to think of it, it is more than I really thought about; there was quite a few. . . . A lot of them lived in the area. I think back to school and I realize that, hey, you know, that guy was a mestizo too." Ricardo met a lot of mestizos in school. The experience strengthened his identity. As he recalled, "Yeah, there were guys that I hung around with that were mestizos. We stayed kind of tight."[99]

Ricardo grew up in the community of Logan Heights. His Filipino father was in the navy and married his mother, who was Mexican. Ricardo grew up alongside Mexicans, Filipinos, and African Americans. As a young man, he was nicknamed "mestizo" by his Mexican and Filipino friends. They saw him as a mestizo, but his physical features highlighted his Mexican heritage. Ricardo identified as a mestizo but also called himself a "Chilipino." Both his self-imposed identity and nickname recognized his multiethnic background.

The term *mestizo* also resonated with both Irene Mena and Freddie Ayap, who grew up in San Diego during the early 1930s and 1940s. Indeed, the term *mestizo* recognized their multiplicity as Filipino and Mexican or Latino (Ayap is Filipino-Panamanian). Their own understanding of the mestizo was reserved for those who were mixed with these ethnicities. In fact, most of the Mexipinos from the 1930s to the 1960s that I interviewed grew up knowing the term *mestizo*, which for them meant being Mexican and Filipino.[100] They did not associate that term with being mixed Filipino-white because the mestizos they knew were Mexican-Filipino. As David Galbiso noted, being mestizo was to be Mexipino.[101] The term *mestizo* equated with what more recent generations called Mexipinos. For these early generations who grew up since the 1940s, mestizo was synonymous with being Filipino-Mexican or Filipino-Latino. Although it was a term that was different from the more recent Mexipino, it meant the same thing for these earlier generations. For those who grew up in the 1970s and 1980s, language was used more frequently as a means to create distinct labels to express this dualistic identity. Terms like "Filicano," "Flipsican," "Jalapino," "Chilipino," "Chicapino,"

"Flippin' Chicano," "fish taco," and the more frequently used "Mexipino" were key language manifestations that described distinct, fluid experiences among contemporary generations of Mexipinos. Psychologist Maria Root, who has written extensively on the multiracial experience, notes that language and self-designation are "important vehicles for self-empowerment of oppressed people. Labels are powerful comments on how one's existence is viewed."[102] Thus, recognizing the multiple layers of connectedness that define this experience, the term *Mexipino* is an affirmation of being both Mexican *and* Filipino.

When interviewing and discussing if they had ever heard of the term *Mexipino,* the generations who came of age from the 1930s to the 1960s had not, but found it amusing. They saw this as a more creative way to identify their experience. What is interesting is that Ricardo frequently used the new term *Mexipino* and used it interchangeably with chilipino and mestizo, thus including it in his existing vocabulary. Ricardo's adoption of the term *Mexipino* connected him to this multigenerational identity; yet he did recognize that coming age during the late 1940s and 1950s, his generation did not have the creative use of language that later generations utilized to define themselves today. Others, like Irene Mena and David Galbiso, also incorporated the term into their existing vocabulary. Although Rosalie Zarate did not know of the term *Mexipino* when she was growing up during the 1940s and 1950s, she did hear of the words "Flipsican" and "halo-halo."[103]

Those who came of age since the 1960s were a part of the "biracial baby boom."[104] This generation was more consciously aware of their identity as being mixed and used language as a creative way to express their multiplicity. Unlike preceding generations that always acknowledged their multiethnic background but did not utilize language to discuss their mixed heritage outside of the pre-existing term *mestizo* and a few other words, newer generations of Mexipinos who were more socialized at home to embrace all their racial/ethnic identities were more likely to play with self-designating terms to capture their multiplicity. Mexipinos thus defined themselves on their own terms. They did not have to consider themselves either/or nor adhere to monoracial categories. Their very existence and the use of self-designating terms were forms of resistance and transformed racial categories, hierarchies, and boundaries.[105] Moreover, despite the ages of my interviewees or which generation they grew up in, the term *Mexipino* bound them all together as individuals who identify with both their Mexican and Filipino ancestries but also recognizes their distinct experiences.[106] Rashaan Meneses talked about the term *Mexipina,* which she grew up using: "I actually love it [Mexipino] because not many people are familiar with it and they don't know what it means. And it feels like . . . it gives you a space where it's set apart from being Mexican or Filipino. And I also know because of my own background that it can mean anything. But even though you're Mexipino you are going to have . . . a different story to tell and different experiences even though we have these shared things. We're the same but different and that's what

Mexipino means—same but different. It gives you that whole psychological space of acceptance on those terms of being the same yet different."[107]

Mexipinos, however, are not the only multiethnic/multiracial individuals to use such language to define their mixed identities. Other racially and ethnically mixed individuals also expressed their multiracial/multiethnic identity by creating terms to describe their own multiplicity, including "Afropino" (African American/Filipino), "Blaxican" (Black and Mexican), "Mexichino" (Mexican/Chinese), "LatiNegra" (Latin American/Black), "Blasian" (Black/Asian), and "Filirican" (Filipino/Puerto Rican).[108] Indeed, *Mexipino* and the other terms that describe this experience are born from a generation that had a growing multiracial population, and thus they were more likely to be socialized to embrace all their identities. They had a more conscious understanding of what these terms symbolized in the process of negotiating their identities. The use of these terms has political implications and plays into current issues of identity politics, particularly in colleges and universities where young Mexipinos and other multiethnic and multiracial students learn to formulate and express their complex heritages and identities. In this context, *Mexipino* is used as a term of empowerment and resistance because, as previously noted, it "acknowledges the multiethnic character of the individual. It takes the two familiar terms, Mexican and Filipino, and transform[s] them into a new concept, *Mexipino*. . . . [T]his new term states that multiethnicity must be addressed and recognized."[109] Other self-identifying terms were also interchanged with Mexipino. Ricardo Romio recalled, "My wife's mother used to call me chilipino. Back then some of the guys would say 'flippin' Chicano.' . . . [T]here was all those other mestizos around that we hung around with together, so we all learned from each other."[110] Similarly, Rashaan Meneses and Gina Lleva called themselves Chicapina or Mexipina. Gina said that she and her sister interchanged these terms all the time.[111]

Growing Up Mexipino

Understanding what it meant to be Mexipino involved a rich cultural experience that blended elements from both parents' cultures. Most of the interviewees with whom I spoke grew up with Mexican mothers and generally spoke Spanish. Both parents were usually Catholic, attended Catholic Churches, and, oftentimes, cooked and expressed an aspect of their culture through food. Their children were exposed to a multiethnic, multicultural upbringing. Their communities, although multiracial, were largely Mexican. This suggests the children had more of a Mexican than Filipino influence and upbringing, not only because of San Diego's proximity to Mexico, but also, even more, because of their Mexican mothers. It was Mexican mothers who taught their Mexipino children cultural traditions and language. It was the women who provided the foundation for the children's cultural upbringing. Filipino men left these aspects of childrearing to the Mexican women, which allowed most of the children to identify more with their mother's culture. This gendered aspect to their identity shows the importance of women to their cultural development and how, despite their pride in being both Mexican and Filipino, Mexipinos had stronger Mexican and Chicano sensibilities.

Indeed, the Mexipinos I interviewed acknowledged that although they were conscious of being both Mexican and Filipino, culturally they were raised Mexican. As Gina Lleva noted, "Since my dad didn't have a lot of connection to his Filipino side, or his family in the Philippines . . . I wasn't raised with a lot of the Filipino side."[112] Thus, Gina identified more with her Mexican side, although she always consciously knew that she was not completely Mexican. Seeing how her family functioned, which she noted was different than her Mexican friends' families, personally confirmed the multiethnic complexity of her family's makeup. Similarly, Lanny Villarin, a Filipino who grew up in Logan Heights, recalled, "I would say they [Filipinos] hang around more with the Mexicans. . . . [A] lot of them went to the FAVA [Filipino American Veterans Association] Hall and became talented musicians. . . . [N]ot everybody was a full-blooded Filipino."[113]

Mexipino children were always conscious of their Filipino fathers and what that identity meant. Being surrounded by many of their fathers' friends, or, as they referred to them, "uncles," and frequenting the Filipino district in San Diego and other social events, many of these Mexipino children were exposed to their father's culture in tangible ways. This differed from what Barbara Posadas stated regarding Filipino-white mestizas, who "acknowledge their parental background, but function more as the products of an American mass culture than of an ethnic enclave. . . . [T]he islands themselves were a distant memory to most."[114] Although American mass culture wiped away the cultural memories of the Filipino-white children she documented, it was not the case for Mexipinos in San Diego. Rather, they embraced their cultural identities and thrived in their multiracial communities.

Even though Mexipino children were raised by Mexican mothers and identified more with their maternal culture, their connection to their fathers instilled pride in being Filipino. Indeed, many of the interviewees recalled memories that they looked upon fondly as being the symbol of their Filipino identity. Ricardo Romio, for example, remembered his father had a ukulele that he used to play all the time. As he recalled, "He just sat in his little corner smoking a cigar. He would play the ukulele and sing."[115] Ricardo also listened attentively to his dad and "uncles" talk, trying to understand their language but bathing himself in the experience, which he holds dear. He said, "My father was always gone. But I never learned to speak Tagalog. I learned to speak Spanish because my grandparents and mother used to speak to me in Spanish, and I would answer in English. . . . My father, when he came home, he would speak Tagalog with all his friends and everything. I knew by the gestures what they were talking about, but I didn't understand the language and I never really learned. I learned to cook from him. I make adobo and pancit."[116] Rafael Patricio also recalled how his father used to play Mexican and Filipino songs on his ukulele for him and his siblings when they were children.[117] Freddie Ayap shared his childhood memories of when he accompanied his father to various social events at FAVA Hall on Market Street in San Diego. There were other Filipinos present at FAVA Hall with their wives, which included other Filipinas, some whites, but principally Mexicans and some Panamanians. He was always proud to say he was Filipino; even to this day, he greets others whom he finds out are Filipino with a welcoming smile and conversation about their shared heritage.[118] All of the Mexipinos I interviewed displayed a strong sense of pride for their Filipino heritage despite the fact that their cultural exposure to Filipino traditions was limited.

Indeed, listening to their father's language also connected them to their Filipino heritage.[119] They heard Tagalog, Ilocano, or other dialects spoken around them. They heard the songs that the countrymen sang in the rondalla groups; they saw the brown faces of these manongs as a reminder of their fathers' homeland and frequently were exposed to the social gatherings and cultural events that the Filipino community organized. Community events also brought together Filipino and mixed couples and reinforced Filipino traditions and customs. This exposure is what converged with the direct influence of their mothers' culture and language. Thus, despite their geographic and emotional distance from the Philippines, Mexipinos were exposed to their Filipino culture. They celebrated those memories, which gave them a sense of pride and a reason why they claimed their multiethnic heritage.[120]

Not all of the Mexipinos interviewed were comprised of Filipino fathers and Mexican mothers. Vanessa Solis, for example, had a Filipina mother and Mexican father. She spent more time with her mother's side of the family and was thus a bit more familiar with Filipino culture. She remembered: "I think growing up I identified with the Filipino side a little bit more because I looked like it [Filipino] and was surrounded more by my Filipino side of the family . . . but now, I identify pretty much as half and half. . . . [M]y mom's Filipino and my dad's Mexican and that's it. I think that I balance out a little more now that I've put myself more in the Mexican culture. . . . [I]t brought more of the Mexican out of me, you can say. But yeah, I pretty much identify myself as half and half. I don't do any one more than the other. . . . Mexipino, that's what I am."[121] Yet Vanessa also acknowledged that her Mexican aunt, who married her Filipino uncle, also influenced her. Vanessa's cousins were also Mexipino. Since she grew up with them, Vanessa was also exposed to Mexican culture. Reflecting on this, Vanessa replied, "They made the food and spoke Spanish around me. I had both, pretty much equal."[122] Rosalie Zarate, who had a Filipino father and Mexican mother, said, "My culture was more, I would say, of a Filipino nature. I ate rice more than I ate beans and tortillas. I could eat rice every day." However, she went on to say, "I feel that I am both cultures."[123] Yet, unlike Vanessa and a few other interviewees who looked more Filipino, many of the Mexipinos interviewed looked phenotypically

Mexican. For some, though, their features were difficult to discern. The responses to how they were accepted by either community were somewhat varied. Although the majority found acceptance in both, it was mostly the Mexican community in which they felt more comfortable because that was the culture in which most of them had been raised, both in the home and in San Diego at large.

These stories demonstrate that longstanding Mexipino residents were almost universally accepted in their communities because of generations of mixing that occurred between Filipinos and Mexicans in San Diego. This is not to suggest that Mexipinos were always accepted. On the contrary, new generations of Mexipinos post 1960s faced identity obstacles primarily within the Filipino community. Filipino immigrants who came after 1965 often questioned the identity of the longtime Mexipino residents who asserted both their Mexican and Filipino identities. This was disturbing to some Mexipinos who were angry at the fact that they were questioned by recently arrived immigrants and others from newer Filipino communities. Filipino immigrants may not have been familiar with or understood what the historical implications of interethnic mixing meant for Mexipinos and the multiethnic communities from which they came. Moreover, this tension between U.S.-born Mexipinos, Mexicans, Filipinos, and immigrants coming from both Mexico and the Philippines created problems between the two groups.[124] Intra-ethnic tensions also exist between Filipinos as well. Resident Lanny Villarin remarked about post-1965 Filipino immigrants, "They kind of segregate themselves from you, and you don't feel loved by your own people, even though you are Filipino too. You feel like an outcast because you're not like them."[125] For Mexipinos, however, it was more complicated. They had to deal with both their Mexican and Filipino sides because they were multiethnic. Yet they asserted their right to be both because their very existence challenged the notion of what it meant to be Mexican *and* Filipino.

At times, Mexipinos still faced questions of cultural authenticity and feelings of rejection because they did not fit Filipino expectations of what being Filipino meant. Oral testimonies suggest that this was one reason why they carved out a separate identity for themselves as multiethnic individuals. They created a separate space that allowed them to identify as mixed, with the intersecting identities of Mexican and Filipino. Although this was something that many of them faced within more contemporary Filipino communities, they often did not face any rejection from Mexican communities. The only time identity came into question was with regards to language and whether the Mexipinos spoke Spanish or not. This was also true for Filipinos who questioned the Mexipinos on this cultural trait. David Galbiso said, "Filipinos would ask me, do you speak the language [Tagalog]. It made me angry because I had just been marginalized." He would respond, "No, my dad was Ilocano. . . . Why would you think I want to speak Tagalog?"[126] His resistance to the authenticity of his ethnic identity rested on his language proficiency and challenged the norm that Tagalog was the official Filipino language. To those concerned with Filipino authenticity, languages helped them legitimize "Filipinoness" and resist marginalization, yet, because the majority of Mexipinos did speak Spanish, it was the Mexican community that was oftentimes more inviting.[127] The identity of Mexipinos who grew up within the older established Mexican-Filipino communities—where they historically shared the same living space—was practically never questioned.

The subtle notions of singling out Mexipinos within their group of friends were also apparent. When Vanessa's Mexican friends introduced her to others, for example, she was known as the "Filipino one." This bothered her because she did not want to be singled out but wanted to be known as both Filipino *and* Mexican.[128] Most people thought Ricardo was just Mexican and not Filipino. But as soon as they found out that he was Filipino, the bond was formed. He said, "The closeness came as soon as they found out that I was [Mexipino], but most of the time they say, 'You don't look Filipino.'" Nonetheless, he was accepted as Filipino.[129] Gina Lleva did not look exactly Mexican according to her peers. She noted, "I didn't take into consideration that I didn't look Mexican, because I always felt I was. You know I never questioned it. . . . [A]s I get older . . . they don't think I'm Mexican and so that's a big shock for me."[130] She was raised by her Mexican mother and lived in a multiethnic community that was predominately Mexican. Gina was also more accepted by the Mexican community. She pointed out: "They [post-1965 Filipinos] would always ask me if I spoke Tagalog or, you know, certain things of the culture that I was not familiar with because I did not have exposure to. I always felt a little less accepted, I would say, or just not as connected . . . from my experiences because I have a lot more contact with Mexicans. I've always felt I've never had a problem. I have always been accepted by that community."[131]

Alan Duran Gonzalez also identified more with his Mexican culture because of his mother, yet he was always aware of his Filipino background. As he recalled: "Primarily, I was raised in a Mexican environment. But my mom did let me know about my Filipino heritage. . . . It wasn't a whole lot because my mom just concentrated on raising me with the Mexican side. . . . Yes, I was raised more by my mom's side and, yes, I am more Latino, but I'm also not going to neglect my Filipino side."[132] Although Alan did not try to take sides, at times his identity was called into question because he did not look completely Mexican or Filipino. He said, "Because I don't speak the language [Tagalog] and I don't know all the culture and sometimes these old ladies [Filipinas] that I see around town just gave me these weird, mean looks." It was also the same within the Mexican community outside of his family. He stated, "There were some Latinos and Mexicans that were like, 'You're not all Mexican.' And in a way, it kind of pissed me off because I didn't have all of the other basic features."[133] Alan's statement is telling because it illustrates the treatment he received from both communities. He did not exactly fit into either ethnic group because of his lack of cultural knowledge and physical features, which is a rare experience for the Mexipinos I interviewed. Alan grew up in the 1980s and his experience is exemplary of the post-1965 attitude of Filipinos toward Mexipinos who lacked the cultural expressions that recently arrived Filipino immigrants looked for.

Similarly, Suzanna Balino Fernandez recalled: "The Mexicans thought you were too 'Oriental' and the Filipinos thought you were too Mexican. If you didn't know Spanish, they [the Mexicans] would make fun of you, and if you didn't know Tagalog, they [the Filipinos] would make fun of you too. It was hard because I had friends in both cultures and all that, but it wasn't easy all the time because you were called half-breed or some other stupid remarks."[134] Suzanna's comments illustrate how difficult it was for some Mexipinos to prove their identity to each respective community based on their cultural authenticity. Despite their sincere efforts to fit in, Mexipinos were just not Filipino or Mexican enough. Although these few examples show some of the extreme alienation or marginalization, their experiences were the minority within the social interactions and acceptance that most other Mexipinos experienced. What these oral testimonies suggest is that although their multiplicity was complex and tensions did exist within their own communities at times, the positive experiences all of the interviewees shared because they grew up in a multicultural household far outweighed the negative treatment they received.

Rafael Patricio, for example, grew up knowing both his Filipino and Mexican cultures although he was raised culturally Mexican. He remembered, "We felt stronger ties to the Mexican side and the language also came first. And we had all our uncles and aunts [who] over the years raised us predominately Mexican with a hint of Filipino culture." Rafael's father did not have any family in the United States and his cultural influence on his children was less prominent. His only contact was with other Filipinos who lived in Tijuana and San Diego who also had Mexican wives.[135] His father's Filipino influence was evident, however, especially with food. Whenever Rafael visited his friends at their houses he would ask, "No hay arroz? [There's no rice?]" They gave him Mexican rice rather than steamed white rice, and, as he recalled, "It took until maybe the fourth or fifth grade that I figured out that I was a little bit different. We had to have rice, and then all the other kids always had tortillas."[136] Phenotypically, everybody assumed he was Mexican and were surprised when he told them he was also Filipino. As he noted, "When you tell them you're half Filipino, they're surprised. But they still treat you the same. And then they say, 'Oh, that explains your eyes . . . [and] that explains why you eat rice so much.'"[137] Marissa Mariscal stated that people would tell her, "You look Mexican but . . ." or, "You look like you're Filipino, but you have . . ."[138] This was a common experience for many of the Mexipinos I interviewed, who forged their identity as being both multiethnic and ethnically ambiguous at the same time.

Growing up in National City, Rafael had a multitude of friends including Mexipinos, Mexicans, and Filipinos. His friendships with other Mexipinos were strong, yet for the larger group of friends that he hung around with, he noted: "In the community that I come from we did a lot of things together. The boyfriends and girlfriends, they mixed. The parties were mixed . . . [but] nowadays there's rivalry between Mexicans and Filipinos in some parts of the community here in San Diego, which is sad because it'd be better if we got along."[139] He blamed this on recent gang violence, which has divided younger post-1965 Mexican and Filipino youth in his community.[140] For his generation, however, they all got along most of the time, except for one incident, which challenged his identity. As Rafael recalled, in the ninth grade the Mexican kids were going to fight the Filipino and African American kids. Half of the school seemed to show up at the park with their sticks and chains. When the fight broke out he just stood there. He said: "I was literally in the middle of the whole thing. . . . [W]hen the Filipino kids came up to me, I remember one kid came up to me with a chain. He looked at me and I looked at him . . . [and] we just said there's no problem, no fight between us. So he just came past me and hit some other kid with the chain. I was torn between the two. . . . I was in the middle of the whole thing and I just stood there. I wasn't going to fight with the Filipino kids because they were my friends, and I wasn't going to fight with the Mexicans."[141] Rafael's choice not to fight illustrates how he recognized both of his cultures and the tension induced by his mixed identity. It was symbolic in that he could not fight for either side but, rather, stood in the middle and negotiated his decision. In the end, both groups respected his decision not to choose sides. By refusing to fight, Rafael's Mexipino identity demonstrates the sociocultural and political resistance he employed against identity politics that often causes other mixed-race individuals to choose sides.

FOOD, CULTURE, AND IDENTITY

One of the largest indicators of how Mexipinos identified with both their Filipino and Mexican cultures was through food. The fact that they literally consumed their cultures was their way of connecting with both of their identities. Food enabled Mexipinos to reinforce and reinterpret their multiethnic identity as a means of survival; it nourished and sustained them culturally. Foods such as *menudo, adobo, empanadas,* and *caldo de arroz* shared their Spanish influence. At the dinner table there was Filipino or Mexican food and, oftentimes, a combination of the two. These included, for example, steamed rice, beans, chicken adobo, tortillas, salsa, soy sauce, *lumpia,* and carne asada, among other delicacies. Ricardo Romio's memories of growing up in San Diego emphasized both cultures and centered on food—what he ate and learned to cook. As he recalled, "With my mother I ate beans, and with my dad I ate rice. But I learned how to make little ribs, sweet and sour ribs, chop suey, and adobo. From my mother, beans, and she used to make empanadas."[142] Sophia Limjoco remembered: "When we have parties, both the Mexican and Filipino sides of our family get together. There are a lot of people there! Our food is a combination of Mexican and Filipino. We have tortillas, beans, salsa, *nopales,* as well as lumpia, rice, *pan de sal,* and sandwiches. It's great!"[143] Vanessa Solis also noted at her family parties, "We got adobo, *pancit,* lumpia, tamales, carne asada, Spanish and white rice . . . all kinds of stuff. Food is one of the large parts . . . one of the main factors of family get-togethers." She also jokingly said that at these same family parties "everyone is invited and everyone brings something. There's always tons of food. That's just how it is with Filipinos and Mexicans. Everyone, of course, is going to show up late [laughing]."[144]

Whether the food they ate from both cultures was served alternatively during the week or mixed at the dinner table, the Mexipinos I interviewed were consistently exposed to their cultures through food. It was, however, more than a surface connection to their culture. Rather, it was an intimate experience that reinforced their multiethnic identity. Having a mixed cuisine was especially prevalent during the holidays and family functions, which included other aspects of Mexican or Latino culture. Rashaan Meneses recalled how at her family functions they had a combination of salsa music and Filipino food.[145] Gina Lleva noted that food connected her to the Filipino culture; cultural awareness was "definitely through food because it was not the language."[146] She recalled her holidays in San Diego: "We always had Mexican food. We would have tamales and then we'd have lumpia, you know. At our house we always had rice, white rice always there, and beans. And then there would be certain foods like *mole* that you would eat normally with beans and tortillas and that we would eat it with white rice."[147] Indeed, for Gina, food was how she was able to connect with her culture since she did not know the language. Alan Duran Gonzalez also described his family meals, which were Mexican and Filipino but made on alternate days: "Like one night would probably be carne asada; the next night would be chicken adobo. The next night would be pancit and then enchiladas."[148] Rashaan also shared her family experiences with food: "She [her mother] would cook Mexican food, Filipino food; my dad would cook both too. He would cook his menudo; they would both cook adobo. . . . They definitely mixed it. We'd have lumpia and homemade enchiladas together . . . [and] adobo was made at least once a week, *machaca* on weekends, or a bowl of menudo."[149]

Rosalie Zarate recalled how both of her parents cooked. It was her mother, however, who used to make Filipino and Mexican food. It was something she learned working in a Filipino restaurant in Los Angeles before moving to San Diego. Rosalie recalled, "Oh, she made excellent Filipino food. She'd make the best *sinagang hipon.* She'd put chili in it."[150] Rafael Patricio also shared his experience with food and how it defined his Mexipino identity in San Diego: "One of my favorite meals is pancit with tamales, the best combination. We get the best of two cultures. Yeah, my dad would make chicken adobo and my mom would make enchiladas de pollo, and they go together very well, . . . I think that maybe the pancit coming with the tamales and the rice and tortillas with chicken adobo on the table summarizes my whole experience. . . . [E]verything complemented each other."[151]

As these numerous examples demonstrate, food was the strongest factor in how Mexipinos in San Diego identified with both cultures and what it meant to be multiethnic. Their meals illustrated their complex identity on the dinner table and during family get-togethers. The consumption of their cultures enabled them to make an important connection, albeit one that may not have always been recognized by others. Food was the occasion that brought them into contact with their Mexican and Filipino families, where stories were told and memories were ingrained, and that, to them, was a Mexipino experience.

MEXIPINO AS "*NEPANTLERAS*": A MULTIETHNIC PERSPECTIVE

For Mexipinos like Rafael Patricio, the experience of being both Mexican and Filipino made him a better, well-rounded person. He saw strength in being mixed. The fact that they were multiethnic made those Mexipinos I interviewed more conscious of their surroundings and more open-minded, as some suggested. Their multiplicity was a reason to be proud. Sophia Limjoco observed: "Our Mexipino culture is unique. Our cultures are so similar. We may deal with some prejudice, but there is a lot more understanding between the two cultures. Being Mexipino also opens us up to learning about other people's cultures and who people are because of what they are. It helps us to associate well with others. It is much different than a black and white racial mix, like my friend, where the two sides are always played against each other culturally. It is not like that with us."[152] Marissa Mariscal also noted the advantages of being a Mexipina. She put it this way: "I think being Mexipino is a total advantage. . . . [Y]ou just become so open-minded, and I notice, with a lot of other people that are mixed, you're not just open-minded to both Mexican and Filipino, but everyone. I think you become open-minded to everything and you see and become attracted to other people. So I love being like this. I just think that it makes you open-minded to other people and cultures."[153]

Mexipinos did not see one side of their ethnic identity as more valuable than the other. Rather, their mixed identity empowered them with the knowledge that they were not culturally inferior to those who identified as monoethnic.[154] Mexipinos thus found that their multiplicity was an advantage that far outweighed any negative experiences they had to endure. Rashaan Meneses, for example, had a distinct experience. Both of her parents went to college and they exposed her to different cultural events and gatherings, especially Filipino. In fact, she did things that, according to her peers, did not seem "Filipino," like joining theater groups and listening to music other than hip hop. Rashaan's decision to try other things did not make her any less Filipina. It was just a different way of being Filipina. Indeed, since Rashaan's mother was Filipina, she felt more familiar with Filipino values. She said, "Going to my grandparents' house in Stockton was like my direct plug into what was Filipino. Waking up in the morning and hearing them speak Visayan and eating their donuts and their coffee, that was what essentially being Filipino was about." As for her Mexican side, she observed, "Going to my grandmother's house, I smelled the menudo, and she'll have the *telenovela* on the station and they'll be kids running around all over the place. . . . [T]hat was what being Mexican was for me."[155] She also noted the advantages of being multiethnic. Rashaan and other Mexipinos in San Diego are the bridges between both cultures because they live a multicultural existence. Multiethnic and multiracial people have already experienced an alternative worldview, which has positive implications. She described it in terms of the future of racial and ethnic mixing: "I think it's inevitable. . . . *Time* magazine put up all the races together to see what it [hypothetical person of the future] would look like, and it looked like a Filipino. You know, it's like we're already there; we've been there. We're just bringing it to the forefront."[156]

Like Rashaan, Gina Lleva saw her multiethnic identity as a positive thing. For Gina, her identity made her more accepting of different cultures and more open-minded. In fact, she recalled how most of her friends were also multiethnic or multiracial: "We had that commonality of not being one or the other."[157] Her experiences in college and her ability to work through the complexity of her life were what reinforced this comfort with her multiplicity. Her experience illustrates the majority of this particular generation of Mexipinos in San Diego born after 1965. Gina noted, "I'm totally OK with being multiracial and, like, I love it. I like having these two cultures. . . . I listen to Mexican music, but, you know, I like Filipino food. It's just embracing who you are, just coming to terms with that."[158]

Irene Mena was always conscious of her identity, being Mexican, Chicana, and also Filipina. She said, "I never denied being Filipino. I was proud to be both."[159] Similarly, for Rafael, his mother taught him to be proud of his heritage: "We were always very proud to announce that we were Filipino. It wasn't like we kind of hid it or denied it, even though we didn't live with a lot of Filipino culture and didn't know the language; but there was a lot of pride. But whenever people ask me what I feel stronger for or what am I more proud of, I say fifty-fifty. Even if I do feel stronger of the Mexican side, the pride is there."[160] Their pride in being both Mexican and Filipino and their assertion of a multiethnic identity as Mexipinos show how this subcommunity within the larger Mexican and Filipino communities was distinct in its own right. Indeed, my study contradicts what sociologist John H. Burma once wrote about Mexipinos. Burma suggested that Filipinos of mixed Mexican-Filipino parentage "will become more and more dilute and eventually may disappear."[161] The fact that Mexipinos have endured over several generations and multiplied their numbers certainly dispels Burma's hasty prediction. The examples of mixed Filipino-Mexican couples and their multigenerational relationships illustrated here attest to a phenomenon that suggests otherwise. Rather, their communities and lived experiences continue to shape multiple racial formations in San Diego in the twenty-first century.

Mexipino identity, then, is also what Karen Leonard calls a "historical construction and reconstruction of identity . . . consciously drawing on multiple cultural traditions."[162] Mexipinos construct and reconstruct an identity that is distinctly Mexipino, fusing the cultural elements of both Mexican and Filipino identity as well as their American upbringing. In the words of Gloria Anzaldúa, this new consciousness enables Mexipinos to "continually walk out of one culture and into another, because I am all cultures at the same time."[163] This in-between or "new middle" is a liminal space where Mexipinos can forge a separate and distinct experience. Mexipinos can thus be considered what Anzaldúa calls "*nepantleras,*" who, as literary scholar AnaLouise Keating writes, "move within and among multiple, often conflicting, worlds and refuse to align themselves exclusively with any single individual, group, or belief system. This refusal is not easy; nepantleras must be willing to open themselves to personal risks and potential woundings which include, but are not limited to, self-division, isolation, misunderstanding, rejection and accusations of disloyalty. Yet the risk-taking has its own rewards, for nepantleras use their movements among divergent worlds to develop innovative, potentially transformative perspectives. They respect the differences within and among the diverse groups and, *simultaneously,* posit commonalities."[164]

Indeed, by embracing their multiplicity, Mexipinos are able to develop an alternate consciousness to express their multiple ancestries in ways that are important for them to understand how they view the world in relation to their multiethnic and multicultural upbringing. Their identity is fluid, never fixed. It is based on a historical bond between two ethnic groups and communities that lived, worked, worshipped, and socialized together on various levels and in multiple contexts. Identity is thus a continual process, which relies on context.[165] As risk takers, Mexipinos challenge their own communities to reconceptualize what it means to be Mexican, Chicano, Filipino, and/or Pinoy.[166]

Filipino-Mexican relationships are illustrative of complex overlapping histories that have fostered several generations of Mexipino children since the 1930s. This is no accident. Filipinos and Mexicans had multiple threads of commonalities and "interzones" that bound them together. The legacy of Spanish colonialism left these two groups with many cultural, linguistic, and religious similarities. By and large, these multiethnic families continued to foster the relationship between both groups as members of their family also married other Mexicans or Filipinos.

What is even more telling about this experience is the gender ratio which finally started leveling out for the Filipino population. First, with Filipino participation in the armed forces in World War II, they were granted U.S. citizenship. With their newfound citizenship, they were able to marry their Filipina girlfriends whom they met in the Philippines and bring them over to the United

States as war brides. Given the phenomenal rise of Filipino marriages in cities like San Diego, these war brides were among the 2,500 percent increase of Filipino immigrants who came to the United States between 1945 and 1946.[167] Second was the 1965 Immigration Act, which initiated a "female-dominated flow" of Filipinas to the United States through the family reunification and special job skills provisions. Despite the gender balance in the Filipino community, intermarriage with Mexicans continued in San Diego well after 1965.[168] Filipinos did marry each other in increasing numbers. Filipino men, however, continued to marry Mexican and Chicana women; and more recently, with the presence of Filipinas, they too began to date and marry Mexican and Chicano men. Such is the case with Vanessa Solis's and Rashaan Meneses's parents. Similarly, Gina Lleva remarked how one of her friends who is Mexican, and whose wife is Filipina, has Mexipino children, and they speak Tagalog because of the mother and are closer to the Filipino side of their family.[169] This is a phenomenon not to ignore.

Moreover, the continued influx of Filipino and Mexican immigrants, along with their U.S.-born children, also perpetuates Mexipino identity in San Diego. New generations of Mexipinos are being born, increasing their numbers. Some of the interviewees have as many as four generations of Mexipinos in their families. The relationship between Filipinos and Mexicans in San Diego is unlike any other type. The complexity generates tension between the two groups at times, but it has not resembled the hostility sparked by individuals who have dared to cross the color line. This tension has played itself out more on the economic level since both Mexicans and Filipinos sought the same types of jobs in areas such as agriculture. In addition, both groups may not have always been in harmony or worked together for common goals. There were real tensions and differences, yet what prevailed were the overlapping histories, numerous similarities, and shared experiences Mexicans and Filipinos had with each other. I contend that unlike other racial and ethnic relationships, theirs seemed to have been the most amicable and successful. It was one where common bonds were tightly woven through their overlapping histories; similar socioeconomic experiences; cultural, religious, and other kinship rituals; labor and civil rights struggles; and social and work cultures where friendships and relationships were formed and reinforced over generations. It is because of this unique dynamic that I find the relationship between Mexicans and Filipinos to be a distinct experience that we can learn from in terms of interethnic relations and the importance of fostering ties between various racial and ethnic groups. Their multiethnic children, who have come of age since the 1930s, continue to serve as cultural mediators by fostering alliances between their communities. Their lives are an example of how prevalent this relationship is in San Diego and other geographic areas where Mexicans and Filipinos coexist.

After examining the lives of Mexipinos, we see how their experiences reflected their interethnic relationships that were forged out of similarities with colonialism, race, immigration, labor, and geographical space. They provide a critical lens to understand how communities function not only as separate entities but also in relationship to each other in larger society. For earlier Mexipinos, their place was never really questioned in their communities. As we will see in the epilogue, with the coming of the post-1965 immigrants from the Philippines and Mexico, tensions increased with U.S.-born Filipinos, Chicanos, and Mexipinos who were longtime residents of San Diego. For Mexipinos, their very existence challenges and redefines what it means to be Mexican *and* Filipino, Chicano *and* Pinoy, even something else, and still be accepted within their communities in San Diego. To marginalize this large group of mixed Mexipinos on either side, as Maria Root notes, is "particularly meaningful, and therefore hurtful." No one has the right to be the gatekeeper of who is Filipino or Mexican, and to do so is to "use the colonizer's tool against each other."[170]

The generations of Mexipinos who have found comfort in both communities, as well as alternate spaces, have contributed to a growing multiracial and multiethnic consciousness. Undoubtedly, they will continue to challenge monoracial and monoethnic thinking that defines identity politics and will force us to acknowledge the diversity of experiences even within our own communities and the multiple spaces we inhabit. Their experiences are distinct, and as new generations of Mexipinos continue to add to the growing numbers that claim multiple identities today, they will "not only redefine ethnic and racial borders, but provide a new way in which to see the world."[171]

This new perspective, forged out of multiracial spaces and comparative/relational histories, will allow us to see how such identities are formed; and rather than choosing to be a separate community, Mexipinos will continue to draw from both Mexican and Filipino elements and function *within* instead of outside of them. They have been the focal point where all these histories and identities converge. They have been the bridge between these two communities as well as the lens by which we view them as historical experiences that resonate today in even more complex ways. This has been their experience, and it is one that we need to examine thoroughly and appreciate if we are to recognize a future that is undeniably becoming more multiracial.

Epilogue

Since 1965, the Filipino and Mexican communities have undergone a series of demographic, geographic, and economic changes. The 1965 Immigration Act, for example, abolished all national origins quotas, allowing for increased immigration of both Filipinos and Mexicans.[1] As a result, Filipino and Mexican communities have mushroomed all over San Diego. Filipinos in San Diego currently number 135,272, while Mexicans number 805,326. The size of their populations has also changed dramatically across the United States. At over 2.3 million, Filipinos are now the nation's second-largest Asian group, while the United States' proximity to Mexico ensures that Mexicans still comprise the largest segment of Latinos in the country.[2] Although census numbers do not provide specific details as to the numbers of Mexipinos in San Diego, given the historical mixing and increasing demographics of Mexicans, Filipinos, and the mixed-race Asian-Latino population, it is likely that their numbers also increased.

Class differences define most Filipino immigrants after 1965. They are predominately professionals who were given occupational preference status and moved to newer, upper-middle-class suburban neighborhoods in San Diego County. These occupations include doctors, nurses, engineers, and other professionals.[3] Moreover, recent suburban Filipino communities were established in the northern area San Diego County (north of the I-8 Freeway), including Mira Mesa (also known as Manila Mesa), Rancho Peñasquitos, Scripps Ranch, Poway, and Murrieta. Many Filipino professionals and some navy retirees also live in the suburban community of East Lake area in Chula Vista, located on the eastern portion of the South Bay.[4] A number of well-to-do Mexican immigrant and U.S.-born Mexican families also reside in the Chula Vista–East Lake area and, like their Filipino counterparts, are also professionals and business owners.[5] Their class status has been much higher than that of earlier Mexican and Filipino residents who initially settled in San Diego prior to 1965. Residents who settled in the Southeast and South Bay areas after 1965 are still primarily working class and reside in the same blue-collar communities with other long-established residents, including a substantial number of navy families. Mexican immigrants and their U.S.-born children, and small pockets of undocumented populations, also live in the rural areas of North County San Diego.[6] Mexican immigrants continue to dominate the county's agriculture, landscaping, construction, and service industries.

Another change that defined the post-1965 generations was the rise of political consciousness through the cultural nationalist movements of the mid-1960s and early 1970s. With the advent of the Chicano movement, for example, Chicano nationalism reigned as the ideological force that bound a large part of the Mexican American community, particularly among the youth who now identify as Chicana and Chicano.[7] Student groups such as M.E.Ch.A. (Movimiento Estuduantil Chicana/o de Aztlán) and community activist groups like the Brown Berets of Aztlán were a part of the larger Chicano movement, which empowered their communities as they fought for self-determination and neighborhood control. In Barrio Logan, the Chicano community and their allies took over a piece of land by the bay that eventually became Chicano Park.[8]

Filipino cultural nationalism also emerged in the mid-1960s and early 1970s, which stemmed from their participation in the Third World Liberation Front (TWLF), which ignited the student strikes at San Francisco State University (SFSU) in 1968 and 1969. Students demanded an education and curriculum that were both relevant and accessible to their communities. Out of this struggle came the first School of Ethnic Studies in the United States. This event occurred during the rise of the Asian American, Chicano, Black Power, and American Indian movements, which were influenced by the larger global Third World movements.[9] Organizing was also directed at particular sites, such as in the fight to save the International Hotel in San Francisco for retired elderly Asian Americans; Filipino students from San Diego organized and fought alongside the elderly. Filipino students also got involved in political affairs in the 1970s, which were intimately tied back to the Philippines. San Diego's Katipunan Demokratikong Ng Mga Pilipino (KDP), for example, organized anti-Marcos protests to denounce martial law in the Philippines and the U.S.-backed dictatorship of President Ferdinand Marcos.[10]

The rise of these cultural nationalist movements created both tension and cooperation between Filipino and Mexican groups, especially when they overlapped with preexisting social or labor movements. One example of the tension that occurred was with the marginalization of Filipino laborers by their Mexican counterparts in the farmworkers' movement of the 1960s and 1970s. This is best illustrated with the rise of the United Farm Workers (UFW), the result of a large coalition of Filipino, Mexican, and other racial and ethnic workers in Delano, California. What is often overlooked, however, is the pivotal role Filipinos played in the movement. It was Filipinos who began the Delano grape strike in 1965, which ignited the movement.[11] United under the UFW, the mostly

Filipino-Mexican coalition gained national and international attention. Both marched together in solidarity under the *huelga* (strike) and Our Lady of Guadalupe banners, symbolizing their class and religious ties. Their struggle resonated with activists in the Chicano movement and from around the world who came to support the farmworkers. This outside attention, though, came at a cost that was detrimental to Filipino farmworkers. Dorothy Fujita-Rony notes, "While these campaigns gave the UFW heightened publicity, it meant that the labor struggle was influenced by the priorities of other people from outside the agricultural workforce, which in turn reshaped the resources and attention given to internal groups like the Filipina/o workers."[12]

Filipino farmworkers and veteran labor organizers such as Larry Itliong, Philip Vera Cruz, Andy Imutan, and Pete Velasco and their rank-and-file workers were also overwhelmed by the increasing numbers of Mexicans who dominated the union. Racial politics soon began to fracture the alliance; this was already becoming apparent in hiring practices, where Filipinos felt left out, and in the fact that Filipino workers were feeling displaced in union meetings, among other issues.[13] The 1965 Immigration Act and its family reunification and professional clauses also changed the class demographics of the Filipino population, who were now professionals such as doctors and nurses. Filipino laborers were no longer coming to the United States, so they had no new bodies to join their ranks. The largely Mexican membership eventually marginalized their Filipino counterparts as César Chávez took center stage. Vera Cruz recalled, "Cesar and the others weren't willing to put the same time and money into organizing the Filipinos as they did with Mexicans." Most of the leadership (such as Itliong and Vera Cruz) and many rank-and-file Filipino farmworkers eventually left the union.[14]

As the Chicano movement utilized César Chávez's image and UFW symbols as its own, the face and historical contributions of Filipinos were almost forgotten. I suggest this also further alienated them from their Mexican counterparts as Chicano nationalism ignored the importance of Filipinos to the farmworkers' movement—a group that historically shared in their struggle and resistance as it pertained to labor. The complex relationship between Filipinos, Mexicans, and Chicanos illustrates the interethnic fractures in this particular historical moment.

There were other instances when both groups came together within these cultural nationalist movements and Mexipinos took center stage. One example is the participation of Mexipinos in the Chicano movement. Paula Crisostomo, for example, is a Mexipina whose life story and involvement in the East Los Angeles school walkouts in 1968 were adapted into the HBO film *Walkout*. What was most likely overlooked in this history until the film's release was her Mexican and Filipino ancestry. Her identity is revealed early on in the film when she has a conversation with her Filipino father, whose response to her newfound Chicana identity is to remind her of her multiethnic background by calling her a

"Chilipina." Her central role in the walkouts demonstrates that Chicanos were not just "full-blooded" but also multiethnic.[15] Indeed, with the participation of individuals such as Paula, there needs to be further analysis of the formation of a Chicano nationalist identity and how Mexipinos and other mixed-race Chicanos have both contributed to and complicated it as key figures in these movements.

Mexipinos were also key figures in San Diego's Chicano movement. This is best exemplified by Irene Mena, a Mexipina who is known as the honorary grandmother of the San Diego Brown Berets of Aztlán. Irene's dedication to the Chicano community of Barrio Logan gained her a solid reputation as a sister in the struggle through her involvement in the Chicano Park takeover in 1970, the Chicano Moratorium in East Los Angeles, and other community struggles in San Diego. Proud to be both Filipina and Mexican, Irene even informed her peers in the Brown Berets about her Filipino ancestry. Their response was one of acceptance. She recalled: "They all accepted me. . . . [S]ome of them didn't even know I was Filipina. Some said, 'Irene, I didn't know you were Filipino.' Well, yeah, I'm half Filipino; I don't deny it. And I'm just as proud being Filipino as I am Mexican. Up to now, most of them do know I'm part Filipino because I'll even announce it. I'll say, 'I'm a mestiza Filipino-Mexican.'"[16]

Their acceptance of her as someone who identified as both Filipina and Chicana is worth noting. In a moment when cultural nationalism took center stage in the Chicano community, you had Mexipinas who, like Irene Mena, were influential, pivotal figures in the movement. Her family continues to be a part of the Brown Berets, with her children and grandchildren as members. In addition to her own family, Irene also noted several other Mexipinos who were involved in the Chicano movement in San Diego. Chicano scholars and activists who lived and went to school during the 1970s in San Diego also verified this fact.[17] There are other instances of Filipino and Chicano solidarity. Mexipina Maite Valladolid was a part of the Zapatista Movement's "La Otra Compaña" (The Other Campaign) in Mexico. Chicanas and Mexipinas have also been involved as allies against the sexual trafficking and violence women face in the Philippines, through organizations such as Gabriela Network.[18] These sorts of alliances have a rich racial and gender complexity to them, which begs for further research.

Today, newer Mexican and Filipino suburban communities remain separated by class and geography within San Diego County. These suburban neighborhoods are quite different from those early Mexican and Filipino communities that lived in segregated areas of South Bay and Southeast San Diego during the early twentieth century. Although there have been some instances of U.S.-born Mexicans and Filipinos still intermarrying and raising Mexipino children in these suburban areas, for the immigrant communities that also share these spaces, there is a disconnect. One result of this disconnect is the fact that many Filipino and Mexican immigrants view each other negatively, a result of how the United States historically racialized and colonized both groups and the ways in which differential racialization impacts how both communities view each other. Given that post-1965 Filipino immigrants are more desired because of their preferred occupational status and because they are more likely to apply for citizenship, they often look down upon their Mexican counterparts, using U.S.-manufactured racial stereotypes. Since Mexican immigrants are given negative media attention and are the subject of heated anti-immigrant rhetoric, many Filipinos have opted to distance themselves from them.[19] Some join in the anti-Mexican rhetoric, claiming their own patriotism, especially if they came to the United States via the U.S. Navy or waited twenty years to gain their legal residency status. By doing so, many Filipinos want to be American and be less associated with a group of people who once shared the same socioeconomic space and racialized status as themselves. I argue that this is the rearticulating of neocolonialism in the Philippines and among recent Filipino immigrants in the United States.

This does not mean that Mexican immigrants and newer Mexican communities that are revitalizing older ones are themselves not guilty of such prejudices. Indeed, they have their own racial views toward Filipinos, oftentimes lumping them together with other Asians and referring to them as "Chinos." Sophia Limjoco, for example, recalled her interaction with a Mexican resident in San Ysidro: "I used to work in San Ysidro, and I talked to this Mexican man one day about politics. As I was speaking to him, I also began to talk to others in Spanish. He was very surprised about this. He saw me at first as some stupid 'China' until we talked. He then had respect for me and felt ashamed about the way he felt. He learned from me."[20]

Such attitudes also reflect the U.S. racial hierarchy that seeks to divide Mexicans and Filipinos into separate entities that should have nothing to do with each other by instilling a historical amnesia, which wipes out their previous relationships in the United States. Their geographic and class separation, as well as their adoption of U.S. racial stereotypes of each other, prohibits some contemporary Mexican and Filipino communities from understanding or acknowledging the sociohistorical and cultural connection that they have with each other. Moreover, these views deny the historical presence and participation of Mexipinos as stark reminders of this rich cultural mixing that occurred in San Diego and other parts of California. These barriers to some degree continue to separate contemporary Filipino and Mexican communities.

One particular moment where their paths diverged was in the immigration debate surrounding the rally on April 9, 2006, when over fifty thousand people marched through downtown San Diego, joining other marches throughout the nation in support of immigrant rights.[21] Although there was a debate going around in the Filipino community press about whether or not to join the march, the end result was that a minimal number of Filipinos participated in the rally. This illustrated a large part of the Filipino community's move to disconnect from the immigration issue, despite the fact there is an undocumented segment within the Filipino population.[22] Filipinos who did participate in the march saw it as a collective issue and not solely a Latino or Mexican one. They were mostly from (or once a part of) these pioneering communities in the South Bay and Southeastern sections of San Diego. Mexipinos who grew up in these communities also participated in the march, reminding others that this issue affected them as a group that identified as both Mexican and Filipino.[23]

Yet not all Filipinos have made that separation. There is often a shared working-class identity between Filipinos and Mexicans who continue to work together as janitors and service workers and in other occupations. Sometimes these same individuals and their children continue to live in the Southeastern and South Bay sections of San Diego County. Many recent immigrants that do come to these communities are actually sponsored by Filipino laborers who have lived in San Diego prior to 1965.[24] To bridge the gap in these particular areas, especially for newly arrived immigrants, there have been various activities and individuals who advocate for mutual friendship and coalition building. One example is the celebration of the Fiesta Filipiana Mexciana in National City. This annual event has been going on for the last eighteen years and is sponsored by Seafood City, a Filipino supermarket, to bring together the Filipino and Mexican clientele and have a day of fun, music, and karaoke.[25] Other Filipino-owned businesses in National City cater to both Filipino and Mexican clientele. One of the local supermarkets in National City, for example, even had mini Filipino and Mexican flags all around the outside of its store to honor its patrons.[26]

Another example is Judy De Los Santos. As a Filipina married to a Mexican, with Mexipino children, she understands the need to bridge both communities and negotiates post-1965 tensions through political activism. Hers is one of the contemporary mixed Mexican-Filipino families living in National City, and she took her personal experiences with her when she ran for city council in 2004. Her campaign focused on appealing to her predominately Mexican and Filipino constituents. Her flyers were printed in brochure form with English, Spanish, and Tagalog messages calling for Mexicans and Filipinos (among other National City residents) to support her candidacy. As Judy noted, her candidacy was to represent Filipino and Mexican residents of National City who made up the majority of the area's population. Since she saw them having similar struggles with housing and education, she appealed to both sides. Judy sees National City as a model of how Filipinos and Mexicans coexist together in an amicable relationship.[27] Judy's experiences in National City did not recall any animosity but, rather, mutual cooperation. She said, "I don't really sense any tension of any sort. There are Filipino restaurants that I've gone to that actually Mexicans go there. They know the food; they know the culture. There's that whole interaction that goes on because it's such a close-knit community."[28]

Her husband, Armando, also pointed out that there were not the same sort of racial tensions between Mexicans and Filipinos as there were with other groups. He saw both Mexicans and Filipinos in National City as part of this long-established area where they have interacted over generations and share a working-class experience. When comparing the Filipino and Mexican communities in National City to those in newer suburban areas like Chula Vista's East Lake area, he pointed out the class difference: "It's very different in East Lake than here in National City. They come from working-class background . . . working-class people that come specifically to work. That's what unites them more than like in East Lake. They come from different backgrounds . . . upper middle class."[29]

His statement is telling because this newer satellite community is comprised mostly of professionals, both Filipino and Mexican. A large number of the Mexican residents in East Lake are also from wealthier families in Mexico. Despite the tensions that do exist between U.S.-born Filipinos, Mexicans, and their immigrant counterparts in the South Bay and Southeast sections of San Diego, they tend to get along better and coexist in a fashion that is conducive for continued interrelationships. As Yen Le Espiritu noted, "this north-south separation also reflects differences in class and immigration history."[30] The continued cohabitation of Mexicans and Filipinos in these communities has contributed to the continual growth of the Mexipino population. New generations are being born in areas such as National City, Chula Vista, San Ysidro, Imperial Beach, Paradise Hills, and other areas where Mexicans and Filipinos have lived for generations. This reflects the continued growth of these communities through familial and kinship networks.[31] As Gina Lleva shared about the Filipinos and Mexicans who continue to live in these areas, "It depends on where the Filipinos are from. If they're from National City or they're from San Ysidro, they go to school with all Mexicanos. A lot of those Filipinos date Mexicana women. My cousin is married to a Filipino right now. He [her husband] grew up in San Ysidro, went to Southwest High . . . so he likes Mexicana women."[32]

Gina's statement illustrates how these communities continue to come together and form relationships in these spaces. But Karen Leonard's study on the Punjabi-Mexican communities in the Imperial Valley showed a different experience. With the introduction of more Punjabi women post-1965, Punjabi men no longer wanted to marry Mexican women. Their multiethnic children also seemed to identify more with their Punjabi identity, thus negating their experiences of also being Mexican. What makes the Mexipino community distinct is that, unlike the Punjabi Mexicans, the contemporary Filipinos and Mexicans that reside in the older areas continue to intermarry. This continues to be the case despite the fact that there has now been a gender balance since 1965, with more Filipina women coming here than men. Moreover, Mexipinos differ in that they identify with both aspects of their parents' cultures.

In addition to Filipino men dating and marrying Mexican women, there is now an increase of Mexican and Chicano men dating and marrying Filipinas.[33] The fact that they still live, work, go to school, and socialize together only reinforces the bonds that were established between these communities generations ago. If some of the more recently settled Filipino and Mexican communities today understood the historical and cultural connections with each other and built on these commonalities, it would cultivate better relations. Indeed, more coalition building could be a possibility with the knowledge that these early generations came together through their shared experiences, stemming from racial isolation, labor struggles and organizing, social and religious life, and a common cultural influence. The narratives of these contemporary communities, then, are but another chapter in a historical web that is now being woven in more complex ways as their relationships, identities, and communities take on new meanings and continue to be shaped and redefined by race, class, gender, and sexual orientation.

The legacy of the early communities that were formed with the manong generation and its Mexican counterparts attests to the overlapping histories that extended well beyond the initial contact between Mexicans and Filipinos during the Acapulco-Manila galleon trade beginning in the sixteenth century. In the twentieth century, these early communities built lasting familial and kinship networks through the bonds of compadrazgo and continued to live, work, worship, and socialize, forming a world of their own in a once racialized space. Their friendships and common labor and civil rights struggles helped forge several generations of Mexipinos who are the living remnants of this rich multicultural heritage. One has but to look at the dinner table in a Mexican-Filipino household to witness the blending of cultural delicacies, family stories, and shared experiences that make the Mexipino story a unique experience in its own right—one that embraces multiplicity in all its complexity. It is a celebration of life and love between two peoples who are different and yet so much alike.

Unless these stories regarding their shared similarities and the history of their communities are told, it is unlikely that more people will come to understand what truly lies behind the meaning of being Mexipino. It is more than a catchy phrase to describe someone who is both Mexican and Filipino. It is a connection that binds two peoples together over time and space as they forge a multiethnic relationship that spans generations of family, kin, friends, and communities, all in order to survive in an environment that was not always welcoming. They share an obvious bond that no one can deny nor ignore. What makes this story unique is that it has not ended. Rather, the experience continues to define subsequent generations of Mexipinos who are being born into these sustained communities, which have deep roots in San Diego. Mexipinos thus embody a collective memory of historical moments. They live in two cultures and, in the process, forge a new identity for themselves. They continually challenge and redefine what it means to be both Mexican and Filipino. Moreover, their multiethnic identity masks how empire, part of this historical process, becomes invisible through the forging of these complex identities. Their lives are the lens by which we see these two communities and the ways in which they interacted over generations to produce this distinct multiethnic experience. In addition, their lives can be seen as a way to critically view how this historical process occurred and continues to unfold in the twenty-first century.

The implications of this study highlight localized comparative and relational approaches to understanding how Mexican and Filipino communities of San Diego formed in relation to one another. Broadly speaking, this story also touches upon the notion that racial and ethnic groups have always functioned in relation to each other, not as separate entities. The story of San Diego's Mexicans, Filipinos, and Mexipinos thus helps us to understand broader narratives of racial and ethnic relations in the United States, multiple racial formations, and how they have historically functioned and maintained their identities and communities into the twenty-first century. Thus, Mexipino is a way of life, not only for those who share this multiethnic background but for the families that came together through struggle, love, conflict, and cooperation, all in the name of living, working, socializing, and surviving so that individuals like myself can honor our multicultural heritage, our history, and our name as we navigate multiple identities and communities. Our collective memories and the stories they have produced are, indeed, worth telling.

Notes

General note: Although I am aware of the gender inclusive "a/o" for Chicana/o, Filipina/o, and Mexipina/o, as shorthand I will use the neutral term (e.g., Chicano or Filipino) to encompass all genders in these populations. However, I will use gendered terms when necessary.

INTRODUCTION

1. "My Vision for America: Speeches by Barack Obama," November 8, 2008, http://www.independent.co.uk/news/race-for-whitehouse/my-vision-for-america-speeches-by-barack-obama-1001275.html (accessed July 8, 2010).

2. For more on the experiences of Mexipinos in San Diego, see Rudy P. Guevarra Jr., "Burritos and Bagoong: Mexipinos and Multiethnic Identity in San Diego, California," in *Crossing Lines: Race and Mixed Race across the Geohistorical Divide*, ed. Marc Coronado, Rudy P. Guevarra Jr., Jeffrey Moniz, and Laura Furlan Szanto (Walnut Creek, CA: Alta Mira Press, 2005), 73–96.

3. U.S. Census Bureau, 2006–2008 American Community Survey, San Diego County, CA, ACS Demographic and Housing Estimates: 2006–2008; U.S. Census Bureau, 2005–2009 American Community Survey, San Diego County, CA, ACS Demographic and Housing Estimates: 2005–2009; Yen Le Espiritu, *Filipino American Lives* (Philadelphia: Temple University Press, 1995), 22.

4. Census numbers provided in Evelyn Hu-DeHart, "Voices of Asian Latinas and Latinos, Historical Perspective, Forced Removal and Displacement, Interesting and Unusual Situations," http://www.jrank.org/cultures/pages/3615/Asian-Latinos.html (accessed March 3, 2011).

5. Richard Griswold del Castillo, ed., *Chicano San Diego: Cultural Space and the Struggle for Justice* (Tucson: University of Arizona Press, 2007); Robert R. Alvarez Jr., *Familia: Migration and Adaptation in Baja and Alta California, 1800–1975* (Berkeley: University of California Press, 1991); Yen Le Espiritu, *Home Bound: Filipino American Lives across Cultures, Communities, and Countries* (Berkeley: University of California Press, 2003); and Espiritu, *Filipino American Lives.*

6. See Adelaida Castillo-Tsuchida, "Filipino Migrants in San Diego, 1900–1946" (MA thesis, University of San Diego, 1979); and James D. Sobredo, "From American

'Nationals' to the 'Third Asiatic Invasion': Racial Transformation and Filipino Exclusion (1898–1934)" (PhD diss., University of California, Berkeley, 1998), 213–28.

7. Scott Kurashige, *The Shifting Grounds of Race: Black and Japanese Americans in the Making of Multiethnic Los Angeles* (Princeton, NJ: Princeton University Press, 2008); Lorrin Thomas, *Puerto Rican Citizen: History and Political Identity in Twentieth-Century New York City* (Chicago: University of Chicago Press, 2010); Mark Wild, *Street Meeting: Multiethnic Neighborhoods in Early Twentieth-Century Los Angeles* (Berkeley: University of California Press, 2005); Karen Isaksen Leonard, *Making Ethnic Choices: California's Punjabi Mexican Americans* (Philadelphia: Temple University Press, 1992); Mae M. Ngai, *Impossible Subjects: Illegal Aliens and the Making of Modern America* (Princeton, NJ: Princeton University Press, 2004); Natalia Molina, *Fit to Be Citizens? Public Health and Race in Los Angeles, 1879–1939* (Berkeley: University of California Press, 2006); Laura Pulido, *Black, Brown, Yellow, and Left: Radical Activism in Los Angeles* (Berkeley: University of California Press, 2006); Paul Spickard, *Almost All Aliens: Immigration, Race, and Colonialism in American History and Identity* (New York: Routledge, 2007); Jonathan Y. Okamura, *Ethnicity and Inequality in Hawai'i* (Philadelphia: Temple University Press, 2008); and Moon-Kie Jung, *Reworking Race: The Making of Hawaii's Interracial Labor Movement* (New York: Columbia University Press, 2006).

8. Omi and Winant refer to racial formations as "the sociohistorical process by which racial categories are created, inhabited, transformed and destroyed." See Michael Omi and Howard Winant, *Racial Formations in the United States from the 1960s to the 1990s* (New York: Routledge, 1994), 55.

9. Pulido, *Black, Brown, Yellow, and Left*, 3.

10. Ibid., 4.

11. Kurashige, *The Shifting Grounds of Race*, 4.

12. For more on the Supreme Court decision of *Loving v. Virginia* (1967), see Peggy Pascoe, *What Comes Naturally: Miscegenation Law and the Making of Race in America* (New York: Oxford University Press, 2009), 287–296; and *Loving v. Virginia*, 388, U.S. 1 (1967).

13. Although Maria Root refers to it as the "biracial baby boom," collectively, individuals who may already be biracial when entering mixed-race or ethnic unions in the United States create a more complex multiracial baby boom experience. See Maria P. P. Root, ed., *The Multiracial Experience: Racial Borders as the New Frontier* (Thousand Oaks, CA: Sage Publications, 1996), xiv.

14. One of the earliest studies done on interracial mixing and mixed-race identity was by sociologist Romanzo Adams, who looked at the Hawaiian Islands as a geographic site for these experiences. See Romanzo Adams, *Interracial Marriage in Hawaii: A Study of the Mutually Conditioned Processes of Acculturation and Amalgamation* (Montclair, NJ: Patterson Smith, 1969). For more on the multiracial baby boom studies to come out after the 1980s, see Paul R. Spickard, *Mixed Blood: Intermarriage and Ethnic Identity in Twentieth-Century America* (Madison: University of Wisconsin Press, 1989); Maria P. P. Root, ed., *Racially Mixed People in America* (Newbury Park, CA: Sage Publications, 1992); Paul R. Spickard and Rowena Fong, "Pacific Islander Americans and Multiethnic Identity: A Vision of America's Future?" *Social Forces* 73, no. 4 (June 1995), 1365–83; Stephen Murphy-Shigematsu, "Addressing Issues of Biracial/Bicultural Asian Americans," in *Reflections on Shattered Windows: Promises and Prospects for Asian American Studies*, ed. Gary Y. Okihiro et al. (Pullman: Washington State University Press, 1988), 111–16; Teresa Williams-León and Cynthia L. Nakashima, eds., *The Sum of Our Parts: Mixed Heritages, Asian Americans* (Philadelphia: Temple University Press, 2001); Velina Hasu Houston and

Teresa Kay Williams, eds., "No Passing Zone: The Artistic and Discursive Voices of Asian-Descent Multiracials," special issue, *Amerasia Journal* 23, no. 1 (1997); Stephen L. Murphy-Shigematsu, "The Voices of Amerasians: Ethnicity, Identity, and Empowerment in Interracial Japanese Americans" (dissertation.com, 1999); Root, ed., *The Multiracial Experience;* Christina Iijima Hall, "The Ethnic Identity of Racially Mixed People: A Study of Black Japanese" (PhD diss., University of California, 1980); George Kitahara Kich, "Eurasians: Ethnic/Racial Identity Development of Biracial Japanese/White Adults" (PhD diss., University of California, 1983); Kip Fulbeck, *Paper Bullets: A Fictional Autobiography* (Seattle: University of Washington Press, 2001); Leonard, *Making Ethnic Choices;* Gloria Anzaldúa, *Borderlands/La Frontera: The New Mestiza* (San Francisco: Aunt Lute Books, 1987); Kevin R. Johnson, *How Did You Get to Be Mexican? A White/Brown Man's Search for Identity* (Philadelphia: Temple University Press, 1999); and Martha Menchaca, *Recovering History, Reconstructing Race: The Indian, Black, and White Roots of Mexican Americans* (Austin: University of Texas Press, 2001).

15. Kurashige, *The Shifting Grounds of Race,* 2, 4.

16. For more on this, see Kevin Mumford, *Interzones: Black/White Sex Districts in Chicago and New York in the Early Twentieth Century* (New York: Columbia University Press, 1997).

17. Most references to the term *indio* in Spanish records regarding the Philippines generally referred to native Filipinos. The same could also be applied for indigenous Mexicans. The term *mestizo* initially referred to both Filipinos and Mexicans who were of indio and Spanish ancestry. These terms, however, were never fixed and changed depending on time and space. For more on these terms, see Edward R. Slack Jr., "Sinifying New Spain: Cathay's Influence on Colonial Mexico via the *Nao de China*," *Journal of Chinese Overseas* 5 (2009): 5–8; Edward R. Slack Jr., "The *Chinos* in New Spain: A Corrective Lens for a Distorted Image," *Journal of World History* 20, no. 1 (2009): 35–67; Arnoldo Carlos Vento, *Mestizo: The History, Culture, and Politics of the Mexican and Chicano* (New York: University Press of America, 1998); C. E. Marshall, "The Birth of the Mestizo in New Spain," *Hispanic American Historical Review* 19, no. 2 (May 1939), 161–84; and Edward Slack Jr., e-mail correspondence with author, January 3–4, 2011.

18. William Lytle Schurz, *The Manila Galleon: The Romantic History of the Spanish Galleons Trading between Manila and Acapulco* (New York: E. P. Dutton, 1959), 263; and Eugene Lyon, "Track of the Manila Galleons," *National Geographic* 178, no. 3 (September 1990): 28–34.

19. Floro L. Mercene, "15 Generations of Filipinos Thriving in Mexico," *Philippine News* (June 21–27, 2000), A15; Floro L. Mercene, *Manila Men in the New World: Filipino Migration to Mexico and the Americas from the Sixteenth Century* (Honolulu: University of Hawai'i Press, 2007), 118–30.

20. Museum Exhibit Display Information, "Crossbreeding or Mestizaje," Museo Histórico de Acapulco Fuerte de San Diego, Acapulco, Mexico. All subsequent references to the museum's exhibit displays will be referred as MEDI. Amalia R. Mamaed, "Distant Cousins," *Hispanic* (January/February 1994): 30–32; Mercene, *Manila Men in the New World,* 122–24.

21. See MEDI, "Contributions of New Spain to the Philippines" and "Crossbreeding or Mestizaje"; Evelyn Ibatan Rodriguez, "Comparing Filipina Debuts and Mexican Quinceañeras," Mexican-Filipino American File, Filipino American National Historical Society, National Pinoy Archives, Seattle, Washington (hereafter cited as FANHS NPA); Carlos Quirino, "The Mexican Connection: The Cultural Cargo of the Manila-Acapulco Galleons" (source unknown), 933–34, Manila Galleons File, FANHS NPA; Mamaed,

"Distant Cousins," 30–32; Marcelino A. Foronda Jr., "Vigan: A Study of Mexican Cultural Influences in the Philippines," *Journal of Social History* (Manila, Philippines) 21, nos. 1–2 (January–December 1976): 1–12; and Mercene, *Manila Men in the New World*, 123–27.

22. Mumford, *Interzones*, xii; and Griswold del Castillo, *Chicano San Diego*, 5.

CHAPTER 1 — IMMIGRATION TO A RISING METROPOLIS

1. Chuey's went out of business in 2009. Quoted from "Chuey's a Big Name over in Barrio Logan," *Currents*, August 23, 1978, D1, D3. See also "Jesus 'Chuey' Garcia, 1907–1995," *San Diego Union Tribune*, October 26, 1995, A1, A9, Folder: Obituaries, Box 1, Logan Heights Historical Society, San Diego.

2. Camille Guérin-Gonzales, *Mexican Workers and American Dreams: Immigration, Repatriation, and California Farm Labor, 1900–1939* (New Brunswick, NJ: Rutgers University Press, 1994), 24–25; Carey McWilliams, *Brothers under the Skin* (Boston: Little, Brown, 1943).

3. The terms *cultural record* and *cultural footprint* came out of conversations with my colleague and friend Robert Soza in July of 2009 while editing this book.

4. Gilbert G. González, *Guest Workers or Colonized Labor? Mexican Labor Migration to the United States* (Boulder, CO: Paradigm Publishers, 2006), 3.

5. See Renato Constantino, "The Miseducation of the Filipino," in *Vestiges of War: The Philippine-American War and the Aftermath of the Imperial Dream, 1899–1999*, ed. Angel Velasco Shaw and Luis H. Francia (New York: New York University Press, 2002), 177–92; Yen Le Espiritu, *Home Bound: Filipino American Lives across Cultures, Communities, and Countries* (Berkeley: University of California Press, 2003), 25–27; Dorothy Fujita-Rony, *American Workers, Colonial Power: Philippine Seattle and the Transpacific West, 1919–1941* (Berkeley: University of California Press, 2002), 51–61.

6. Fujita-Rony, *American Workers, Colonial Power*, 51–61.

7. Mae M. Ngai, *Impossible Subjects: Illegal Aliens and the Making of Modern America* (Princeton, NJ: Princeton University Press, 2004), 11–13, 94–95.

8. Ronald Takaki, *Strangers from a Different Shore: A History of Asian Americans* (New York: Little, Brown, 1998); Sucheng Chan, *Asian Americans: An Interpretive History* (New York: Twayne Publishers, 1991).

9. "Filipinos Displacing Japanese," *Philippine Republic*, March 1924, 18, Labor File, National Pinoy Archives, Filipino American National Historical Society, Seattle, Washington. All subsequent citations will be noted as FANHS, NPA. See also "Growers' Convention Votes to Import Filipino Labor," *Los Angeles Times*, May 17, 1917, II:1; Paul S. Taylor, *Mexican Labor in the United States* (New York: Arno Press, 1970); and Ngai, *Impossible Subjects*, 103.

10. Ngai, *Impossible Subjects*, 94.

11. California Department of Finance, *California Statistical Abstract—Population*, http://www.ca.gov/About/Facts/Population.html (accessed January 23, 2004); Philip R. Pryde, *San Diego: An Introduction to the Region*, 4th ed. (San Diego, CA: Sunbelt Publications, 2004), 75; Espiritu, *Home Bound*, 17.

12. Richard Griswold del Castillo, ed., *Chicano San Diego: Cultural Space and the Struggle for Justice* (Tucson: University of Arizona Press, 2007), 2.

13. U.S. Census Bureau, "2006–2008 American Community Survey, San Diego County, California," ACS Demographic and Housing Estimates: 2006–2008; San Diego Association of Governments (SANDAG), "Mapping the Census: Race and Ethnicity in the San Diego Region," *SANDAG Info 1* (April 2002), www.sandag.org/uploads/publicationid/ publicationid_722_1120.pdf; Griswold del Castillo, *Chicano San Diego*, 2; and Espiritu, *Home Bound*, 17.

14. For more on Horton, Kettner, Spreckels, and other "founding fathers" of San Diego, see Carl H. Heilbron, ed., *History of San Diego County* (San Diego: San Diego Press Club, 1936), 1–314; Iris H. W. Engstrand, *San Diego: Gateway to the Pacific* (Houston: Pioneer Publications, 1992), 29–41.

15. "San Diego Headquarters Eleventh Naval District," *Standard Oil Bulletin* (April 1922), 7–12, Folder 18—Armed Forces, Navy, General #1, Lateral Files, San Diego Historical Society; and Rear Admiral Thomas J. Senn, "The History of the Navy in San Diego," in *History of San Diego County*, ed. Heilbron, 370–76.

16. Richard Pourade, *The Glory Years: The Booms and Busts in the Land of the Sundown Sea* (San Diego, CA: Union Tribune Publishing Company, 1966), 120–21; and R. B. Davy, M.D., "The Climate of San Diego," in *San Diego: The City and the County*, ed. San Diego Chamber of Commerce (San Diego, CA: Gould and Hutton, 1888), 22–29. For more on population statistics, see *U.S. Census Reports, 1900–1960* (Washington: GPO, 1901, 1913, 1922, 1932, 1942, 1952, and 1961); San Diego Chamber of Commerce, "Civilian Population," *San Diego Business* (February 1943), San Diego Historical Society.

17. Nicholas Mirkowich, "Urban Growth in the San Diego Region," *Economic Geography* 17, no. 3 (July 1941): 310; Clarence Alan McGrew, *City of San Diego and San Diego County: The Birthplace of California* (Chicago: American Historical Society, 1922), 347–75.

18. Roger W. Lotchin, *Fortress California, 1910–1961: From Warfare to Welfare* (Chicago: University of Illinois Press, 2002), 1–41; Kevin Starr, *The Dream Endures: California Enters the 1940s* (New York: Oxford University Press, 1997), 90–114; Norman W. Tolle, ed., "The Navy and San Diego: The Story of a Vital Link in the Nation's Defense Chain," *Union Title–Trust Topics* 2, no. 2 (March–April 1953): 2–19; Anthony W. Corso, "San Diego: The Anti-City," in *Sunbelt Cities: Politics and Growth Since World War II*, ed. Richard M. Bernard and Bradley R. Rice (Austin: University of Texas Press, 1983), 329–30; Bruce Linder, *San Diego's Navy: An Illustrated History* (Annapolis, MD: Naval Institute Press, 2001); Christine Killory, "Temporary Suburbs: The Lost Opportunity of San Diego's National Defense Housing Projects," *Journal of San Diego History* 39, no. 1–2 (Winter/Spring 1993): 34; Mary Taschner, "Boomerang Boom: San Diego 1941–1942," *Journal of San Diego History* 28, no. 1 (Winter 1982): 2.

19. Carey McWilliams, "The Boom Nobody Wanted," *New Republic*, June 30, 1941, 882; Taschner, "Boomerang Boom," 1–2; Lucinda Eddy, "War Comes to San Diego," *Journal of San Diego History* 39, no. 1–2 (Winter/Spring 1993): 51; Gerald Nash, *The American West Transformed: The Impact of the Second World War* (Lincoln: University of Nebraska Press, 1985), vii, 17, 56–59.

20. Starr, *The Dream Endures*, 90–91.

21. Abraham Shragge, "A New Federal City: San Diego during World War II," *Pacific Historical Review* 63, no. 3 (August 1994): 336–37.

22. Ibid., 355, 360–61; McWilliams, "The Boom Nobody Wanted," 882; Taschner, "Boomerang Boom," 1–2; Eddy, "War Comes to San Diego," 51; Nash, *The American West Transformed*, vii, 17, 56–59.

23. I also recognize that before the area which is now San Diego was a part of Mexico, it was inhabited by the Kumeyaay people, who are indigenous to the area. For more on this, see Griswold del Castillo, *Chicano San Diego*, 12–39; and Robert R. Alvarez Jr., *Familia: Migration and Adaptation in Baja and Alta California, 1800–1975* (Berkeley: University of California Press, 1991).

24. Wayne Cornelius, quoted in Richard Louv, "U.S. Magnet Lures Mexican Migrants," *San Diego Union*, November 25, 1979, A14, Lateral File: Hispanic Heritage, Thelma Hollingsworth Local History Room, National City Public Library.

25. See Michael J. Gonzales, *The Mexican Revolution, 1910–1940* (Albuquerque: University of New Mexico Press, 2002); Michael C. Meyer, William L. Sherman, and Susan M. Deeds, *The Course of Mexican History* (New York: Oxford University Press, 1999), 467–615; Matt S. Meier and Feliciano Ribera, *Mexican Americans/American Mexicans: From Conquistadors to Chicanos* (New York: Hill and Wang, 1993), 108–10; Manuel G. Gonzales, *Mexicanos: A History of Mexicans in the United States* (Bloomington: Indiana University Press, 1999), 114–20.

26. Consuelo "Connie" Zuniga, interview with author, San Diego, CA, August 20, 2001.

27. Home Missions Council, *A Study of Social and Economic Factors Relating to Spanish-Speaking People in the United States,* 6, Untitled Folder, Box 63, George P. Clements Papers, Special Collections and University Archives, University of California, Los Angeles; Paul S. Taylor, "Some Aspects of Mexican Immigration," *Journal of Political Economy* 38, no. 5 (October 1930): 609–15, Folder: 1932–1933 Mexican Labor and Immigration, Box 80, George P. Clements Papers, Special Collections and University Archives, University of California, Los Angeles; Mary Catherine Miller, "Attitudes of the San Diego Labor Movement toward Mexicans, 1917–1936" (MA thesis, San Diego State University, 1974), 1; Guérin-Gonzales, *Mexican Workers and American Dreams,* 25–47; Manuel Gamio, *Mexican Immigration to the United States: A Study of Human Migration and Adjustment* (New York: Dover Publications, 1971); Lawrence A. Cardoso, *Mexican Emigration to the United States, 1897–1931* (Tucson: University of Arizona Press, 1980), 38–39; Max Sylvius Handman, "Economic Reasons for the Coming of the Mexican Immigrant," *American Journal of Sociology* 35, no. 1 (January 1930): 601–11.

28. Mexican anthropologist Manuel Gamio documented it as another crucial time period of Mexican immigration to the United States. See Manuel Gamio, *The Life Story of the Mexican Immigrant: Autobiographical Documents* (New York: Dover Publications, 1971), 1; Gamio, *Mexican Immigration to the United States;* James L. Slayden, "Some Observations on Mexican Immigration," *Annals of the American Academy of Political and Social Science* 93 (January 1921): 123; Meier and Ribera, *Mexican Americans/American Mexicans,* 114–17; David G. Gutiérrez, ed., *Between Two Worlds: Mexican Immigrants in the United States* (Wilmington, DE: SR Books, 1996).

29. Will J. French, dir., *Mexicans in California: Report of Governor C. C. Young's Fact-Finding Committee* (San Francisco: State of California Department of Industrial Relations, 1930), 35–45.

30. As Matt Meier and Felicano Ribera noted, an estimated one million Mexicans came to the United States as a result of the Mexican Revolution. See U.S. Bureau of the Census, *Population Census 1930* (Washington: GPO, 1933), 498; Meier and Ribera, *Mexican Americans/American Mexicans,* 109; Manuel P. Servín, "The Pre–World War II Mexican-American: An Interpretation," *California Historical Society Quarterly* (1966): 327.

31. French, *Mexicans in California,* 51; Taylor, "Some Aspects of Mexican Immigration," 609–15; Marion Towle, "Mexican Population in San Diego," Minority Survey, circa 1936, Folder 704: Mexicans, 1935 and 1938, Box 16, Federal Writers' Project Collection, Bancroft Library, University of California, Berkeley.

32. Constantine Panunzio, "How Mexicans Earn and Live: A Study of the Incomes and Expenditures of One Hundred Mexican Families in San Diego, California," *University of California Publications in Economics* 13, no. 1 (May 1933): 3–4. Both writer Carey

McWilliams and historian Albert Camarillo noted that census data are just estimates, due to the fact that they only include Mexicans who are Spanish speaking. Actual populations are higher than what is reported. See "Mexican Population of California," Folder 3 (Mexicans—California), Box 27, Carey McWilliams Papers, Special Collections and University Archives, University of California, Los Angeles; Albert Camarillo, *Chicanos in a Changing Society: From Mexican Pueblos to American Barrios in Santa Barbara and Southern California, 1848–1930* (Cambridge, MA: Harvard University Press, 1996).

33. Arthur G. Coons and Arjay R. Miller, *An Economic and Industrial Survey of the Los Angeles and San Diego Areas Summary* (Sacramento: California State Planning Board, 1942), 314.

34. See Griswold del Castillo, *Chicano San Diego*, 3; and Mike Davis, Kelly Mayhew, and Jim Miller, *Under the Perfect Sun: The San Diego Tourists Never See* (New York: New Press, 2003).

35. I attended a family reunion in 2006, which enabled me to see the extent that Niland, the Imperial Valley, and San Diego are connected. See David Galbiso, interview with author, Chula Vista, CA, August 4, 2006; and David Galbiso, "Sakada in California's Imperial Valley," 1–5, Galbiso Family Collection, Filipino American National Historical Society (hereafter cited as FANHS), San Diego Chapter Archives.

36. Emory S. Bogardus, "The Mexican Immigrant," *Journal of Applied Sociology* 11 (1926): 471; Mirkowich, "Urban Growth in the San Diego Region," 308–9; and McGrew, *City of San Diego and San Diego County*, 372, 399, and 416–17.

37. See Richard V. Dodge, "San Diego's 'Impossible Railroad,'" *Dispatcher*, no. 6, June 29, 1956, Railway Historical Society, http://www.sdrm.org/history/sda/history.html (accessed July 3, 2005).

38. Griswold del Castillo, *Chicano San Diego*, 92.

39. "U.S. Magnet Lures Mexican Migrants," *San Diego Union*, November 25, 1999, A14, Lateral File: Hispanic Heritage, Thelma Hollingsworth Local History Room, National City Public Library.

40. Pryde, *San Diego*, 79.

41. Lanny Villarin, interview with author, National City, CA, May 5, 2004. For more on the experiences of Filipina nurses, see Catherine Ceniza Choy, *Empire of Care: Nursing and Migration in Filipino American History* (Durham, NC: Duke University Press, 2003).

42. Ngai, *Impossible Subjects*, 100.

43. See "Fruit Interests Need More Abundant Labor," *Pacific Rural Press*, November 17, 1917, 498; "California's Labor Situation in a Nutshell," *Los Angeles Times*, May 27, 1917, 3; "Growers' Convention Votes to Import Filipino Labor," *Los Angeles Times*, May 17, 1917, 3.

44. Filipinization was the compromising of U.S. colonialism with regards to Filipinos and how they fashioned democracy under U.S. rule while maintaining a sense of traditional Filipino customs and practices. See Teodoro A. Agoncillo, *History of the Filipino People* (Quezon City, Philippines: Garotech Publishing, 1990), 298–313.

45. See McWilliams, *Brothers under the Skin*, 234; Takaki, *Strangers from a Different Shore*, 58.

46. See William Alexander Sutherland, *Not by Might* (Las Cruces, NM: Southwest Publishing Company, 1953); Catherine Ceniza Pet, "Pioneers/Puppets: The Legacy of the Pensionado Program" (BA thesis, Pomona College, 1991); Fred Cordova, *Filipinos: Forgotten Asian Americans* (Seattle: Demonstration Project for Asian Americans, 1983), 125–26; Benicio T. Catapusan, "Problems of Filipino Students in America," *Sociology and Social Research* 26, no. 2 (November–December 1941): 146–53.

47. "Filipino Students Will Arrive November 10th," *San Diego Union,* November 5, 1903, 3.

48. See "Filipino Youths Have Arrived," *San Diego Union,* November 13, 1903; "Filipino Students Will Arrive November 10th," *San Diego Union,* November 5, 1903, 3; "Filipinos Arrive to Be Educated," *Evening Tribune,* November 9, 1903, 1; "Filipino Boys: Nineteen of Them Here for an Education," *San Diego Sun,* November 13, 1903, 1; Sutherland, *Not by Might,* 148–49.

49. "Filipino Students Will Arrive November 10th," *San Diego Union,* November 5, 1903, 3; and "Filipino Boys Hard at Work," *San Diego Union,* November 17, 1903.

50. "Filipino Youths Have Arrived," *San Diego Union,* November 13, 1903.

51. Ibid.

52. "Our New Students," *National City News,* November 12, 1903, 1.

53. "Report of the Philippine Commission," source unknown, 926–27, Binder 2: San Diego County Pensionados—St. Louis World's Fair 1904—Non Pensionado Articles, Ron Buenaventura Collection, FANHS, San Diego Chapter Archives.

54. "Farewells Said by Filipino Students," *San Diego Union,* June 23, 1904, 6; and Adelaida Castillo-Tsuchida, "Filipino Migrants in San Diego, 1900–1946" (MA thesis, University of San Diego, 1979), 43.

55. Service Record of Ciriaco Poscablo, National Personnel Records Center, St. Louis, MO, record obtained December 24, 2004.

56. Leonard Dinnerstein and David M. Reimers, *Ethnic Americas: A History of Immigration* (New York: Columbia University Press, 1999), 88.

57. Riz A. Oades, *Beyond the Mask: Untold Stories of U.S. Navy Filipinos* (National City, CA: KCS Publishing, 2004); Jocelyn Agustin Pacleb, "Gender, Family Labor, and the United States Navy: The Post–World War II San Diego Filipina/o American Immigrant Navy Community" (PhD diss., University of California, Irvine, 2003), 47.

58. Cordova, *Filipinos,* 84–86.

59. Pacleb, "Gender, Family Labor, and the United States Navy," 52.

60. Statement of Brig. Gen. F. LeJ. Parker, Chief of the Bureau of Insular Affairs, before the House Committee on Immigration and Naturalization, *Hearings on H.R. 8708,* April 11, 1930, 88, taken from Bruno Lasker, *Filipino Immigration to Continental United States and Hawaii* (Chicago: University of Chicago Press, 1931), 25.

61. Felix Budhi, quoted in Castillo-Tsuchida, "Filipino Migrants in San Diego" (thesis), 41; and Adelaida Castillo-Tsuchida, "Filipino Migrants in San Diego, 1900–1946," *Journal of San Diego History* 22, no. 3 (Summer 1976): 31.

62. "U.S.S. Boston" (#230-A), San Diego, CA, March 6, 1907, Navy Folder, Photograph Collection, San Diego Historical Society; and Castillo-Tsuchida, "Filipino Migrants in San Diego," 43–46.

63. Judy Patacsil, Rudy Guevarra Jr., and Felix Tuyay, *Filipinos in San Diego* (San Francisco: Arcadia Publishing, 2010), 58, 67–69.

64. Ricardo Romio, interview with author, Lakeside, CA, May 4, 2004.

65. Freddie Ayap, interview with author, National City, CA, August 5, 2004.

66. Fujita-Rony, *American Workers, Colonial Power,* 35–36.

67. According to Yen Le Espiritu, of the one hundred Filipinos she interviewed for her study, approximately 50 percent settled in San Diego because of a parent or other relative who was in the navy. See Espiritu, *Home Bound,* 111; Oades, *Beyond the Mask,* 25.

68. Espiritu, *Home Bound,* 99; and Lasker, *Filipino Immigration to the Continental United States and to Hawaii,* 62–63.

69. Takaki, *Strangers from a Different Shore*, 318.

70. See Lasker, *Filipino Immigration to the Continental United States and to Hawaii*, and Will J. French, dir., *Facts about Filipino Immigration into California, Special Bulletin No. 3* (San Francisco: California Department of Industrial Relations, 1930).

71. Linda España-Maram, *Creating Masculinity in Los Angeles's Little Manila: Working-Class Filipinos and Popular Culture, 1920s–1950s* (New York: Columbia University Press, 2006), 39.

72. Linda Nueva España-Maram, "Negotiating Identity: Youth, Gender, and Popular Culture in Los Angeles's Little Manila, 1920s–1940s" (PhD diss., University of California, Los Angeles, 1996), 22; Fujita-Rony, *American Workers, Colonial Power*, 93–95; and Lasker, *Filipino Immigration to the Continental United States and to Hawaii*, 21.

73. See Castillo-Tsuchida, "Filipino Migrants in San Diego" (article), 28.

74. Castillo-Tsuchida, "Filipino Migrants in San Diego" (thesis), 27, 41. For more photo documentation of early Filipino settlement in San Diego, see Patacsil, Guevarra, and Tuyay, *Filipinos in San Diego*, 11–67.

75. In Ronald S. Buenaventura, "San Diego's Manongs of the 1920s and 1930s," *Filipino American National Historical Society Journal* 5 (1998): 30.

76. Nena Amaguin, interview with author, San Diego, CA, July 6, 2004.

77. Vicki L. Ruiz, *From Out of the Shadows: Mexican Women in Twentieth-Century America* (New York: Oxford University Press, 1998).

78. Irene Rivas, interview with author, San Diego, CA, August 21, 2001.

79. French, *Facts about Filipino Immigration into California*, 12.

80. Ibid., 32, 42. This report also noted that both Mexicans and Filipinos had a large influx to the United States, which began in 1923.

81. Immigration and Naturalization Records, Vols. 1–3, San Diego State University Special Collections. See also Alvarez, *Familia*; J. Blaine Gwin, "Immigration along Our Southwest Border," *Annuals of the American Academy of Political and Social Science* 93 (January 1921): 128.

82. French, *Facts about Filipino Immigration into California*, 17, 23. For additional statistics, see Lasker, *Filipino Immigration to the Continental United States and to Hawaii*, 347–53.

83. McWilliams, *Brothers under the Skin*, 235. One of the most famous Filipino labor leaders to come out of Hawai'i was Pablo Manlapit. He was deported to the U.S. mainland as a result of his labor activities in Hawai'i. For more on Pablo Manlapit, see Melinda Tria Kerkvliet, *Unbending Cane: Pablo Manlapit, a Filipino Labor Leader in Hawai'i* (Honolulu: University of Hawai'i Press, 2002).

84. Paul Scharrenberg, "The Philippine Problem: Attitude of American Labor toward Filipino Immigration and Philippine Independence," *Pacific Affairs* 2, no. 2 (February 1929): 49.

85. Alvarez, *Familia*, 57–59 and 95–98.

86. Ibid., 110.

87. Ngai, *Impossible Subjects*, 64.

88. "Report to the Labor Council Mexican Immigration Committee," *San Diego Labor Leader*, February 14, 1930, 1, 8, San Diego–Imperial Counties Labor Council Collection, San Diego State University Special Collections.

89. See H. Brett Melendy, "Filipinos in the United States," *Pacific Historical Review* 3, no. 4 (November 1974): 524; Espiritu, *Home Bound*, 101; Lasker, *Filipino Immigration to the Continental United States and to Hawaii*, 21–22; C. M. Goethe, "Filipino Immigration Viewed as a Peril," *Current History* 34 (June 1931): 353.

90. Goethe, "Filipino Immigration Viewed as a Peril," 353.

91. Michael Andrew Lewis, "Ethnic and Racial Violence in San Diego, 1880–1920" (MA thesis, San Diego State University, 1991), 51; and Ngai, *Impossible Subjects,* 108.

92. Ngai, *Impossible Subjects,* 118–26.

93. See *Commonwealth* 5, no. 45 (November 5, 1929): 306–79; Francisco E. Balderrama and Raymond Rodríguez, *Decade of Betrayal: Mexican Repatriation in the 1930s* (Albuquerque: University of New Mexico Press, 1996), 53–54; J. M. Saniel, ed., *The Filipino Exclusion Movement, 1927–1935,* Occasional Papers no. 1 (Quezon City, Philippines: Institute of Asian Studies, University of the Philippines, 1967), 9, 32–33; Judge George J. Steiger, "The Filipinos as I Meet Them," *Organized Labor,* March 8, 1930; Ngai, *Impossible Subjects,* 116–17; Melendy, "Filipinos in the United States," 543–45; and Castillo-Tsuchida, "Filipino Migrants in San Diego" (thesis), 90.

94. See "Filipino Exclusion," *Wall Street Journal,* April 1, 1930, 17; Scharrenberg, "The Philippine Problem," 49–52; Melendy, "Filipinos in the United States," 543–45; Daniel R. Williams, "Philippine Exclusion," *Pacific Affairs* 2, no. 5 (May 1929): 281–83; and "Making Aliens of Citizens of the Filipinos," *Honolulu Advertiser,* January 22, 1929, File 2, Series 2, Box 1, RASL Clippings, Romanzo Adams Social Research Library, University Archives and Manuscripts, University of Hawai'i at Manoa. For more on the issues surrounding Philippine independence, see Fred C. Fisher, "The Moral Aspects of the Philippine Question," *Pacific Affairs* 3, no. 5 (May 1930): 460–69.

95. "Comments on Filipino Exclusion Bill," *Filipino Nation,* May 1930, 43; and James D. Sobredo, "From American 'Nationals' to the 'Third Asiatic Invasion': Racial Transformation and Filipino Exclusion (1898–1934)" (PhD diss., University of California, Berkeley, 1998), 220.

96. Samuel Shortridge, quoted in "How the United States Senate Stands on Filipino Exclusion," *Filipino Nation,* May 1930, 42.

97. Ibid.; and Scharrenberg, "The Philippine Problem," 53.

98. Shortridge, quoted in "How the United States Stands on Filipino Exclusion," 42.

99. Aaron M. Sargent, "Survey of Filipino Immigration—Report of Immigration Section," *The Commonwealth* 5, no. 45 (November 5, 1929): 319.

100. Helen W. Walker, "Mexican Immigrants and American Citizenship," *Sociology and Social Research* 13 (1929): 467.

101. For more on the racialization of health, see Natalia Molina, *Fit to Be Citizens? Public Health and Race in Los Angeles, 1879–1939* (Berkeley: University of California Press, 2006).

102. Filipino newspapers, such as the *Filipino Nation,* which was published by the Filipino Federation of America, Inc., had several editorials and commentary pieces attesting to their loyalty to the United States and their desire to be a part of America.

103. See Howard DeWitt, *Anti-Filipino Movements in California: A History, Bibliography, and Study Guide* (San Francisco: R and E Research Associates, 1979); Howard DeWitt, *Violence in the Fields: California Filipino Farm Labor Unionization during the Great Depression* (San Francisco: Century Twenty-One Publishing, 1980); H. Brett Melendy, "California's Discrimination against Filipinos, 1927–1935," in *Racism in California: A Reader in the History of Oppression,* ed. Roger Daniels and Spencer Colin Jr. (New York: Macmillan, 1972), 147–48.

104. Carlos Bulosan, *America Is in the Heart* (Seattle: University of Washington Press, 1990), 121; and Carlos Llaralde, "Roberto Galvan: A Latino Leader of the 1940s," *Journal of San Diego History* 52, no. 3 and 4 (Summer–Fall 2006): 154.

105. Saniel, *The Filipino Exclusion Movement*, 4.

106. "Candidate for Assembly District for Curtailment of Immigration," *San Diego Labor Leader*, March 14, 1930, 1, San Diego–Imperial Counties Labor Council Collection, Special Collections and University Archives, San Diego State University.

107. For more on the Tydings-McDuffie Act, see B. Powell, "The Commonwealth of the Philippines," *Pacific Affairs* 9, no. 1 (March 1936): 33–43; Sobredo, "From American 'Nationals' to the 'Third Asiatic Invasion'"; Takaki, *Strangers from a Different Shore*, 331–32; Chan, *Asian Americans*, 55–56.

108. See James S. Allen, "The Philippine Problem Enters a New Phase," *Pacific Affairs* 11, no. 2 (June 1938): 159–70.

109. Between 1923 and 1929, an average of 4,177 Filipinos came per year. See French, *Facts about Filipino Immigration into California*, 11.

110. Benicio T. Catapusan, "Filipino Immigrants and Public Relief in the United States," *Sociology and Social Research* 23, no. 4 (March 1939): 546–54.

111. See Manuel Buaken, *I Have Lived with the American People* (Caldwell, ID: Caxton Printers, Ltd., 1948), 155–66; and "Filipino Repatriation Movement," 90–100, Repatriation File, NPA, FANHS, Seattle, Washington; and "Repatriation of Filipinos Offered," File 8:2, Carton 3, Federal Writers' Project on Migratory Labor, Bancroft Library, University of California, Berkeley.

112. Ngai, *Impossible Subjects*, 121.

113. John F. Wehman, dir., "Filipino Americans: Discovering Their Past for the Future," Filipino American National Historical Society Program Series, 1994.

114. España-Maram, *Creating Masculinity in Los Angeles's Little Manila*, 42–43.

115. Letter to Carey McWilliams from Henry B. Hazard, U.S. Department of Justice, Immigration and Naturalization Service, July 27, 1942, Folder 3, Box 8, Carey McWilliams Papers, Bancroft Library, University of California, Berkeley; Emory S. Bogardus, "Filipino Repatriation," *Sociology and Social Research* 21, no. 1 (September–October 1936): 67–71; "Petition to President Roosevelt," *Philippines Mail*, October 8, 1934, in *Asian Americans: Opposing Viewpoints*, ed. William Dudley (San Diego: Greenhaven Press, 1997), 131–34; Carey McWilliams, "Exit the Filipino," *The Nation*, September 4, 1935, 265, Folder 2–20 (Minorities—Filipino), Box 15, Carey McWilliams Papers, Special Collections and University Archives, University of California, Los Angeles; Luciano Mangiafico, *Contemporary Asian Immigrants: Patterns of Filipino, Korean, and Chinese Settlement in the United States* (New York: Praeger, 1988), 37; Melendy, "Filipinos in the United States," 543–45; Ngai, *Impossible Subjects*, 120–25.

116. "Filipinos Expected to Be Repatriated," *San Diego Union*, March 8, 1936, 10.

117. Castillo-Tsuchida, "Filipino Migrants in San Diego" (thesis), 24; Paul G. Cressey, *The Taxi-Dance Hall: A Sociological Study in Commercialized Recreation and City Life* (New York: Greenwood Press, 1968), 163; Ngai, *Impossible Subjects*, 122.

118. Ngai, *Impossible Subjects*, 125; and Zaragosa Vargas, *Crucible of Struggle: A History of Mexican Americans from Colonial Times to the Present Era* (New York: Oxford University Press, 2011), 217.

119. Vargas, *Crucible of Struggle*, 217.

120. "Mexican Situation," Los Angeles Chamber of Commerce Interdepartmental Memo to Dr. Clements from Mr. Arnoll, June 16, 1931, Unnamed Folder, Box 80, George P. Clements Papers, Special Collections and University Archives, University of California, Los Angeles; "Mexicans Prefer United States to Free Trip Home," *San Diego Union*, April 22, 1934, 7; Guérin-Gonzales, *Mexican Workers and American Dreams*, 77–94; and Griswold del Castillo, *Chicano San Diego*, 94–95.

121. Consuelo "Connie" Zuniga, interview with author; Joe Lerma, interview by Rene Zambrano, San Diego, CA, n.d., *U.S. Latinos and Latinas and World War II Oral History Project,* University of Texas at Austin, http://utopia.utexas.edu/explore/latino (accessed October 7, 2005).

122. Jesus Ochoa, interview by Rene Zambrano, San Diego, CA, April 6, 2001, in *U.S. Latinos and Latinas and World War II Oral History Project,* University of Texas at Austin, http://www.lib.utexas.edu/voces/browse-locale.html?locale=World+War+II (accessed October 7, 2005); Joe Lerma, interview by Rene Zambrano, San Diego, CA, n.d., in *U.S. Latinos and Latinas and World War II Oral History Project.*

123. "Memo to C. P. Visel, Los Angeles Chamber of Commerce," January 8, 1931, Folder: 1932–33 (Mexican Labor and Immigration), Box 80, George P. Clements Papers, Special Collections and University Archives, University of California, Los Angeles.

124. Vargas, *Crucible of Struggle,* 215–20; Balderrama and Rodríguez, *Decade of Betrayal,* 54–64; Abraham Hoffman, *Unwanted Mexican Americans in the Great Depression: Repatriation Pressures, 1929–1939* (Tucson: University of Arizona Press, 1976), 56–66; Rodolfo Acuña, *Occupied America: A History of Chicanos* (New York: HarperCollins, 1988), 202–6; Douglas Monroy, *Rebirth: Mexicans in Los Angeles from the Great Migration to the Great Depression* (Berkeley: University of California Press, 1999), 147–51; and Paul Spickard, *Almost All Aliens: Immigration, Race, and Colonialism in American History and Identity* (New York: Routledge, 2007), 301–2.

125. Griswold del Castillo, *Chicano San Diego,* 95.

126. "Memorandum Regarding Mexican Repatriation in California," n.d. (circa 1930s), Untitled Folder, Box 80, George P. Clements Papers, Special Collections and University Archives, University of California, Los Angeles; letter to Ortiz Rubio, President of Mexico, from J.A.H. Kerr, Los Angeles Chamber of Commerce, June 8, 1931, Folder: 1932–1933 (Mexican Labor and Immigration), Box 80, George P. Clements Papers, Special Collections and University Archives, University of California, Los Angeles; Emory S. Bogardus, "Mexican Repatriates," *Sociology and Social Research* 18, no. 2 (November–December 1933): 174–75, and George Sánchez, *Becoming Mexican American: Ethnicity, Culture, and Identity in Chicano Los Angeles, 1900–1945* (New York: Oxford University Press, 1993), 214.

127. For more on these statistics, see Ngai, *Impossible Subjects,* 72–75; Griswold del Castillo *Chicano San Diego,* 94; Balderrama and Rodríguez, *Decade of Betrayal;* Paul Taylor, "Mexican Labor in the United States: Migration Statistics 4," *University of California Publications in Economics* 12, no. 3 (1934): 23–50; Hoffman, *Unwanted Mexican Americans in the Great Depression;* Guérin-Gonzales, *Mexican Workers and American Dreams.*

128. "Jose 'Joe' Galvan Delgado, 89; Began Working Career at Age 12," *San Diego Union-Tribune,* August 23, 1998, B7, Lateral Files: Galvan, Thelma Hollingsworth Local History Room, National City Public Library.

129. John Rubalcava, interview by Rene Zambrano, September 10, 2000, Chula Vista, CA, in *U.S. Latinos and Latinas and World War II Oral History Project.*

130. Herb Ibarra, quoted in Richard Louv, "U.S. Magnet Lures Mexican Migrants," *San Diego Union,* November 25, 1979, A14, Lateral File: Hispanic Heritage, Thelma Hollingsworth Local History Room, National City Public Library.

131. Letters and reports from Mexican consuls in Mexico City, Archivo de la Secretaria de Relaciones Exteriores (AREM), "Repatriation" files, courtesy of Camille Guérin-Gonzales, June 20, 2006. See also Guérin-Gonzales, *Mexican Workers and American Dreams,* 84, 145.

132. "Indigent Aliens Cost S.D. $16,000 Monthly, Report," *San Diego Union*, July 27, 1934; "Survey of Alien Mexicans to Aid in Repatriation," *San Diego Union*, August 10, 1934; "City Asks U.S. to Provide Funds to Deport Aliens," *San Diego Union*, December 30, 1930, 7.

133. Guérin-Gonzales, *Mexican Workers and American Dreams*, 84–89; and Griswold del Castillo *Chicano San Diego*, 95–96.

134. Balderrama and Rodríguez, *Decade of Betrayal*, 105–6; Bogardus, "Mexican Repatriates," 169–76.

135. Ngai, *Impossible Subjects*, 75 and 120–21.

CHAPTER 2 — THE DEVIL COMES TO SAN DIEGO

1. Manuel Buaken, *I Have Lived with the American People* (Caldwell, ID: Caxton Printers, 1948), 68–70.

2. George Lipsitz, *The Possessive Investment in Whiteness: How White People Profit from Identity Politics* (Philadelphia: Temple University Press, 1998), 24–33.

3. Frank Norris, "Logan Heights: Growth and Change in the Old 'East End,'" *Journal of San Diego History* 29, no. 1 (Winter 1983): 32.

4. Laurence I. Hewes Jr. and William Y. Bell Jr., *Intergroup Relations in San Diego: Some Aspects of Community Life in San Diego Which Particularly Affect Minority Groups* (San Francisco: American Council on Race Relations, 1946), 5.

5. George J. Sánchez, "What's Good for Boyle Heights Is Good for the Jews: Creating Multiracialism on the East Side during the 1950s," in *Los Angeles and the Future of Urban Cultures: A Special Issue of American Quarterly*, ed. Raul Homero Villa and George J. Sánchez (Baltimore, MD: The John Hopkins University Press, 2005), 137.

6. Filipinos held status as U.S. nationals until the 1934 Tydings-McDuffie Act, which changed their status to that of "aliens ineligible for citizenship." It would not be until World War II that Filipino soldiers were eligible to become naturalized citizens because of their contributions to the war effort. For more on the complexity of their status, see "Race Discrimination in Naturalization," *Iowa Law Bulletin* 8, no. 3 (March 1923): 155–56; "Filipinos in United States Neither Aliens nor Citizens," *Filipino Nation*, March 1930, 21, 47; "Filipinos—Eligible for U.S. Citizenship," Folder: Philippines—American Rule, n.d., Box 17, David Barrows Papers, Bancroft Library, University of California, Berkeley; Linda España-Maram, *Creating Masculinity in Los Angeles's Little Manila: Working-Class Filipinos and Popular Culture, 1920s–1950s* (New York: Columbia University Press, 2006), 150–51; Paul Spickard, *Almost All Aliens: Immigration, Race, and Colonialism in American History and Identity* (New York: Routledge, 2007), 308.

7. Spickard, *Almost All Aliens*, 150.

8. The ambiguous nature of whiteness and citizenship among Mexican Americans can be traced back to the provisions of the Treaty of Guadalupe Hidalgo in 1848, where Mexican residents living in the conquered territories of the present-day U.S. Southwest who elected to stay after the U.S.-Mexican War would be granted U.S. citizenship and all civil and property rights associated with it. Although they were granted these rights, such as the vote for "every white, male citizen of Mexico who shall have elected to become a citizen of the United States," the majority of Mexican Americans who did not look white did not experience these protections. Rather, they endured continued racial discrimination and violence at the hands of white Americans, who continued to see them as foreigners regardless of citizenship. See Richard Griswold del Castillo, *The Treaty of Guadalupe Hidalgo: A Legacy of Conflict* (Norman: University of Oklahoma Press, 1990), 62–72; William Deverell, *Whitewashed Adobe: The Rise of Los Angeles and the Remaking of Its*

Mexican Past (Berkeley: University of California Press, 16–18; Spickard, *Almost All Aliens,* 148–50; Zaragosa Vargas, *Crucible of Struggle: A History of Mexican Americans from Colonial Times to the Present Era* (New York: Oxford University Press, 2011), 102.

9. For more on white racial ideology, see Stephen J. Pitti, *The Devil in Silicon Valley: Northern California, Race, and Mexican Americans* (Princeton, NJ: Princeton University Press, 2003); Lisbeth Haas, *Conquests and Historical Identities in California, 1769–1936* (Berkeley: University of California Press, 1995); Tomás Almaguer, *Racial Fault Lines: The Historical Origins of White Supremacy in California* (Berkeley: University of California Press, 1994).

10. Michael Omi and Howard Winant, *Racial Formation in the United States: From the 1960s to the 1990s* (New York: Routledge, 1994), 55–56.

11. Sánchez, "What's Good for Boyle Heights," 137–38.

12. Lawrence Herzog, *Where North Meets South: City Space and Politics on the United States–Mexican Border* (Austin: University of Texas Press, 1990), 172–73; Leroy E. Harris, "The Other Side of the Freeway: A Study of Settlement Patterns of Negroes and Mexican Americans in San Diego, California" (PhD diss., Carnegie-Mellon University, 1974), 88; Mike Davis, Kelly Mayhew, and Jim Miller, *Under the Perfect Sun: The San Diego Tourists Never See* (New York: New Press, 2003).

13. Jim Miller, quoted in Davis, Mayhew, and Miller, *Under the Perfect Sun,* 166.

14. Ibid., 167.

15. I borrowed these patterns from Leroy Harris's study of the African and Mexican American communities of San Diego. See Harris, "The Other Side of the Freeway," 200.

16. Albert Camarillo, *Chicanos in a Changing Society: From Mexican Pueblos to American Barrios in Santa Barbara and Southern California, 1848–1930* (Cambridge, MA: Harvard University Press, 1996), 117–26.

17. Sánchez, "What's Good for Boyle Heights," 157–58.

18. Wendy Hsin Cheng, "Episodes in the Life of a Place: Regional Racial Formation in Los Angeles's San Gabriel Valley" (PhD diss., University of Southern California, 2009), 29.

19. Mexicans and Filipinos use the term "barrio" to mean neighborhood, while white residents usually equate it with being a ghetto.

20. Camarillo, *Chicanos in a Changing Society,* 209–10; Haas, *Conquests and Historical Identities in California,* 168.

21. Herzog, *Where North Meets South,* 174.

22. Consuelo "Connie" Zuniga, interview with author, San Diego, CA, August 20, 2001.

23. Augie Bareño, "Logan Heights Memory Book," *Logan Heights Historical Society Memory Album,* 1, Logan Heights Historical Society; Harris, "The Other Side of the Freeway," 112; Castillo-Tsuchida, "Filipino Migrants in San Diego, 1900–1946" (MA thesis, University of San Diego, 1979), 41–42.

24. See Sociedad Beneficia Mexicana "Benito Juarez," de National City, circa 1900s, and National City class photo, circa 1906, Photograph Collection, Thelma Hollingsworth Local History Room, National City Public Library.

25. Joe Montijo, interview by S. Hurley, National City, CA, March 11, 1982, Oral History Collection, San Diego Historical Society; National City class photo, circa 1906, Photograph Collection, Thelma Hollingsworth Local History Room, National City Public Library; Leslie Trook, *National City: Kimball's Dream* (National City, CA: National City Chamber of Commerce, 1992), 52.

26. Robert Holmes, interview by Edgar F. Hastings, March 16, 1959, Oral History Collection, San Diego Historical Society; Marivi Soliven Blanco, *An Annotated*

Bibliography of Filipino and Filipino-American History Resources in the San Diego Historical Society Research Archives (Spring 2002), FANHS San Diego Chapter Archives; Donald H. Estes, "Before the War: The Japanese in San Diego," *Journal of San Diego History* 24, no. 4 (Fall 1978): 425–56. In Blanco's annotated bibliography there is information about this particular oral history; the author mentions that Filipinos settled in Chula Vista around 1912. This coincides with the introduction of winter celery by the Japanese in the area in 1912, which eventually made Chula Vista the "Celery Capital of the World." See also Castillo-Tsuchida, "Filipino Migrants in San Diego" (thesis), 41; and Castillo-Tsuchida, "Filipino Migrants in San Diego, 1900–1946," *Journal of San Diego History* 22, no. 3 (Summer 1976): 31.

27. Herzog, *Where North Meets South,* 180–81.

28. Ibid., 174, 179; and Judy Patacsil, Rudy Guevarra Jr., and Felix Tuyay, *Filipinos in San Diego* (San Francisco: Arcadia Publishing, 2010), 11–30.

29. See Harris, "The Other Side of the Freeway," 91; Constantine Panunzio, "How Mexicans Earn and Live: A Study of the Incomes and Expenditures of One Hundred Mexican Families in San Diego, California," *University of California Publications in Economics* 13, no. 1 (May 1933); Hewes and Bell, *Intergroup Relations in San Diego;* Federal Writers' Project, *San Diego: A California City* (San Diego: San Diego Historical Society, 1937); and Will J. French, dir., *Mexicans in California: Report of Governor C. C. Young's Fact-Finding Committee* (San Francisco: State of California Department of Industrial Relations, 1930).

30. Stephanie Sansom, "Mexicans Were Once Unwanted in Lemon Grove School System," newspaper unknown, August 26, 1982, 4A, Vertical File 353: Lemon Grove, Lemon Grove Historical Society; Patacsil, Guevarra, and Tuyay, *Filipinos in San Diego,* 27; Richard Griswold del Castillo, ed., *Chicano San Diego: Cultural Space and the Struggle for Justice* (Tucson: University of Arizona Press, 2007), 80; and Herzog, *Where North Meets South,* 174.

31. Federal Writers' Project, *San Diego,* 16; and Harris, "The Other Side of the Freeway," 112.

32. Harris, "The Other Side of the Freeway," 116; and Kevin Delgado, "A Turning Point: The Conception and Realization of Chicano Park," *Journal of San Diego History* 44, no. 1 (Winter 1998): 50.

33. Harris, "The Other Side of the Freeway," 116–17.

34. Griswold del Castillo, *Chicano San Diego,* 79.

35. Lanny Villarin, interview with author, National City, CA, May 5, 2004; Rudy Guevarra Sr., interview with author, San Diego, CA, March 26, 2005; Home Owners' Loan Corporation (HOLC) area descriptions, San Diego, CA, October 20, 1936, National Archives, courtesy of Richard Marciano; and R. Marciano, D. Goldberg, and C. Hou, "T-RACES: A Testbed for the Redlining Archives of California's Exclusionary Spaces," http://salt.unc.edu/T-RACES (accessed May 1, 2010). All subsequent citations of Home Owners' Loan Corporation will be cited as HOLC.

36. Harris, "The Other Side of the Freeway," 150.

37. College Woman's Club, *Pathfinder Social Survey of San Diego: Report of Limited Investigations of Social Conditions in San Diego, California* (San Diego: Labor Temple Press, 1914), 12–13.

38. Harris, "The Other Side of the Freeway," 138–39; and Rick Bonus, *Locating Filipino Americans: Ethnicity and the Cultural Politics of Space* (Philadelphia: Temple University Press), 75.

39. Hewes and Bell, *Intergroup Relations in San Diego,* 8.

40. Panunzio, "How Mexicans Earn and Live," 40; Harris, "The Other Side of the Freeway," 157–61; Karl Taeuber and Alma Taeuber, *Negroes in Cities* (Chicago: Aldine Publishing Co., 1965), 34–35.

41. Norris, "Logan Heights," 36; Herzog, *Where North Meets South,* 176–77; Harris, "The Other Side of the Freeway," 128–29.

42. Harris, "The Other Side of the Freeway," 146.

43. Ibid., 147.

44. See Norris, "Logan Heights," 28–40.

45. Harris, "The Other Side of the Freeway," 165; Oscar Handlin, *Fire-Bell in the Night: The Crisis in Civil Rights* (Boston: Beacon Press, 1964), 97; Gary Fowler, "The Urban Settlement Patterns of Disadvantaged Migrants," *Journal of Geography* (May 1972): 276.

46. Ronald Takaki, *Strangers from a Different Shore: A History of Asian Americans* (Boston: Little, Brown, 1998), 13.

47. Statement of Edwin B. Tilton, Assistant Superintendent of Schools, San Diego, February 15, 1929, Carton 10, Folder 10:5 (Mexican Labor in the U.S. Field Notes: Series B, Set 1, 1927–29), Paul S. Taylor Papers, Bancroft Library, University of California, Berkeley (hereafter cited as Taylor Papers).

48. Frank Penuelas, quoted in Mark T. Sullivan, "Dark Ages to Daylight: City's Racial Tale," *San Diego Tribune,* November 18, 1991, A5, Folder 510: Race Relations in San Diego, San Diego Historical Society.

49. Sullivan, "Dark Ages to Daylight."

50. Hewes and Bell, *Intergroup Relations in San Diego,* 19, and Castillo-Tsuchida, "Filipino Migrants in San Diego" (thesis), 69.

51. Armando Rodriguez, quoted in Sullivan, "Dark Ages to Daylight."

52. A. B. Santos, quoted in Simeon G. Silverino Jr., "The Filipino Old Timers," *San Diego Asian Journal,* November 16–30, 1989, 6, 11, File: Ethnic Groups— Asian—Filipinos—SD, California Room, Vertical File Collection, San Diego Public Library.

53. See George J. Sánchez, *Becoming Mexican American: Ethnicity, Culture, and Identity in Chicano Los Angeles, 1900–1945* (New York: Oxford University Press, 1993); Linda Nueva España-Maram, "Negotiating Identity: Youth, Gender, and Popular Culture in Los Angeles's Little Manila, 1920s–1940s" (PhD diss., University of California, Los Angeles, 1996), 53.

54. French, *Mexicans in California,* 176.

55. Richard Griswold del Castillo, *The Los Angeles Barrio, 1850–1890: A Social History* (Berkeley: University of California Press, 1979), 150.

56. Harris, "The Other Side of the Freeway," 165–74; Handlin, *Fire-Bell in the Night,* 97; Fowler, "The Urban Settlement Patterns of Disadvantaged Migrants," 276.

57. "Statement by Elmer Heald; District Attorney, Imperial Valley," 75, Carton 10, Folder 10:4 (Mexican Labor in the U.S. Field Notes, Series A, Set 1), Taylor Papers.

58. Emory S. Bogardus, "The Mexican Immigrant and Segregation," *American Journal of Sociology* 36, no. 1 (July 1930): 78; Emory S. Bogardus, "Current Problems of Mexican Immigrants," *Sociology and Social Research* 25 (1940): 168; Castillo-Tsuchida, "Filipino Migrants in San Diego" (thesis), 58; España-Maram, *Creating Masculinity in Los Angeles's Little Manila,* 154.

59. "Across the Tracks," *Time,* September 6, 1943, 25.

60. Lillian Lim, interview with author, Chula Vista, CA, March 20, 2004.

61. Norris, "Logan Heights," 170.

62. Kevin J. Mumford, *Interzones: Black/White Sex Districts in Chicago and New York in the Early Twentieth Century* (New York: Columbia University Press, 1997), xvii, 175–76.

63. Mary Ting Yi Lui, *The Chinatown Trunk Mystery: Murder, Miscegenation, and Other Dangerous Encounters in Turn-of-the-Century New York City* (Princeton, NJ: Princeton University Press, 2005), 5.

64. Norris, "Logan Heights," 36.

65. Cynthia J. Shelton, "The Neighborhood House of San Diego: Settlement Work in the Mexican Community, 1914–1940" (MA thesis, San Diego State University, 1975), 28; and Camarillo, *Chicanos in a Changing Society*, 210.

66. Harris, "The Other Side of the Freeway," 174.

67. Ibid., 170–71.

68. Sullivan, "Dark Ages to Daylight."

69. Hewes and Bell, *Intergroup Relations in San Diego*, 15.

70. Summary of Interview—Hope and Bernardo Hernandez, interview by Sylvia Morales, March 14, 1999, 4, Logan Heights History Project, Special Collections and University Archives, San Diego State University.

71. Lauro Vega, interview by Rene Zambrano, Chula Vista, CA, October 8, 2000, in *U.S. Latinos and Latinas and World War II Oral History Project*, University of Texas at Austin, http://www.lib.utexas.edu/voces/browse-locale.html?locale=World+War+II (accessed October 7, 2005).

72. Charito Balanag, interview with author, San Diego, CA, June 28, 2004.

73. French, *Mexicans in California*, 177.

74. Panunzio, "How Mexicans Earn and Live," 40–43; and Lipsitz, *The Possessive Investment in Whiteness*, 33.

75. Delgado, "A Turning Point," 50.

76. Jesus Hernandez, "The Residual Impact of History: Connecting Residential Segregation, Mortgage Redlining, and the Housing Crisis," in *Kirwan Institute for the Study of Race and Ethnicity* (Columbus: Ohio State University, 2009), 7.

77. Terry Pettus, "Greed of Real Estate Interests Reason for 'Racial Covenants,'" *New World*, February 5, 1948; and Kathie L. Taylor, "Shadow of Segregation Haunts City," *San Diego Tribune*, November 18, 1991, A5, Folder 510: Race Relations in San Diego, San Diego Historical Society.

78. Hewes and Bell, *Intergroup Relations in San Diego*, 15.

79. See "Navy Housing in San Diego," in Fred Cordova, *Filipinos: Forgotten Asian Americans* (Seattle: Demonstration Project for Asian Americans, 1983), 83.

80. Harris, "The Other Side of the Freeway," 176.

81. See chart on racial restrictive covenants in Harris, "The Other Side of the Freeway," 178–80.

82. These housing price lists were gathered from 1914 through 1926 and show the early move to restrict nonwhites from moving into surrounding neighborhoods that were newer and made specifically for white residents. The only exception to these clauses was for whites who kept "non-Caucasians" as servants. See Arlington Price List, May 20, 1914, and Loma Portal Price List, April 1, 1922, Folder A (Brochures and Price Lists), Box 1, Regine Thorne Subdivision Collection, San Diego Historical Society; and Taylor, "Shadow of Segregation Haunts City."

83. "Reasons for Restrictions," source unknown, 1934, A5, Folder 510: Race Relations in San Diego, San Diego Historical Society.

84. This is similar to what occurred in the Boyle Heights community of Los Angeles. See Sánchez, "What's Good for Boyle Heights," 140–41.

85. Harris, "The Other Side of the Freeway," 182.

86. Stuart Palmer, "The Role of Real Estate Agent in the Structuring of Residential Areas: A Study of Social Control" (PhD diss., Yale University, 1955), 1; Harris, "The Other Side of the Freeway," 183; Herman H. Long and Charles S. Johnson, *People vs. Property: Race Restrictive Covenants in Housing* (Nashville: Fisk University Press, 1947), 56.

87. Davis, Mayhew, and Miller, *Under the Perfect Sun*, 165.

88. "Report of Committee on Minorities," United Community Defense Services, June 1952, 6, Box 10, Carlin Integration Case Records, San Diego State University Special Collections; Lawrence B. Glick, "The Right to Equal Opportunity," in *La Raza: Forgotten Americans,* ed. Julian Samora (Norte Dame: University of Norte Dame Press, 1966), 109; Taylor, "Shadow of Segregation Haunts City"; Davis, Mayhew, and Miller, *Under the Perfect Sun,* 165.

89. According to Richard Marciano, director of Sustainable Archives and Leveraging Technologies (SALT), HOLC and FHA shared information, which indicates that HOLC influence was imbedded in both FHA and VA loans. For more on redlining maps, see Kenneth T. Jackson, *Crabgrass Frontier: The Suburbanization of the United States* (New York: Oxford University Press, 1985); and Taylor, "Shadow of Segregation Haunts City."

90. Luigi Laurenti, *Property Values and Race: Studies in Seven Cities* (Berkeley: University of California Press, 1960), 22–25; E. Frederick Anderson, Napoleon A. Jones Jr., Burdett B. Plumb, and David A. Schneider, "An Investigation of Discrimination against Negroes in Housing in the City of San Diego" (MA thesis, San Diego State College, 1967), 18–19; J. William Leasure and David H. Stern, "A Note on Housing Segregation Indexes," *Social Forces* 46, no. 3 (March 1968): 406–7.

91. Lipsitz, *The Possessive Investment in Whiteness,* 7; and Rudy Guevarra Jr., field notes regarding racial segregation in San Diego, January 10, 2007.

92. Ralph Guzman and Joan Moore, "Mexican-Americans, A Background Paper," paper prepared for Conference on Mexican-American Problems, October 29, 1965, sponsored by the Center for the Study of Democratic Institutions, Santa Barbara, California, 7, Folder 14 (Mexican-Americans-History), Box 28, Julian Nava Collection, Special Collections and Archives, California State University, Northridge.

93. Marciano, Goldberg, and Hou, "T-RACES: A Testbed for the Redlining Archives of California's Exclusionary Spaces"; and Hernandez, "The Residual Impact of History," 9.

94. HOLC area descriptions, San Diego, California, October 20, 1936, National Archives, courtesy of Richard Marciano, and Marciano, Goldberg, and Hou, "T-RACES: A Testbed for the Redlining Archives of California's Exclusionary Spaces." (All subsequent citations of Home Owners' Loan Corporation will be cited as HOLC.)

95. Ibid.; and Hernandez, "The Residual Impact of History," 10.

96. Long and Johnson, *People vs. Property,* 39.

97. Golden Hills at the time was a predominately white community. It lies north of Logan Heights and Sherman Heights. See Consuelo "Connie" Zuniga, interview with author.

98. Harris, "The Other Side of the Freeway," 180.

99. "Letter to Governor regarding racial restrictive covenants from J. Chinn," April 29, 1947, 1–2, Folder F3640:3657, Earl Warren Papers, California State Archives.

100. See Harris, "The Other Side of the Freeway," 178–79; Anderson, Jones, Plumb, and Schneider, "An Investigation of Discrimination against Negroes in Housing," 7–8; United Community Defense Services, "Report of Committee on Minorities" (June 1952), 5,

Box 10, Carlin Integration Case Records, Special Collections and University Archives, San Diego State University; Sullivan, "Dark Ages to Daylight."

101. Castillo-Tsuchida, "Filipino Migrants in San Diego" (thesis), 101.

102. Of the twenty-seven cases, only eleven were given corrective action. See Anderson, Jones, Plumb, and Schneider, "An Investigation of Discrimination against Negroes in Housing," 29.

103. Harris, "The Other Side of the Freeway," 185–86.

104. Ibid., 186–87.

105. Ibid., 190.

106. Lipsitz, *The Possessive Investment in Whiteness*, 30.

107. "Prejudice: Our Postwar Battle," *Look* magazine, May 1, 1945, 49.

108. Carlos Bulosan, *America Is in the Heart* (Seattle: University of Washington Press, 1990), 143.

109. Ricardo Romio, interview with author, Lakeside, CA, May 4, 2004.

110. See also Consuelo "Connie" Zuniga, interview with author; Albert López Pulido, "Nuestra Señora de Guadalupe: The Mexican Catholic Experience in San Diego," *Journal of San Diego History* 37, no. 4 (Fall 1991): 237–39. For more on Mexican Catholics in San Diego, see Alberto L. Pulido, "Searching for the Sacred: Conflict and Struggle for Mexican Catholics in the Roman Catholic Diocese of San Diego," *Latino Studies Journal* 5, no. 3 (September 1994): 37–59.

111. Lanny Villarin, interview with author; and Patacsil, Guevarra, and Tuyay, *Filipinos in San Diego*, 46.

112. According to Chancellor Rodrigo Valdivia of the San Diego Catholic Diocese, parish records show that whites oftentimes had their own churches. This has led to the current racial composition of many churches in San Diego today. More research needs to be done with regards to the racial makeup of non-Catholic churches in the San Diego area. See personal field notes, June 24, 2005.

113. Cordova, *Filipinos*, 157.

114. Mumford, *Interzones*, xii.

115. Haas, *Conquests and Historical Identities in California*, 199–201.

116. Ting Yi Lui, *The Chinatown Trunk Mystery*, 6.

117. Carol Hemminger, "Little Manila: The Filipino in Stockton Prior to World War II," part 2, *Pacific Historian* 24 (Spring 1980): 214.

118. Lazaro Lupian, interview by Rene Zambrano, San Diego, CA, December 3, 2000, *U.S. Latinos and Latinas and World War II Oral History Project*, University of Texas at Austin, http://www.lib.utexas.edu/voces/browse-locale.html?locale=World+War+II (accessed October 7, 2005).

119. Angel, quoted in Hemminger, "Little Manila," 215.

120. Bonus, *Locating Filipino Americans*, 57.

121. Ibid., 57–91.

122. *Manong* means "older brother." It is a term of respect and endearment for the majority of elder Filipinos, who were bachelors in the United States.

123. Nena Amaguin, interview with author, San Diego, CA, July 6, 2004.

124. Ibid.

125. Jona Cruz, Jessica Sarsoza, Ronald S. Buenaventura, and Fidencio S. Pampo, "A Sailor's Sacrifice: The Navy Steward," *Kalayaan* 3, no. 3 (March 1997): 6.

126. Lanny Villarin, interview with author. See also family photos, circa 1940s, Lanny Villarin Photo Collection, personal.

127. Sánchez, *Becoming Mexican American*, 11.

128. See Rudy P. Guevarra Jr., "Skid Row: Filipinos, Race, and the Social Construction of Space in San Diego," *Journal of San Diego History* 54, no. 1 (Winter 2008): 26–38; Paul G. Cressey, *The Taxi-Dance Hall: A Sociological Study in Commercialized Recreation and City Life* (New York: Greenwood Press, 1968), 145. For more on the activities of Filipinos in the taxi dance halls, see Roberto V. Vallangca, *Pinoy: The First Wave* (San Francisco: Strawberry Hill Press, 1977), 50–53; Rhacel Salazar Parreñas, "'White Trash' Meets the 'Little Brown Monkeys': The Taxi Dance Hall as a Site of Interracial and Gender Alliances between White Working-Class Women and Filipino Immigrant Men in the 1920s and 1930s," *Amerasia Journal* 24, no. 2 (1998): 118–21; España-Maram, *Creating Masculinity in Los Angeles's Little Manila*, 105–33.

129. Castillo-Tsuchida, "Filipino Migrants in San Diego" (thesis), 52–53.

130. Rolando Mata, interview with author, La Puente, CA, September 1, 2004; Guevarra, "Skid Row," 3; Castillo-Tsuchida, "Filipino Migrants in San Diego" (thesis); and Ronald Buenaventura, "San Diego's Manongs of the 1920s and 1930s," *Filipino American National Historical Society Journal* 5 (1998): 31.

131. Yen Le Espiritu, *Home Bound: Filipino American Lives across Cultures, Communities, and Countries* (Berkeley: University of California Press, 2003), 112–13.

132. Castillo-Tsuchida, "Filipino Migrants in San Diego" (thesis), 106.

133. Virgil Garcia, interview with author, Lemon Grove, CA, August 21, 2001.

134. España-Maram, *Creating Masculinity in Los Angeles's Little Manila*, 110.

135. Consuelo "Connie" Zuniga, interview with author.

136. Rolando Mata, interview with author.

137. Notes from personal conversations with Rudy Guevarra Sr., San Diego, CA, July 5, 2001. See also, Guevarra, "Skid Row," 26–38.

138. Patacsil, Guevarra, and Tuyay, *Filipinos in San Diego*, 21; Cruz, Sarsoza, Buenaventura, and Pampo, "A Sailor's Sacrifice," 6.

139. Patacsil, Guevarra, and Tuyay, *Filipinos in San Diego*, 21; *Polk's San Diego City Directories*, 1920–1965 (San Diego County, California); Buenaventura, "San Diego's Manongs of the 1920s and 1930s," 31.

140. *Rondalla* are Filipino string bands that include guitars, banjos, and the "kudyapi" (a small guitar that has its origins in the Philippines during the 1500s). For more on the barbershop and its activities, see Castillo-Tsuchida, "Filipino Migrants in San Diego," (thesis), 81–82.

141. "Photograph of Bataan Café, 1946," Kistner, Custado, Redondo Collection, Box 1, San Diego Historical Society; and Rolando Mata, interview with author.

142. Cooperativa Mexicana, Inc., 1929 (O.P. 15523), Book 1: Mexican Americans, Box 155, Photograph Collection, San Diego Historical Society.

143. Most early listings of businesses include the name of the owner, rather than the name of the business. I have collected business information based on Spanish surnames for both Mexicans and Filipinos. I have also listed businesses with names that appear to be Filipino. For more on this, see *Polk's San Diego City Directories, 1920–1965*.

144. Consuelo "Connie" Zuniga, interview with author.

145. Rosalie Toledo Zarate, interview with author, National City, CA, November 16, 2005; and Patacsil, Guevarra, and Tuyay, *Filipinos in San Diego*, 56–57.

146. España-Maram, "Negotiating Identity," 48–50. For more on the concept of "mobile homes," see Espiritu, *Home Bound*.

147. Castillo-Tsuchida, "Filipino Migrants in San Diego" (thesis), 42.

148. Haas, *Conquests and Historical Identities in California*, 201.

149. *Chicano Park,* prod. Marilyn Mulford and Mario Barrera, dir. Marilyn Mulford, 59 min., Redbird Films, 1989, videocassette.

150. Cordova, *Filipinos,* 195.

CHAPTER 3 — SURVIVAL AND BELONGING

1. See Jon D. Cruz, "Filipino-American Community Organizations in Washington, 1900s–1930s," in *Peoples of Color in the American West,* ed. Sucheng Chan, Douglas Henry Daniels, Mario T. Garcia, and Terry P. Wilson (Lexington, MA: D. C. Heath, 1994), 235–45.

2. Ibid., 244–45.

3. Ibid., 245.

4. Ibid.

5. Zaragosa Vargas, *Labor Rights Are Civil Rights: Mexican American Workers in Twentieth-Century America* (Princeton, NJ: Princeton University Press, 2005), 5.

6. See Filipino Oral History Project, Inc., *Voices: A Filipino American Oral History* (Stockton, CA: Filipino Oral History Project, Inc., 2000), 39.

7. "Filipinos Getting Their Bearings in South Bay," *San Diego Union Tribune,* December 4, 1983, Lateral File: Filipino Americans, Thelma Hollingsworth Local History Room, National City Public Library.

8. David G. Gutiérrez, *Walls and Mirrors: Mexican Americans, Mexican Immigrants, and the Politics of Ethnicity* (Berkeley: University of California Press, 1995), 36.

9. "San Diego Mexican and Chicano History," http://www-rohan.sdsu.edu/dept/mas/chicanohistory/chapter06/c06s04.html (accessed June 3, 2005).

10. "Mexican Fraternal Society," *San Diego Union,* January 29, 1900, 6.

11. The Sociedad Beneficia Mexicana "Benito Juarez" de National City was a chapter of a larger national organization. There are no written records of the National City branch of this organization, other than a photograph. See "The Sociedad Beneficia Mexicana 'Benito Juarez' de National City," De Mara Family Photograph Collection, Local History Room, National City Public Library.

12. Richard Griswold del Castillo, ed., *Chicano San Diego: Cultural Space and the Struggle for Justice* (Tucson: University of Arizona Press, 2007), 75.

13. "Los Festejos Patrios en S. Diego, Cal.," *El Hispano Americano,* September 16, 1934, 8; "Las Fiestas del Cinco de Mayo en San Diego, Calif.," *El Hispano Americano,* May 12, 1934, 1.

14. "Un Brillante Programa se Desarrollará los Días 15 y 16 en el Parque Balboa," *El Hispano Americano,* September 11, 1935, 1.

15. "L. F. Castro, New Mexican Consul, Reception Host," *San Diego Union,* September 16, 1934, 5; "Mexicans Celebrate Independence Day," *San Diego Union,* September 16, 1938, 3; "S.D. to Observe Mexican Holiday," *San Diego Union,* September 15, 1943, 4; "S.D. to Join in Celebration of Mexican Independence," *San Diego Union,* September 5, 1943, 10; "Mexican Fiesta Celebrates Day of Independence," *San Diego Union,* September 16, 1935, 5; "L. F. Castro, New Mexican Consul, Reception Host," *San Diego Union,* September 16, 1936, 5; "Mexicans Celebrate Independence Day," *San Diego Union,* September 16, 1938, 3.

16. George B. Mangold and S. Lucile Thompson, *Community Welfare in San Diego* (San Diego: Community Welfare Council of San Diego, 1929), 171–75.

17. "S.D. to Observe Mexican Holiday," *San Diego Union,* September 15, 1943, 4; "S.D. to Join in Celebration of Mexican Independence," *San Diego Union,* September 16, 1943, 10.

18. For more on the Alianza Hispano-Americana, see Kaye Lynn Briegel, "Alianza Hispano-Americana, 1984–1965: A Mexican American Fraternal Insurance Society" (PhD diss., University of Southern California, 1974).

19. Briegel, "Aliana Hispano-Americana," 9.

20. Ibid., 69, and 128–34. Although I came across mention of a San Ysidro lodge (Lodge No. 146) in 1933, Alianza records show no such branch. See "Allianza [sic] Hispano Americana Elect New Officers," San Ysidro Border Press, 1933, 1, Newspaper Room, San Diego Public Library.

21. "Allianza [sic] Hispano Americana Elect New Officers"; "Un Brillante Programa se Desarrollará los Días 15 y 16 en el Parque Balboa," 1.

22. Brielgel, "Alianza Hispano-Americana," 176. See also "photograph of Alianza Hispano Americana, September 15–16, 1924," Book 1: Mexican Americans, Box 155, Photograph Collection, San Diego Historical Society.

23. For more on the Mexican American Movement, see "Mexican American Movement: Its Scope Origin and Personnel" pamphlet, Folder 7, Box 14, Series 3, Subseries A, Ernesto Galarza Papers, Special Collections and University Archives, Stanford University; and Albert R. Lozano, "Progress through Education," 16–17, Folder 01:29, Box 1, Supreme Council of the Mexican American Movement Collection, Special Collections and Archives, California State University, Northridge.

24. See "La Hermandad Mexicana Nacional," File: Mexican Americans, Vertical File Collection, California Room, San Diego Public Library.

25. "The History of MAPA and the Mexican-American in California" and "Governor's Meeting with Mexican-American Community Roster," Folder 11, Box 14, Series 3, Subseries A, Ernesto Galarza Papers, Special Collections and University Archives, Stanford University. For more on the life of Armando Rodriguez, see Armando Rodriguez, as told to Keith Taylor, From the Barrio to Washington: An Educator's Journey (Albuquerque: University of New Mexico Press, 2007).

26. "National Hero to Be Honored," San Diego Union, December 28, 1930, 4.

27. Untitled clipping, San Diego Union, December 28, 1934, 4; untitled clipping, San Diego Union, March 8, 1936, 10, untitled clipping, San Diego Union, December 31, 1937, 2; and Adelaida Castillo-Tsuchida, "Filipino Migrants in San Diego, 1900–1946" (MA thesis, University of San Diego, 1979), 70.

28. "Program Commemorating 23rd Anniversary of the Death of Dr. Jose Rizal, The Philippine Organization of San Diego, California, December 30, 1919," in Castillo-Tsuchida, "Filipino Migrants in San Diego," 54. Original document can be found at the San Diego Historical Society.

29. Ibid. The program was also conducted both in English and Spanish, which could indicate that there were Mexican members involved in this organization, including Mexican wives of Filipino members.

30. City directory information shows that in 1921 the Filipino Club was an active club, with P. E. Arriola as secretary-president. See Polk's San Diego City Directory, 1921; and Castillo-Tsuchida, "Filipino Migrants in San Diego" (thesis), 51.

31. Polk's San Diego City Directories, 1920–1965; Castillo-Tsuchida, "Filipino Migrants in San Diego" (thesis), 53; and Castillo-Tsuchida, "Filipino Migrants in San Diego, 1900–1946," Journal of San Diego History 22, no. 3 (Summer 1976): 32.

32. "S.D. Filipinos in Celebration," San Diego Sun, November 16, 1935; "Filipinos to Observe Island Anniversary," San Diego Sun, November 13, 1936, 1; "Coronado Filipino Club to Celebrate," San Diego Sun, November 14, 1926; "Filipinos Open Freedom Fete,"

San Diego Sun, November 14, 1936. For more on Rizal Day, see "Ceremony to Honor Heró of Philippines," *San Diego Sun,* December 30, 1935.

33. "Philippine Independence Rites Slated," *San Diego Union,* June 10, 1965, A29.

34. See "Barangay in America," *The Philippine Press,* August 1987, 7, Caballeros de Dimas-Alang 1 File, NPA, FANHS, Seattle, Washington.

35. For more on the Caballeros de Dimas-Alang, see "Articles of Incorporation of Caballeros de Dimas-Alang," Folder: Caballeros de Dimas-Alang 94077, California State Archives; "Luna Lodge No. 8 Convention Program," December 22, 1930, 14, Caballeros de Dimas-Alang 2 File, NPA, FANHS, Seattle, Washington.

36. Ibid.

37. Michael Cullinane, "The Filipino Federation of America: The Prewar Years, 1925–1940," *Crossroads* 1, no. 1 (February 1983): 74–85, Filipino Federation of America, Inc. File, NPA, FANHS, Seattle, Washington; "A Message to Both Filipinos and Americans from the Filipino Federation of America, Inc.," Filipino Federation of America, Inc. File, NPA, FANHS, Seattle, Washington.

38. "Filipino Federation, Branch No. 9 Opens in San Diego," *Filipino Nation,* July 1928, 14; "Directory of Branches of the Filipino Federation of America, Inc.," *Filipino Nation,* January 1929, 3; "Hawaii Member Transferred to California," *Filipino Nation,* January 1931, 44.

39. "Filipino Center Plans Outlined," *San Diego Union,* August 23, 1931, 10.

40. Judy Patacsil, Rudy Guevarra Jr., and Felix Tuyay, *Filipinos in San Diego* (San Francisco: Arcadia Publishing, 2010), 82.

41. Del Labao, "My Memories of FAVA, Filipino-Americans of San Diego: The Early Years," *Philippine and World Report,* April 1999, 1.

42. "Filipino Association Plans Christmas Party," *San Diego Union,* December 9, 1934, 4; and Patacsil, Guevarra, and Tuyay, *Filipinos in San Diego,* 25–27.

43. "Filipino Inter-Community Organization of the Western States Member Communities List," Folder F3640:3655, Earl Warren Papers, California State Archives; "Filipino Group Will Meet Here," *San Diego Union,* August 26, 1946, B1; "Filipinos Will Open Conclave Here Today," *San Diego Union,* August 28, 1946, A2; "Grand Ball Ends Filipino Parley," *San Diego Union,* September 1, 1946, A3.

44. "Constitution and By-Laws of the Filipino Women's Club of San Diego, California," January 13, 1949, Virginia Gomez Personal Collection; "History of the Filipino American Women's Club of San Diego County (FAWC), 1949–2004," *55th Anniversary Installation Dinner and Ball of the Filipino American Women's Club of San Diego County,* February 14, 2004, 44, Virginia Gomez Personal Collection; "The Filipino American Women's Club," *FANHS San Diego Chapter Newsletter* 2, no. 4 (Winter 1998): 6, Filipino American Women's Club Folder, FANHS San Diego Chapter Archives; Ronald S. Buenaventura, "Our History Is No Mystery," *Kalayan,* October 1996, San Diego File, NPA, FANHS, Seattle, Washington.

45. "Constitution and By-Laws of the Filipino Women's Club of San Diego, California," January 13, 1949, Virginia Gomez Personal Collection; "San Diego's Oldest FAWC Marks 35th Year," *The Filipino-American,* April 6–12, 1984, 3, Virginia Gomez Personal Collection; and "History of the Filipino American Women's Club of San Diego County (FAWC), 1949–1999," *50th Golden Anniversary Gala Program,* March 13, 1999, 1, Charito Pelaez Balanag Personal Collection; Yen Le Espiritu, *Home Bound: Filipino American Lives across Cultures, Communities, and Countries* (Berkeley: University of California Press, 2003), 112–13.

46. Charito Balanag, interview with author, San Diego, CA, June 28, 2004; and Espiritu, *Home Bound,* 112.

47. Charito Balanag, interview with author; and Espiritu, *Home Bound*, 112–13.

48. Virginia Gomez, interview with author, San Diego, CA, July 6, 2004.

49. "Get-Together Set," *San Diego Union*, April 12, 1969, D2, Virginia Gomez Personal Collection; and Patacsil, Guevarra, and Tuyay, *Filipinos in San Diego*, 89.

50. "Philippine Independence Rites Slated," *San Diego Union*, June 10, 1965, A29; and Espiritu, *Home Bound*, 113.

51. Charito Balanag, interview with author.

52. Espiritu, *Home Bound*, 114.

53. Virginia Gomez, interview with author; and Freddie Ayap, interview with author, National City, CA, August 5, 2004.

54. Newspapers report that more than 80 percent of the Mexican schoolchildren were U.S. born. Anthropologist Roberto Alvarez Jr. notes that the Mexican parents clarified that 95 percent of the students were American citizens. See "Pupils Strike Over Special Schoolhouse," *San Diego Sun*, February 10, 1931, 3; and Robert R. Alvarez Jr., "The Lemon Grove Incident: The Nation's First Successful Desegregation Court Case," *Journal of San Diego History* 32, no. 2 (Spring 1986): 134.

55. I borrowed this title from the documentary of the same name produced by Paul Espinosa.

56. Superior Court of the State of California, County of San Diego, Petition for Writ of Mandate No. 66625, February 13, 1931. According to Roberto Alvarez Jr., this is the only official record of the court case that still exists. See Alvarez, "The Lemon Grove Incident," 116 and fn. 8; Billie Sutherland, "Making a Difference," *The Californian Lifestyles*, February 7, 1991, C2; and Griswold del Castillo, *Chicano San Diego*, 85. See also *Brown v. Board of Education*, 347 U.S. 483 (1954); and *Westminster School Dist. of Orange County v. Mendez*, 161 F. 2d 774 (1947).

57. Lemon Grove School Board minutes, July 1930, Vertical File 353: Lemon Grove, Lemon Grove Historical Society; and "Mexicans Were Once Unwanted in Lemon Grove School System," *Daily Californian*, August 26, 1982, 4A, Vertical File 353: Lemon Grove, Lemon Grove Historical Society.

58. Lemon Grove School Board minutes, August 13, 1930, Vertical File 353: Lemon Grove, Lemon Grove Historical Society; "Mexicans Were Once Unwanted," 4A, Vertical File 353: Lemon Grove, Lemon Grove Historical Society.

59. Alvarez, "The Lemon Grove Incident," 121; and "Lemon Grove School Strike Still Going On," *San Diego Sun*, February 11, 1931, 1.

60. Lemon Grove School Board minutes, December 16, 1930; and "Mexicans Were Once Unwanted," 4A, Vertical File 353: Lemon Grove, Lemon Grove Historical Society.

61. "International Complications in School Strike," *La Mesa Scout*, February 13, 1931, Vertical File 353: Lemon Grove, Lemon Grove Historical Society; Byron L. Netzley, "Personal History of the Lemon Grove School District," Vertical File 353: Lemon Grove, Lemon Grove Historical Society; "Mexican Pupils Go On 'Strike' in Lemon Grove, *San Diego Union*, January 9, 1931, 1; "Lemon Grove School Strike Still Going On," *San Diego Sun*, February 11, 1931, 1, Griswold del Castillo, *Chicano San Diego*, 85.

62. "Roberto Alvarez, 84; Businessman Made History in 1931 with Landmark School Integration Suit," *Los Angeles Times*, February 26, 2003, Vertical File 353: Lemon Grove, Lemon Grove Historical Society; "In Memorium: Don Roberto Ricardo Alvarez," *La Prensa San Diego*, February 28, 2003; "Mexicans Were Once Unwanted," 4A, Vertical File 353: Lemon Grove, Lemon Grove Historical Society; Alvarez, "The Lemon Grove Incident," 118, 125.

63. For more on the Alvarez family, see Roberto R. Alvarez Jr., *Familia: Migration and Adaptation in Baja and Alta California, 1800–1975* (Berkeley: University of California Press, 1987); Alvarez, "The Lemon Grove Incident," 125; and Griswold del Castillo, *Chicano San Diego,* 86.

64. "Mexicans Were Once Unwanted," 4A, Vertical File 353: Lemon Grove, Lemon Grove Historical Society.

65. "Roberto Alvarez, 84; Businessman Made History in 1931 With Landmark School Integration Suit"; "In Memorium: Don Roberto Ricardo Alvarez"; Alvarez, "The Lemon Grove Incident," 130–31.

66. "Orders Mexican Pupils Admitted at Lemon Grove," *San Diego Union,* March 12, 1931, 10; "In Memorium: Don Roberto Ricardo Alvarez"; Alvarez, "The Lemon Grove Incident," 131.

67. Lemon Grove School Board minutes, March 12, 1931, Vertical File 353: Lemon Grove, Lemon Grove Historical Society.

68. Griswold del Castillo, *Chicano San Diego,* 88.

69. "Roberto Alvarez, 84; Businessman Made History in 1931 with Landmark School Integration Suit"; and Alvarez, "The Lemon Grove Incident," 132.

70. See *Kari Carlin et al. v. Board of Education, San Diego Unified School District,* No. 303, 8000, 1967, Folder C-1967 (Legal Doc 1–2), Box 1, Carlin Integration Case Records, San Diego State University Special Collections; Larry D. Carlin and Earnest E. Hartzog, "School Segregation in San Diego," Folder CC (Presentations Re. SDUSD), Box 10, Carlin Integration Case Records, San Diego State University Special Collections; "A Brief History of the Carlin Case," Folder: Carlin Integration Case Collection, Box 1, Carlin Integration Case Records, San Diego State University Special Collections.

71. Although Filipinos are not pictured or mentioned in newspaper articles as members, given their history of fighting for labor and civil rights, it is likely that they were also involved in the organization. For more on members in the organization, see "photo of elective officers, San Diego Race Relations Society, 1947, San Diego, California" and "photo of board of directors of the San Diego Race Relations Society, 1947, San Diego, California," Folder F3640:3657, Earl Warren Papers, California State Archives.

72. "Letter to Governor Earl Warren from Dennis V. Allen, San Diego Race Relations Society," March 21, 1944, Folder F3640:3655, Earl Warren Papers, California State Archives; and "Affair Planned at Memorial," *San Diego Union,* February 24, 1943.

73. "Race Relations Commission—California Session Information Sheet, 1937," Folder F3640:3655, Earl Warren Papers, California State Archives.

74. "Letter to Randall M. Dorton, Deputy Director of Finance, from Dennis V. Allen, President, San Diego Race Relations Society regarding Birth and History of The California Race Relations Commission," March 4, 1946, 1–2, Folder F3640:3657, Earl Warren Papers, California State Archives.

75. Ibid., 2; and "Letter to Earl Warren from Dennis V. Allen," March 25, 1944, Folder F3640:3656, Earl Warren Papers, California State Archives.

76. "Letter to Mayor Edgar E. Clover from Ricardo Castro Sainz, San Diego Race Relations Society regarding braceros in Escondido," September 1944; and "Letter to Governor Earl Warren from Dennis V. Allen, San Diego Race Relations Society regarding Mexican Nationals," September 4, 1944, Folder F3640:3656, Earl Warren Papers, California State Archives.

77. This case seems to have been an isolated incident, which resulted in victory prior to the Supreme Court ruling in 1948 that deemed racial restrictive covenants as not enforceable. See Castillo-Tsuchida, "Filipino Migrants in San Diego" (thesis), 101.

78. Dora Hollman Garcia, interview with author, Spring Valley, CA, September 15, 2004; Delia Chavez, interview with author, San Diego, CA, August 23, 2001.

79. Dora Hollman Garcia, interview with author.

80. Delia Chavez, interview with author.

81. Rodriguez, *From the Barrio to Washington*, 36.

82. Noel Osment, "A Joyful Reunion of the Girlfriends," *San Diego Union*, January 20, 1980, D1, D7, File: Filipinos—San Diego (city), Vertical File Collection, California Room, San Diego Public Library.

83. Ibid.

84. Ibid.

85. Photograph of the Toltec Club, 1947, Freddie Ayap Family Photograph Collection; Freddie Ayap, interview with author, Imperial Beach, CA, September 23, 2004; and "Coach Augie Escamilla, 'Coach of Coaches' Program," April 17, 1999, Freddie Ayap Personal Collection.

86. See Douglas Henry Daniels, "Los Angeles Zoot: Race 'Riot,' the Pachuco, and Black Music Culture," *Journal of Negro History* 82, no. 2 (Spring 1997): 201–20.

87. *Logan Heights Historical Society Memory Album,* 43, Logan Heights Historical Society Collection.

88. Linda España-Maram, *Creating Masculinity in Los Angeles's Little Manila: Working-Class Filipinos and Popular Culture, 1920s–1950s* (New York: Columbia University Press, 2006), 137–38.

89. Luis Alvarez, "Zoot Violence on the Home Front: Race, Riots, and Youth Culture during World War II," in *Mexican Americans and World War II*, ed. Maggie Rivas-Rodriguez (Austin: University of Texas Press, 2005), 144.

90. Ibid.

91. See Alvarez, "Zoot Violence on the Home Front," 141–75; Edward J. Escobar, *Race, Police, and the Making of a Political Identity: Mexican Americans and the Los Angeles Police Department, 1900–1945* (Berkeley: University of California Press, 1999); Luis Alvarez, *The Power of the Zoot: Youth Culture and Resistance during World War II* (Berkeley: University of California Press, 2009); and Catherine S. Ramírez, *The Woman in the Zoot Suit: Gender, Nationalism, and the Cultural Politics of Memory* (Durham, NC: Duke University Press, 2009).

92. "Zoot-Suiters Hunted in S.D.," *San Diego Union,* June 10, 1943, A1; "Zooters Escape San Diego Mob," *Los Angeles Examiner,* June 1943, in Zoot Suiters [microform]: A Compilation of Clippings, Reports and Documents Collected by Carey McWilliams [Los Angeles, 1930–1940], University of California, Los Angeles Library; Alvarez, *The Power of the Zoot,* 202–3.

93. "Zoot-Suit Fracas Hits San Diego," *Chicago Defender,* June 19, 1943, 20.

94. "S.D. Zoot-Suit Tension Eases," *San Diego Union,* June 12, 1942, A1.

95. Frank Penuelas, quoted in Mark T. Sullivan, "Dark Ages to Daylight: City's Racial Tale," *San Diego Tribune,* November 18, 1991, A5, Folder 510: Race Relations in San Diego, San Diego Historical Society; and Griswold del Castillo, *Chicano San Diego,* 103.

96. "CIO Council Acts Against Race Incitement," in Zoot Suiters [microform]: A Compilation of Clippings, Reports and Documents Collected by Carey McWilliams [Los Angeles, 1930–1940], University of California, Los Angeles Library.

97. With the passing of the Tydings-McDuffie Act of 1934, Filipinos became "aliens ineligible for citizenship." For more on the participation of Filipinos and Mexicans in World War II, see Filipinos Ditoy, Hawai'i brochure, *Philippine Islands War Relief Fund Iti National War Fund,* 1945, Hawaiian Sugar Planters' Association Archives, University of

Hawai'i at Manoa (hereafter cited as HSPA Archives); Ronald Takaki, *Democracy and Race: Asian Americans and World War II* (New York: Chelsea House Publishers, 1989), 27–37; Lorraine Jacobs Crouchett, *Filipinos in California: From the Days of the Galleons to the Present* (Cerritos, CA: Downey Place Publishing House, 1982), 46; Rivas-Rodriguez, *Mexican Americans and World War II*; Zaragosa Vargas, *Crucible of Struggle: A History of Mexican Americans from Colonial Times to the Present* (New York: Oxford University Press, 2011), 255–59; Ronald Takaki, *Double Victory: A Multicultural History of America in World War II* (New York: Little, Brown, 2000), 82–90, 120–25; Alex S. Fabros, "California's Filipino Infantry," http://www.militarymuseum.org/Filipino.html (accessed January 12, 2007).

98. George J. Sánchez, *Becoming Mexican American: Ethnicity, Culture, and Identity in Chicano Los Angeles, 1900–1945* (New York: Oxford University Press, 1993), 267; and Alvarez, "Zoot Violence on the Home Front," 165.

99. "Prejudice: Our Postwar Battle," *Look*, May 1, 1945, 48; Vargas, *Crucible of Struggle,* 259–60, 267; Takaki, *Double Victory,* 123.

100. Salvador Torres, quoted in *Logan Heights Historical Society Memory Album,* 43, Logan Heights Historical Society Collection.

101. Jack Williams, "Henry Diaz; Lifetime Booster of Logan Heights," *San Diego-Union Tribune,* May 9, 2003, B7, File: Obituaries, Box 1, Logan Heights Historical Society; and "Henry L. 'Leaky' Diaz; Founder of the Logan Heights Historical Society," File: Obituaries, Box 1, Logan Heights Historical Society.

102. Freddie Ayap, interview with author; Consuelo "Connie" Zuniga, interview with author, San Diego, CA, August 20, 2001.

103. Ricardo Romio, interview with author, Lakeside, CA, May 4, 2004.

104. Ibid.

105. Ibid.

106. Ibid.

107. George Lipsitz, *Rainbow at Midnight: Labor and Culture in the 1940s* (Chicago: University of Illinois Press, 1994), 305–7.

108. Douglas Henry Daniels, *Pioneer Urbanites: A Social and Cultural History of Black San Francisco* (Berkeley: University of California Press, 1990), 144–46.

109. For more on popular youth culture and the role of music, see Lipsitz, *Rainbow at Midnight,* 304–33; Sánchez, *Becoming Mexican American;* Guthrie P. Ramsey Jr., *Race Music: Black Cultures from Bebop to Hip-Hop* (Berkeley: University of California Press, 2003); Robin D. G. Kelley, *Race Rebels: Culture, Politics, and the Black Working Class* (New York: Free Press, 1996), 161–81; Daniels, "Los Angeles Zoot," 201–20.

110. Lanny Villarin, interview with author, National City, CA, May 5, 2004.

111. Ibid.; Doral Hollman Garcia, interview with author.

112. Rachael Ortiz, Rachael and the Chorals (45 single), "You Don't Know," Rachael Ortiz Collection, Logan Heights Historical Society; and *Logan Heights Historical Society Memory Album,* 39–45.

113. Ricardo Romio, interview with author.

114. Personal notes on conversation with Rachael Ortiz, June 14, 2006; "The Original Angel Baby Rosie Hamlin," *Logan Heights Historical Society Memory Album,* 24; and J. J. Rocha, "Rosie: Still an Original after All These Years," *El Sol de San Diego,* June 25, 1987, 5.

115. David Hinckley, "Rosie: 'Angel Baby' Still Singing," *Press-Enterprise,* July 1, 1991, A5; Rosie Hamlin, "The Biography of Rosie Hamlin," http://rosieandtheoriginals.com/main/rosiehamlin.htm (accessed October 28, 2006); Yvette Urrea, "NC Native Credited

for Classic Hit," http://rosieandtheoriginals.com/newspaper/yvetteurrea.htm (accessed October 28, 2006).

116. Alan Freed, quoted in Hamlin, "The Biography of Rosie Hamlin."

117. Hinckley, "Rosie," A5.

118. Rosie Hamlin eventually settled a million-dollar lawsuit in 1988 to regain control over her royalties for writing "Angel Baby." See "Singer, 16, Settles $1 Million Suit," http://rosieandtheoriginals.com/newspaper/sandiegounion.htm (accessed October 28, 2006); and Urrea, "NC Native Credited for Classic Hit."

119. Rocha, "Rosie," 5; and John Lennon, quoted in Hamlin, "The Biography of Rosie Hamlin."

120. Lanny Villarin, interview with author.

121. See David Reyes, *Land of a Thousand Dances: Chicano Rock'n'Roll from Southern California* (Albuquerque: University of New Mexico Press, 2009); and Anthony Macías, *Mexican American Mojo: Popular Music, Dance, and Urban Culture in Los Angeles, 1935–1968* (Durham, NC: Duke University Press, 2008).

122. Daniels, *Pioneer Urbanites*, 160.

123. Bell Hooks, *Killing Rage: Ending Racism* (New York: Owl Books, 1995), 6.

CHAPTER 4 — RACE AND LABOR ACTIVISM IN SAN DIEGO

1. Chris Mensalvas helped organize the Filipino Labor Union (FLU) in Salinas, then worked to establish other local chapters throughout California. Although most studies that mention Mensalvas leave out San Diego as one of the areas where FLU was present, I was able to find some mention of it in San Diego newspapers, showing the only known evidence of Chris Mensalvas's and FLU's activities in the region. See "Accord Reached for Settlement of Pickers' Row," *San Diego Union*, February 23, 1936, 1–2; "Celery Workers' Strike Set Today," *San Diego Union*, February 16, 1936, 1; "Workers' Union Strike Captain Cites Objective," *San Diego Union*, February 23, 1936, 2; "Arrest Looms for Woman in Celery Strike," *San Diego Sun*, February 24, 1936, 1.

2. "Accord Reached for Settlement of Pickers' Row," *San Diego Union*, February 23, 1936, 1–2; and "Deportations Is Warning to S.D. Celery Pickets," *San Diego Evening Tribune*, February 21, 1936, Vertical File 93–2, Vertical File Collection, San Diego Historical Society.

3. David Reid, quoted in Mike Davis, Kelley Mayhew, and Jim Miller, *Under the Perfect Sun: The San Diego Tourists Never See* (New York: New Press, 2003), 16.

4. I borrow the concept of a colonized workforce from Gilbert G. González, *Guest Workers or Colonized Labor? Mexican Labor Migration to the United States* (Boulder, CO: Paradigm Publishers, 2006).

5. Laura Pulido, *Black, Brown, Yellow, and Left: Radical Activism in Los Angeles* (Berkeley: University of California Press, 2006), 24.

6. See Adrian Cruz, "There Will Be No 'One Big Union': The Struggle for Interracial Labor Unionism in California Agriculture, 1933–1939," *Cultural Dynamics* 22, no. 1 (2010): 29–48.

7. Gang labor describes groups of men that were organized into "gangs" to work specific crops.

8. This observation was the result of conducting research in the San Diego–Imperial Valley Counties Labor Council Collection and its extensive newspaper holdings of the *San Diego Labor Leader*. Most of the information in these newspapers dealt with skilled, white labor, with very few articles touching upon issues regarding agricultural workers or other unskilled and semi-skilled positions.

9. A. B. Santos, quoted Yen Le Espiritu, *Filipino American Lives* (Philadelphia: Temple University Press, 1995), 40–41.

10. Manuel Buaken, *I Have Lived with the American People* (Caldwell, ID: Caxton Printers, 1948), 78.

11. Will J. French, dir., *Facts about Filipino Immigration into California, Special Bulletin No. 3* (San Francisco: California Department of Industrial Relations, 1930), 72.

12. See Adelaida Castillo, "Filipino Migrants in San Diego, 1900–1946," *Journal of San Diego History* 22, no. 3 (Summer 1976): 31; Adelaida Castillo-Tsuchida, "Filipino Migrants in San Diego, 1900–1946" (MA thesis: University of San Diego, 1979), 69; *Polk's 1955 San Diego City Directory*, 650; *Polk's 1960 San Diego City Directory*, 392; Ronald S. Buenaventura, "San Diego's Manongs of the 1920s and 1930s," *Filipino American National Historical Society Journal* 5 (1998), 31.

13. Castillo-Tsuchida, "Filipino Migrants in San Diego" (thesis), 81.

14. Buaken, *I Have Lived with the American People,* 82.

15. See "Hotel Chef Dishes Up Memories," *San Diego Evening Tribune,* November 14, 1977; "El Cortez to End Its Towering Role in City's History," *San Diego Evening Tribune,* July 10, 1978, B1, B4; and "El Cortez Turns Back Clock on 50th Birthday," *San Diego Union,* November 24, 1977, F1, F6, Vertical File 288–12: Hotels/Motels, El Cortez, Vertical File Collection, San Diego Historical Society.

16. Kitchen, campus, and groundskeeper staff were not included in staff pages in the Bishop High School annuals until 1964. *El Miradero,* Bishop's High School Annual, La Jolla, CA, 1964, 7; and *El Miradero,* Bishop's High School Annual, La Jolla, CA, 1965, 90, La Jolla Historical Society.

17. Rudy Guevarra Sr., interview with author, San Diego, CA, March 26, 2005; Alma Gonzalez (pseudonym), interview with author, Tracy, CA, August 29, 2004; HOLC area descriptions, San Diego, California, October 20, 1936, National Archives, courtesy of Richard Marciano; and Marciano, Goldberg, and Hou, "T-RACES: A Testbed for the Redlining Archives of California's Exclusionary Spaces," http://salt.unc.edu/T-RACES (accessed May 1, 2010).

18. There is a dearth of historical records documenting their employment. I had to rely on previous oral testimonies, photographs, and other sources. For example, an archivist at the Hotel Del Coronado informed me that they had no records of either Mexicans or Filipinos, except for two photographs. See "photo of Mexican waiters, circa 1960" and "photo of Filipino bartenders and cooks, circa 1960," Photograph Collection, Hotel Del Coronado, San Diego.

19. HOLC area descriptions, San Diego, CA, October 20, 1936, National Archives, courtesy of Richard Marciano; Marciano, Goldberg, and Hou, "T-RACES"; and Castillo-Tsuchida, "Filipino Migrants in San Diego" (thesis), 98.

20. French, *Facts about Filipino Immigration into California,* 72; and Buaken, *I Have Lived with the American People,* 189.

21. See Philip R. Pryde, *San Diego: An Introduction to the Region* (San Diego, CA: Sunbelt Publications, 2004), 145.

22. Ibid., 154–56.

23. For more on the contributions of Chinese, Japanese, and Koreans to California agriculture, see Sucheng Chan, *This Bitter Sweet Soil: The Chinese in California Agriculture, 1860–1910* (Berkeley: University of California Press, 1986); Donald H. Estes, "Before the War: The Japanese in San Diego," *Journal of San Diego History* 24, no. 4 (Fall 1978): 425–56; Ronald Takaki, *Strangers from a Different Shore: A History of Asian Americans* (Boston: Little, Brown, 1998).

24. George P. Clements, "Should Mexican Immigration Be Restricted?," May 12, 1926, 4, Untitled Folder, Box 80, George P. Clements Papers, Special Collections and University Archives, University of California, Los Angeles.

25. Larry R. Salomon, *Roots of Justice: Stories of Organizing in Communities of Color* (Berkeley: Chardon Press, 1998), 13.

26. For an example of sources showing the presence of early Mexican and Filipino communities in these areas, see "Spring Valley, 1947" (photo of Mexican agricultural workers), Alicia S. Valadez album, Book 1—San Ysidro, CA, Box 295, Photograph Collection, San Diego Historical Society; "Lemon Grove, 1934" (photo of Mexican men), Number 80:5239, Book 1—Lemon Grove, CA, Box 270, Photograph Collection, San Diego Historical Society; David Galbiso, interview with author, Chula Vista, CA, August 4, 2006; Robert R. Alvarez Jr., *Familia: Migration and Adaptation in Baja and Alta California, 1800–1975* (Berkeley: University of California Press, 1987).

27. Alvarez, *Familia*, 141–51.

28. Encanto is a small town south of and adjacent to Lemon Grove. See Bertha Ramirez, interview with author, San Diego, CA, August 22, 2001; and Freddie Ayap, interview with author, National City, CA, August 5, 2005.

29. Joe Montijo, interview by S. Hurley, National City, CA, March 11, 1982, Oral History Collection, Thelma Hollingsworth Local History Room, National City Public Library; Marivi Soliven Blanco, *An Annotated Bibliography of Filipino and Filipino-American History Resources in the San Diego Historical Society Research Archives* (Spring 2002), FANHS San Diego Chapter Archives; Robert Holmes, interview by Edgar F. Hastings, Chula Vista, CA, March 16, 1959, Oral History Collection, San Diego Historical Society

30. Dorothy Fujita-Rony's insightful study on Filipinos in Seattle, for example, mentions San Diego as a location where Filipinos migrated to the urban sector for employment. The rural sector, however, was not mentioned, despite having a much larger labor force that employed thousands of agricultural workers. See Dorothy Fujita-Rony, *American Workers, Colonial Power: Philippine Seattle and the Transpacific West, 1919–1941* (Berkeley: University of California Press, 2002), 92, 114; Bruno Lasker, *Filipino Immigration to the Continental United States and to Hawaii* (Chicago: University of Chicago Press, 1931); French, *Facts about Filipino Immigration into California*; Castillo-Tsuchida, "Filipino Migrants in San Diego" (thesis); Carlos Bulosan, *America Is in the Heart* (Seattle: University of Washington Press, 1990); Richard Griswold del Castillo, ed., *Chicano San Diego: Cultural Space and the Struggle for Justice* (Tucson: University of Arizona Press, 2007), 81; Paul S. Taylor and Edward J. Rowell, "Patterns of Agricultural Labor Migration within California," *Monthly Labor Review of the Bureau of Labor Statistics, U.S. Department of Labor* (November 1938): 1–11, Folder 2–20, Box 8, Carey McWilliams Papers, Special Collections and University Archives, University of California, Los Angeles (hereafter cited as McWilliams Papers).

31. For more on the Alaskeros, see Bruno Lasker, "In the Alaska Fish Canneries," *Mid-Pacific* 43 (April 1932): 335–38; "Alaskeros," CW FLU Local No. 7, 1–8, Alaskeros File, NPA, FANHS Seattle, Washington; and Thelma Buchholdt, *Filipinos in Alaska, 1788–1958* (Anchorage, AK: Aboriginal Press, 1996).

32. Bulosan, *America Is in the Heart.*

33. Paul S. Taylor and Tom Vasey, *California Farm Labor,* Bureau of Research and Statistics, Federal Writers' Project, January 1937, 15, Folder 2–24, Box 9, McWilliams Papers.

34. Asian immigration was curtailed with the Chinese Exclusion Act of 1882, then the Gentlemen's Agreement in 1907–1908, and finally the Immigration Acts of 1917 and 1924,

which signaled the end of Chinese, Japanese, Indian, and other Asian laborers coming to California. See Takaki, *Strangers from a Different Shore;* Sucheng Chan, *Asian Americans: An Interpretive History* (New York: Twayne Publishers, 1991).

35. Mae M. Ngai, *Impossible Subjects: Illegal Aliens and the Making of Modern America* (Princeton, NJ: Princeton University Press, 2004), 106.

36. See John E. Pickett, "The Farm Labor Problem Grows Acute," *Pacific Rural Press,* May 9, 1936, 602; and Clements, "Should Mexican Immigration Be Restricted?"

37. Taylor and Vasey, *California Farm Labor,* 12–13.

38. William H. Metzler, "Making Stoop Labor Available for and Acceptable to Domestic Farm Labor," Farm Production Economics Division, U.S. Department of Agriculture, 1–7, Folder 27, Box 43, Paul Taylor Papers, Bancroft Library, University of California, Berkeley (hereafter cited as Taylor Papers).

39. "Letter to the Editor from Luis Agudo," February 18, 1930, 3, Filipino Survey, 1925–1930, Department of Industrial Relations—Division of Labor Laws Enforcement, F3275, Selected Archives, Box 118–2, California State Archives; and Carey McWilliams, "Exit the Filipino," *The Nation,* September 4, 1935.

40. Mary Catherine Miller, "Attitudes of the San Diego Labor Movement toward Mexicans, 1917–1936" (MA thesis, San Diego State University, 1974), 5–6.

41. "Statement of S. P. Frisselle," n.d., 4, Folder 2–24, Box 9, McWilliams Papers.

42. George P. Clements, quoted in John E. Pickett, "The Farm Labor Problem Grows Acute," *Pacific Rural Press,* May 9, 1936, 602, Folder: Pacific Rural Press, Box 17, McWilliams Papers.

43. Emory S. Bogardus, "The Mexican Immigrant," *Journal of Applied Sociology* 11 (1926): 477.

44. Takaki, *Strangers from a Different Shore,* 324.

45. Will J. French, dir., *Mexicans in California: Report of Governor C. C. Young's Fact-Finding Committee* (San Francisco: State of California Department of Industrial Relations, 1930), 92.

46. Helen W. Walker, "Mexican Immigrants and American Citizenship," *Sociology and Social Research* 13 (1929): 466.

47. C. C. Young, quoted in Roger Daniels and Harry H. L. Kitano, *American Racism: Exploration of the Nature of Prejudice* (Englewood Cliffs, NJ: Prentice Hall, 1970), 70.

48. Bogardus, "The Mexican Immigrant," 477.

49. Ibid., 479.

50. See Tomás Almaguer, "Racial Domination and Class Conflict in Capitalist Agriculture: The Oxnard Sugar Beet Workers' Strike of 1903," *Labor History* 25 (1984): 325–50; Richard Steven Street, *Beasts of the Field: A Narrative History of California Farmworkers, 1769–1913* (Stanford, CA: Stanford University Press, 2004), 440–69; Juan Gómez-Quiñones, *Mexican American Labor, 1790–1990* (Albuquerque: University of New Mexico Press, 1994), 76–77.

51. Gómez-Quiñones, *Mexican American Labor,* 132–33.

52. Ibid., 67.

53. Ibid., 67–68.

54. Miller, "Attitudes of the San Diego Labor Movement toward Mexicans," 4.

55. Samuel Gompers, who headed the AFL from its inception in 1886 until 1924, was vehemently anti-Asian and anti-Mexican, despite the fact he was also an immigrant. See Miller, "Attitudes of the San Diego Labor Movement toward Mexicans," 5, 10–11.

56. "Mexicans in Urban California," 15, Folder 4, Box 58, Subseries 1, Ernesto Galarza Papers, Special Collections and University Archives, Stanford University.

57. "Mass Meeting and Demonstration against Attack upon Filipino Workers," *Filipino Survey, 1925–1930*, Department of Industrial Relations—Division of Labor Laws Enforcement, F3275, Selected Archives, Box 118–2, California State Archives. "White casual workers" were defined as single, migratory white men who were known more commonly as "hobos" or "bindle-stiffs." Growers considered them unorganized and unreliable when compared to Asian and Mexican labor. For more on this, see Stuart Jamieson, dir., *Labor Unionism in American Agriculture* (Washington, DC: Government Printing Office, 1945), 55–58.

58. Given that Miller relied primarily on the *San Diego Labor Leader,* an organ of the AFL, her conclusions may have been biased. The paper suggests an amicable relationship between the AFL and Mexican workers in San Diego agriculture. A more careful look at its content, however, reveals that the paper primarily focused on skilled and semi-skilled white labor, not agriculture, which was oftentimes considered an occupation for unskilled nonwhite labor. If anything, her arguments are more applicable to the fish canning industry in San Diego, which was predominately AFL affiliated. Since the *San Diego Labor Leader* was an AFL paper, it is highly likely that it would not report the extent of the violence aimed at nonwhite workers. Ultimately, it was the voice of the AFL. When considering the turbulent times of the 1930s, one only has to look at Stuart Jamieson's report *Labor Unionism in American Agriculture* for examples on how effective the Communist Party and UCAPAWA were at organizing farm workers. These unions took on the task of organizing those that the AFL did not want in their ranks. See Miller, "Attitudes of the San Diego Labor Movement toward Mexicans," 58–63; and Jamieson, *Labor Unionism in American Agriculture.*

59. Miller, "Attitudes of the San Diego Labor Movement toward Mexicans," 33.

60. Ibid., 36.

61. Salomon, *Roots of Justice,* 12–13.

62. Jamieson, *Labor Unionism in American Agriculture,* 74.

63. Ibid., 75.

64. Ibid., 74–75.

65. For more on the various Filipino and Mexican unions see Howard DeWitt, "The Filipino Labor Union: The Salinas Lettuce Strike of 1934," *Amerasia Journal* 5, no. 2 (1978): 1–21; Salomon, *Roots of Justice,* 16–19; Peter W. Stanley, "Exiled in California," *This World,* July 19, 1981, 19, File: Demography—CA, NPA, FANHS, Seattle, Washington; Jamieson, *Labor Unionism in American Agriculture;* Cruz, "There Will be No 'One Big Union,'" 42.

66. "Report to Senator Robert F. Wagner from J. L. Leonard, Will J. French, and Simon J. Lubin," February 11, 1934, 16, Folder: Imperial Valley, Box 5, Records of the National Labor Relations Board (RG 25), National Archives and Records Administration, Laguna Niguel. All subsequent citations will me noted as NARA, Laguna Niguel.

67. See Ronald Takaki, *Pau Hana: Plantation Life and Labor in Hawaii* (Honolulu: University of Hawai'i Press, 1984); and Edward D. Beechert, *Working in Hawaii: A Labor History* (Honolulu: University of Hawai'i Press, 1985).

68. French, *Facts about Filipino Immigration into California,* 60–61.

69. Daniels and Kitano, *American Racism,* 70.

70. Jamieson, *Labor Unionism in American Agriculture,* 74; McWilliams, "Exit the Filipino," 265.

71. Camille Guérin-Gonzales, *Mexican Workers and American Dreams: Immigration, Repatriation, and California Farm Labor, 1900–1939* (New Brunswick, NJ: Rutgers University Press, 1994), 22; Cletus E. Daniel, *Bitter Harvest: A History of California Farmworkers, 1870–1941* (Berkeley: University of California Press, 1981), 109.

72. Jamieson, *Labor Unionism in American Agriculture*, 129; Linda C. Majka and Theo J. Majka, *Farm Workers, Agribusiness, and the State* (Philadelphia: Temple University Press, 1982), 65; Howard DeWitt, *Violence in the Fields: California Filipino Farm Labor Unionization during the Great Depression* (Saratoga, CA: Century Twenty One Publishing, 1980), 16; Salomon, *Roots of Justice*, 13; Takaki, *Strangers from a Different Shore*, 198–200.

73. William Becker, "Conflict as a Source of Solidarity," *Journal of Social Issues* 9, no. 1 (1953): 26.

74. *Unionization of Filipinos in California Agriculture*, 13–14, Folder: Filipinos, Box 16, Federal Writers' Project on Migratory Labor, Bancroft Library, University of California, Berkeley.

75. Moon-Kie Jung, *Reworking Race: The Making of Hawaii's Interracial Labor Movement* (New York: Columbia University Press, 2006), 6–7, 190.

76. See Jung, *Reworking Race*; and Yen Le Espiritu, *Home Bound: Filipino American Lives across Cultures, Communities, and Countries* (Berkeley: University of California Press, 2003), 17. See also addendum to notes, 225.

77. For more on this topic, see Rudy P. Guevarra Jr., "Mabuhay Compañero: Filipinos, Mexicans, and Labor Organizing in Hawai'i and California, 1920s–1940s," in *Transnational Crossroads: Remapping the Americas and the Pacific*, ed. Camilla Fojas and Rudy P. Guevarra Jr. (Lincoln: University of Nebraska Press, 2012), 171–197.

78. See Salomon, *Roots of Justice*, 9–20; David G. Gutiérrez, *Walls and Mirrors: Mexican Americans, Mexican Immigrants, and the Politics of Ethnicity* (Berkeley: University of California Press, 1995), 106; and Guevarra Jr., "Mabuhay Compañero."

79. Rufino Deogracias, "Filipino Agricultural Workers Must Fight against the Contract System," *The Agricultural Worker*, December 20, 1933, 6.

80. *Unionization of Filipinos in California Agriculture*, 4, Folder: Filipinos, Box 16, Federal Writers' Project on Migratory Labor, Bancroft Library, University of California, Berkeley.

81. The Communist Party wanted to organize elements of the working class that were untouched by the AFL and its "craft-conscious" conservatism. These included unskilled and semi-skilled workers in industries such as agriculture, mining, and textiles. Thus, the Communist Party set out to organize migratory seasonal farmworkers. Under its Trade Union Unity League (TUUL), the Communist Party established a new farm labor organization, the Cannery and Agricultural Workers Industrial Union (CAWIU) in 1930. See Jamieson, *Labor Unionism in American Agriculture*, 19–20; DeWitt, *Violence in the Fields*, 49–69; Majka and Majka, *Farm Workers, Agribusiness, and the State*, 65–69. With regards to Mexican and Filipino labor unions, although they were predominately ethnic based prior to 1930, in many instances they remained so, but worked together under interethnic alliances. See Joseph Maizlish, "California Agricultural Labor Unionism and the Agricultural Workers Organizing Committee," 5, Folder 9, Box 3, Series 3, Subseries A, Agricultural Labor, Ernesto Galarza Papers, Special Collections and University Archives, Stanford University.

82. Davis, Mayhew, and Miller, *Under the Perfect Sun*, 201.

83. Jamieson, *Labor Unionism in American Agriculture*, 83, 129.

84. Guérin-Gonzales, *Mexican Workers and American Dreams*, 70; Gutiérrez, *Walls and Mirrors*, 100; and Devra Anne Weber, "The Organizing of Mexicano Agricultural Workers: Imperial Valley and Los Angeles, 1928–1934: An Oral History Approach," *Aztlán* 3, no. 2 (Fall 1972): 314–16.

85. Jamieson, *Labor Unionism in American Agriculture*, 75.

86. Ibid., 74; Carey McWilliams, *Brothers under the Skin* (Boston: Little, Brown, 1964), 239–40; Ernesto Galarza, *Farm Workers and Agribusiness in California, 1947–1960* (Norte Dame: University of Norte Dame Press, 1977), 199; Sonia Emily Wallovits, "The Filipinos in California" (MA thesis, University of Southern California, 1966), 28–29; Roberto V. Vallangca, *Pinoy: The First Wave, 1898–1941* (San Francisco: Strawberry Hill Press, 1977), 23; DeWitt, *Violence in the Fields*, 101.

87. Gómez-Quiñones, *Mexican American Labor*, 131; and Jamieson, *Labor Unionism in American Agriculture*, 111.

88. "Report of Complaints Filed by Mexican Laborers with the California State Labor Commission in San Diego–Imperial County District for the Year January 1, 1926 to December 31, 1926," Folder 1, Box 9, Taylor Papers; and "Letter to Paul S. Taylor from Stanley Gue, Deputy Labor Commissioner, Bureau of Labor Statistics, State of California, July 14, 1927," Folder 10:1, Box 10, Taylor Papers.

89. "Statistical Summary of Agricultural Strikes in California 1933," 1–7, Folder 36 (Strikes), Box 20, McWilliams Papers.

90. Jamieson, *Labor Unionism in American Agriculture*, 130.

91. For more on statewide strikes, see Federal Writers' Project, "California Agriculture," in *Oriental Labor Unions and Strikes: California Agriculture* (Oakland, CA: n.p., n.d.), 24; Jamieson, *Labor Unionism in American Agriculture*, 107–10; "Orderly Strike of 2000 Field Workers Awakens Admiration," *Philippines Mail*, August 27, 1934, 1; Alex S. Fabros and Annalissa Herbert, eds., *The Filipino American Newspaper Collection: Extracts from 1906–1953* (Fresno, CA: The Filipino American Research Project, 1994), 120; Carey McWilliams, *Factories in the Field: The Story of Migratory Farm Labor in California* (Boston: Little, Brown, 1939), 133; Benicio Catapusan, "The Filipino Labor Cycle in the United States," *Sociology and Social Research* 19 (September 1934): 63; and Davis, Mayhew, and Miller, *Under the Perfect Sun*, 202. Although white workers were also involved in some of these strikes, they posed several problems. As Juan Gómez-Quiñones points out, white workers did not have a militant organizing tradition like Mexicans and Filipinos, nor did they really identify with farm labor. Rather, they tried to negotiate separately with the owners for better jobs in agriculture. This favoritism guaranteed them the comforts of the packing sheds. On other occasions, they left farm work altogether to find employment in the city. See Gómez-Quiñones, *Mexican American Labor*, 135; Takaki, *Strangers from a Different Shore*, 322.

92. Many of the strikes were mentioned in San Diego's newspapers, but the articles did not always indicate if the strikes were actually settled. See "Agitators Urge Wage Raise for Field Workers," *Chula Vista Star News*, January 6, 1933, 1; and "Celery Workers Form Union in San Diego," *Western Worker*, January 30, 1933, 1, Folder 704: Mexicans, 1933–34, Box 16, Federal Writers' Project on Migratory Labor, Bancroft Library, University of California, Berkeley.

93. See "Los Angeles Regional Labor Board List of Cases," Folder: List of Cases, 1933–35, Box 16, Records of the National Labor Relations Board, Record Group 25, NARA, Laguna Niguel.

94. "Striking Celery Men to Present Case at Hearing," *San Diego Union*, January 12, 1935, 1–2; and "Mexican Celery Workers' Strike Ends with Vote," *San Diego Union*, January 14, 1935, 1.

95. Although Japanese growers did work in concert with white growers to curtail labor organizing in other areas of California, sources indicate that Japanese growers in San Diego County were usually the first ones to concede to worker demands. See "Los Angeles Regional Labor Board List of Cases," Folder: List of Cases, 1933–35, Box 16, "Report from

the Regional Labor Board regarding new cases filed during week of June 8, 1935," Folder: New Cases Filed, Box 14, and "Agreement between Japanese Celery and Vegetable Growers in San Diego County and Workers, July 6, 1934," Folder 5460–45 (Labor Agreements), Box 14, "Weekly Report Ending December 2, 1933," Los Angeles Labor Board, Box 14, Folder: New Cases Filed, all in Records of the National Labor Relations Board, Record Group 25, NARA, Laguna Niguel; "Mexican Workers Await Wage Ruling," *San Ysidro Border Press*, n.d. (circa 1934), 1, Newspaper Collection, San Diego Public Library; Cruz, "There Will Be No 'One Big Union,'" 35–38.

96. "Strikes Hit Farm Region," *Los Angeles Times*, June 9, 1934, 4.

97. "Picketing of Melon Fields Halted Here," *Chula Vista Star News*, June 29, 1934, 1; and "Wage Dispute Settled after Board Hearing," *Chula Vista Star News*, July 6, 1934, 1, 8.

98. "Los Angeles Regional Labor Board List of Cases," Folder: List of Cases, 1933–35, Box 16; "Report from the Regional Labor Board regarding new cases filed during week of June 8, 1935," Folder: New Cases Filed, Box 14; and "Agreement between Japanese Celery and Vegetable Growers in San Diego County and Workers, July 6, 1934," Folder 5460–45 (Labor Agreements), Box 14, all in Records of the National Labor Relations Board, Record Group 25, NARA, Laguna Niguel.

99. *Unionization of Filipinos in California Agriculture*, Folder: Filipinos, Box 16, Federal Writers' Project on Migratory Labor, Bancroft Library, University of California, Berkeley; "Mass Meeting and Demonstration Against Attack Upon Filipino Workers," Filipino Survey, 1925–1930, Department of Industrial Relations—Division of Labor Laws Enforcement, F3275, Selected Archives, Box 118–2, California State Archives; and Federal Writer's Project, *Oriental Labor Unions and Strikes: California Agriculture*, 23. For more on death of Aristo Lampky and other acts of terrorism against Filipinos, see "Valley Bomb Blast Injures Four Filipinos," *San Diego Tribune*, December 9, 1930, 1; "Valley Filipinos Near Panic; One Dies from Blast," *San Diego Tribune*, December 10, 1930, 1; "Bomb Outrage at Imperial, California," *Filipino Nation*, January 1931, 21–27; Howard DeWitt, "The Watsonville Anti-Filipino Riot of 1930: A Case Study of the Great Depression and Ethnic Conflict in California," *Southern California Quarterly* 61, no. 3 (1979): 291–301; Howard DeWitt, *Anti-Filipino Movements in California: A History, Bibliography, and Study Guide* (San Francisco: R and E Research Associates, 1976), 50–52; "Reimbursement Bill," *Filipino Nation*, March 1930, 7.

100. Jamieson, *Labor Unionism in American Agriculture*, 31.

101. "Stop Imperial Valley Terror," *Open Forum*, April 7, 1934, 2–3, Folder 2–20, Box 8, McWilliams Papers; James Rorty, "Lettuce—with American Dressing," *The Nation*, May 15, 1935, 576, Folder 1–2, Box 8, McWilliams Papers; Lew Levenson, "California Casualty List," *The Nation*, August 29, 1934, 243–244, Folder 17, Box 24, McWilliams Papers; Norman Mini, "That California Dictatorship," *The Nation*, 226, Folder 17, Box 24, McWilliams Papers; and Davis, Mayhew, and Miller, *Under the Perfect Sun*, 203–6.

102. Chester Williams, "Imperial Valley Crisis Nears," *Open Forum*, April 14, 1934, 1–2, Folder 2–20, Box 8, McWilliams Papers; Chester Williams, "Imperial Valley Prepares for War," *The World Tomorrow*, April 26, 1934, 199–201; and "California's Greatest Industry," *Pacific Weekly*, June 15, 1936, 343, Folder: Misc., Box 16, McWilliams Papers.

103. Davis, Mayhew, and Miller, *Under the Perfect Sun*, 199.

104. Rorty, "Lettuce—with American Dressing"; Levenson, "California Casualty List"; Mini, "That California Dictatorship"; "Agriculture—California's Biggest of Big Industries," *North Bay Labor Herald*, March 25, 1938, Folder 28, Box 1, McWilliams Papers; Jamieson, *Labor Unionism in American Agriculture*, 107–10; and Bulosan, *America Is in the Heart*, 144.

105. Levenson, "California Casualty List"; Davis, Mayhew, and Miller, *Under the Perfect Sun*, 203–5; Williams, "Imperial Valley Prepares for War,"; Ella Winter, "Fascism on the West Coast," *The Nation*, 242, Folder 17, Box 24, McWilliams Papers; Campbell MacCulloch, Regional Labor Board, "Labor Conditions in the Imperial Valley," January 19, 1934, 4, Folder: Imperial Valley, Box 5, Records of the National Labor Relations Board (RG 25), NARA, Laguna Niguel; Gilbert G. González, *Mexican Consuls and Labor Organizing: Imperial Politics in the American Southwest* (Austin: University of Texas Press, 1999), 178–79.

106. "Glassford Hits Valley Lawlessness," *Open Forum*, April 21, 19344, 1, Folder 2–20, Box 8, McWilliams Papers.

107. "Valley Vigilantes on Rampage Again," *Open Forum*, May 12, 1934, 1, Folder 2–20, Box 8, McWilliams Papers.

108. Miller, "Attitudes of the San Diego Labor Movement toward Mexicans," 49–50; Mini, "That California Dictatorship," 226; Williams, "Imperial Valley Prepares for War"; González, *Mexican Consuls and Labor Organizing*, 159–96; "Red Ouster Move Looms," *Los Angeles Times*, March 20 (circa 1930s), Folder 1–20, Box 8, McWilliams Papers.

109. "Blows Dealt Reds in Valley," paper unknown, circa 1934, Folder 1–20, Box 8, McWilliams Papers; González, *Mexican Consuls and Labor Organizing*, 184–85; "Annex Imperial Valley to United States," *San Diego Labor Leader*, April 6, 1934, 1, San Diego–Imperial Counties Labor Council Collection, Special Collections and University Archives, San Diego State University.

110. "A List of the Agricultural Unions and Strikes in the United States," Folder 8, Box 48, Taylor Papers; Jamieson, *Labor Unionism in American Agriculture*, 109; "Mexican Consul again Betrays Strikers," *Agricultural Worker*, December 20, 1933, 3.

111. González, *Mexican Consuls and Labor Organizing*, 180.

112. In his report, Campbell MacCulloch also noted an alliance of Mexican and Filipino tomato pickers who organized together against Japanese growers in San Diego County, which contradicts his suggestion that they hated each other. See MacCulloch, "Labor Conditions in the Imperial Valley"; "Glassford Hits Valley Lawlessness."

113. Williams, "Imperial Valley Prepares for War," 199.

114. "Labor Asks That Labor Board Hold Imperial Valley Election," *San Diego Labor Leader*, May 4, 1934, 1.

115. González, *Mexican Consuls and Labor Organizing*, 192–93.

116. See "Democracy Called 'Red' Plot," *Open Forum*, May 5, 1934, 1, Folder 2–20, Box 8, McWilliams Papers.

117. González, *Mexican Consuls and Labor Organizing*, 159–96; and Patricia Zavella, *Women's Work and Chicano Families: Cannery Workers of the Santa Clara Valley* (Ithaca, NY: Cornell University Press, 1987), 41–42. For more on the "Great Strike" in San Francisco, see Jamieson, *Labor Unionism in American Agriculture*, 113–14; and Mini, "That California Dictatorship."

118. Although Filipinos were also involved in these strikes, this quote was specific to Mexican workers. See Miller, "Attitudes of the San Diego Labor Movement toward Mexicans," 50–51.

119. "Labor Protests Use of State Police as Strike Breakers," *San Diego Labor Leader*, January 19, 1934, 1; "Labor Council Learns Firsthand Imperial Valley Labor Conditions," *San Diego Labor Leader*, January 26, 1934, 1; "Unions Back Labor Commissioners," *San Diego Labor Leader*, February 9, 1934, 1, 4; "Annex Imperial Valley to United States," *San Diego Labor Leader*, April 6, 1934, 1; and "Tyranny Ruled Imperial Valley Workers," *San Diego Labor Leader*, June 29, 1934, 1, San Diego–Imperial Counties Labor Council

Collection, Special Collections, San Diego State University; Davis, Mayhew, and Miller, *Under the Perfect Sun*, 201.

120. Levenson, "California Casualty List."

121. Davis, Mayhew, and Miller, *Under the Perfect Sun*, 206.

122. Jamieson, *Labor Unionism in American Agriculture*, 123–30.

123. "A List of Agricultural Unions and Strikes in the United States," 33, Folder 8, Box 48, Taylor Papers; Jamieson, *Labor Unionism in American Agriculture*, 124; Miller, "Attitudes of the San Diego Labor Movement toward Mexicans," 54.

124. Jamieson, *Labor Unionism in American Agriculture*, 124.

125. *Unionization of Filipinos in California Agriculture*, 12, Folder: Filipinos, Box 16, Federal Writers' Project on Migratory Labor, Bancroft Library, University of California, Berkeley.

126. Jamieson, *Labor Unionism in American Agriculture*, 120.

127. "Mexican Field Union Affiliates to CIO," *Western Worker*, July 19, 1937, File 8:1, Carton 3, Federal Writers' Project on Migratory Labor, District No. 8 Records, Bancroft Library, University of California, Berkeley.

128. Alvarez, *Familia*, 156. For more on FALA, see Salomon, *Roots of Justice*, 19; Jamieson, *Labor Unionism in American Agriculture*, 179–86; DeWitt, *Violence in the Fields*.

129. Jamieson, *Labor Unionism in American Agriculture*, 132.

130. Ibid., 40.

131. By 1939, the fish-canning industry was the city's major industry outside of the navy. See Arthur G. Coons and Arjay R. Miller, *An Economic and Industrial Survey of the Los Angeles and San Diego Areas* (Sacramento: California State Planning Board, 1941), 341; Edward S. Soltesz, "Pole Fishing for Tuna, 1937–1941," *Journal of San Diego History* 37, no. 3 (Summer 1991): 163–64; Iris W. Engstrand, *San Diego: California's Cornerstone* (San Diego, CA: Continental Heritage Press, 1990), 113.

132. Anthony Millican, "A League of Their Own," *San Diego Union Tribune*, September 6, 1998, B6; and Canice Gardner Ciruzzi, "India Street and Beyond: A History of the Italian Community of San Diego, 1850–1980" (MA thesis, University of San Diego, 1980), 75.

133. "Production Record Set for Sun Harbor," *Sun Harbor Catch & Can News* 4, no. 4 (Christmas–New Year's, 1947–1948): 5; and "Sun Harbor Has Biggest Payroll in Its History," *Sun Harbor Catch & Can News* 4, no. 11 (August 1948): 1, Folder: Cannery Newsletters, Box 1, Logan Heights Historical Society.

134. Ciruzzi, "India Street and Beyond," 73.

135. See Mellisa Garza, "San Diego's Big Catch: The Tuna Industry" (MA thesis, University of San Diego, 2001), 11–12. For more on the Japanese and other ethnic groups in San Diego's fishing industry, see Daniel M. Shapiro, "The 'Pork Chop Express': San Diego's Tuna Fleet, 1942–1945" (MA thesis, University of San Diego, 1993), 7; Michael K. Orbach, *Hunters, Seamen, and Entrepreneurs: The Tuna Seinermen of San Diego* (Berkeley: University of California Press, 1977), 1–2; Ciruzzi, "India Street and Beyond," 68–69; William C. Richardson, "Fishermen of San Diego: The Italians," *Journal of San Diego History* 27, no. 4 (Fall 1982): 214–17; Don Estes, "Kondo Masaharu: And the Best of All Fishermen," *Journal of San Diego History* 23, no. 3 (Summer 1977): 1–19; Arthur F. McEvoy, "In Places Men Reject: Chinese Fishermen at San Diego, 1870–1893," *Journal of San Diego History* 23, no. 4 (Fall 1977): 12–24.

136. Ciruzzi, "India Street and Beyond," 74; Richardson, "Fishermen of San Diego," 214–17; Estes, "Kondo Masaharu," 1–19.

137. Ciruzzi, "India Street and Beyond," 75.

138. Ibid., 11.

139. Charito Balanag, interview with author, San Diego, CA, June 28, 2004.

140. Although Filipinas were also employed in the canneries, their numbers were minimal prior to the 1965 Immigration Act. Mexican women comprised the largest numbers, yet both groups lived in the same community of Logan Heights. Santiago Solis, "Mexican-American Women in the Work Force during World War II: Working Document," Summer 1995, 34, Special Collections and University Archives, San Diego State University.

141. Other occupations that provided the greatest sources of employment included construction laborers and service workers. See personal database compiled from California Superior Court (San Diego County), *Naturalization Records, 1935–1948*, Vols. 1–3, Special Collections and University Archives, San Diego State University; Federal Writers' Project of the Works Project Administration for the State of California, *California: A Guide to the Golden State* (New York: Hastings House, 1939), 259–60; Millican, "A League of Their Own," B1.

142. State of California, Department of Employment, Area VI, Research Statistics, *Annual Uses 274 Labor Market Report for San Diego, California Area*, May 1948, 15–16, File 69–506: Employment-Administrative-Research and Statistics, Community Labor Market Surveys, 1963–1966, California State Archives.

143. Salvador Torres, quoted in Roberto Alvarez, "The Logan Heights Ethnography Project: Identifying Institutions," 69, Spring 2004, Department of Ethnic Studies, University of California, San Diego, Box 1, Logan Heights Historical Society.

144. See Vicki L. Ruiz, *Cannery Women, Cannery Lives: Mexican Women, Unionization, and the California Food Processing Industry, 1930–1950* (Albuquerque: University of New Mexico, 1987), 32; and Zavella, *Women's Work and Chicano Families*, 99–129.

145. Ruiz, *Cannery Women, Cannery Lives*, xiii–xvi.

146. *Sun Harbor Can & Catch News* 4, no. 3 (December 1947); 4, no. 4 (Christmas–New Year's 1947–1948); 4, no. 9 (June 1948); 5, no. 2 (November 1948); and 5, no. 8 (May 1949); *Van Vamp News* 3, no. 9; and *Tuna Topics* 4, no. 4 (February 1956), Folder: Cannery Newsletters, Box 1, Logan Heights Historical Society. Photographs from the San Diego Historical Society also show large numbers of Mexican women in the canneries.

147. Roberto Qunitana, "The Pillar Remembered: The Story of the Cannery Workers," *La Prensa San Diego*, August 14, 1998; and Solis, "Mexican-American Women in the Work Force," 102–3.

148. Alvarez, "The Logan Heights Ethnography Project," 67.

149. Emma Lopez, quoted in Solis, "Mexican-American Women in the Work Force," 29.

150. Bertha Ramirez, interview with author, San Diego, CA, August 22, 2001.

151. Millican "A League of Their Own," B6; "Sue A. Talamantez Memorial Card, 1914–2003, File: Obituaries, Box 1, Logan Heights Historical Society; "Remodeled Can Washer in Operation," *Sun Harbor Catch & Can News* 5, no. 8 (May 1949): 1; "photo of warehouse crew," *Sun Harbor Catch & Can News* 6, no. 1 (October 1949): 2; *Tuna Topics* 4, no. 4 (February 1956): 4, File: Cannery Newsletters, Box 1, Logan Heights Historical Society; photo of cannery workers, Van Camp Cannery, circa 1940s, Photograph Collection, Logan Heights Historical Society.

152. Virgil Garcia, interview with author, Lemon Grove, CA, August 21, 2001; Consuelo "Connie" Zuniga, interview with author, San Diego, CA, August 20, 2001.

153. As white women left the canneries, Mexican women filled their places as packers, eventually dominating this position. Elvira Esparza, quoted in Solis, "Mexican-American Women in the Work Force," 34.

154. See "Van Camp's Fish Cannery Signs Contract with Local 64 UCAPAWA," *UCAPAWA News,* July 1939, 4. For more on the discussion of gendered wage disparities, see Zavella, *Women's Work and Chicano Families,* 57–62.

155. Solis, "Mexican-American Women in the Work Force," 101–3; Ruiz, *Cannery Women, Cannery Lives,* 14–17; Zavella, *Women's Work and Chicano Families,* 133–48.

156. Ruiz, *Cannery Women, Cannery Lives,* 32; and Zavella, *Women's Work and Chicano Families,* 11–17.

157. Although women were paid by piecework, cannery news in the *San Diego Labor Leader* and *UCAPAWA News* also notes that cannery workers, both men and women, were paid hourly, with men earning more than women. Hortencia Carrazco, quoted in Solis, "Mexican-American Women in the Work Force," 72.

158. Millican, "A League of Their Own," B1.

159. Jenny Dominguez, phone interview with author, San Diego, CA, July 13, 2000.

160. Consuelo "Connie" Zuniga, interview with author.

161. Ricardo Romio, interview with author, Lakeside, CA, May 4, 2004.

162. "Workers Thanked," *Sun Harbor Catch & Can News* 5, no. 2 (November 1948): 4. For more on personal news regarding workers, see collection of *Sun Harbor Catch & Can News; Tuna Topics* 4, no. 4 (February 1956): 3; and *Van Camp News,* all in Folder: Cannery Newsletters, Box 1, Logan Heights Historical Society; Alvarez, "The Logan Heights Ethnography Project," 71; Zavella, *Women's Work and Chicano Families,* 148–54.

163. John Cota, quoted in Quintana, "The Pillar Remembered: The Story of the Cannery Workers."

164. Virgil Garcia, interviewed with author; and Alvarez, "The Logan Heights Ethnography Project," 18.

165. Although both women mention mackerel, it may have been tuna since that was the main fish canned at the time in San Diego. See Bertha Ramirez, interview with author; Hortencia Carrazco, quoted in Solis, "Mexican-American Women in the Work Force," 71.

166. Delia Chavez, interview with author, San Diego, CA, August 23, 2001.

167. Carrazco, quoted in Solis, "Mexican-American Women in the Work Force," 71.

168. Ricardo Romio, interview with author.

169. Millican, "A League of Their Own," B1.

170. Minnie Ybarra, phone interview with author, San Diego, CA, July 14, 2000.

171. Ricardo Romio, interview with author.

172. Virgil Garcia, phone interview with author, San Diego, CA, July 12, 2000.

173. Millican, "A League of Their Own," B6.

174. Delia Chavez, interview with author.

175. Carrazco, quoted in Solis, "Mexican-American Women in the Work Force," 71.

176. Elvira Esparza, quoted in Solis, "Mexican-American Women in the Work Force," 40.

177. Bea Avina, quoted in Quintana, "The Pillar Remembered."

178. Salvador Torres, quoted in Alvarez, "The Logan Heights Ethnography Project," 70.

179. Alvarez, "The Logan Heights Ethnography Project," 70.

180. Virgil Garcia, interview with author.

181. Alvarez, "The Logan Heights Ethnography Project," 71.

182. Ricardo Romio, interview with author.

183. "Letter to Charles H. Cunningham from Peter J. Taylor," April 12, 1934; "Letter to Campbell MacCulloch from O. C. Heitman," April 24, 1934; and "Letter to Towne

Nylander from A. K. Johnson," April 27, 1934, all in Folder 5382–14, Box 8, Records of the National Labor Relations Board, Record Group 25, NARA, Laguna Niguel.

184. "Letter to L.A. Regional Labor Board from Peter J. Taylor," May 1, 1934, Folder 5382–14, Box 8, Records of the National Labor Relations Board, Record Group 25, NARA, Laguna Niguel.

185. Ibid.

186. Gutiérrez, *Walls and Mirrors*, 110.

187. According to Vicki Ruiz, the breach between the CIO and AFL did not occur until November 1938, but the CIO was functioning as a separate union prior to that. For more on this, see Ruiz, *Cannery Women, Cannery Lives*, 42–43. For more on the CIO, see Congress of Industrial Organizations, *CIO: 1935–1955* (Washington, DC: Congress of Industrial Organizations, 1955).

188. "Mexicans in Urban California," 15, Folder 4, Subseries 1: Other Subjects, 1929–1978, Box 58, Ernesto Galarza Papers, Stanford University Special Collections; and Miller, "Attitudes of the San Diego Labor Movement toward Mexicans," 32–40.

189. Ruiz, *Cannery Women, Cannery Lives*, 43–45.

190. Ibid., 77–79.

191. According to Hortencia Carrazco, a San Diego resident and former cannery worker, over 75 percent of the cannery workers were Mexican women. Salvador Torres, quoted in Solis, "Mexican-American Women in the Work Force," 71; and Alvarez, "The Logan Heights Ethnography Project," 72.

192. For more on Luisa Moreno and Robert Galvan, see Carlos Larralde and Richard Griswold del Castillo, "Luisa Moreno and the Beginnings of the Mexican American Civil Rights Movement in San Diego," *Journal of San Diego History* 43, no. 3 (Summer 1997): 158–75; Carlos Larralde and Richard Griswold del Castillo, "Luisa Moreno: A Hispanic Civil Rights Leader in San Diego," *Journal of San Diego History* 41, no. 4 (Fall 1995): 284–311; Ruiz, *Cannery Women, Cannery Lives*, 81; Carlos Larralde, "Roberto Galvan: A Latino Leader of the 1940s," *Journal of San Diego History* 52, no. 3 and 4 (Summer–Fall 2006): 151–78; and "San Diego Man's Deportation Upheld by High Court," *Evening Tribune*, May 24, 1954, A1–A2.

193. Higher wages in the canneries were still based on gender, with men earning sixty cents an hour, while women earned fifty-five cents. For more on UCAPAWA's activities in San Diego, see "Van Camp's Fish Cannery Signs Contract with Local 64 UCAPAWA," *UCAPAWA News*, July 1939, 4; "Van Camp Workers Smash Attempt to Break Union," *UCAPWAW News*, August 1939, 16; Ruiz, *Cannery Women, Cannery Lives*, 81; and Zaragosa Vargas, *Labor Rights Are Civil Rights: Mexican American Workers in Twentieth-Century America* (Princeton, NJ: Princeton University Press, 2005), 153.

194. "Local 64 Gains Many New Members," *UCAPAWA News*, December 1939, 9; and Larralde and Griswold del Castillo, "Luisa Moreno and the Beginnings of the Mexican American Civil Rights Movement," 160–61.

195. See Larralde and Griswold del Castillo, "Luisa Moreno: A Hispanic Civil Rights Leader," 290–91.

196. Ibid., 284–311; Larralde and Griswold del Castillo, "Luisa Moreno and the Beginnings of the Mexican American Civil Rights Movement," 158–75.

197. "Van Camp Signs Improved Pact with UCAPAWA," *UCAPAWA News*, May–June 1940, 5.

198. "Local 64 Gains Many New Members," *UCAPAWA News*, December 1939, 9.

199. In their article on Luisa Moreno, Larralde and Griswold del Castillo note that Moreno and Galvan organized hundreds of cannery workers in San Diego, in canneries

such as California Packing Corporation, Marine Products Company, Old Mission Packing Corporation, and Van Camp Sea Food Company. It is not known if they actually were able to secure a closed shop at those particular canneries. Carlos Larralde obtained what information was available regarding their organizing efforts from an oral interview with Luisa Moreno among other sources. For more on this, see Larralde and Griswold del Castillo, "Luisa Moreno and the Beginnings of the Mexican American Civil Rights Movement," 160; Larralde and Griswold del Castillo, "Luisa Moreno: A Hispanic Civil Rights Leader," 290.

200. Although Larralde and Griswold del Castillo suggest that Moreno was able to have contracts signed with most of the canneries in San Diego, after excavating additional sources, what I found was that Local 64 only had control over the Van Camp cannery. Examining the *San Diego Labor Leader,* the official paper of the local AFL and its umbrella organization, the San Diego Labor Council, provided a different view. According to the *San Diego Labor Leader,* the AFL controlled all of canneries in San Diego except for Van Camp. For more on this, see Larralde and Griswold del Castillo, "Luisa Moreno and the Beginnings of the Mexican American Civil Rights Movement," 158–75; Larralde and Griswold del Castillo, "Luisa Moreno: A Hispanic Civil Rights Leader," 284–311. For more on AFL activities in the canneries, see "Cannery Worker Notes," *San Diego Labor Leader,* October 11, 1940, 2; and "Cannery Worker Notes," *San Diego Labor Leader,* November 1, 1940, 3, San Diego–Imperial Counties Labor Council Collection, Special Collections and University Archives, San Diego State University.

201. Ruiz, *Cannery Women, Cannery Lives,* 46, 102.

202. Ibid., 46.

203. According to Ruiz, testimony given before the House on Un-American Activities Committee "linked the labor organization [UCAPAWA] with Communist intrigue." For more on this, see Ruiz, *Cannery Women, Cannery Lives,* 46.

204. Ruiz, *Cannery Women, Cannery Lives,* 116; and Larralde, "Roberto Galvan," 151–78.

205. Miller, "Attitudes of the San Diego Labor Movement toward Mexicans," 62.

206. See Carlos M. Larralde and Richard Griswold del Castillo, "San Diego's Ku Klux Klan, 1920–1980," *Journal of San Diego History* 46, no. 2–3 (Spring/Summer 2000): 75–76; and Larralde, "Roberto Galvan," 154.

207. According to the *San Diego Labor Leader,* Westgate Cannery was under the AFL since 1938. See "Westgate Peace Threatened," *San Diego Labor Leader,* March 15, 1940, 1; "No Vote at Westgate; CIO Out!," *San Diego Labor Leader,* April 26, 1940; "Cannery Workers Notes," *San Diego Labor Leader,* August 16, 1940, 2; and "S.D. Canneries in AFL Pact," *San Diego Labor Leader,* October 25, 1940, 1–4, all in San Diego–Imperial Counties Labor Council Collection, Special Collections and University Archives, San Diego State University.

208. "Cannery Workers Notes," *San Diego Labor Leader,* August 16, 1940, 2; "New Gains Loom for AFL Cannery Workers Militant AFL Union Shows Big Membership Increases In '40," *San Diego Labor Leader,* September 2, 1940, 9, 11, San Diego–Imperial Counties Labor Council Collection, Special Collections and University Archives, San Diego State University.

209. "Cannery Workers Notes," *San Diego Labor Leader,* October 11, 1940, 2, and October 18, 1940, 2; "S.D. Canneries in AFL Pact," *San Diego Labor Leader,* October 25, 1940, 1, San Diego–Imperial Counties Labor Council Collection, Special Collections and University Archives, San Diego State University.

210. "Cannery Workers Notes," *San Diego Labor Leader,* November 1, 1940, 3; and "AFL Win Seen at Van Camps," *San Diego Labor Leader,* May 30, 1941, 1, 3, San

Diego–Imperial Counties Labor Council Collection, Special Collections and University Archives, San Diego State University.

211. Lemon pickers in El Cajon, who were part of Citrus and Vegetable Workers Local 19274, were one example of this. In the course of my research, I have yet to find other instances in which the AFL organized agricultural workers, who were predominately Mexican. This is especially true since the United States relied primarily on the Bracero Program for its labor in the agricultural fields, among other industries, after 1942. For more on this, see "AFL Citrus Union Back in Council!," *San Diego Labor Leader*, February 9, 1940, 1; and "Citrus Workers in Pay Victory," *San Diego Labor Leader*, January 30, 1942, 1, 4, San Diego–Imperial Counties Labor Council Collection, Special Collections and University Archives, San Diego State University.

212. Memorial program for Sue A. Talamantez, 1914–2003, File: Obituaries, Box 1, Logan Heights Historical Society.

213. "Fish Tales," *San Diego Labor Leader*, n.d. (circa 1940), San Diego–Imperial Counties Labor Council Collection, Special Collections and University Archives, San Diego State University.

214. Ruiz, *Cannery Women, Cannery Lives*, 21–39; and Gutiérrez, *Walls and Mirrors*, 106.

215. See "Ten Cent Increase Won at Van Camps," *UCAPAWA News*, January 15, 1942, 7; "Six S.D. Canneries Ink AFL Pay Raise Contract," *San Diego Labor Leader*, January 16, 1942, 1, San Diego–Imperial Counties Labor Council Collection, Special Collections, San Diego State University; "No Strikes for Duration of War!," *San Diego Labor Leader*, January 2, 1942, 3, San Diego–Imperial Counties Labor Council Collection, Special Collections and University Archives, San Diego State University.

216. "Fishermen Join Cannery Workers," *San Diego Labor Leader*, September 24, 1943, 3, San Diego–Imperial Counties Labor Council Collection, Special Collections and University Archives, San Diego State University.

217. According to Vicki Ruiz, UCAPAWA changed its name to the Food, Tobacco, Agricultural, and Allied Workers of America (FTA) in 1944 to reflect the importance of tobacco workers to the union. See Ruiz, *Cannery Women, Cannery Lives*, 57.

218. Ruiz, *Cannery Women, Cannery Lives*, 103–13.

219. For more on the end of UCAPAWA/FTA, see ibid., 117.

220. Ibid., 114–15; "Cannery Workers Ballot in NLRB Election Test," *San Diego Labor Leader*, October 26, 1950, 1, San Diego–Imperial Counties Labor Council Collection, Special Collections and University Archives, San Diego State University; Larralde and Griswold del Castillo, "Luisa Moreno and the Beginnings of the Mexican American Civil Rights Movement," 170; Larralde and Griswold del Castillo, "Luisa Moreno: A Hispanic Civil Rights Leader," 298–300.

221. The extent of UCAPAWA Local 64's activities in San Diego since its beginning in the late 1930s cannot really be ascertained in greater detail because UCAPAWA records, which were stored in a basement of a garment workers' local, were destroyed in a flood. See Vicki L. Ruiz, e-mail correspondence with author, September 27, 2005.

222. Ruiz, *Cannery Women, Cannery Lives*, 55–56.

223. For more on the participation of Mexican women in the defense industry, see Solis, "Mexican-American Women in the Work Force"; and Griswold del Castillo, *Chicano San Diego*, 106–10.

224. For more on the Bracero Program, see Carey McWilliams, *North from Mexico: The Spanish-Speaking People of the United States* (New York: Praeger, 1990), 237–42; and Rodolfo Acuña, *Occupied America: A History of Chicanos* (New York: HarperCollins Publishers, 1988), 260–66.

225. Congress of Industrial Organizations, *CIO*, 29.

226. Garza, "San Diego's Big Catch," 44; Richardson, "Fishermen of San Diego," 213–26; Estes, "Kondo Masaharu," 1–19.

227. Ruiz, *Cannery Women, Cannery Lives*, 113–17; Larralde and Griswold del Castillo, "Luisa Moreno and the Beginnings of the Mexican American Civil Rights Movement," 170–71; Larralde and Griswold del Castillo, "Luisa Moreno: A Hispanic Civil Rights Leader," 299–300; and Larralde, "Roberto Galvan," 169–70.

228. Ruiz, *Cannery Women, Cannery Lives*, 57, 117.

229. Garza, "San Diego's Big Catch," 89, 96.

230. Alessandro Bonanno and Douglas Constance, *Caught in the Net: The Global Tuna Industry, Environmentalism, and the State* (Lawrence: University of Kansas Press, 1996), 154–55; Quintana, "The Pillar Remembered"; "Tuna Processing Sites to Be Razed," *San Diego Union Tribune*, December 15, 2003, B3.

231. Alvarez, "The Logan Heights Ethnography Project," 77.

232. Vargas, *Labor Rights Are Civil Rights*.

CHAPTER 5 — FILIPINO-MEXICAN COUPLES AND THE FORGING OF A MEXIPINO IDENTITY

1. Although Mexicans were considered "white" by law, their social realities and treatment were similar to other nonwhites because of how they were racialized. By 1930 the U.S. census would also classify "Mexican" as a racial category.

2. Certificate of Marriage for Ciriaco Poscablo and Felipa L. Castro, June 25, 1938, County of San Diego, County Recorder, San Diego, CA.

3. Peggy Pascoe, *What Comes Naturally: Miscegenation Law and the Making of Race in America* (New York: Oxford University Press, 2009), 19–30; Paul R. Spickard, *Mixed Blood: Intermarriage and Ethnic Identity in Twentieth-Century America* (Madison: University of Wisconsin Press, 1989), 286–88; Maria P. P. Root, *Love's Revolution: Interracial Marriage* (Philadelphia: Temple University Press, 2001), 34–40; Randall Kennedy, *Interracial Intimacies: Sex, Marriage, Identity, and Adoption* (New York: Pantheon Books, 2003), 243–80; the Staff of the Asian American Studies Center, the University of California, "Antimiscegenation Laws and the Filipino, 1920–1960s," in *Peoples of Color in the American West*, ed. Sucheng Chan, Douglas Henry Daniels, Mario T. Garcia, and Terry P. Wilson (Lexington, MA: D. C. Heath, 1994), 336–44.

4. Pascoe, *What Comes Naturally*, 13; and the Staff of the Asian American Studies Center, "Antimiscegenation Laws and the Filipino," 337–38.

5. Pascoe, *What Comes Naturally*, 6.

6. Ibid., 4, 33.

7. See ibid., 122–32. As Peggy Pascoe notes, the status of Mexicans and Mexican Americans was wrought with contradictions as it pertained to issuing of marriage licenses. Since bureaucrats, lawyers, and judges could not find a consensus on how to classify them legally with regards to miscegenation laws, licensing clerks were left with the task of guessing whether they were too white or dark, depending on the spouse. Even then, confusion and uncertainties still occurred since Mexicans, although legally "white," were still discriminated against due to their ancestry and/or skin color.

8. Root, *Love's Revolution*, 2.

9. Pascoe, *What Comes Naturally*, 207–18, 280–84; and the Staff of the Asian American Studies Center, "Antimiscegenation Laws and the Filipino," 336–44.

10. I will use the term "Mexican" to describe the experiences of ethnic Mexicans, both immigrant and U.S.-born, in this chapter as they relate to Filipino-Mexican couples.

I will also use the term "Mexican American" when needed, depending on the context. I use David G. Gutiérrez's position on labeling them as such for the purpose of this study. I will also use the term "Filipino" to discuss the collective experiences of both immigrants and U.S.-born. I will refer to their citizenship status when necessary to distinguish intra-group experiences. For more on this, see David G. Gutiérrez, *Walls and Mirrors: Mexican Americans, Mexican Immigrants, and the Politics of Ethnicity* (Berkeley: University of California Press, 1995), 218n3.

11. Maria P. P. Root, "Contemporary Mixed-Heritage Filipino Americans: Fighting Colonized Identities," in *Filipino Americans: Transformations and Identity*, ed. Maria P. P. Root (Thousand Oaks, CA: Sage Publications, 1997), 84; and Karen Isaksen Leonard, *Making Ethnic Choices: California's Punjabi Mexican Americans* (Philadelphia: Temple University Press, 1992).

12. Although I am aware of the gender inclusive "a/o" for Mexipina/o, as a shorthand, I will use the neutral term (Mexipino) to encompass all genders in these populations. However, I will use gendered terms when necessary.

13. Bruno Lasker, *Filipino Immigration to Continental United States, and to Hawaii* (Chicago: University of Chicago Press, 1931), 119–20; Ronald Takaki, *Strangers from a Different Shore,: A History of Asian Americans* (Boston: Little, Brown, 1998), 341.

14. Lasker, *Filipino Immigration to Continental United States and to Hawaii*, 10.

15. "Filipinos Getting Their Bearings in South Bay," *San Diego Union Tribune*, December 4, 1983, Lateral File: Filipino Americans, Thelma Hollingsworth Local History Room, National City Public Library. The common Spanish and American influences can be attributed to the fact that both Mexico and the Philippines were involved in wars of independence and/or expansion with both Spain and the United States. This led both Filipinos and Mexicans to be, as Jeffrey Moniz noted, "double colonized." See personal notes from discussion with Jeffrey Moniz, Santa Barbara, CA, June 3, 2003.

16. Rolando Mata, interview with author, La Puente, CA, September 1, 2004.

17. John H. Burma, *Spanish-Speaking Groups in the United States* (Detroit: Blaine Ethridge, 1974), 152.

18. Rafael, Regidor, and Maximiana Patricio, interview with author, Chula Vista, CA, December 28, 2003.

19. Consuelo "Connie" Zuniga, interview with author, San Diego, CA, August 20, 2001.

20. Burma, *Spanish-Speaking Groups in the United States*, 138–55.

21. In urban areas like Chicago, for example, Filipino-white families were ostracized and lived in marginal areas of the city. Historian Barbara Posadas notes that in Chicago they were "too few in number to establish a fully viable community." See Barbara M. Posadas, "Mestiza Girlhood: Interracial Families in Chicago's Filipino American Community since 1925," in *Making Waves: An Anthology of Writings by and about Asian American Women*, ed. Diane Yen-Mei Wong and Emilya Cachapero (Boston: Beacon Press, 1989), 278; Paul G. Cressey, *The Taxi-Dance Hall: A Sociological Study in Commercialized Recreation and City Life* (Chicago: University of Chicago Press, 1932), 171; Benicio T. Catapusan, "Filipino Intermarriage in the United States," *Sociology and Social Research* 22 (January 1938): 269; Takaki, *Strangers from a Different Shore*, 341–42.

22. Although I focus on Mexican women, Panamanians and other Latinas also comprised a substantial number of brides for Filipino men in San Diego. This particular topic begs for further research. For more on photographic evidence regarding Filipino interethnic marriages and families in San Diego, see Judy Patacsil, Rudy Guevarra Jr., and Felix Tuyay, *Filipinos in San Diego* (San Francisco: Arcadia Publishing, 2010).

23. Niland is a town in Imperial Valley County, California. The multiracial families that made up the communities Josephine describes included Mexicans, whites, Spaniards (from New Mexico), and indigenous peoples. See David Galbiso, "He Was the Prettiest Thing I Had Ever Seen," biography of Josephine "Fita" Stevens, Galbiso Family File, FANHS San Diego Chapter Archives.

24. Although these communities were predominately nonwhite, there would be a few white ethnic families that lived among them. See Ricardo Romio, interview with author, Lakeside, CA, May 4, 2004.

25. Mexican-Filipino relationships and families also formed in other areas where agriculture and various industries brought them together, such as Yakima, Washington; and Los Angeles, Salinas, Stockton, and other areas of California.

26. Given that I could not gain access to the San Diego County recorder's database of marriage licenses, I had to rely on oral testimonies, archival evidence, and personal observations to document the frequency and size of Filipino-Mexican intermarriages and unions in San Diego. I also relied on comparative studies done on interracial couples in Los Angeles. Although John Burma's research noted that Filipino-white couples comprised slightly larger numbers, followed by Filipino-Mexican, scholars such as Benicio T. Catapusan recorded that, of the racial composition of Filipino intermarriages in Los Angeles, "most of these mixed unions are Filipino-Mexican." Catapusan also collected questionnaires from Filipinos he surveyed and found that Filipino-Mexican unions were the most preferred at 29.3 percent, followed by Filipino-mulatto at 20.3 percent. His findings were similar to what Bruno Lasker observed regarding the success among intermarriages between Filipinos and Mexicans. See Benicio T. Catapusan, "The Social Adjustment of Filipinos in America" (PhD diss., University of Southern California, 1940), 79–81; Catapusan, "Filipino Intermarriage in the United States," 267; John H. Burma, "Research Note on the Measurement of Interracial Marriage," *American Journal of Sociology* 57, no. 6 (May 1952): 587–89; Lasker, *Filipino Immigration to the Continental United States and to Hawaii*, 119; Robert M. Jiobu, *Ethnicity and Assimilation* (Albany: State University of New York Press, 1988); James D. Sobredo, "From American 'National' to the 'Third Asiatic Invasion': Racial Transformation and Filipino Exclusion (1898–1934)" (PhD diss., University of California, Berkeley, 1998), 216; Root, "Contemporary Mixed-Heritage Filipino Americans," 86; Susan Koshy, *Sexual Naturalization: Asian Americans and Miscegenation* (Stanford, CA: Stanford University Press, 2004), 10; Paul Spickard, *Almost All Aliens: Immigration, Race, and Colonialism in American History and Identity* (New York: Routledge, 2007), 306; and Karen Leonard, "Intermarriage and Ethnicity: Punjabi Mexican Americans, Mexican Japanese, and Filipino Americans," *Explorations in Ethnic Studies* 16, no. 2 (July 1993): 149.

27. Gina Lleva, interview with author, San Diego, CA, September 21, 2004.

28. For more on the ways in which Mexipinos have been mistaken as other ethnic groups, see Rudy P. Guevarra Jr., "Burritos and Bagoong: Mexipinos and Multiethnic Identity in San Diego, California," in *Crossing Lines: Race and Mixed Race Across the Geohistorical Divide*, ed. Marc Coronado, Rudy P. Guevarra Jr., Jeffrey Moniz, and Laura Furlan Szanto (Walnut Creek, CA: Alta Mira Press, 2005), 84–86.

29. See Carlos Bulosan, *America Is in the Heart* (Seattle: University of Washington Press, 1973); and Manuel Buaken, *I Have Lived with the American People* (Caldwell, ID: Caxton Printers, 1948).

30. See Buaken, *I Have Lived with the American People*, 138; and Takaki, *Strangers from a Different Shore*, 328.

31. Takaki, *Strangers from a Different Shore*, 328–29.

32. See David Barrows, "The Desirability of the Filipino," *Commonwealth* 5, no. 45 (November 5, 1929): 322; Sonia Emily Wallovits, "The Filipinos in California" (MA thesis, University of Southern California, 1966), 58; Takaki, *Strangers from a Different Shore*, 329.

33. Judge Rohrback, quoted in Takaki, *Strangers from a Different Shore*, 327.

34. Ibid., 327–29.

35. Vaughan MacCaughey, "The Filipino and Our Cheap Labor Problem," *The Commonwealth* 5, no. 45 (November 5, 1929): 341. For early information regarding white fear of racial mixing, see Kenneth L. Roberts, "Kenneth L. Roberts and the Treat of 'Mongrelization' in America, 1922," in *In Their Place: White America Defines Her Minorities, 1850–1950*, ed. Lewis H. Carlson and George A. Colburn (New York: John Wiley and Sons, 1972), 311–13.

36. C. M. Goethe, "Filipino Immigration Viewed as a Peril," *Current History* 34 (June 1931): 354.

37. See Howard DeWitt, *Anti-Filipino Movements in California: A History, Bibliography, and Study Guide* (San Francisco: R and E Research Associates, 1976); Emory S. Bogardus, *Anti-Filipino Race Riots: A Report Made to the Ingram Institute of Social Science of San Diego* (Los Angeles: University of Southern California, May 15, 1930), 88–111; Wallovits, "The Filipinos in California," 65–73; Rhacel Salazar Parreñas, "'White Trash' Meets the 'Little Brown Monkeys': The Taxi Dance Hall as a Site of Interracial and Gender Alliances between White Working Class Women and Filipino Immigrant Men in the 1920s and 1930s,'" *Amerasia Journal* 24, no. 2 (1998): 116; Ana Marcelo, "Sex and the Single Manong," *Filipinas,* October 2004, 43, 46; Alex S. Fabros Jr., "When Hilario Met Sally," *Filipinas,* February 1995, 51; and Takaki, *Strangers from a Different Shore*, 327–28.

38. Filipinos were the main targets of white male sexual fear, more so than Mexican men because Mexican men had more gender balance within their communities and tended to marry within their ethnic group. See Ruby C. Tapia, "Just Ten Years Removed from a Bolo and a Breech-cloth: The Sexualization of the Filipino 'Menace,'" in *Positively No Filipinos Allowed: Building Communities and Discourse*, ed. Antonio T. Tiongson Jr., Edgardo V. Gutierrez, and Ricardo V. Gutierrez (Philadelphia: Temple University Press, 2006), 61–70. Although Mexican women were sometimes included with white women, research indicates it only applied to those who were light-skinned. For more on this, see Linda España-Maram, *Creating Masculinity in Los Angeles's Little Manila: Working-Class Filipinos and Popular Culture, 1920s–1950s* (New York: Columbia University Press, 2006), 125; and Takaki, *Strangers from a Different Shore*, 327.

39. Nellie Foster, "Legal Status of Filipino Intermarriages in California," *Sociology and Social Research* 16, no. 5 (May 1932): 449.

40. For more on Filipinos and taxi dance halls, see Parreñas, "'White Trash' Meets the 'Little Brown Monkeys,'" 115–34; Takaki, *Strangers from a Different Shore*, 338–39; "Taxi-Dance Girls Start Filipinos on Wrong Foot," *Los Angeles Times*, February 2, 1930, A1; España-Maram, *Creating Masculinity in Los Angeles's Little Manila*, 105–33; Cressey, *The Taxi-Dance Hall*, 172.

41. Foster, "Legal Status of Filipino Intermarriages in California," 448; "Filipino-White Girl Tie Upheld Due to Lack of Legal Precedent," *Daily Transcript*, September 11, 1931, 1; the Staff of the Asian American Studies Center, "Antimiscegenation Laws and the Filipino," 341; Leti Volpp, "American Mestizo: Filipinos and Anti-Miscegenation Laws in California," in *Mixed Race America and the Law: A Reader*, ed. Kevin R. Johnson (New York: New York University Press, 2003), 90–91.

42. "Aqui No Se Permiten Uniones de Blancas con Filipinos (unions between white women and Filipinos are not permitted here)," *El Hispano Americano*, July 27, 1934, 1.

43. In numerous court cases, Filipinos argued, sometimes successfully, that because they were Malay and not Mongoloid, they were exempt from anti-miscegenation laws. The term "Malay" was not included in law that sought to exclude them. That changed in 1933, however, when Malay was included in those exempt from marrying white women. It was not until 1948 in *Perez v. Sharp* that miscegenation laws were ruled as unconstitutional in the California State Supreme Court. In 1967 the U.S. Supreme Court followed suit, also ruling that miscegenation laws were unconstitutional with *Loving v. Virginia*. For more on this, see Peggy Pascoe, "Miscegenation Law, Court Cases, and Ideologies of 'Race' in Twentieth-Century America," *Journal of American History* 83, no. 1 (June 1996): 44–69; the Staff of the Asian American Studies Center, "Antimiscegenation Laws and the Filipino," 342–44; Volpp, "American Mestizo," 91–92; Takaki, *Strangers from a Different Shore*, 330–31; *Perez v. Sharp*, 32, Cal. 2d 711 (1948); and *Loving v. Virginia*, 388, U.S. 1 (1967).

44. Yen Le Espiritu, *Home Bound: Filipino American Lives across Cultures, Communities, and Countries* (Berkeley: University of California Press, 2003), 67.

45. España-Maram, *Creating Masculinity in Los Angeles's Little Manila*, 105–33; Parreñas, "'White Trash' Meets the 'Little Brown Monkeys,'" 120–21; "Filipino Americans Missing One Complete Generation," *Sacramento Bee*, April 13, 1974, A2, Interracial Marriage File, NPA, FANHS, Seattle, Washington.

46. Although Riz Oades noted that Barbara Quines was a U.S.-born Mexican, she was, in fact, a U.S. born Mexipina. See Riz A. Oades, *Beyond the Mask: Untold Stories of U.S. Navy Filipinos* (National City, CA: KCS Publishing, 2004), 42–43; Patacsil, Guevarra, and Tuyay, *Filipinos in San Diego;* Adelaida Castillo-Tsuchida, "Filipino Migrants in San Diego, 1900–1946" (MA thesis, San Diego State University, 1979), 44.

47. Espiritu, *Home Bound*, 114.

48. Castillo-Tsuchida, "Filipino Migrants in San Diego," 70.

49. Edwin Almirol's study seemed to focus on the Filipino "old-timers" who were married between the 1930s and 1950s. Although Almirol did not devote too much attention to the subject, the few pages he provided focused on their perceived differences, tensions, and the negative stereotypes Filipinos had toward Mexicans, which were likely influenced by white racial stereotypes. See Edwin B. Almirol, *Ethnic Identity and Social Negotiation: A Study of a Filipino Community in California* (New York: AMS Press, 1985), 85–89.

50. Lasker, *Filipino Immigration to Continental United States and to Hawaii,* 119.

51. Personal research notes, discussion with Fred and Dorothy Cordova, Seattle, Washington, September 25, 2003.

52. Galbiso, "He Was the Prettiest Thing I Had Ever Seen."

53. Under spouse's country of origin, those listed were under "Philippine Islands." See California Superior Court (San Diego County), *Naturalization Records, 1935–1948*, Vols. 1–3, Special Collections and University Archives, San Diego State University.

54. Lanny Villarin, interview with author, National City, CA, May 5, 2004.

55. Charito and Ben Balanag, interview with author, San Diego, CA, June 28, 2004.

56. Gina Lleva, interview with author.

57. Rafael Patricio, interview with author, National City, CA, December 11, 2003.

58. See Leonard, *Making Ethnic Choices.*

59. There was only one divorce noted out of the two dozen Mexipino and Filipino-Mexican couples that I interviewed. Another case involved a couple that had a child out of wedlock and did not stay together. Photographs from Filipino-Mexican families in San Diego who are still together also suggest high success rates. This number does not

include the numerous families that were mentioned in the interviews, which provided no indication of any other divorces because longstanding communities of Filipino-Mexican couples in San Diego, Tijuana, and the Imperial Valley still exist. See Box 1, Folder: Filipino Families, FANHS San Diego Chapter Archives. For more on the issue of love, marriage, and divorce in the Punjabi-Mexican community, see Leonard, *Making Ethnic Choices*, 101–20.

60. Leonard, *Making Ethnic Choices*, 90–91.

61. Koshy, *Sexual Naturalization*, 9.

62. Espiritu, *Home Bound*, 114.

63. Castillo-Tsuchida, "Filipino Migrants in San Diego," 25.

64. Gina Lleva, interview with author.

65. Ibid. This is not to suggest that all Mexican men were bad spouses or followed a patriarchal structure, but Gina Lleva observed that Filipino men were not domineering with their wives. She recalled her parent's relationship as more egalitarian, which was what her mother and other Mexican women noted about their Filipino husbands, who shared in household duties and other responsibilities. This is something sociologist Benicio Catapusan noted in 1938 when he surveyed Mexican wives, who overwhelmingly considered Filipinos to be better spouses than Mexicans. For more on this see Catapusan, "The Social Adjustment of Filipinos in America," 82–83.

66. Maria Theresa "Maite" Valladolid, interview with author, Bonita, CA, June 8, 2007.

67. Gina Lleva, interview with author. Karen Leonard also describes this in her study on Punjabi-Mexican couples: how Mexican women married Punjabi men not only to escape the patriarchal structures of their homes, but also for class mobility. Filipino-Mexican couples were usually of the same socioeconomic background. See Leonard, *Making Ethnic Choices*, 69–71.

68. Although this couple was not from San Diego, I use them as an example of how families accepted and/or rejected marriages between Filipinos and Mexicans. See Jim Dickey, "Pair Celebrate 55 Years of Love," *San Jose Mercury*, February 14, 1995, Interracial Marriage File, NPA, FANHS, Seattle, Washington.

69. Rafael Patricio, interview with author; and Regidor, Maximiana, and Rafael Patricio, interview with author.

70. Regidor, Maximiana, and Rafael Patricio, interview with author.

71. Rolando Mata, interview with author.

72. Ricardo Romio, interview with author.

73. Roberto R. Alvarez Jr., *Familia: Migration and Adaptation in Baja and Alta California, 1800–1975* (Berkeley: University of California Press, 1991), 2.

74. Alvarez, *Familia*, 57–59, and Leonard, *Making Ethnic Choices*, 90–92.

75. For more on the Filipino practice of *compadrinazgo*, see Donn V. Hart, *Compadrinazgo: Ritual Kinship in the Philippines* (Dekalb: Northern Illinois University Press, 1977).

76. Although there are Filipinos and Mexicans who are not Catholic, the majority of the Mexicans and Filipinos that I interviewed are Catholic. Their stories illustrated this experience. See Gina Lleva, interview with author; and Alan Duran Gonzalez, interview with author, San Diego, CA, December 10, 2003.

77. As a child I remember going to mass at Saint Mary's in National City. I observed at a young age the number of Filipino and Mexican parishioners in our church. I also attended catechism with other Filipino, Mexican, and Chamorro children. Some of these parishes also offer mass in English, Spanish, and Tagalog, which illustrates the communities they cater to.

78. Baptism Index, Books 1–3, September 17, 1961, to April 1966, Saint Anthony of Padua Parish Records, National City, CA; Baptism and Marriage Records, Reel 31, Saint Anthony of Padua, National City, CA, Archives, San Diego Diocese.

79. Maria Theresa "Maite" Valladolid, interview with author.

80. Gina Lleva, interview with author.

81. Rafael Patricio, interview with author; Ricardo Romio, interview with author; Irene Mena, interview with author, Lemon Grove, CA, January 26, 2007.

82. Espiritu, *Home Bound,* 120.

83. Catapusan, "Filipino Intermarriage Problems in the United States," 269–71; Takaki, *Strangers from a Different Shore,* 342–43; Cressey, *The Taxi-Dance Hall,* 170.

84. Bruce Rowan and Katherine "Puggy" Balino Rowan, interview with author, San Marcos, CA, December 14, 2003.

85. Rachael Ochoa-Tafoya, interview with author, Santa Barbara, CA, January 5, 2002. Originally cited in Guevarra, "Burritos and Bagoong," 82.

86. Rafael Patricio, interview with author.

87. Rashaan Meneses, interview with author, National City, CA, December 26, 2003.

88. Cressey, *The Taxi Dance Hall,* 167–68.

89. Ibid., 172.

90. Ibid., 86.

91. Posadas, "Mestiza Girlhood," 277–78.

92. For more on these experiences regarding both the social and psychological implications of inclusion and/or exclusion for American mestizos and growing up in a interracial family, see Michelle Remoreras Watts, "Not White Enough, Not Filipino Enough: A Young Mestiza's Journey," in *Pinay Power: Theorizing the Filipina/American Experience,* ed. Melinda L. De Jesús (New York: Routledge, 2005); Root, "Contemporary Mixed-Heritage Filipino Americans," 80–94; Patricia Justiniani McReynolds, *Almost Americans: A Quest for Dignity* (Santa Fe, NM: Red Crane Books, 1997); Posadas, "Mestiza Girlhood," 276–82.

93. Alma Gonzalez (pseudonym), interview with author, Tracy, CA, August 29, 2004.

94. Rolando Mata, interview with author.

95. Virgil Garcia, interview with author, Lemon Grove, CA, August 21, 2001.

96. Consuelo "Connie" Zuniga, interview with author.

97. Ibid.

98. Irene Mena, interview with author.

99. Ricardo Romio, interview with author.

100. Maria Root notes that the term *mestizo* has been used to include "almost all mixes of Filipinos." In the Philippines and Mexico, it usually was reserved for those who were of indigenous and Spanish descent. Most notably in the Philippines, though, mestizo was used to signify those of Filipino-white ancestry. This was in direct contrast to what my interviewees defined as mestizo. See Irene Mena, interview with author; Ricardo Romio, interview with author; Root, "Contemporary Mixed-Heritage Filipino Americans," 81.

101. Personal notes from conversation with David Galbiso, November 11, 2004. See also David Galbiso, interview with author, Chula Vista, CA, August 4, 2006.

102. Maria P. P. Root, ed., *The Multiracial Experience: Racial Borders as the New Frontier* (Thousand Oaks, CA: Sage Publications, 1996), xxiii.

103. Halo-halo is a Filipino dessert that is a mixture of crushed ice, ice cream, jelly candies, and other delights. Its mixed consistency has thus been used to describe multiracial Filipinos. See Rosalie Zarate, interview with author, National City, CA, November 16, 2005; Ricardo Romio, interview with author.

104. Root, *The Multiracial Experience*, xiv, 237–38.

105. Rebecca Romo, "Between Black and Brown: Blaxican (Black-Mexican) Multiracial Identity in California," *Journal of Black Studies* 42, no. 3 (April 2011): 405; and G. Reginald Daniel and Joseph Manuel Castañeda-Liles, "Race, Multiraciality, and the Neoconservative Agenda," in *Mixed Messages: Multiracial Identities in the "Color-Blind" Era*, ed. David L. Brunsma (Boulder, CO: Lynne Rienner, 2006), 125–45.

106. Of the several self-designated terms used to describe those of mixed Mexican-Filipino descent, I chose to use *Mexipino* to include all generations who identify with their Mexican heritage, including Chicana/os. Using other terms like *Chicanpina/o*, for example, recognizes a Chicano identity, which pre-1960s generations may not relate to politically.

107. Rashaan Meneses, interview with author.

108. For more on the various experiences mentioned, see Root, *The Multiracial Experience*; Maria P. P. Root, ed., *Racially Mixed People in America* (Newbury Park, CA: Sage Publications, 1992); Spickard, *Mixed Blood*; "No Passing Zone," *Amerasia Journal* 23, no. 1 (1997); Teresa Williams-León and Cynthia L. Nakashima, eds., *The Sum of Our Parts: Mixed Heritage Asian Americans* (Philadelphia: Temple University Press, 2001); Paul Spickard and W. Jeffrey Burroughs, eds., *We Are a People: Narrative and Multiplicity in Constructing Ethnic Identity* (Philadelphia: Temple University Press, 2000); Coronado, Guevarra, Moniz, and Szanto, *Crossing Lines*; Romo, "Between Black and Brown," 402–26; "The Pursuit of Hapa-ness," *aMagazine* (June/July 2001): 34–39; "Chopsticks and Chitlins," *Mavin Magazine* (Fall 1999): 48–51; "Soul Searching: Recognizing Filipinos of Black Heritage," *Kalayaan* (February 1997): 6–7.

109. Guevarra, "Burritos and Bagoong," 78.

110. Ricardo Romio, interview with author.

111. Gina Lleva, interview with author; and Rashaan Meneses, interview with author.

112. Gina Lleva, interview with author.

113. Lanny Villarin, interview with author.

114. Posadas, "Mestiza Girlhood," 282.

115. Ricardo Romio, interview with author.

116. Ibid.

117. Rafael, Regidor, and Maximiana Patricio, interview with author.

118. Freddie Ayap, interview with author, National City, CA, August 5, 2004.

119. Leonard, *Making Ethnic Choices*, 171–76.

120. In all of my interviews, I did not meet one individual who was ashamed or denied his or her Filipino identity, despite the fact that most of them either looked mixed, could be mistaken as another ethnicity, or physically did not look Filipino to most outsiders.

121. Although Vanessa is not from San Diego, I use her story to illustrate the multicultural upbringing and multiethnic identity formations that most Mexipinos experience. See Vanessa Solis, interview with author, Santa Barbara, CA, July 20, 2005.

122. Ibid.

123. Rosalie Zarate, interview with author.

124. Historian David G. Gutiérrez also notes similar intra-ethnic tensions between U.S.-born Mexicans and Mexican immigrants. See Gutiérrez, *Walls and Mirrors*.

125. Lanny Villarin, interview with author.

126. David Galbiso, interview with author.

127. Whether this had to do with them being more culturally Mexican or phenotypically looking like one is a topic that needs to be further explored.

128. Vanessa Solis, interview with author.

129. Ricardo Romio, interview with author.

130. Gina Lleva, interview with author.

131. Ibid.

132. Alan Duran Gonzalez, interview with author.

133. Ibid.

134. Suzanna Balino Fernandez, interview with author, San Diego, CA, December 30, 2001. Originally cited in Guevarra, "Burritos and Bagoong," 87.

135. Rafael Patricio, interview with author.

136. Ibid.

137. Ibid.

138. Marissa Marsical, interview with author, Santa Barbara, CA, February 8, 2002. Originally cited in Guevarra, "Burritos and Bagoong," 84.

139. Rafael Patricio, interview with author.

140. For more on Filipino youth gangs and their tensions with Mexicans, see Bangele D. Alsaybar, "Filipino American Youth Gangs, 'Party Culture,' and Ethnic Identity in Los Angeles," in *The Second Generation: Ethnic Identity among Asian Americans,* ed. Pyong Gap Min (Walnut Creek, CA: Alta Mira Press, 2002), 133–40.

141. This incident was a one-time thing that occurred, but for the most part they always mixed together and hung out as friends. See Rafael Patricio, interview with author.

142. Ricardo Romio, interview with author.

143. Sophia Limjoco, telephone interview with author, January 8, 2002. Originally cited in Guevarra, "Burritos and Bagoong," 82.

144. Vanessa Solis, interview with author.

145. Rashaan Meneses, interview with author. This was something that I also shared in my article on growing up Mexipino in San Diego. I noted how at some of our family parties we would have Mexican music playing while we ate Filipino food. For more on this, see Guevarra, "Burritos and Bagoong," 73.

146. Gina Lleva, interview with author.

147. Ibid.

148. Alan Duran Gonzalez, interview with author.

149. Rashaan Meneses, interview with author.

150. *Sinigang hipon* is shrimp in sour soup with vegetables. Rosalie Zarate, interview with author.

151. Rafael Patricio, interview with author.

152. Sophia Limjoco, telephone interview with author.

153. Marissa Mariscal, interview with author.

154. Dario Deguzman Villa, *The Bridge Generation: Sons and Daughters of Filipino Pioneers* (San Diego, CA: Dario D. Villa, 1996), 2.

155. Rashaan Meneses, interview with author.

156. Ibid.

157. Gina Lleva, interview with author.

158. Ibid.

159. Irene Mena, interview with author.

160. Rafael Patricio, interview with author.

161. Burma, *Spanish-Speaking Groups in the United States,* 155.

162. Leonard, *Making Ethnic Choices,* 214–15.

163. Gloria Anzaldúa, *Borderlands/La Frontera: The New Mestiza* (San Francisco: Aunt Lute Books, 1987), 77.

164. AnaLouise Keating, "From Borderlands and New Mestizas to Nepantlas and Nepantleras: Anzaldúan Theories for Social Change," *Human Architecture: Journal of*

the Sociology of Self-Knowledge 4 (Summer 2006): 6; and Anzaldúa, *Borderlands/La Frontera*, 77.

165. Leonard, *Making Ethnic Choices*, 215.

166. According to Benito Vergara, *Pinoy* (and the feminine counterpart *Pinay*) are slang terms that early Filipino migrants used to differentiate themselves from Filipinos who lived in the Philippines. See Benito M. Vergara Jr., *Pinoy Capital: The Filipino Nation in Daly City* (Philadelphia: Temple University Press, 2008).

167. Vince Reyes, "The War Brides," *Filipinas*, October 1995, 22–24.

168. Philippine Resource Center, *In the Belly of the Beast: The Filipino Community in the United States* (Berkeley: Philippine Resource Center, 1985), 20; Espiritu, *Home Bound*, 145; and Patacsil, Guevarra, and Tuyay, *Filipinos in San Diego*, 32.

169. Gina Lleva, interview with author.

170. Root, "Contemporary Mixed-Heritage Filipino Americans," 92.

171. Guevarra, "Burritos and Bagoong," 88.

EPILOGUE

1. The 1965 Immigration Act (Hart-Cellar Act) provided a quota of 170,000 immigrants from the Eastern Hemisphere and 120,000 from the Western Hemisphere. Immediate family members were not a part of the quota. The majority of those eligible within the quota had family reunification and occupational preferences. Despite the quota, undocumented Mexican immigrants also came in substantial numbers. For more on the 1965 Immigration Act, see Mae M. Ngai, *Impossible Subjects: Illegal Aliens and the Making of Modern America* (Princeton, NJ: Princeton University Press, 2004), 258–64; Ronald Takaki, *Strangers from a Different Shore: A History of Asian Americans* (Boston: Little, Brown, 1998), 419–20; Paul Spickard, *Almost All Aliens: Immigration, Race, and Colonialism in American History and Identity* (New York: Routledge, 2007); Reed Ueda, *Postwar Immigrant America: A Social History* (Boston: Bedford/St. Martin's Press, 1994), 44–46.

2. U.S. Census Bureau, 2005–2009 American Community Survey, San Diego County, CA, ACS Demographic and Housing Estimates: 2005–2009. In 2000, Chinese were the largest Asian group in the United States at over 2.7 million people. No new census data is available for 2010 regarding the Asian population of the United States. As of 2010, Mexicans comprised an estimated 31.8 million people, making them the largest Latino group in the United States. See U.S. Census Bureau, *The Asian Population 2000: 2000 Census Brief* (Washington, DC: U.S. Census Bureau, 2002), 1–10; and U.S. Census Bureau, *The Hispanic Population 2010: 2010 Census Brief* (Washington, DC: U.S. Census Bureau, 2001), 1–7.

3. There were also some retired navy families in these areas. For more on post-1965 Filipino immigrants, see John M. Liu, Paul M. Ong, and Carolyn Rosenthein, "Dual Chain Migration: Post-1965 Filipino Immigration to the U.S.," in *Asians in America: The Peoples of East, Southeast, and South Asia in American Life and Culture*, ed. Franklin Ng (New York: Garland Publishing, 1998), 487–513; Juanita Tomayo Lott, "Demographic Changes Transforming the Filipino American Community," in *Filipino Americans: Transformation and Identity*, ed. Maria P. P. Root (Thousand Oaks, CA: Sage Publications, 1997), 11–38; Catherine Ceniza Choy, *Empire of Care: Nursing and Migration in Filipino American History* (Durham, NC: Duke University Press, 2003); Yen Le Espiritu, "Filipino Navy Stewards and Filipina Health Care Professionals: Immigration,

Work, and Family Relations," *Asian and Pacific Migration Journal* 11, no. 1 (2002): 47–66; Yen Le Espiritu, *Home Bound: Filipino American Lives across Cultures, Communities, and Countries* (Berkeley: University of California Press, 2003), 116.

4. Espiritu, *Home Bound*, 120–21.

5. These were observations I made during a two-year period when I resided in one of the suburban communities of the Chula Vista–East Lake area. More research is required to see how the Chula Vista–East Lake area has functioned with regards to Filipino-Mexican relations.

6. These areas include Escondido, Oceanside, San Marcos, Vista, and Fallbrook.

7. "Chicana/o" is a sociopolitical term that was used as a means of self-empowerment for Mexican American youth who were coming of age during the turbulent era of the 1960s and 1970s, when cultural nationalism and a rejection of assimilation to U.S. society were the ideological forces behind these movements. For more on Chicano identity and the Chicano movement, see George Mariscal, *Brown-Eyed Children of the Sun: Lessons from the Chicano Movement, 1965–1975* (Albuquerque: University of New Mexico Press, 2005); Tony Castro, *Chicano Power: The Emergence of Mexican America* (New York: E. P. Dutton, 1974); Ignacio M. García, *Chicanismo: The Forging of a Militant Ethos among Mexican Americans* (Tucson: University of Arizona Press, 1997); Carlos Muñoz Jr., *Youth, Identity, Power: The Chicano Movement* (New York, Verso, 1989); Juan Gómez-Quiñones, *Chicano Politics: Reality and Promise, 1940–1990* (Albuquerque: University of New Mexico Press, 1990); F. Arturo Rosales, *Chicano! The History of the Mexican American Civil Rights Movement* (Houston: Arte Público Press, 1997).

8. Barrio Logan is also known as Logan Heights. For more on the history of Chicano Park, see Kevin Delgado, "A Turning Point: The Conception and Realization of Chicano Park," *Journal of San Diego History* 44, no. 1 (Winter 1998): 48–61; *Chicano Park*, prod. and dir. by Marilyn Mulford and Mario Barerra, 59 min., Redbird Films, 1989, videocassette.

9. See Karen Umemoto, "'On Strike!' San Francisco State College Strike, 1968–1969: The Role of Asian American Students," in *Contemporary Asian America: A Multidisciplinary Reader,* ed. Min Zhou and James V. Gatewood (New York: New York University Press, 2000), 49–79; William Wei, *The Asian American Movement* (Philadelphia: Temple University Press, 1993); and Veronica Verzosa, "Last Night of the I-Hotel," *Filipinas* (October 1997): 55–57.

10. See Madge Bello and Vincent Reyes, "Filipino Americans and the Marcos Overthrow: The Transformation of Political Consciousness," *Amerasia* 13, no. 1 (1986–1987): 73–83; and Judy Patacsil, Rudy Guevarra Jr., and Felix Tuyay, *Filipinos in San Diego* (San Francisco: Arcadia Publishing, 2010), 92–106.

11. See Craig Scharlin and Lilia V. Villanueva, *Philip Vera Cruz: A Personal History of Filipino Immigrants and the Farmworkers Movement* (Seattle: University of Washington Press, 2000); Peter Matthiessen, *Sal Si Puedes (Escape If You Can): Cesar Chavez and the New American Revolution* (Berkeley: University of California Press, 200); Susan Ferriss and Ricardo Sandoval, *The Fight in the Fields: Cesar Chavez and the Farmworkers Movement* (New York: Harcourt Brace, 1997); Rosales, *Chicano!*, 130–51; Juan Gómez-Quiñones, *Mexican American Labor, 1790–1990* (Albuquerque: University of New Mexico Press, 1994), 242–54; Andrew Kopkind, "The Grape Pickers' Strike: A New Kind of Labor War in California," *New Republic,* January 29, 1966, 12–15.

12. Dorothy Fujita-Rony, "Coalitions, Race, and Labor: Rereading Philip Vera Cruz," *Journal of Asian American Studies* 3, no. 2 (June 2000): 152.

13. For more on this, see Adrian Cruz, "Racialized Fields: Asians, Mexicans, and the Farm Labor Struggle in California" (PhD diss., University of Illinois at Urbana-Champaign, 2009), 126–63.

14. For more on the role of Filipinos in the UFW, see Scharlin and Villanueva, *Philip Vera Cruz;* Alex S. Fabros Jr. and Daniel P. Gonzalez, "Filipinos—Forgotten Heroes of the UFW," *Filipinas,* April 2005, 24–28; Emelyn Cruz Lat, "Paving the Way for UFW," *San Francisco Examiner,* October 19, 1997, C1, C3; Fujita-Rony, "Coalitions, Race, and Labor," 147; Cruz, "Racialized Fields," 126–63.

15. Edward James Olmos, dir., *Walkout* (HBO Films, 2006).

16. Irene Mena, interview with author, Lemon Grove, CA, January 26, 2007.

17. Ibid. Anthropologist Carlos Velez-Ibañez, who lived and went to graduate school during the 1970s, also verified this phenomenon. He noted that anywhere from 5 to 10 percent of the students he knew who were a part of the Chicano movement were multiethnic Mexipinos. See also personal notes, discussion with Carlos Velez-Ibañez, September 15, 2008.

18. Maria Theresa "Maite" Valladolid, interview with author, Bonita, CA, June 8, 2007. For more on the Gabriela Network, see http://www.gabnet.org.

19. See Marcos Portales, *Crowding Out Latinos: Mexican Americans in the Public Consciousness* (Philadelphia: Temple University Press, 2000); Leo R. Chavez, *Covering Immigration: Popular Images and the Politics of the Nation* (Berkeley: University of California Press, 2001); Otto Santa Ana, *Brown Tide Rising: Metaphors of Latinos in Contemporary American Public Discourse* (Austin: University of Texas Press, 2002).

20. Sophia Limjoco, telephone interview with author, January 8, 2002. Originally cited in Rudy P. Guevarra Jr., "Burritos and Bagoong: Mexipinos and Multiethnic Identity in San Diego, California," in *Crossing Lines: Race and Mixed Race across the Geohistorical Divide,* ed. Marc Coronado, Rudy P. Guevarra Jr., Jeffrey Moniz, and Laura Furlan Szanto (Walnut Creek, CA: Alta Mira Press, 2005), 87–88.

21. For more on this, see "50,000 Throng Downtown in Immigrant Rights March," *San Diego Union Tribune,* April 10, 2006, http://www.signonsandiego.com/uniontrib/ 20060410/news_1n10march.html (accessed April 11, 2006).

22. Although the Filipino community at times tries to disassociate itself from the undocumented immigration issue, the fact is that as of 2006, over 280,000 undocumented Filipinos reside in the United States; most purposely overstayed their visa in order to live in the United States. Known as "TNTs" or "*tago, tago*" (to keep on hiding), they are rarely discussed among the Filipino communities in San Diego and elsewhere. See Concepcion A. Montoya, "Living in the Shadows: The Undocumented Immigrant Experience of Filipinos," in *Filipino Americans,* ed. Root, 112–20. For more on the debate regarding the immigrant rights march, see Alfonso B. Villamora, "Why Must Filipinos Join the April 9 'March for Dignity, Respect, and Hope,'" *Filipino Press,* April 8–14, 2006, 7, 20, and 22; and Aaron Terrazas, "Filipino Immigrants in the United States," September 2008, *Migration Information Source,* http://migrationinformation.org/usfocus/display. cfm?id=694 (accessed January 15, 2010).

23. Patacsil, Guevarra, and Tuyay, *Filipinos in San Diego,* 107; and author's personal photo archive and observations of the event, April 9, 2006.

24. Espiritu, *Home Bound,* 118.

25. For more on this annual celebration, see "Fiesta Filipina-Mexicana Marks 7th Year," *Philippine Mabuhay News,* November 1–15, 1999, A1, A8; and "Fiesta Filipina-Mexicana Marks 8th Year," *Philippine Mabuhay News,* October 1–15, 2001, A1, A3, Mexican-Filipino American File, NPA, FANHS, Seattle, WA; and "The 18th Annual Fiesta

Filipiana Mexicana Karaoke Competition, October 23, 2010," http://www.seafoodcitysing-galingcontest.com/how-to-join (accessed May 23, 2010).

26. This independent supermarket was located in National City on E. Eighth Street and Palm Avenue when I initially visited it in 2001. The supermarket is no longer there.

27. Rosalie Toledo Zarate, a Mexipina, is currently a city council member in National City and is a strong advocate for the residents of her community.

28. Judy De Los Santos and Armando Abundis, interview with author, National City, CA, September 17, 2004.

29. Ibid.

30. Espiritu, *Home Bound*, 118.

31. Most Filipino and Mexipino families have moved out of Logan Heights and into other areas like National City that are more multiethnic with large Mexican and Filipino communities. Since 1970, Logan Heights, or "Barrio Logan," has become a predominately Mexican immigrant and Chicano community.

32. Gina Lleva, interview with author, San Diego, CA, September 21, 2004.

33. I personally know at least a dozen recent Filipino-Mexican and Mexican-Filipina couples that I grew up with; they come from these working-class communities in San Diego.

ADDENDUM TO NOTES

New information came to my attention while this book was in production regarding the information in note 76 to chapter 4 (page 203). Despite Pablo Manlapit's efforts at creating an interethnic coalition between Filipino and Japanese sugar plantation workers in Hawai'i, the reality was the Japanese community was divided over the issue. Not only was the coalition fragile, it ended up being a failure because of the lack of cooperation between the groups. Filipinos, however, brought those experiences of interethnic organizing with them to California. Seeing the potential that could exist with Mexican workers, they utilized those tools and were more successful. I would like to thank Jonathan Okamura for providing me with recent information written by Ruben Alcantara on this relationship. For more on this, see http://scholarspace.manoa.hawaii.edu/handle/10125/17651 (accessed November 16, 2011).

Index

Page numbers in *italics* refer to figures and tables.

About the Author

Rudy P. Guevarra Jr. is an assistant professor of Asian Pacific American Studies at Arizona State University. He is coeditor of *Transnational Crossroads: Remapping the Americas and the Pacific* (2012) and coauthor of *Filipinos in San Diego* (2010).